Lightnin'
Hopkins

Also by Alan Govenar

Nonfiction

Texas Blues: The Rise of a Contemporary Sound

Untold Glory: African Americans in Pursuit of
Freedom, Opportunity and Achievement

The Early Years of Rhythm and Blues

Stoney Knows How: Life as a Sideshow Tattoo
Artist

Masters of Traditional Arts: A Biographical
Dictionary

African American Frontiers: Slave Narratives and
Oral Histories

Portraits of Community: African American
Photography in Texas

Deep Ellum and Central Track: Where the Black
and White Worlds of Dallas Converged (with
Jay F. Brakefield)

American Tattoo

Meeting the Blues: The Rise of the Texas Sound

Flash From the Past: Classic American Tattoo
Designs 1890–1965 (with Ed Hardy)

A Joyful Noise: A Celebration of New Orleans
Music (with Michael P. Smith)

Living Texas Blues

For Young Readers

Extraordinary Ordinary People: Five American
Masters of Traditional Arts

Stompin' at the Savoy

Osceola: Memories of a Sharecropper's Daughter

Essay Collections

Juneteenth Texas: Essays in African-American
Folklore (with Francis Abernethy and
Patrick B. Mullen)

Artist Books

Hotung Shadows

Pachinko Stops

Tour Bus Tanka

Umbrellas in Beijing

For Boys Who Dream of War

Daddy Double Do Love You

Cold Earth

Midnight Song

The Blues and Jives of Dr. Hepcat

Daddy Double Do Love You

Casa di Dante, Arcadian Press

The Light in Between

The Life and Poems of Osceola Mays

Paradise in the Smallest Thing

Lightnin' Hopkins

His Life and Blues

Alan Govenar

CHICAGO
REVIEW
PRESS

The Library of Congress has cataloged the hardcover edition as follows:

Govenar, Alan B., 1952–
 Lightnin' Hopkins : his life and blues / Alan Govenar.
          p. cm.
 Includes bibliographical references.
 ISBN 978-1-55652-962-7 (hardcover)
1. Hopkins, Lightnin', 1912-1982. 2. Blues musicians—United States—
Biography. I. Title.

 ML420.H6357G68 2010
 781.643092—dc22
 [B]   2009048798

Cover and interior design: Jonathan Hahn
Front cover image: © Les Blank

Printed in the United States of America

Contents

Acknowledgments

Writing this book spread over more than fifteen years. While there were days and months that I set the manuscript aside, I knew I'd come back to it and complete what I had set out to do. The amount of inaccurate information on Lightnin' Hopkins made me especially vigilant, and numerous people helped me through the arduous process of establishing a cohesive biography.

Andrew Brown propelled my work forward by sharing his voluminous research and then reading and critiquing several drafts of the manuscript. Chris Strachwitz of Arhoolie Records made available his archive and record collection, and my frequent conversations with him clarified many inconsistencies. Jane Phillips, whom I first talked to more than a decade ago, made valuable suggestions as she shared her memories of Lightnin' during the 1960s. David Benson openly discussed Lightnin's day-to-day life during his last years. Paul Oliver and Pat Mullen aided me in contextualizing the cross-cultural appeal of Lightnin's blues. Laurent Danchin translated various articles published in French and engaged me in a dialogue I had not foreseen.

I am also grateful to Les Blank of Flower Films, Jeff Place of the Smithsonian Center for Folklife and Cultural Heritage, John Wheat of the Center for

American History at the University of Texas, Dan Morgenstern of the Institute of Jazz Studies at Rutgers University, Bill Belmont of Prestige Music Archives/ Concord Music Group, and many others who offered their assistance, including Sam Charters, Mack McCormick, Paul Oliver, Roger Armstrong, Barbara Dane, David Evans, Kip Lornell, John Broven, Ed Pearl, Bernie Pearl, Carroll Peery, Bruce Bromberg, Paul Drummond, Jay Brakefield, Stan Lewis, Don Logan, Joe Kessler, Eric Davis, Eric LeBlanc, Andre Hobus, Krista Balatony, Ray Dawkins, Clyde Langford, Alan Hatchett, Francis Hofstein, Norbert Hess, and Alan Balfour.

My wife, Kaleta Doolin, and my children, Breea and Alex, were a constant source of encouragement as my efforts moved forward, bringing a counterpoint to my work that has enriched my life.

Introduction

I been making up songs all my life. I could get out among people 'cause this here's a gift . . . to me. An old lady told me, "Son, your mother had music in her heart when she was carrying you." You know what that mean, don't you? When I come into this world I was doin' this.[1]

S am "Lightnin'" Hopkins, at the time of his death in 1982, may have been the most frequently recorded blues artist in history. He was a singular voice in the history of the Texas blues, exemplifying its country roots but at the same time reflecting its urban directions in the years after World War II. His music epitomized the hardships and aspirations of his own generation of African Americans, but it was also emblematic of the folk revival and its profound impact upon a white audience.

What distinguished Lightnin' Hopkins was his virtuosity as a performer. He soaked up what was around him and put it all into his blues. He rambled on about anything that came into his mind: chuckholes in the road, gossip on the street, his rheumatism, his women, and the good times and bad men he met along the way. In his songs he could be irascible, but in the next verse he might be self-effacing. He prided himself on his individuality, even if it meant he was full of inconsistencies. He often poured out his feelings in his songs with a heart-wrenching pathos, but it could be hard to tell if he was truly sincere. He peppered his lyrics with few actual details about his own life, but he was at once raw, mocking, extroverted, sarcastic, and deadly serious. Most of the time, Lightnin' appeared to trust no one, yet he knew how to endear himself to his audience. While he voiced the hardships, yearnings, and foibles of African Americans in the gritty bump and grind of the juke joints of Third Ward Houston, he could be cocky and brash in his performances for white crowds at the Matrix in San Francisco, or at the New Orleans Jazz and Heritage Festival, or a concert hall in Europe, where he was in complete control and was adored.

Lightnin's down-home blues did not adhere strictly to a traditional, three-line, AAB verse form, but rather he improvised a form that suited the song he was singing or composing on the spot and expressed what he was feeling at that moment. If Lightnin' held a line for one or two extra beats, if he abbreviated the musical time between lines, or if he lost his place during an instrumental riff, he was never fazed. But this is what made it so difficult for bassists and drummers to play with him, and his timing got more erratic as the years went by. He wasn't schooled in the complex harmonic structures and precision of rhythm and blues, but instead stayed with a basic three-chord (tonic, subdominant, dominant) guitar pattern to accompany his vocal phrasing. In doing so, his vocal lines did not always agree metrically with his guitar lines. But for Lightnin' the basis of his songs was rarely structure. It was the essence of the blues that he was after. "I come along, long about the time that the people first put the blues on this earth for the people to go by," Lightnin' said. "Well, I'm one in the number and the rest of them is dead and gone. I got in that number at a young age . . . and I just keeps it up 'cause the blues is something that the people can't get rid of. And if you ever have the blues, remember what I tell you. You'll always hear this in your heart: That's the blues."[2]

Lightnin' played both acoustic and electric guitars and was steeped in the Texas country blues tradition. From Blind Lemon Jefferson and Alger "Texas" Alexander, Lightnin' absorbed stylistic and repertoire elements that included a melismatic singing style rooted in the field holler, mixing long-held notes with loose, almost conversational phrasing.[3] Musically, "Short Haired Woman," which Lightnin' recorded for the first time around May 1947, established the signature sound that he used in just about every song, whether it was a fast instrumental boogie/shuffle or a slow blues. In his guitar playing Lightnin' had an open and fluid style with his right hand, using a thumb pick and his index finger. He kept his right hand loose so he could move from playing sharp notes near the bridge to playing wider open chords up near the fingerboard.

Lightnin' usually tuned his guitar in the key of E, though not necessarily to a concert pitch. He utilized what ZZ Top guitarist Billy Gibbons has called "that turnaround. . . . It's a signature lick. . . . He'd come down from the B chord and roll across the top three strings in the last two bars. He'd pull off those strings to get a staccato effect, first hitting the little open E string then the 3rd fret on the B string and the 4th fret of the G string. He would then resolve on the V chord after doing his roll. It's a way to immediately identify a Lightnin' Hopkins tune."[4]

Lightnin' was tremendously appealing for aspiring blues guitarists to emulate because his signature turnaround was relatively easy to learn, but it was extremely hard to replicate his sound because of his distinctive held notes, pauses, string bending, and shortened and lengthened measures. Sometimes, as bluesman Michael "Hawkeye" Herman points out, Lightnin' "played it in triplets, sometimes as a quarter note, sometimes as an eighth note. . . . He knew how to play the same lick/riff forward, backward, from the middle to the front, from the middle to the back, from the back to the front . . . each effort creating a completely huge guitar vocabulary."[5] Ultimately, it didn't matter what kind of guitar he was playing, acoustic or electric. "He just had this feel," guitarist and luthier Sam Swank maintains, echoing the sentiments of so many Lightnin' devotees. "There aren't that many blues guitar players in the world that when you drop the needle on the record, anybody who's anybody knows who that is. Lightnin' Hopkins is one of those guitar players."[6]

Most people thought Lightnin' was making up the words to his songs as he went along, and that his lyrics were completely original. But he was actually doing something more amazing and subtle. He was instantly accessing hundreds of floating lyrics from his memory and inserting them when and where they seemed appropriate. Many blues singers did this to a certain extent, but

Lightnin's ability seemed to exceed all of his peers. His capacity for improvisation was uncanny, and regardless of the source of his lyrics, he was able to make each of his songs his own by performing them in his inimitable voice and his signature guitar style.

If there were a dominant theme in his blues, it was the ever-changing and often-tumultuous relationships between men and women. Lightnin' could turn the simplest phrase into sexual innuendo, and, just as easily, express the pain of being mistreated and the despair of being betrayed. He often bragged about his exploits with women in his songs, but other than identifying some names, he said little about his actual relationships. While he sang in the first-person, remarkably little of his repertoire was truly autobiographical.

I saw Lightnin' perform once at the Austin nightclub Castle Creek in 1974, and when he came on stage, I was drawn into his performance like everyone else. But he was so different from what I had expected from having listened to his records. Every gesture seemed so measured—the placement of the guitar, the positioning of his hat, the towel around his neck, the half pint of liquor that he pulled up to his lips, the big, gold-toothed grin, and the dark sunglasses that kept him a mystery. By the time the show was over, I wasn't sure how to respond. Still, his presence was indelible, and in many ways my memory of that night, that image of Lightnin' in the spotlight, made me want to know more. Lightnin' was an enigma. He was both compelling and disturbing. To what extent did the white audience listening to him shape his performance, and how did it relate to his roots in East Texas? How would it have been different in a juke joint on a backcountry road or in a little dive in Houston?

Years later, in the mid-1980s, Chris Strachwitz and Les Blank, two giants in the field of American roots music, talked to me at length about Lightnin's importance as a bluesman and his significance in each of their lives. Chris, after hearing Lightnin' in Houston, decided to start Arhoolie Records and he has since released hundreds of recordings of blues and American roots music; Les, after seeing Lightnin' at the Ash Grove in Los Angeles, was inspired to make his first full-length documentary film. And for both of them, Lightnin's passing marked the end of an era. They recognized the need for a biography, but they weren't going to do it themselves. Les offered me the use of his interviews and outtakes from his films *The Blues According to Lightnin' Hopkins* and *The Sun's Gonna*

Shine. Chris made himself available for countless conversations, sharing what he remembered and introducing me to people he thought I should interview.

Initially I was reluctant to begin work on a biography. Dr. Cecil Harold, who was Lightnin's manager for more than a decade, and Antoinette Charles, who was his long-time companion, refused to be interviewed. I called Dr. Harold on several occasions but was repeatedly rebuffed. The first time he asked me to make a financial offer and said that "Mrs. Hopkins" might accept ten thousand dollars, but he then recanted. The next year he told me that "Mrs. Hopkins isn't doing any more interviews," and two years later he reiterated that "Mrs. Hopkins isn't interested." Three years after that, he explained that "it's too painful for Mrs. Hopkins," and in my last attempt, he asked me to write a letter in which I explained that I was completing a biography of Lightnin' Hopkins and asked what terms for a conversation and/or interview might be acceptable. A few weeks later, I received a hand-written reply that stated: "Mrs. Hopkins . . . declines further interviews. She wishes to simply say . . . no more reviews of life with Lightnin'."[7] Then it occurred to me that I needed to see Lightnin's probated will, and when I finally got a copy it all began to make sense. Antoinette was never Mrs. Hopkins. She had an affair with him that lasted an estimated thirty-five years, and during much of that time she was married to someone else with whom she had children. What mattered most to Antoinette was her privacy.

Finally, in 1995, after studying and writing about Texas blues for nearly two decades, I started talking to people in Centerville, Texas, where Lightnin' grew up. I was trying to get a handle on how Lightnin' was remembered where he grew up. At Ellis's Drive-In on State Highway 7, near the intersection with U.S. Highway 75, eighty-three-year-old Estelle Sims leaned on the front counter with her elbows and smiled when asked about Lightnin'. The light from the street shone on her bristly white hair and the deep wrinkles of her face as she spoke in a solemn tone. "I remember hearing him play at a black-eyed pea festival not too far from here back in the thirties. He was good, but it's been so long that I forget what it was that he actually played." Then she looked up and pointed across the street. "I suspect that man over there might be able to tell you more. He's a Hopkins."

I thanked her and walked across the street, the July heat drawing a sticky asphalt smell from the pavement. Oland Hopkins was sitting in the shade of a post oak tree beside a rusty pick-up truck filled with hay and a few watermelons that he was casually trying to sell to passersby. As I got closer to him, he stood up abruptly and asked, "Can I help you, sir?"

I explained that I was looking for information about Lightnin' Hopkins, and he muttered, "I'm a distant relation of his, but I don't know too much. I used to hear him play at church association picnics and suppers, but that's about it. You ought to talk to J. D. Kelly. Now, he should be able to tell you more."

The pay phone next to Ellis's Drive-In was hot and clammy. I dialed Kelly's number quickly, and he answered after the second ring. Kelly had a hoarse but friendly voice and was eager to share what he knew. "That's right," he said, "I growed up with him. We just went from place to place to play all over this countryside. He had a guitar slung on his shoulder, and he picked and sang at ring-play parties. He was a playboy. All he wanted to do was pick." He told me if I wanted to find out anything else, I should give Oscar Davis a call. He was a cousin of Lightnin's and his last remaining kin in Centerville.

Davis, however, was more suspicious than the other two. He stammered, "Who are you? And what do you want?" I tried to answer, but before I could finish my sentence, he grumbled, "Talk to my wife. I'm hard of hearing." When his wife got on the telephone, she was even more suspicious than he had been. "Sure, I remember Lightnin' Hopkins. What's it to you? I remember Lightnin' Hopkins. He come to our house. He was my husband's first cousin, but I didn't really know him. You need to talk to Oscar's brother and he's right here beside me, getting ready to go to Houston." There was a short pause, and then the brother got on the phone and said, "I'm too young. I didn't really know Lightnin'. Sorry, I can't help you. Thank you and good-bye."

I hung up and walked back to my car, and I saw Oland Hopkins was staring at me. "May I have your card?" he asked in amicable way, "I'd like to help you if I can. If I find out anything more, I'll call you." I handed him my card and told him he could call me collect if he wanted to, but I've never heard from him. At that point in 1995, it appeared all that remained of Lightnin' in Centerville were spotty recollections. I decided to set the idea of writing a biography of Lightnin' Hopkins aside, though I did continue to collect stories about him whenever I got the chance. I interviewed Paul Oliver, the British blues aficionado who had traveled to Houston to meet Hopkins with Chris Strachwitz in 1960, as well as Francis Hofstein, the French psychoanalyst who had met Lightnin' when he appeared with the American Folk Blues Festival tour in Strasbourg in 1964. I spoke with John Jackson, the Piedmont bluesman who was at the Newport Folk Festival a year later when Lightnin' performed.

In 2002 the musician and impresario Pip Gillette called me and asked me if I wanted to give the keynote speech at the dedication of a Lightnin' Hopkins memorial statue created by the sculptor Jim Jeffries. I agreed, and much to my surprise, more than three hundred people came to the event on Camp Street in Crockett, Texas, where Lightnin' had performed in the 1930s and '40s. Pip introduced me to Lightnin's daughter, Anna Mae Box, who lived in Crockett, and to Frank Robinson, who had played with Lightnin' in the 1950s. I also had a chance to meet Wrecks Bell, who had played with Lightnin' in the 1970s, and David Benson, who had been Lightnin's traveling companion and road manager during the last decade of his life. Benson helped me to get a clearer sense of his personal life, especially as it related to his relationship with Antoinette and Dr. Harold during a period when he performed less, got paid more, and failed to produce any new recordings.

After speaking in Crockett, my work on the Lightnin' biography had a new momentum. I went to Centerville to meet Clyde Langford, whom I had read about a couple of years earlier.[8] Clyde had grown up across the road from Lightnin's mother, Frances Hopkins, and had learned to play guitar from his brother Joel. Clyde lived in a small wood-frame house on FM 1119 and was eager to tell his story and what he knew about Lightnin'. When I asked Clyde about other people who might know something about Lightnin' he was uncertain, but one time he mentioned Ray Dawkins. Dawkins, born in 1928, is eight years older than Langford, and his memories of Lightnin' were vivid. Lightnin's early years were coming into clearer view. I was beginning to cut through the hearsay to get a stronger sense of what actually transpired over the course of his life. But each time I returned to Centerville, I came away with a slightly different impression. I realized that it was in those varying perceptions that the truth about Lightnin' Hopkins lies. Inconsistencies about the details of his biography abound, fueled as much by the idiosyncrasies of his own memory as his capacity to reconstruct his past to meet his more immediate needs.

For most people, Hopkins was simply known as Lightnin', but he was sometimes called Lightning. However, he didn't get his nickname until November

1946, when an Aladdin Records executive (probably one of the Mesner brothers) decided during his first recording session to dub him "Lightnin'" and his accompanist, Wilson Smith, "Thunder" to enhance their presence in the marketplace. In discussing Hopkins's life prior to 1946, I refer to him by his given name, Sam, for clarity.

Hopkins often referred to himself as Po' Lightnin' in his songs, not only to elicit sympathy, but to identify himself with the plight of those who were listening. Lightnin' was the lifeblood of his own myth. In this book, the stories he told and the accounts of others provide a base for understanding how myth and memory merge into the blues that ultimately defined the man.

1

Early Years

Leaving Centerville on Leon County Road 113, midway between Dallas and Houston, the landscape of Sam Hopkins's early years comes into view. Patches of mesquite interspersed with red bud trees and groves of hickory, elm, and oak spread through the rolling hills and grassy plains. The ranches are small, and longhorns graze in pastures abutting subsistence farms, which yield to rockier soil that is parched and cracked, even in the cool January sun. The road is still unpaved, and loose gravel rattles against the wheel rims as we near Warren's Bottom, where Hopkins was born.

"Yes sir, the closer you get to the Trinity River, the terrain is rough. This was sharecropper land," Ray Dawkins explains.[1] In his denim overalls and flannel shirt, Dawkins emanates a bygone era. For a man of eighty, he has few wrinkles and still seems physically active. He drives a pickup truck and lives in a small apartment in town.

Between 1870 and 1960, 40 percent of the residents of Leon County were African American, but by 1980, the percentage dropped to 20 percent, and in 1990 to 12.8 percent. Dawkins says it's difficult keeping young people in town.

There are more job opportunities in Dallas and Houston, and the population of Centerville has continued to decline, from 961 in 1950 to 903 in 2000.

"Back when Sam was a boy," Dawkins remembers, "black folks didn't have opportunities. You did what you had to, that is, to get by."

Little is known about the details of Sam's early years. Even his birth date is disputed. In his Social Security application, dated January 24, 1940, Sam stated that he was born on March 15, 1912, a date that he reiterated in his song "Going Home Blues (Going Back and Talk to Mama)," as well as in numerous interviews over the course of his life.[2] However, the Social Security Death Index lists his birth date as March 15, 1911, and his death certificate says it was March 12, 1912. Adding to the confusion is the fact that the Texas Birth Index recorded the birth of a Sam Hopkins on March 15, 1911, in Hopkins County, which is in northeast Texas, nowhere near Leon County. It's possible that this was a clerical error, but it may also be a coincidence that another man named Sam Hopkins was born on that day. It's difficult to say which date is actually correct; no birth certificate has ever been found. Still, by all accounts, Sam spent the first years of his life in Warren's Bottom. Today all the sharecropper shacks are gone, and a chain link fence with a NO TRESPASSING sign posted on its gate blocks our way.

Outside the car, the dust subsides. The land appears relatively fertile, but clearly Warren's Bottom was in the flood plain, and much of the loamy topsoil has been washed away. Historically there were more small subsistence farms in Leon County raising vegetables, hogs, and cattle than large plantations, but once the cotton culture took hold, the number of slaves grew rapidly from 621 in 1850 to 1,455 in 1855. "Slave property was the most important possession of the majority of Leon County citizens," Frances Jane Leathers wrote in *Through the Years: A Historical Sketch of Leon County* (1946). In 1855, slaves had "a value of $757,296, which was $300,000 more than the assessed value of all the taxable land in the county."[3]

During the Civil War, this area of Central Texas was a stronghold of the Confederacy, and local historian W. D. Wood wrote in 1899 that "Leon County furnished 600 soldiers for the Confederate armies. . . . The fact is that everybody in Leon County, men and women, were doing their best in some way, to hold up the hands of the soldier, and sustain the Confederate cause. Even the slave at home, not only nobly protected the family of his soldier master, but was industriously engaged in making meat and bread for the soldier on the firing line."[4]

Emancipation brought promise and hope, but the advances of Reconstruction were short-lived. Racism was rampant. J. Y. Gates and H. B. Fox wrote in *A History of Leon County* (1936) that a "lynching occurred in Reconstruction days when a negro was hanged on the tree [called "The Tree of Justice"] and allowed to swing two nights and a full day. Old timers can recall how the negro, swollen from long hanging, 'bounced when he hit the ground,' when he finally was cut down."[5] In 1910 the *New York Times* reported that Frank Bates was "lynched by hanging in the jail at Centerville" after trying to escape his jail cell where he was awaiting trial on a murder charge.[6] In 1915, according to G. R. Englelow, writing in a Centerville newspaper called the *Record*, another man, suspected of murder, was tracked down and arrested without resistance, but the next day he was found with a noose around his neck, hanging from the limb of a large oak tree in the square in front of the Leon County courthouse.[7] In 1919 a black preacher was hung for reputedly killing a white farmer after delivering "a sermon Sunday night. . . . The two had an argument the previous Saturday over cotton. A posse sought the Negro a week along the bottom lands . . . before he was found and brought to jail. When the sheriff was out of town, a mob made a key and opened the jail and hanged the Negro to the tree."[8]

In this climate of racially motivated violence, the Hopkins family, like the others in their community, kept to themselves and worked their little parcel of land on shares, forced to pay the landowner one-third or one-half of the crop each year. But the rocky soil in Warren's Bottom was tough to farm, and they could barely eke out a living growing cotton, peanuts, corn, and peas.[9]

Sam said that his grandfather was a slave who hung himself because he was "tired of being punished."[10] But Sam didn't seem to know much more about his grandfather, or his other grandparents, though he did talk about his parents, Abe and Frances Hopkins. Abe was born in 1873 in Leon County and was working as a sharecropper when he met 15-year-old Frances Washington around 1900.[11] They married, and Frances gave birth to their first son, John Henry, in 1901. According to the 1910 census (taken before Sam was born), Frances and Abe had four children: John Henry (age eight), Joel (age seven), Abe Jr. (age four), and Alice (age two). None of the Hopkins family was able to read or write.[12]

Sam called his father "a rough man" who "peoples didn't like. . . . He'd fight right smart. . . . He killed a man. So, he went to the penitentiary, and he come back and married my mother, and from then on he started this family."[13] Clyde Langford, a distant cousin of the Hopkins family, grew up across FM 1119 from Sam's mother. He says that she spoke fondly of her husband. She described him as a "tall, slender fella with a heavy voice," who intimidated those who didn't know him but who was "a man who wouldn't hurt anyone." [14]

Frances Hopkins, Langford recalls, "was a little old skinny woman" who was "real fiery, frisky" though she didn't say much. He met her when he was a boy of about ten or eleven. "My daddy would take me by her house," Langford says, "and she talked to me. She kept a smile on her face most all the time. She was a church-going woman. She didn't really go for her kids playing the blues, but there wasn't much she could do about it. Sam looked a little like her, but from what I can gather, more like his dad. She was a dark brown, but she wasn't as black-skinned as Sam, not a high yella, but a medium brown–complexioned person. She dressed like a housewife, more or less; she wore an apron just about everywhere she went. She had what she called an everyday apron that she wore around the house, and then she had what she called her dressy apron that she would wear to church, or when she got ready to go up town. She put her work apron down and put on her 'Sunday-go-meetin' apron.' All of her Sunday dresses would be neatly starched and ironed, but now her everyday aprons she never put irons on them. They'd just be wrinkly. She said it didn't matter. She wasn't going anywhere. The aprons were made from flour sacks. . . . You'd go to town and get a fifty-pound sack of flour and the sacks would be beautiful, with different designs and flowers. And her dresses were homemade, long, down to the floor. They would be different colors. She loved something flashy like pink, something with red, yellow, high yellow, some loud, flashy color."[15]

When Sam was three years old, his father was shot and killed by a man named Floyd Johnson, Langford says, "over a buffalo nickel. They were in a card game called Pitty Pat. And they were playing for a nickel, and Floyd won that nickel and Abe picked it up and put it in his pocket. And Floyd killed him. Abe tried to bluff him out of it, and they scuffled and Floyd shot him." [16] Sam, however, believed that the killing of his father was a conspiracy. "They put someone up to kill him because he was rough," Hopkins said. "He raised good crops and he gambled, and . . . he'd win people's cotton and all such as that. And they didn't like him for it. . . . He didn't love nothing but gambling and [he'd] drink whiskey and fight and shoot . . . so that's the way his life was taken, see. So, that left nobody but my mother to raise us children."[17]

Not long after the death of Abe Hopkins, Sam's oldest brother, John Henry, left home because he said that if he stayed, he'd kill the man who had murdered his father.[18] In time, Warren's Bottom flooded out and the Hopkins family moved to Leona, another small farming community about seven and a half miles south of Centerville. Lee Gabriel was one of Sam's friends in Leona until the age of sixteen. Leona, Gabriel said, "was a little country place. It wasn't an organized town," but it had little stores where sharecroppers and landowners could buy groceries and clothes. "The biggest grocery was owned by Mr. Tom Nash. . . . He was the leading food store. And he carried some clothing. When the store had something to wear, Sam would buy something. They had a good understanding. Nobody went around with a chip on his shoulder. He [Sam] bought his shoes there. . . . Lurie Thompson had the post office in his store. He was a grocery store too. Each store had a little hardware. There wasn't much variety in the 1920s."[19]

Life in the country was hard, and boys were expected to work in the field alongside their parents. "I worked," Gabriel said, "Sam did too. Farm work, cotton and corn. I learned to plow with a horse and mule. I even plowed with oxen. That was hard work. . . . It would take several days to plow a five-acre patch."[20]

Growing up, Gabriel and Sam attended a one-room schoolhouse that had two teachers; one was a woman named Miss Davis, and the other was the principal in addition to being a teacher. Gabriel, who was the son of a circuit preacher, was well-behaved, but he said Sam often got into trouble and was strapped, spanked with a thick leather strap, for not behaving.[21]

When Gabriel and Sam had a little free time, they often went hunting together. "We went rabbit hunting," Gabriel said, "or for any other small animal. The last time we went we found a mink and killed him, skinned his pelt and sold it, got big money—$1.75." Occasionally they went horseback riding, though Gabriel recalls, "Sam was not a very good horseman. . . . Sam liked to ride, but not as well as I did. . . . The big thing then was for kids to race. But Sam didn't race. Sam liked to gamble. It was customary back then. There were lots of boys who gambled, mostly dice . . . craps . . . and the older boys played cards and bet on them local horse races." Sam also got into fights. "Once in a while, boys get too idle," Gabriel said. "Sam and this boy had a scuffle over a girl friend . . . kind of a push and wrestle. A lot of pretty girls back then."[22]

Because Gabriel's father was a preacher, his activities outside of school were restricted. However, on Saturday nights, he'd sometimes meet up with Sam at square dances. "Somebody would call the dances for each set—two-steps and waltzes," Gabriel said. "Each dance lasted five or six minutes. They called them dances 'breakdowns.' They had fiddles and sometimes guitars. The guy who called the dance was Tom Butler. He was an older man. And at the end of the set, he'd say, 'Hands in your pocket, go to the candy stand.' Either get you a sandwich or get a plate for the ones who really wanted to buy dinner. They always had some kind of food, fishes or any of the meats. And they made corn liquor. That was during Prohibition. And I knew Sam to be guilty of drinkin' corn liquor."[23]

Lorine Washington was also a friend of the Hopkins family, but she didn't remember any fiddles at the square dances that she went to in the area around Leona and Centerville. "There'd be two guitars," she says, "sometimes one, and they did flat-foot dancing."[24]

While Washington and Gabriel differ in their memories of the square dances, it seems clear that the music performed depended on the musicians who were available. The square dances were often held outside or in the front room of someone's house, Washington says, and "they'd have to move the furniture out into the yard or into a back room." Frequently, Sam recalled, the square dances were family gatherings that were organized around "country suppers," where everyone brought a dish.

Musically, the country suppers mixed blues with a kind of music that Sam described as "fast old stomp time." "That's dance," Sam said in 1967. "You get out there and dance. You see Scruggs [*Flatt and Scruggs TV Show*] and how they get to jumpin' that hillbilly thing they get stompin'? That's the way everybody dance when you get to playing 'Oh, my baby, take me back' or 'Old Stomp Time.' You be two or three out there dancing against one another . . . and the one [who] out dances the other get a quarter, four bits, sometimes a dollar if it's well off white guys be down there. . . . Buck dancin', they called it. Buck and wing . . . and them people dance on Saturday night, Sunday they go to church, Monday they go to the field."[25]

Sam loved the country suppers and square dances, and, as he got older, he started bringing his guitar. "I'd go from farm to farm," he said. "They have them dances why, because they been workin' hard all the week, makin' them big crops. . . .There were singers and players, quite a few . . . because near about everybody around them square dances could near about play for them. All you had to do was rap on your guitar and they'd pat and holler. Ole sister would shout, 'You swing mine and I'll swing yours!' and all that. And sometimes they would have the blues played, but they mostly was really dancin' you see. Have fast songs like 'Oh, my baby, take me back' and 'You swing mine and I'll swing Sue, We're goin' down to the barbecue. . . .' That's jumpin' at that time."[26]

The square dances that Sam described were organized in a way that was quite similar to those of their white counterparts. Historically, African American musicians had played for the white balls in the big plantation houses in the years before emancipation, and this tradition continued. Moreover, black fiddlers, guitarists, and banjo players performed at barn dances or on the cornshucking grounds of plantations and farms for what were called "Saturday night frolics." They played the tunes for the quadrilles, cotillions, and set dances that were popular in white rural communities, and the musical repertory of black musicians influenced their white counterparts. In the 1920s white musicians like the Texan Eck Robertson, Riley Puckett, Fiddlin' John Carson, and Gid Tanner made commercial recordings of country dance music, though relatively few black musicians playing this style were ever recorded. [27]

Henry Thomas, an East Texas guitarist and quill player who often used a banjo tuning, was a rare exception, and his 1928 recording for Vocalion of a song called "Old Country Stomp" featured his singing of couplets and single lines that evoked the spirit of the square dances for which he had undoubtedly performed.

> Get your partners, promenade
> Promenade, boy, round and round
> Hop on, you started wrong
> Take your partner, come on the train
> I'm going away, I'm going away [28]

While Thomas's recording does not illustrate the particular dance forms associated with his music, it does create a kind of composite picture of the instrumental accompaniment. Clearly, in performance, some of the dances were structured and patterned after established sets and quadrilles; others were more individualistic and rooted in African American tradition.

Langford says that in addition to playing guitar and singing at country dances, Sam was a dancer too. "Sam had one step that was out of sight, an extraordinary mixture of tap and the buck dance. Sam was also good at hambone [a style of dance that involves stomping as well as slapping and patting the arms, legs, chest, and cheeks] and Joel [his brother] was good too. One be on the guitar, one be doin' hambone. And if someone said Joel was better, it would be fist city."[29]

In the Hopkins family everyone played some kind of music or sang. Gabriel even recalled Sam playing the pump organ when he came by the church, though he didn't remember him singing church songs. Yet Sam said that he not only played the pump organ but also that he participated in church services. "I come up in Sunday school too. I played organ in Sunday school, and I played piano in Sunday school. It was fine. . . . I opened up the church [service] with the piano. . . . They didn't teach me them songs. They made 'em up. Fact of the business, they sing 'em. I played 'em. . . . All they do is give me the tune. . . . But you see I wouldn't be singing, I just be playing it. When my chorus come in, I just play it."

Sam said that he learned to play the piano by sounding out the notes on that pump organ in church. "My piano playin' . . . just come into life after I got out of church playing them songs about 'Jesus Will You Come by Here' ["Now Is the Needy Time"] and 'Just Like You Treated Your . . . By the Water' and all them songs. . . . Piano, you got to kinda thump it. But organ you pump it."[30]

Sam learned to play the guitar as a child by watching his older brothers John Henry and Joel, as well as other musicians in his community. His mother's cousin, Tucker Jordan, played the fiddle, and his wife was a guitarist, and they often played together at house parties and square dances. Albert Holley was a blues musician Sam remembered singing a song to his mother: "I heard him play, he was sitting on the foot of the bed. He was saying, 'Baby, come sit down on my knee. I got something to tell you that keeps on worrying me.' And he was saying that to Mama. I just listened. I just picked up on what he was saying. The song appealed to me and made me feel good. . . . So that give me some ideas how to sing too."[31]

The first guitar Sam played belonged to his older brother, Joel, though he said he'd also made his own instrument out of a cigar box and screen wire.[32] One day, when he was playing Joel's instrument, Sam got caught, but Joel was impressed with his ability to play. Sam recalled, "I was too little to chop cotton. They come out the field and I was pickin' the guitar one day—[Joel] give me that guitar. . . . They come in for dinner, and I'm sittin' down with that guitar across my lap pickin' it, and he wanted to know what I was doin' with his guitar. I told him I was pickin' it. He told me, 'Let me see what you do.' And I went on and played songs better than him. He said, 'You can have that [guitar]. I'll get me another one.'"[33]

Sam learned the guitar quickly, and when he was still only eight years old, he met the legendary Blind Lemon Jefferson, who was playing at the annual meeting of the General Baptist Association of Churches, commonly referred to as "the Association," in Buffalo, Texas, about sixteen miles northwest of Centerville. In attendance at the Association were people from the surrounding communities, who brought their children each day for about a week for worship and fellowship. "That's where all the delegates, preachers—they'd get there and they'd have a wonderful time," Sam said. "Well, they'd have church in the tabernacle. And they'd sell sody water out on the grounds."[34]

Ray Dawkins recalled that his father, Ike Dawkins, was on the board of the Association, and that in addition to "preaching and singing three times a day," there were barbecues and social events. One of the primary goals of the annual meeting, Dawkins says, was to raise money for Mary Allen College, which was founded in 1886 on ten acres of land in Crockett, Texas, as a two-year school. It was originally known as Mary Allen Seminary and was established for the education of black women by the Presbyterian Board of Missions for Freedmen. "So every year they'd have the Association in Buffalo, and they'd have different singers and performers. I don't know how many years Blind Lemon played there."[35]

While Blind Lemon had only recorded two Christian songs for Paramount under the pseudonym Deacon L. J. Bates, anecdotal evidence suggests that he was, in fact, well known for his capacity to sing both blues and religious music.[36] "That was one thing about Lemon," Wortham postmaster Uel L. Davis told a *Waco Tribune-Herald* reporter. "He'd be singing in church one day, singing at a house of ill repute the next."[37] Sam didn't say what song Jefferson was playing when he approached him, but he did emphasize its significance: "I run up on Blind Lemon Jefferson. He had a crowd of peoples around him. And I was standing there looking at him play, and I went to playing my guitar, just what he was playing. So he say, 'Who is that playing that guitar?' So, they say, 'Oh, that's just a little boy here knocking on that guitar.' He say, 'No, he playing that guitar.' Say, 'Where he at? Come here, boy.' And I went on over there where he was, and he was feeling for me. And I was so low, he reached out, say, 'This here was picking that guitar?' Say, 'Yeah.' So, he say, 'Do that again.' So, I did a little note again, same one he done. He say, 'Well, that's my note.' He say, 'Boy, you keep that up, you gonna be a good guitar player.' So, he went on and then commenced to playing, so I went to playing right on with him. So, I was so little and low, the peoples couldn't see me. And we were standing by a truck. They put me up on top of the truck, and Blind Lemon was standing down by the truck, and me and him, man, we carried it on. And the excitement was me, because I was so little. And I was just picking what he was. I wasn't singing, but I was playing what he was playing. That's right."[38]

Sometimes when Sam told the story, he said that Blind Lemon was displeased when he heard him play and shouted, "You got to play it right!" But when he realized the musician was only eight years old, he hoisted the child onto the truck and let him play. In another version, Sam said the meeting occurred in 1925, which would have made him about thirteen years old, not eight. It's likely that Sam had his dates mixed up, but the fact that he had met Blind Lemon was important to him. By linking himself to Blind Lemon, who was the most successful male blues singer to record in the 1920s, Sam was able to elevate his own stature and lay a cornerstone in the myth he was creating for himself.[39]

Interestingly enough, Sam said that by the time he met Blind Lemon, his brother Joel had already left home and was staying with the Jefferson family. "That was in Mexia, Wortham, Waxahatchie, Buffalo, and another little old place I can't 'call the name. Blind Lemon Jefferson played at those places. He

had a brother named Marcella Jefferson, George Jefferson, and the old lady . . .
well, they used to dance and play."[40]

In researching Blind Lemon's life and career, there are no other accounts
of either Marcella or George Jefferson. Nevertheless, Sam claimed that after
meeting Jefferson he left home and did his best to follow him, going from town
to town in East Texas. "People would see me 'cause I traveled when I was young
with a guitar all over them areas," Sam said, "Buffalo, Oakwood, Palestine, Ben
Hur, and all. Mama didn't think nothing about it. She just know it was all right
'cause I taken care of my mama all my life. From a kid up I taken care of Lady
Frances. I buried her. Out of all the kids she had, I'm the one."

What is clear is that Sam wanted to find a way out of the sharecropper life.
"It wasn't nothing on the end of the hoe handle for me," Sam said. "Choppin'
cotton for six bits a day. Plowin' the mules . . . that wasn't in store for me.
I went on with what the good lord gave me."[41] Once on his own, Hopkins's
musical skills evolved rapidly. As a child, he saw the influence that both the
preacher and the blues singer could have. "You go to church," Sam said, "and
a real preacher is really preaching the Bible to you, he's honest to God trying
to get you to understand these things. That's just the same as singing the blues.
The blues is the same thing. When they get up there and put their whole soul
in there and feel it, it's just like a preacher."[42] And for Sam, the blues singer had
as much power as the preacher in people's lives. "Course I'm like a preacher,"
he claimed, "I got to keep hearing that 'Amen!' from my congregation just the
same as a preacher."[43]

It was not uncommon for blues singers to compare themselves to preachers, though Sam rarely played religious songs. In fact, the only spiritual he ever
recorded as a solo artist was identified as "Needed Time" on RPM.[44] The actual
title is "Now Is the Needy Time," and had been recorded by the Wiseman Sextet
for Victor in 1923 (unissued) and later by two other artists in 1928 and 1930,
though it's likely that the spiritual was traditional and predates any recordings.
Sam did not record another spiritual until the 1960s, when he teamed up with
Barbara Dane on "Jesus, Won't You Come by Here" (which was actually "Now Is
the Needy Time" under a different title) and with Big Joe Williams and Brownie
McGhee on "I've Been 'Buked (and Scorned)." In other recordings, such as
"Prayin' Ground Blues," "Devil Is Watching You," "Sinner's Prayer," and "I'm

Gonna Build Me a Heaven of My Own," there are passing references to religion, but the songs are not spirituals.[45]

Sam, like so many blues singers, believed that "when you born in this world, you born with the blues. Upset is the blues. Worry is the blues. The blues come by what you love. . . .You have the blues by anything. You can have a car and wake up in the morning and have a flat. You get to walking and nobody helps you; you ain't got nothing like the blues. You gonna walk until you find somebody who says they'll try to help you. Trouble is the blues. You can have the blues about being broke, about your girl being gone. You can have the blues so many different ways till it's hard to explain. But whenever you get a sad feeling, you can tell the whole rotten world you got nothing but the blues."[46]

Sam often bragged that he started writing his songs at an early age: "I been making up songs all my life, ever since I was eight years old when I got out on my own."[47] He never identified any songs he wrote at that age, but he did have a gargantuan memory.

Lightnin' said that the first time he got paid for performing was when he had just turned fourteen years old, and he met up with Jabo Bucks about two miles from the Association grounds in Buffalo. Bucks was a fiddler who agreed to go with him into town and play for tips in front of a cafe, and they were soon invited inside. From Buffalo, he and Bucks headed on to the nearby towns of Oakwood and Jewett, stopping when and wherever they could to play for pocket change.

People in the black parts of town in the rural areas of East and Central Texas responded well to Lightnin's guitar picking and singing. But if he got the chance, he said, he "would go around to the white people's houses," where they might invite him inside to play the piano for them and pay him ten or fifteen cents, or even a quarter. [48] While the laws of separate accommodation in Leon County were viciously enforced, black musicians were sometimes welcomed into the homes of white families to entertain them, a tradition that dated back to the years of slavery. The *History of Leon County, Texas*, mentioned a group called the Serenaders, usually consisting of a fiddler, guitar player, and mandolin player, who walked through the streets of Centerville. "About the first Serenader I heard," one unnamed resident recalled, "was Rob Dunbar, a left-handed Negro fiddler and a guitar accompanist [who] came to our house about Christmas time, and that was the sweetest music I had ever heard."[49]

Mabel Milton, who grew up in Centerville, remembered that Lightnin' also liked to visit the homes of the black families he knew. "Sometimes he play just walkin' around, come to your house, and if you got him, he played for tips. He'd have his guitar with him. He just sit and talk, swap stories, tell jokes, maybe play a couple of songs, and folks give him a glass of lemonade, or a tea cake. He wouldn't stay too long, two or three hours, and then he go on some place else. He was neat dresser, keep his hair lookin' pretty all the time. Nice and clean."[50]

Sam did the best he could to avoid working in the fields. With the little money he made from tips, he was able to support himself and help his mother, but he also got deeper into gambling. And it wasn't long before he got himself into trouble: "I been on a chain gang four times. I was bridge gang. I wore ball and chain. That was in my young days. I used to didn't stand no cheatin'. You ever heard 'My baby don't stand no cheatin'?' I ain't lying. That done growed up in me."

No records have ever been found of exactly what crimes Hopkins committed to lead to him being sentenced to a chain gang. He did say, "The first time I went to jail . . . me and my little cousin and a guy got into it. Fact of the business, the man was older than we was, and he just thought he was going to knock us boys around. My cousin had a razor in his pocket and I hit the guy, and he had my cousin choking him, and I said, 'Cut him.' And he kind of slice him in the sides. Man, I tell you, that was a full Sunday." Sam and his cousin left the man bleeding and took off, but they didn't go very far. They were able to get work "choppin' cotton" about twenty miles away. About a week later, they were arrested in the "cotton patch," and brought to jail, but they stayed only one night because Sam's brother Joel paid "the fine." From then on, Sam said people called him "Jailbird" because he continued to get into trouble. "I went crazy," he said, "Jail didn't mean nothing to me then. You could put me in there every day." But Sam knew, no matter how hard he tried, he couldn't run from the law. "If I do something," he said, "I go give up. Because that learnt me a lesson. Don't. Never know that you did something and try to run away from it. It may be twenty years [for them] to get you, and then it's worse. So, just go on and give up."[51]

As often as Hopkins expressed his disdain for the law, the time he spent "chained up" forced him to control his temper. He once spent two hundred days on a bridge gang, toiling from dawn to dusk on bridge construction and repair and chained to a post every night in his bed.[52] Another time, after getting into a fight in Grapeland, he was sentenced to time on a Houston County road crew. He somehow managed to escape but was picked up in Leon County and returned to the chain gang.[53] Sam knew that he had to change his ways. "Mess with me a little bit," he said, "I'd start me a little fight in a minute. So they was throwing a rope on me and puttin' me in the joint and going on. I had to calm down. Wearing that ball and chain ain't no good."[54]

Sam's time in jail and on the chain gang became fodder for the songs he later performed. He recorded the first, "Jail House Blues," in 1949:

> Well, I wouldn't mind staying in jail
> But I've gotta stay there so long
> Thirty days in jail
> With my back turned to the wall

This rendition of "Jail House Blues" borrowed heavily from Bessie Smith's 1923 song of the same title, and while Sam made it sound as if it conveyed his personal experience, only the final verse appeared to be his own:

> Hey, mister jailer
> Will you please sir bring me the key
> I just want you to open the door
> 'Cause this ain't no place for me

Sam's song "I Worked Down on the Chain Gang" was more of a talking blues, in which he recounted his experience with a ball and chain around his leg and emphasized the cold indifference of the guards: "I said, 'Please don't drive me too hard, I'm an old man.'/ They say, 'We don't pay no attention to the age.'" But he concluded by falling back on the refrain to "Jail House Blues" and reiterated his plea: "I says I just want you to open the door/ 'Cause this ain't no place for me."

For a man who claimed to be in and out of jail a lot during the 1930s, Sam sang remarkably few, if any, original lyrics about his incarceration. Songs about prison experiences or run-ins with the law were fairly common in prewar blues, and were means for blues singers to present themselves as victims. While Sam may have exaggerated his jail time, he did indeed have tangible proof of his experiences, and when he started touring to festivals, folk clubs, and the white college circuit, he liked to show off the scars around his ankles.[55] Back stage, he sometimes rolled up his pant leg and asked whomever he was talking to if they knew what those scars were from. Ultimately, what we know about Sam's jail and chain-gang time is limited by what he decided to tell about those experiences, which actually isn't very much. However, the large blank spots in his biography from 1930 to 1946 suggest the possibility of more jail time than Sam would later care to admit in the very selective interviews he gave. One has to wonder what got Sam sentenced to two hundred days on a bridge gang. Clearly he had a vicious temper and was prone to violence and aggravated assault during this period of his life, though it would not have taken much to land him in jail. Even a rather minor crime could have gotten a harsh sentence from a racist judge, and many completely innocent blacks served long sentences for things they didn't do.

In his songs and in interviews, Sam usually shifted the focus from the crime to the punishment. He realized that it was in his best interest to portray himself as a victim who was able to triumph over his adversity. For example, in discussing one of his chain gang experiences, he began by asking, "You drive up around Crockett on them roads?" He then elaborated, "Well, I built roads by myself with a chain locked around this ankle. See the scar there, festering and scabby, ain't it? Back in '37 or so. That judge came and says to turn me loose after I'd sung him a song about 'How bad and how sad to be a fool.'"[56] Here, Sam was in effect demonstrating his ability to adapt the Leadbelly prison release legend to his own purpose, as had Texas Alexander before him.[57] Jail and the chain gang were integral to the persona he wanted to project and to the myth he built for himself. Hardship and suffering engaged the listener, and the ironic humor with which he articulated his plight in his lyrics boosted his stature as a man of words. Certainly, Sam did his best to stay out of jail, but the hardheaded recklessness that got him there also energized his music.

Perhaps Sam's physical appearance played a role in the way he presented himself. He was of average height, but he was frail and skinny and could have easily been overcome in a fistfight. Maybe he adopted his knife- and gun-toting persona as a defense mechanism and as a means to establish that he could take care of himself if he needed to in the rough and violent worlds of the juke joints that were the lifeblood of his music.

Hopkins grew up fast, and by the time he was a teenager, he was ostensibly an adult; he had served jail time, worked as a farm worker, played music on the streets for tips, and traveled around East and Central Texas as a hobo. On September 21, 1928, at age sixteen, he married Elamer Lacy, also known as "Noona." A year later, on August 29, his daughter Anna Mae was born.[58] "My dad was a person that everybody liked that knew him," Anna Mae recalled. "He'd sit there with his leg crossed and look out the window. And they'd come by and holler at him. He was a joyful person."[59] But he hated working in the fields. "It was hard times," Sam said. "I was working in the fields, trying to take care of my wife, me, and my mother. Six bits a day. And that was top price. And I swear, I'd come in the evening, and look like I'd be so weak till my knees would be clucking like a wagon wheel. I'd go to bed, I'd say, 'Baby, well I just can't continue like this.'"[60]

But it wasn't only the farm work that was a problem for Sam. "Me and my first wife were together fourteen years, and I never seen her naked in my life," Sam said. "Wasn't nothing wrong with her and I know it. She told me that it was something that she was born with, to never get naked with no man, regardless to whom, husband or anyone else. You understand me? We were together, but she was never showing me, just like you get up here and pull your clothes off naked. 'You get it under the covers. You can pull off anything and you still won't see me naked.' And she never walked in front of me naked in her life. Now, I'm not lying to you."[61]

Anna Mae said that her parents split up when she was five: "Mama left and went out to the country. We stayed with Daddy's mother [Frances]. Daddy always loved his music. And he always let nothing or nobody keep him from it."[62] After Sam and Elamer separated, Anna Mae had very little contact with her father, "with him coming and going," though she did say she always enjoyed seeing her grandmother, who was then living on Ike Dawkins's farm.

"Folks were close-knit back then," Ray Dawkins says. "Mama Frances was in Leona, Texas, down here. She got into some kind of debt and Daddy cleared it and moved her onto our farm. And she had a grey horse and a buckskin horse. We had two houses on the place. The big house was where we lived, and another house was down below. Daddy bought that farm in 1931. He give $900 for 80 acres, eight miles southeast of Centerville on the other side of Nubbin Ridge across Keechi Creek. I was a little bitty boy of five or six when I first remember meeting Sam—he was a tall, kind of slender man. I guess he was about nineteen or twenty, and he come back to help his mama. And in the evenings, he used to sit me on his knee and play and sing. I wanted to imitate everything that he did, but I couldn't. So I became a dancer, and at house parties I'd tap or buck dance. Just about everyone had someone in the family who played guitar or piano. Not too many people could afford a radio. One or two had wind-up Victrolas. But playing music was the big entertainment. People would ride in a wagon if they had one. They go from one house to the next on Saturdays, and to church on Sunday. And if they didn't have a wagon, they'd ride a horse or walk."[63]

Sam didn't spend much time with his mother because he was "always going off somewhere to play music or gamble," Dawkins says, but he "did as much as he could to help her." From the Dawkins farm, Frances Hopkins moved to Guy Store Prairie a few miles away. "They went to Herman Mannings's place," Dawkins says, "and when they left from there, they went to Ben Coleman's place. Ben Coleman was white; Herman Mannings was white. Sam farmed down there, but he never did work too much. He played music all the time, and the white people had him playing music around the house, piano, guitar, organ. It didn't make him no difference."[64]

According to Dawkins, Sam stayed "some with his mother," but also with Ida Mae, who lived about a mile and a half away from his father's farm. "Ida Mae was a light-skinned girl," Dawkins says, "and they lived together for I don't know how long." In Sam's song "Ida Mae," recorded for the Gold Star label in 1947, he sang, "Yes, you know that woman name Ida Mae/ Folks say she good to me all the time," but then implies that she was unfaithful, drawing upon a traditional blues verse that had been used by Robert Johnson, among others: "Yes, you don't think cause Ida Mae got every man in town/ Baby, you know ain't doing nothing but tearing your reputation down."[65] However, Sam, on different occasions, said that Ida Mae was his wife, though there are no records that prove they were ever actually married. In another version of the song, Sam extolled her virtues and his devotion.

> You know, Ida Mae's a good girl
> Folks say she don't run around at night (x2)
> Yeah, you know, you can bet your last dollar
> Oh, Ida Mae will treat you right[66]

Ida Mae, identified by blues and jazz researcher Mack McCormick (who would later play a pivotal role in Lightnin's career) as Ida Mae Gardner, appears to have been involved with Sam through the 1950s, even though their relationship was at times tumultuous. By some accounts they had a vicious fight around 1937, and Sam stabbed her. But when Sam was sentenced to two years in the Crockett County jail and served his time on the chain gang, McCormick maintains she "got a job cooking for the prisoners in order to be close enough to Lightnin' to attend to his wants and at the same time pay off his fine."[67] However, Dawkins says that he knew Ida Mae for many years and that she lived out her life in Guy Store. To his knowledge, she never married, and when asked about these contradictions, Dawkins speculated that there might have been more than one Ida Mae. Certainly, Sam's loose attitude toward the term *wife* is a complicating factor in trying to sort out the women in his life. He often bragged about how many women he had over the years. "They just be around," he liked to say, "don't you know, I'm some bad man?"[68]

Sam's exploits with women were well known in the African American community of Leon County. People recognized that he was gifted as a guitarist and singer who carried forward the musical culture in which he was raised, but many disapproved of his behavior. Dawkins and Langford were among the many who marveled at his capacity as a performer, but understated his reckless and at times violent conduct. As a person, Sam was scurrilous. He was affable and sharp-witted, but introverted; wary, but sly. He was a backslider by church standards, a drinker and a brawler who lied and gambled, doing anything he could to stay away from the chain gang and the cotton field. Yet he was apparently never completely ostracized, and over the course of his life, he never forgot his country roots. Sam's blues gave voice to the hardships and foibles that he and so many in his community were experiencing, but by the early 1930s, he had gotten himself into enough trouble that he had to move on.

2

~~~^^^~~~

Travels with Texas Alexander

Sam Hopkins was about twenty years old when he met Alger "Texas" Alexander at a baseball game in Normangee, about seventeen miles southwest of Centerville. Normangee was playing against a team from Leona, but off to the side of the field, Hopkins heard someone shouting the blues. "So, I got down there," Sam said, "and I seen a man standing up on a truck with his hand up to his mouth, and man, that man was singing. . . . He like to broke up the ballgame. People was paying so much attention to him. They was interested in him."

Baseball had been a popular sport among African Americans in Texas since the late 1880s. The numerous attempts to organize a viable, professional black baseball association culminated with the formation of the Lone Star Colored Baseball League of Texas in 1897 with clubs representing Galveston, Palestine, Beaumont, Lagrange, Temple, Austin, and Houston.[1] The Normangee and

Leona teams were not formally part of this league. They were likely amateur, or, in a sense, semi-professional, where the players aspired to advance their careers, but were not necessarily paid. Local teams got some local sponsorship to help defer the costs of equipment, and the games attracted people from the surrounding communities. A blues singer, like Texas Alexander, seized the opportunity to perform for tips.

Sam claimed that Alexander was his cousin, but no direct kinship has ever been established. Sam had a very loose definition of the term "cousin" that he tended to use more as an expression of endearment than a statement of fact. Texas Alexander was born on September 12, 1900, in Jewett, Texas, in Leon County, about seven miles from Centerville. He eventually settled in Normangee, a small town that grew up around the railroad stop on the Houston and Texas Central Railway established in 1905 at the intersection of Farm Roads 39 and 3. He was raised by his grandmother because his own mother was "rowdy" and "runnin' around." Growing up he toiled as a field hand, but by 1927 he had moved to Dallas, where he worked as a store man in a warehouse and made "spending change" by singing in cafes and on the streets of the Deep Ellum and Central Track area of the city.

Deep Ellum was the area of Elm Street in Dallas, north of downtown, where immigrants to the city flocked. The spelling Ellum resulted from the mix of dialects of the people who settled there—African Americans displaced by the ravages of the boll weevil in East Texas and Eastern European Jews fleeing the pogroms and persecution in their homeland. The juncture of Elm Street and Central Avenue was where day laborers were picked up and dropped off, taken to the cotton fields of Collin County or to do other jobs. Many of the black businesses were strung out along Central Avenue, which ran alongside the railroad tracks. Black show business and musical activity flourished in Deep Ellum. As early as 1908, John "Fat Jack" Harris opened the Grand Central Theater there and featured local and touring acts. The Grand Central was followed by the Swiss Airdome, the Star, the Circle, and the Palace. The Park Theater was operated by vaudevillians Chintz and Ella B. Moore and offered "high class vaudeville and moving pictures." Black vaudeville entertainment took various forms, including the "tab" or "tabloid" musical comedy show, as well as touring minstrel and stock companies; novelty acts such as the five-hundred-pound Cleo-Cleo and Jack Rabbit, the hoop contortionist; comedians such as Little Jimmie Cox, a Charlie Chaplin imitator; high-kicking dancers; duos such as Butterbeans and Susie; and musicians and singers.[2] In 1920, Chintz Moore and about thirty other black Southern and Midwestern theater owners established the premier black vaudeville circuit, the Theater Owners Booking Association (TOBA), which grew to more than eighty theaters and eventually became known as the "Chitlin' Circuit." Performers often joked that the acronym stood for "Tough on Black Asses" because contracts heavily favored management and the conditions of work were often harsh.

Pianist Sam Price, who worked at R. T. Ashford's shine parlor and record shop on Central Avenue in Dallas and was instrumental in the discovery of Blind Lemon Jefferson, was looking for new talent when he heard Texas Alexander singing on the street. "Texas Alexander had an uncanny voice," Price said, "but he couldn't keep time. That was one of the things I had to teach him."[3] With Ashford's help, arrangements were made for Alexander to go to New York to record in August 1927 and for Lonnie Johnson to accompany him.

Texas Alexander's slow moaning style and his inability to sing in meter made it especially difficult for Johnson, who remarked, "He was liable to jump a bar, or five bars, or anything. You just had to be a fast thinker to play for Texas Alexander. When you been out there with him you done nine days work in one! Believe me, brother, he was hard to play for."[4]

Despite the irregularities of his singing, Alexander's emotionally charged vocal style had great appeal, and the sales of his records were unexpectedly high. He was invited back to the OKeh studios, and between 1927 and 1930 he recorded fifty-two songs with a wide range of accompanists, from Eddie Lang and Lonnie Johnson, who were already established as two of the best guitarists of the era, to an ensemble that included the great King Oliver, Clarence Williams, and Eddie Heywood, to lesser-known regional guitarists like Carl Davis and Little Hat Jones, and even the legendary Mississippi Sheiks with Bo Chatman (Carter) on violin, Sam Chatman on guitar, and Walter Vinson on second guitar. Unlike his other accompanists, the Mississippi Sheiks, a popular and influential guitar and fiddle group of the 1930s, provided Alexander with a rare string band setting that was uncompromising, forcing him to discipline his singing into an uncharacteristic swing.[5]

By the mid-1930s, when Sam met him, Alexander's recording career had tapered off because of the Great Depression, but he was still highly regarded as a performer, and wherever he sang, he had a commanding presence. Hopkins recalled, as did others, that Texas Alexander carried a guitar with him so that anyone who wanted to accompany him could do so. Alexander didn't play the guitar himself, and Sam picked up the instrument and showed him what he could do. "He come . . . ready with that singing. He couldn't play no music," Sam said. "Never played an instrument in his life. But he'd tote a guitar; he'd buy a guitar. But he'd tote it in case he'd run up on you or me or somebody could play, and he'd sing. And he kept a guitar because if he asked could you play a guitar and you say 'Yeah.' Well, he got one, see. And then y'all tear it off."[6] Before long, Hopkins was traveling with Texas Alexander and accompanying, or following, him on guitar. Given that Alexander often broke time, Sam must have struggled at first to keep up, but was apparently able to eventually learn his songs sufficiently to play with him. Clearly, Alexander was not that particular when he showed up at a little juke joint or cafe in East and Central Texas ready to perform.

Texas Alexander showed Sam that he could make a living singing blues. By the 1930s, Sam was fed up with farm work. "I didn't make too much picking cotton," he said. "I'm telling you the truth because they wasn't paying but fifty cents a hundred [pounds of cotton picked]. Man, I'd make me two dollars and something. I was picking four and five hundred [pounds]. But you know, man, I'm telling you the truth, if you just know what it takes to get two dollars out of that cotton patch. . . . But I wasn't on that farm much longer. I left."[7]

While Sam was used to performing for tips, he was beginning to figure out how to get paid for his music. "I commenced to playing for dances," he said. "See, when I got good, and when I went to finding them there places where they barrelhouse [drinking and dancing], I didn't know. I just had to run up on them places, see, around Jewett, Buffalo, and Crockett. And they had little old joints for Saturday nights, you know. But what you gonna do through the week? I found Mart and out there and around Coolidge and where they had one every night, man, I did all right for myself because that was my business. Those joints, cafe joints, you know, where they'd get back in this part and they'd do a little dancing in there, and they'd drink a little. And I was getting three and a half

[$3.50] in Coolidge, Texas. Got pretty good, and so they raised it to around six dollars to go to Mart, making six dollars a night."[8]

With Texas Alexander, Hopkins was able to even earn more. Alexander was known as a recording artist, so he tended to attract bigger audiences wherever he went. Hopkins followed Texas Alexander through the East and Central Texas towns of Crockett, Grapeland, Palestine, Oakwood, Buffalo, Centerville, Normangee, and Flynn. For Sam, Texas Alexander became a kind of mentor, who, like Blind Lemon Jefferson, who played novelty songs and country tunes, in addition to blues.

Once Prohibition ended in 1933, juke joints and barrelhouses on the outskirts of little towns, which had essentially functioned as speakeasies, became more public. However, the laws related to the sale and consumption of liquor varied from county to county, and bootlegging was still rampant. The little joints where Sam and Texas Alexander performed were likely not licensed to sell liquor and probably served booze illegally. They were places where sharecroppers and day laborers alike found some reprieve from the hardships and suffering of the Great Depression, proffering booze, women, music, dancing, and gambling. It was in these gritty, smoke-filled shacks that Sam honed his skills as a guitarist and singer, composing and performing the blues that gave voice to what those around him were feeling and experiencing. While he ventured off on his own at times, he often played with Texas Alexander.

While Sam never recorded with Alexander, he was influenced by his songs, which not only evoked a poignant sense of what life and work must have been like at that time, but also expressed a bitter sense of irony. In "Levee Camp Moan," Texas Alexander's extended hums and moans drawn out over unevenly spaced measures punctuated the lyrics. "Section Gang Blues" combined elements of a traditional work song that might have been shouted by gandydancers lining out railroad track with a sarcastic commentary: "Nigger lick molasses and the white man likes it too/ Lord, I wonder what in the world is the Mexican gonna do." In "Boe Hog Blues," [a mistitling of "Boar Hog Blues"] a sexual explicitness underscored the song's strident sense of humor:

> Oh tell me mama, how d'ye want your rollin' done (x2)
> Says, your face to the ground and your poodle up to the sun

> She got little bitty legs, gee, but below her thighs (x2)
> She's got something on-a-yonder works like a bo' hog's eye
> Says, "I'll be your doctor, pay your bills" (x2)
> Says, "If the doctor won't cure you, I've got something will"

From Texas Alexander, Hopkins learned to emphasize lyrics and the need to rhyme, often at the expense of meter. Alexander rarely sang in meter, though he could turn a phrase and extend his lyrics into a looser, more sprawling structure that might have an extra measure, or thirteen or fourteen bars instead of twelve. By taking this approach, Alexander demonstrated to Sam the power of improvisation, and how ordinary speech could become the fodder of a song lyric.

Moreover, Texas Alexander gave Hopkins a tangible sense of the benefits that making records might bring. Alexander drove a Cadillac, and it made Sam realize that even a black musician from a small town in Texas could be successful in the music business. "First Cadillac that I was known to be," Hopkins said, "one them expensive cars, you know, he went somewhere and he showed up in Normangee and that was longest and most ugly car. Long Cadillac—one of those the first made, you know. Cuz colored people they didn't have even T-Model Fords then. He come in a Cadillac. Texas was doing all right for hisself."[9] To own a Cadillac at the onset of the Great Depression was impressive, but apparently Texas Alexander's records had sold quite well in the late 1920s to rural audiences, as well as among people who had started moving to the city but still enjoyed a taste of the older country styles.

In his song "Deceitful Blues" he sang, "I'm gonna trade this Lincoln, get me a Cadillac eight." In these 1934 recordings, Texas Alexander was trying to keep up with the times, most significantly by adding a small jazz combo, but in the end, his efforts were in vain: his lyrics and singing remained as rural as before. In "Blues in My Mind" the lyrics had more conventional, and even sentimental lines, such as "I'm crying, with tears in my eyes." But he still retained his irreverent edge in "Polo Blues," in which he sang:

> You can hand me my pistol, shotgun and some shells
> I'm gonna kill my woman, send the poor gal to hell

You can get your milk from a polo [an animal that had had its horns
    removed], cream from a jersey cow
Your pigment from your pig, and your bacon from a no-good sow

In "Prairie Dog Hole" he took pride in his irreligious life: "Lord, My Father,
Lord Thy Kingdom come/ Send me back my baby and my will be done," and
then declared, "I went to church and the people called on me to pray/ I set down
on my knees and forgot just what to say."[10]

According to Sam, some time in 1934, probably after Texas Alexander's
second session for the Vocalion label in Fort Worth, they made it to Houston to
audition for a radio station. They were joined by harmonica player Billy Bizor,
another of Sam's purported cousins, but it's unclear whether or not they were
actually given a radio spot. "First time into Houston," Sam said, "I just went to
Houston because I heard the name of Houston, and what a town it was. . . . Texas
and I worked on West Dallas Street [in the thriving Fourth Ward]. . . . Texas an'
I'd work up and down the street, him and me."[11] The city piqued his interest,
but he didn't go back for nearly five years. At this point in his life, Sam wasn't
ready to leave the country. Life was tough in Leon County, but he knew his way
around. "Big cities," he said, "I hadn't been used to 'em. I'd been used to little
three or four stores, and they call it Centerville and Leona."[12]

By the late 1930s, Hopkins and Texas Alexander had gone their separate
ways. Sam was in and out of jail. He was still hell-bent on pursuing his own
music career, though working the juke joints wasn't easy. He ended up getting in
fights over booze, women, and gambling that got him arrested and sent back to
the chain gang. "I was getting cooped up and knocked around pretty good," Sam
said, "I always somehow or another, I'd be lucky and manage to get out. And one
time, I run away."

Sam made his way to Mississippi. "I went to Clarksdale. That's right, hoboing with one dime in my pocket."[13] The details of what happened next are not
entirely clear. In Clarksdale, Sam recalled that he met up with his "wife" and
her brother, though it's unknown whether or not it was the same wife [Elamer]
he had left in Texas. But he didn't stay in Clarksdale very long. He found a job
"picking up those pecans. They was getting nice money . . . dollar and a half a
hundred [pounds]." When he wasn't gathering pecans, he went off to a place

called the Bullpen near the place where his "wife" and her brother were living. The Bullpen was, Sam said, "a hobo jungle. . . . It was under a shed, like. . . . So, I'd go down there. They'd gamble and pick guitars and drink. They had plenty to drink. So, I'd go down and play that guitar for them and make me three or four dollars and sometimes [get] women, twelve, fifteen of them. I done good . . . [and] walked away."

When Sam got back to Texas, he wanted to see his mother, but he was only in Centerville for a short time. He continued to ramble around. "I caught a freight train in Crockett going to Palestine, Texas," Sam said, "but I had a little weak string on my guitar around my neck, and that wind hit that guitar, and I ain't seen that guitar since. But that's the only time I got a freight train; that's right. I taken my sister with me. She was sitting up there with me when that guitar said, 'Whoop!' Gone, man. I ain't joking."[14]

Frank Robinson recalls meeting Hopkins when he came to his hometown of Crockett, Texas around 1935. "My uncle [Clyde Robinson] was running around with him," Robinson says, "and he had a daughter, which is Anna Mae Box [who lived in Crockett]. We grew up together, and he would always come and visit. My uncle, he couldn't play, but he loved guitar music, so whenever a gui-tar picker would come to town, he would always bring them by the house. My family loved to hear guitar music, and I grew up knowing him. . . . Well, they drank and gambled together, but my uncle, he couldn't play. He could sing, but he couldn't play at all."[15]

Robinson recalled that Hopkins had a deep voice and that "he was real friendly, but he liked to drink, and when he'd get to drinking, well, he was quite outspoken. . . . But other than that, he was really nice. Me and him, we talked. He said never a hard word to me the whole time I knowed him. And I looked up to him just like I did my daddy and my uncle, surely."

In 1939, when Robinson's family went to Arizona to pick cotton, Hopkins went along, but he didn't spend much time picking cotton. "He liked to gam-ble," Robinson remembers. "Gambling was legal at that time, out there, and they would all go gambling. We'd peep at them and go on about our business. And at last one day, we didn't see Sam no more."

Where Sam went after leaving Arizona is uncertain, but it's likely that he went back to Texas to stay with his mother in Centerville and play on the street for tips and in little joints and cafes. He may have gone looking for Texas Alexander, but around 1939, Texas Alexander got into trouble. According to bluesman Frankie Lee Sims, Texas Alexander committed a double murder and was sentenced to prison. Pianist Buster Pickens maintained that Texas Alexander served time in the Ramsey State Farm around 1942. However, there are no prison records to substantiate either Sims's or Pickens's claims.

Guitarist Lowell Fulson said Texas Alexander had told him that he had been sentenced to life in Huntsville Penitentiary, but said that he was only incarcerated "three months and twenty-one days" because "he sung his way out of there. They run him off, telling him, 'Come back down here again, and we'll kill you.' He said what happened was that they couldn't stop him singing. He sang that old mourning-type stuff. Nobody wanted to be in the place where he was. He just got next to them all, so they let him go. They run him out of there."[16]

Fulson maintained that he met up with Texas Alexander in 1939: "I worked in a string band for a while in Ada, Oklahoma—Dan Wright and his string band. I couldn't get the blues feel for the type of music they were playing. So Texas Alexander came through there, and he wanted a guitar player. So he heard me. . . . I went on a trip with him to Texas. First, we started out in Western Oklahoma and played Saturday night fish fries and whatever else they had going on. They'd cut the nickelodeon [jukebox] if they thought you sounded pretty good. They let you play there, and they passed the hat around, take up a little collection."[17]

Texas Alexander insisted that he had been in prison twice, once with a sentence of ten years on Ramsey Farm for murder or attempted murder "over some woman," and then a second time, for singing the "obscene" song "Boar Hog Blues." However, no prison records have survived to establish that Alexander was ever in prison. In fact, he may never have served prison time, but told people that to establish a badass credibility that even Sam found appealing.

Sam never talked much about Texas Alexander's crimes, or how long or where he was in jail, though he did confirm that he was punished for singing "Boar Hog Blues." However, when Mack McCormick asked him if they put Alexander in prison, Sam was vague: "Well, I don't know. That's what they tell me."[18]

Texas Alexander made a huge impression on Sam, even though in the overall scope of Alexander's career, Sam was a relatively minor accompanist. The peak of his popularity was probably between 1927 and 1929, but he continued to have a following that extended into Oklahoma and was concentrated in the small towns of East and Central Texas and the segregated wards of Houston. Alexander never exuded optimism in his songs. His music was always more unsettling than it was entertaining, and while he dwelled heavily upon the difficulties he claimed to have experienced, his actual biography remains inscrutable. Whether or not Texas Alexander was forthright in his songs wasn't important. His lyrics had a resonance that moved those who identified with the hard luck and bad times that he sang about, and from Alexander, Sam learned that it wasn't necessarily the truth of the song that mattered so much as the emotions it evoked.

Hopkins's rambling vocal style is heavily indebted to Alexander, but Sam seemed to know few of his songs, at least the ones he recorded. Texas Alexander may have discouraged him or warned him not to imitate him, but then again, Sam may simply not have liked his songs, or perhaps was only interested in certain lines. As Sam matured as a singer and guitarist, the recordings of Big Bill Broonzy, John Lee "Sonny Boy" Williamson, Lonnie Johnson, and Tampa Red, among other popular blues artists, figured more heavily in his development. To Sam, Texas Alexander's music probably seemed dated, and he wanted to keep up with his peers whom he heard on jukeboxes. Yet, on a personal level, Sam admired Texas Alexander, who demonstrated what success as a bluesman might bring—booze, women, and even a Cadillac car—but also made explicit the perils of a self-destructive life.

3

The Move to Houston

With the growth of Houston as an oil-rich shipping port and industrial center, the African American population increased rapidly to meet the needs of an expanding work force. By 1920 there were an estimated 35,000 African Americans in Houston, and by 1940 the number had swelled to roughly 86,000 out of a total population of 384,000. In 1945 the Port of Houston was the fourth busiest in the United States, and by 1948, it was second only to New York in overall tonnage. While Houston embraced and promoted a Western image for itself (replete with rodeos and cowboy culture), it was very much a Southern city during the first half of the twentieth century, with everything that entailed, even as the burgeoning oil industry supplanted the cotton economy that had helped Houston flourish. The sharecropping system of the surrounding rural areas was collapsing as African Americans moved to the city looking for jobs and a better way of life. Houston's black community was spread across principally the Third, Fourth and Fifth Wards. While the ward system of government was dissolved by the City of Houston in the early 1900s, the names remained, and as the city evolved over the years, so did the geographical boundaries of the neighborhoods they defined.

Racism was rampant in Houston. The separate-but-equal principle, upheld by the United States Supreme Court in *Plessy v. Ferguson* (1896), legalized racial discrimination, and Houston, like other cities throughout Texas, passed Jim Crow laws that restricted African American access to public facilities and permeated every social, political, and economic institution in the city, including housing, education, and employment.

On August 23, 1917, years of racial tension erupted in a deadly riot that was triggered by the arrest of a black soldier stationed at Camp Logan on the outskirts of the city, for interfering with the arrest of a black woman in the Fourth Ward. Though the soldier was released, rumors spread to Camp Logan that he had been executed, and more than one hundred black soldiers marched on the city in protest, killing sixteen whites, including five policemen. The consequences of the riot were severe; nineteen black soldiers were hanged and sixty-three received life sentences in federal prison, and the separation of blacks and whites across the city was strictly enforced and more carefully monitored.[1]

Lower-, middle-, and upper-class African Americans lived and worked in close proximity to one another, but the level of education and income of the residents in the wards varied greatly. Articles in the *Houston Informer*, founded as the *Texas Freeman* in 1893 and still publishing today, attest to the diversity of life in the segregated wards, and point out the complexities of social, economic, political, and cultural growth among all sectors of the black population in which Sam Hopkins lived and worked.[2]

The Fourth Ward, established as a freedman's town after the Civil War, was the site of the first black church, high school, and medical facility in the city. As it grew, so did the degree of stratification within the community there. It developed its own musical identity early on. It was home to what was known as the Santa Fe Group, a loosely knit assemblage of blues pianists in the 1920s and '30s which included Robert Shaw, Black Boy Shine, Pinetop Burks, and Rob Cooper. Together and individually, these pianists frequented the roadhouses along the Santa Fe railroad that sold "chock" (bootleg liquor) and prostitution, playing a distinctive style of piano that combined elements of blues with the syncopation of ragtime.

According to Shaw, there were so many blues pianists in Houston during this period that each neighborhood had its own particular style. In the Fifth

Ward, the most well-known pianists and vocalists were members of the George W. Thomas family. The eldest child George Thomas Jr. was born about 1885, followed by his sister Beulah, better known as Sippie Wallace, and brother, Hersal. Their style of piano playing involved more fully developed bass patterns than those of the Santa Fe Group.[3]

The Fifth Ward of Houston also had an area known as Frenchtown, where about five hundred blacks of French and Spanish descent migrated from Louisiana in 1922. As the population grew, the music performed there reflected both Creole and African American influences, not only in blues but in the emerging zydeco style. African American businesses, from restaurants, pharmacies, and doctors' offices to undertakers, beauty parlors, and barbershops, flourished on Lyons Avenue and served the people who lived in the area, many of whom worked for the nearby Southern Pacific Railroad or on the Houston Ship Channel.

During the 1930s, the acclaimed music program of Phillis Wheatley High School in the Fifth Ward vied with Jack Yates High School in the Third Ward for local recognition. Their marching bands were a breeding ground for aspiring musicians, and the competition between them reflected the breadth of the Houston blues and jazz scene. Student members of the marching bands played at football and basketball games, and orchestra students played at all school functions. On weekends, many of the school band directors performed around the city (and some, like Abner Jones, Sammy Harris, and later Conrad Johnson, led jazz orchestras). Student musicians were often featured at church socials and at events sponsored by civic organizations, such as Jack and Jill of America, and Links, and by the numerous sororities and fraternities in the African American community.

By the late 1930s the *Informer* had started to use the phrase "Heavenly Houston" to describe the can-do attitude of the upwardly mobile African American population pulling out of the Great Depression. The Third Ward had the highest concentration of African Americans, and Dowling Street became the main street of black Houston. Lined with churches and African American owned businesses, it was the epicenter of community life. The opening of the El Dorado Ballroom on December 5, 1939, on the second floor of a Deco-style professional building at the corner of Elgin and Dowling Streets was a banner day for African Americans in Houston.[4] C. A. Dupree, treasurer of the El Dorado Social Club and an employee of the very exclusive (white) River Oaks Country Club, was the driving force behind the building. The El Dorado Social Club was in existence for many years prior to the formation of the ballroom and lent it their name and support. The ballroom was comanaged by Dupree and his wife Anna and quickly became the showplace of the Third Ward, if not all of black Houston. "The El Dorado Ballroom made us feel like we were kings and queens," blues vocalist Carolyn Blanchard recalled. "When you went there, from the moment you walked through the door, everything was taken care of. Anna and Mr. Dupree didn't let you want for anything. They would get whatever you wanted for you. We always held our heads a little higher after leaving the El Dorado."[5]

Black social clubs and fraternal organizations dominated the El Dorado Ballroom, and the *Houston Informer* usually covered their festivities. On March 9, 1940, for example, the *Informer* reported: "Amid a conglomeration of laughter, colorful gowns, well-fitted tuxedos and good music, sepia Houstonians came to the realization, last Tuesday evening at the swank El Dorado Ballroom, that this hitherto flat and backward Southern town has definitely broken into the glorious realm of glamorous and chic society. Seven hundred or more socialites were present to witness the advent of this great phenomena, a strictly formal affair given by the El Dorado Social Club, one of the oldest and yet one of the most active organizations."

The El Dorado Ballroom featured touring stars and local performers, as well as talent shows and teen dances. Some of the top bands that performed there were the I. H. Smalley Orchestra, the Sammy Harris Orchestra, the Sherman Williams Orchestra, and the Milton Larkin Orchestra, which was a breeding ground for aspiring musicians, such as Arnett Cobb, Illinois Jacquet, Cedric Haywood, Wild Bill Davis, and Tom Archia. These local big bands, six to twelve pieces deep, played the music of Count Basie, Duke Ellington, Lionel Hampton, Louis Jordan, and the orchestrated swing-era hits of the time. And when they weren't performing at the El Dorado, they might be found at other clubs around the city. The Downtown Grill, Pyramid Club, the Rendezvous Club, the Harlem Grill (a.k.a. Sportsman's Club), Tick Tock Tavern, Southgates, and Abe and Pappy's (a white club) all featured black bands on weekends and special occasions. Bigger-name national acts, like Jimmie Lunceford, Erskine Hawkins, Count Basie, and Duke Ellington, often picked up sidemen in Houston for shows at the Pilgrim Temple in the Fourth Ward or at the City Auditorium downtown.

Houston was rife with musical talent, and there were numerous orchestras and bands that, as early as the late 1930s, featured a mix of Texas-area performing artists, from Ivory Joe Hunter to Eddie Taylor, Henry Sloan, T. H. Crone, Giles Mitchell, Tack Wilson, Bob Williams, Jerry Moore, Joe Pullum, and the Prairie View Collegians. Pullum was one of the few to actually make records prior to World War II; most of these bands were ignored by the major labels recording in Texas at the time because company executives didn't feel the music was commercially viable. Yet Pullum had a hit on Bluebird in 1934 with "Black Gal What Makes Your Head So Hard," a song that Sam Hopkins covered and recorded in 1961.[6]

By the time Sam made his way to Houston in the early 1940s, the Third Ward was teeming with nightlife. But to middle- and upper-class residents of the Third Ward, Hopkins was probably invisible. He was one of the many poor rural blacks trying to get a foothold in the city, frequenting the lower-class bars, some of which, according to the *Informer*, were part of a bigger social problem. In a March 2, 1940, editorial, the *Informer* wrote: "County Judge Roy Hofheinz has announced a fight on honky tonks which sell strong drinks to minors. . . . There are Negro places that knowingly sell beer to minors. . . . There are some places which permit marijuana to be sold to minors in their places. Every Negro should endorse the campaign to close such places of business."

Sam was not known to smoke marijuana, but he did play in the kind of honky tonks referenced in this editorial. In another article in the *Informer*, columnist Ted Williams gave a more visual description of the honky tonks, though he had a very condescending tone: "Yes Honky Tonks [sic], where one sees the other side of Houston's nightlife. For these places are rendezvous for those who like the enjoyment in a crude way. Clothes are of the least importance. The men and women who frequent these places are usually in their work clothes. . . . Lacking in modern furnishings they make up for it with hilarity. The jocund strains of guitar music ringing from the nickelodeon sends the crowd there in to dances that crosses between the swing-out of today and the native dance of the dark continent. Women swing and shake their bodies, while the men do their numbers.

Words of all description can be heard among the throng. Though somewhat primitive, it is an interesting spectacle."[7]

During his early years in Houston, Lightnin' also performed on the street and did whatever he could to eke out a living. "I stuck around there awhile," he said, "and they come to find out that I was playing up and down Dowling Street there. So that began to get around, see, and I began to ride the buses free. The bus driver stopped and picked me up anywhere he'd see me with that guitar. And they'd have a big time on that bus. . . . I'd pick up quarters, halves, dollars. He'd even shill me a couple of dollars. . . . And one thing that the bus driver did—God in heaven knows that I'm not lying—he knowed that I drank, so he stopped at the liquor store on the corner of Dowling and Leeland at his own risk. Sent me in that liquor store and I got me a half a pint of liquor and he wait till I come back and then he takes on off. He brought me on back to Elgin and Dowling, and I goes on down to Holman, and I told him, 'Now, I wants to get off here.' And he say, 'Well, I'm gonna let you off here. . . . But you try to catch me on my next round.' And every day, I'd catch that same man. And that's the way that I'd ride them buses and didn't pay nary a dime. Just get on there with that guitar. And one night, I looked for us all to get arrested. They had a dance on the bus. I got to playing that 'Little Schoolgirl' [referring to John Lee 'Sonny Boy' Williamson's 'Good Morning, Little School Girl,' recorded in 1937]. They all got up and went to swinging on the bus. Bus driver drive slow; he just had as much fun as anybody."[8]

Sam didn't move to Houston until about 1945. He was living in Grapeland, about 130 miles north of Houston in January 1940, when he filled out his Social Security application, but it is unclear exactly when he left. He did say that Lucien Hopkins, a family friend, lent him the money to buy a new guitar and urged him to go to the city. In interviews, Sam often jumped between time periods for the sake of telling a good story. One time, Sam said he got on a bus in Houston around 1940 and played a song that he said he had made up called "Play With Your Poodle," but the girls listening to it didn't know what he meant. However, Tampa Red actually composed "Let Me Play With Your Poodle" and recorded it on February 6, 1942. But for Sam it didn't matter. He wanted to talk about those girls who apparently didn't understand the lasciviousness of his song. "I'd see them little school girls come by," he recalled, "and I'd say, 'I want to play with your poodle.' And they'd say, 'Listen to that man. That man saying that.' 'I wants to play with your poodle. I mean your little poodle dog.'"[9]

As much as Sam bragged about the tips he made from his music during the early 1940s, it was barely enough to support himself, and he often went back to Leon County to stay with his mother. "She'd always take him in," Clyde Langford says. "He might bring her a little something, maybe help buy a few groceries. He'd do what he could, though in those years, my daddy said it wasn't much."[10]

Sam never served in World War II, though he did say he was drafted. But on the night before his induction, he said, prior to moving to Houston, he was stabbed in a fight after winning all the money in a crap game, and his injuries made him unfit for military service.[11] However, if he had indeed served time in jail or on a chain gang, he would never have been drafted in the first place. It's likely he invented the stabbing story during the 1940s. It was another way for Sam to cast himself as a victim to elicit the sympathy of his audience. Moreover, it was means for him to save face; a man of his age and generation who didn't serve in the armed forces was looked down upon.

Sam did sing "European Blues," apparently about World War II, but he didn't record it until 1949.[12] In the first stanza, the tone was at once a lament and an admonition.

> Yeah, you know there's people raidin' in Europe
> They're raidin' on both sea, land, and air (x2)
> Yes, you better be mighty careful, little girl
> Your man might have to go over there

But then, in the second stanza, Sam admitted:

> You know, my girlfriend got a boyfriend in Europe
> That fool's already crossed the sea (x2)
> You know, I don't hate it so bad
> That's a better break for me

In the last stanza, he alluded to what might have been a draft notice, and even if it wasn't his, he sang in the first person: "Yes, I got a letter this morning/

Sayin' practically all these boys got to go," and then ended the song by advising those who don't want to serve to move away (so that Uncle Sam doesn't catch them): "Yes, if you're goin' live bad, son, don't live here no more."

The fact that Sam never served in the military during World War II probably contributed to his decision to move to Houston, where he could get away from his past and build a new life for himself. He rented a room in a boarding house in the Third Ward.[13] While Sam said he was married at the time, he never identified which of his "wives" was with him. Years later, he liked to boast that he'd written songs about "practically every wife" he ever had and often named Ida Mae, Katie Mae, Mary, and Glory Be, even though he was never legally married to any of them. In most instances, he referred to these women as common-law wives, though it appears that he used the title *wife* in the same sense that men use *girlfriend* today, meaning somebody he was sleeping with but not married to. Certainly, at that time living with a woman out of wedlock was considered sinful, and his use of the term *wife* was probably just a ruse to cover these illicit affairs. "I been married to ten common-law wives," he said, but for him, his first wife had special significance: "The first woman that you marry, that was your wife until she die. . . . But you know, that's just an old saying. You can grab a license and marry twenty times. But the first wife is the only one."

However, he claimed, "Every time I get ready to go, I just throw the divorce money up on the table and the paper's already signed. I'm gone. I done bought about seven divorces. I love these women. You know what I mean? But if they make me mad, I'm gone. Good-bye, honey, because there's another somewhere else, just like the saying goes, 'For the flower that blooms, there's another of a different color.' White flowers, blue flowers, I can pick any kind I want. And if I got a blue one that makes me mad, I go get me a red one. I kind of like to pick my flowers, and if I get hot, I pick a good one."[14]

No records of any of Sam's "divorces" have ever been found. His daughter from his first wife, Anna Mae Box, had in her possession the marriage certificate for Hopkins and her mother, Elamer, but wasn't sure whether or not they were ever legally divorced, which might explain why there are no records of any of Sam's other "marriages."[15] Hopkins did his best to avoid the judicial system by moving around, and his desire to play music, gamble, and carouse trumped being a responsible father and raising a family. Once Sam moved to Houston, Anna Mae lost contact with him.

During his first year in Houston, Sam mainly played in the little cafes and honky tonks, like those ridiculed in the *Houston Informer*, near where he lived in the Third Ward, though he did venture off into the Fourth and Fifth Wards as well as the surrounding areas. "I used to sing on Dowling Street," he explained, and then "go to Fourth Ward and Fifth Ward, and back to the Third Ward. That was my run. I'd get money. They would give it to me. Sometimes two dollars, just to hear one song and all that. I was doing pretty good at that time. Sometimes, I'd make a round from Third Ward to Fourth Ward. I'd go on a bus out there and back and I'd have seventy dollars. See the people that were living there, they didn't know how much I was making with them little fifty cents and two bits and dimes. All you have to do is keep working, and then go count your money."[16]

Generally Sam worked by himself, but sometimes he'd make his rounds with a friend. "I had a friend play with me by the name of Luther Stoneham. We was playing on the corner of Pierce and Dowling. We walked to Harrisburg [Boulevard] and every joint we play they want us and we get in that joint and play. When we got back from Harrisburg, we counted up on the corner Pierce and Dowling a hundred and eighty-one dollars. And that was just from that corner. But when we put out all that money on the concrete, here come a load of cops. They want to know where we got this money. That's the only time I was ever questioned on Dowling Street. We had it down on the concrete. We had to divide it, you see. I had to call a man [to tell them] that I played in his cafe for them to know that we made that money like that. They thought we had done robbed something. I told them it would be silly for me, if I had robbed something, to count my money down on the street. I was talking to the cop and they called two more carloads of cops. I wasn't intending for them to take it. So they told us, 'Y'all get that money off the street and go to your house and count it.' They knowed I was a musician."[17]

Sam never played at the El Dorado Ballroom or any of the more "respectable" clubs in the Third, Fourth, or Fifth Wards. His talking blues spoke to the experiences of the people who listened to him on the street and in the cafes or bars that he frequented—the day laborers, the domestics, the custodians, and others who toiled long hours for low wages. He was building a reputation for himself, and in 1946 word of mouth about him attracted the attention of Lola Ann Cullum, who was married to the respected dentist Dr. Samuel J. Cullum and was well known in the African American community for her abiding interest in blues and jazz.

As early as 1940, Lola Cullum had organized a musical program for the Retail Beer Dealers Association, under the auspices of the Alpha Kappa Alpha sorority, in the hope of getting radio station KPRC to "replace the music by records, now heard on the Saturday night programs for colored, with that of local talents."[18] According to the *Houston Informer*, the program included a public school teacher and a quartet featuring Novelle and Leonard Randle, as well as Percy Henderson and the young blues guitarist Lester Williams.

On March 26, 1946, the *Houston Informer* reported in a front-page story that Dr. and Mrs. Cullum were the hosts of W. C. Handy, who came to Houston for the first time in forty-eight years to perform at Don Robey's Bronze Peacock Dinner and Dance Club with the Wiley College Log Cabin Theatre. While Cullum had helped to plan musical programs around Houston, her first foray into the record business was with Amos Milburn. She had heard Milburn in a San Antonio nightclub, and was so impressed with his vocal capacity that she asked him to come see her when he was next home in Houston. When they finally got together, she made "some crude paper-backed tapes" of his singing and sent them to the Mesner brothers at Aladdin Records, who invited her to bring Milburn to California.[19] Cullum had probably heard about the Mesners from Houston blues pianist Charles Brown, who was already an established star on the Aladdin label by the time she found Milburn.

Guitarist Johnny Brown, who worked as a guitarist and sideman for Milburn, recalls, "Mrs. Cullum was a full-figured woman. She was light skinned. And she had them Indian features. She had straight, long hair. Mrs. Cullum must have been around five ten; she wore all kinds of fancy clothes. She was a fancy-dressing person."[20]

Brown met Cullum in 1946, shortly after moving to Houston. Brown says, "One club in particular where I played at was Shady's Playhouse [then called Jeff's Playhouse] on Simmons Street in the Third Ward. It was the most popular club in the Third Ward at that time. And Mrs. Cullum kind of found out. She went looking for young musicians. She was the kind of person who took the young musicians and kept them busy, kept them working."[21]

Lola Cullum also let Milburn rehearse with his band at her house in the Third Ward. "She had a beautiful home at that time," Brown says. "She had one of the upper-class houses in Third Ward, and she would make sure everything was just right. And if they [the sidemen] weren't wearing the right clothes, she get them something. She used to take the doc's [her husband's] white shirts and put them on musicians."[22]

Milburn's first session for Aladdin on September 12, 1946 was well received. Sid Thompson of the *Informer* said that when Milburn returned to Texas, he had "crashed the movie and musical capital with his particular brand of blues. He cut six sides for Aladdin Recording Company . . . and is back here for a rest."[23] A month later, Thompson wrote: "Amos Milburn, newest recording star to flash across the jukebox world, has really hit big time with his boogie woogie singing and piano playing. . . . He is under the management of Lola Ann Cullum. This brings to mind the little known fact this lady is a song writer of excellence with several hit numbers to her credit. 'Twas she who got the lucrative contracts for Milburn, who is quite a youngster and just out of the Navy."[24]

With the success of Milburn's records, Eddie Mesner from Aladdin encouraged Cullum to look for more local talent. She found out about the scene on Dowling Street, where Sam Hopkins sometimes played on the sidewalk with his old partner from pre-war days, Texas Alexander. Cullum told blues researchers Mike Leadbitter and Larry Skoog in a 1967 interview that she liked Hopkins's music and that she made some test recordings to send to Aladdin.

While country blues, performed by such artists as Big Boy Crudup and Big Bill Broonzy, was dying on the charts, the Mesners thought Hopkins might stand a chance in the marketplace. Initially, Hopkins wanted to bring Texas Alexander because of his longtime association with him, but once Cullum heard a rumor that Alexander had just been released from the penitentiary, she was worried about his marketability and replaced him with Wilson Smith, an accomplished barrelhouse piano player. Cullum also had to make Hopkins more presentable, and gave him some money to get new clothes before she drove him and Smith to Los Angeles.[25]

Sam told the story of how Cullum discovered him countless times, but with each telling, he tended to embellish the details. To Sam Charters, he recalled in 1965 that he was shooting craps at home when a friend told him that a lady outside was honking her horn wanting to speak to him. When he went outside, she identified herself as a talent scout and asked him to get his guitar and play one song for her, after which she offered him one thousand dollars to come with her to make records. Two years later, during the filming of *The Blues According to Lightnin' Hopkins*, Sam exaggerated even further and said Cullum, after hearing him play, gave him ten one-hundred-dollar bills before he even got in the car to go with her. A thousand-dollar advance was astronomical in 1946, especially for an unknown singer.

Clyde Langford says that when he was a child in Centerville, he heard a radically different version of the story, not only from his parents, but also from Sam's mother, Frances Hopkins: "That lady out of Houston [Cullum] first saw him in Centerville. He'd sit on the front porch and play his guitar sometimes. And he used to play on the street up there in town, on Highway 7, down toward the Lacy Grocery, toward FM 1119. . . . And that's where he was picked up when he got his start. . . . He was sitting there thumpin' an old, beat up guitar with a pair of run-over shoes on, no socks, overalls with all the tail ends of them tore out, an old, raggedy sundown hat, and she seen him and pulled over and stopped. And she asked him to get in and he got in and she drove off with him. He started to get into the front and she told him, 'No, she didn't want no trouble. He better get on the back seat,' and that's what he did. . . . And they went on into California and she bought him a gorgeous suit of clothes . . . and had that ole kinky hair, they call it conked. And he said she gave him a pocket full of money, it might not a been over fifty dollars . . . and he slipped away from her. She didn't know when he left. He slipped away from her and went back to Houston and that's where he made his home."[26]

While Langford's account is hard to believe, given it's based on hearsay from the perspective of a child, it does underscore the way in which Sam had become larger than life in his hometown. Sam was a kind of folk hero in Centerville, and this rags to riches story, even if it does distort the facts, is nonetheless revealing about how he was remembered.

Cullum, in her interview with Leadbitter and Skoog, was adamant about the fact that she had discovered Hopkins in the Third Ward, though she never said how much he was paid. When they got to Los Angeles, Eddie Mesner decided to record eight sides in a session on November 9, 1946, four that featured Hopkins on vocals, and four with Smith. While they were in the studio, according to Cullum, one of the producers, presumably Eddie Mesner, dubbed Hopkins "Lightnin'" and Smith "Thunder."[27]

Years later, Lightnin' told different naming stories. To *Dallas Morning News* columnist Frank Tolbert, he maintained that "Blind Lemon said [in the 1920s] when I played and sang I electrified people. He was the one that started calling me Lightnin'."[28] But in the 1970s he told drummer Doyle Bramhall that he got his nickname when he was sitting on his porch and "got hit by lightning."[29] In many ways, how Lightnin' recounted his life paralleled his approach to his music. He was free form, at once confiding, endearing, and deceiving, saying and singing whatever he felt. He was a man of the moment, and by changing his story or improvising a new verse or line to an old song, he was able to take control of his own destiny and to engage the listener with details no one else had ever heard.

For Lightnin's first release on Aladdin 165, he played guitar accompaniment for Thunder Smith, who sang "West Coast Blues" and "Can't Do Like You Used To." Aladdin 166 was attributed to only Thunder Smith, and for Aladdin 167 Lightnin' accompanied himself on guitar and sang "Katie Mae Blues" and "Mean Old Twister." On Aladdin 168, Lightnin' sang "Rocky Mountain Blues" and "I Feel So Bad." For this session Lightnin' played acoustic guitar, which he would record with only a few more times until 1959.

Of these recordings, "Katie Mae Blues" was one of Lightnin's favorites, and he performed it often. Katie Mae was one of Lightnin's "wives," and while he extols her virtues when he sings, "Yeah, you know Katie Mae is a good girl, folks, and she don't run around at night," he admits that even though, "she walks like she got oil wells in her backyard," she isn't quite as good as what people think: "Yeah, you know some folks say she must be a Cadillac, but I say she must be a T-Model Ford / Yeah, you know she got the shape all right, but she can't carry no heavy load." The mixing of metaphors related to oil, cars, and sexual innuendo was traditional in blues, and in this song, Lightnin' seized the opportunity to give the lyrics his own twist by establishing a solid call and response with the guitar, accompanied by Smith on piano and an unidentified drummer. Smith's barrelhouse sound, however, is almost incompatible with Lightnin's country flair, and it's not surprising in future recordings that the piano is rarely ever used as accompaniment to his guitar, though he sometimes liked to have a bass and drums. Lightnin' was not a finger-style guitarist like Mance Lipscomb and other country bluesmen. He tried to play bass and melody runs simultaneously with a thumb pick and a finger pick on some recordings in the 1960s, but nearly everything he played was single-string guitar style, without a slide, whether he was using an acoustic or electric instrument.

It's difficult to say how well the first Aladdin records sold, since nothing from the session ever charted. But the fact that Lightnin' was not invited back to record for nearly a year is a good indicator that they didn't do very well. By contrast, Amos Milburn was back in the studio after only three months. Still, when Lightnin' returned to Texas he was proud of what he had accomplished, and he went back to Centerville as soon as he could to tell his mother and friends that his records were going to be issued soon. Ray Dawkins recalled, "We was there at Jack Marshall's farm. Everybody wanted to hear him play. And he told us about how he made up that song 'Rocky Mountain' after he saw someone being buried when they were passing through West Texas. And he told us how it was going to be hitting the deck in the next two weeks, how they were putting it out and how he had finally made it."[30]

After Hopkins and Smith returned to Houston, they essentially parted ways. "Lightnin' never tied himself down too long with anybody," Brown says. "He was kind of freelance."[31] Brown got to know Hopkins at Lola Cullum's house in the Third Ward. "I remember when he started doing tunes [after his first session]," he says. "I remember the times we'd be sitting there in her den, and Lightnin' would be going through some of the things that she and Lightnin' put together."[32] Cullum helped Lightnin' write out his songs and corrected his bad pronunciation of words that she transcribed.

Brown wasn't sure if Lightnin' could actually read or write, but it's likely that he was mostly illiterate. Lightnin' bragged that he left home at age eight, and there was never much indication of how much schooling he actually had. He was able to sign his name, as evidenced by some of the contracts he agreed to—though his distrust of contracts that persisted throughout his life no doubt related to the difficulty he had in understanding them. No contracts with

Aladdin have ever been located; certainly Cullum was responsible for negotiating the terms.

Years later Lightnin' complained that Aladdin had cheated him, but he claimed that the label had also paid him one thousand dollars for his first session. We have no way of knowing how much or how little Lightnin' actually got paid for these records, but generally Mesner was held in fairly high esteem by other musicians who recorded for him. About Mesner, Houston blues singer Peppermint Harris (a.k.a. Harrison D. Nelson) said, "It's hard to describe my feelings for him. He was like a father or a brother. He was the most important man in my life as far as my career was concerned. He did more for me than anyone I've ever been associated with. He was beautiful to me. It's like Ella Fitzgerald felt about Chick Webb. Eddie Mesner showed me the way. He paved the way for me. He was straight about everything. Including royalties. I had no problems. If I wanted a new car, Eddie Mesner got it for me. He did things for me, like the only reason I'm a BMI writer now is because of him. . . . The only regret I have about Eddie Mesner is that the man died."[33]

Lightnin's interactions with Mesner and Aladdin were much more limited than Harris's, but Hopkins was apparently looking for a better deal and a way to record closer to home, since he didn't like traveling. He'd heard about Bill Quinn, possibly from Dowling Street record store owner Eddie Henry, who distributed Quinn's early releases.

With a background in radio and electronics, Bill Quinn moved to Houston in 1939 and started a repair shop called Quinn's Radio Service. By the early 1940s he expanded his small business to establish the Quinn Recording Company, located at 3104 Telephone Road on Houston's east side. He began producing radio commercials and jingles, but saw the potential for producing records, though the materials needed were scarce. "The war had made materials short," Mack McCormick observed, "and the four major companies had a practical monopoly on the manufacturing process. The independent labels of that period came into existence because of people like Bill Quinn. He invented his own method of making records. Somehow, he bought or confiscated an old pressing machine. He'd been experimenting and thinking about the process for years before he actually did it. The precise material—that is, the biscuit that goes into the pressing machine—was an industry secret. They called it 'shellac,' which is a mixture of insect matter and other resins and fillers. . . . One of the solutions he tried was to melt down other people's records. Eventually, he found an independent way to go from the studio to the warehouse—recording, mastering, electroplating, and pressing his own records, and so was free to put regional talent in record stores."[34]

Quinn soon joined forces with another radio repairman, Frank Sanborn, and a Houston-based hillbilly singer, Bennie Hess, and together, they founded the Gulf Record Company on July 14, 1944. But after a handful of releases, beginning around August 1945, including blues singers Jesse Lockett and Inez Newell (nothing by her was actually released, as far as we know), Quinn started his own label, which he called Gold Star, in the summer of 1946.[35] His first release on Gold Star had the catalog number 1313, which was his address on Dumble Street in Houston, and featured Harry Choates, whose song "Jole Blon" exceeded all expectations. "Jole Blon" was a traditional Cajun waltz that had been recorded before, but Choates's version accelerated the tempo and added prominent piano. It became a giant hit because it was done in the contemporary Western swing style of Bob Wills and was sung in such a charismatic way that it was immediately accessible. Quinn was not prepared by the response he got from that record, and it went to #4 on the *Billboard* folk charts twice in 1947. That same year, Quinn, who imprinted his label with the slogan "King of the Hillbillies" under the name Gold Star, decided to branch out.

The discs that Quinn produced were uneven and ranged from unlistenable to passable, but he was not deterred. Even *Billboard* magazine, as early as April 1944, had observed, "It is generally agreed that the public is not too particular about quality—either in the record (durability, etc.) or in the production. The indies say that a hot tune and a good ork [orchestra] will sell that are not the gems of perfection." Quinn's quality steadily improved, and by 1949 he was pressing good-sounding records on high-quality vinyl.

Lightnin's debut release on the Gold Star label ushered in a new sound for him and simultaneously helped lead the direction that country blues would take after World War II. In a significant departure from his Aladdin session, his guitar was now amplified—a novelty that Quinn seized upon by printing ELECTRIC GUITAR in bold capital letters on the label, hoping it would catch the fleeting attention of retailers and jukebox operators. Arthur "Big Boy" Crudup had enjoyed some recent country blues hits featuring electric guitar, but his popularity was fading. Muddy Waters had cut an amplified session for Columbia in 1946, but it was left unissued, and he was still months away from recording his debut for Aristocrat Records. John Lee Hooker would not put out his first record for another year and a half. The country-born bluesman with an electric guitar, still finding his way during these immediate postwar years, was about to blend the old with the new into an alchemy that would force the record industry—and eventually the world—to take notice.[36]

The record Lightnin' made was "Short Haired Woman" backed with (b/w) "Big Mama Jump," for which Quinn gave the catalog number 3131, reversing the numbers 1313. "Short Haired Woman" immediately staked a presence on the jukebox with its unexpectedly bold and direct opening riff—barely amplified by modern standards, but commanding enough at the time when heard through large jukebox speakers. It was basically the same riff he had used on "Rocky Mountain Blues" and "Katie Mae Blues," and had probably been playing for years. But amplification and the absence of a distracting piano now brought it starkly into focus.

Lightnin' cut his usual twelve-to-sixteen bar introduction in half so he could declare:

> I don't want no woman if her hair ain't no longer'n mine (x2)
> Yes, you know she ain't no good for nothin' but trouble
> That keep you buying rats all the time

As a white producer with little familiarity with African American slang or diction, Quinn had no idea what Lightnin' was singing about, but black record buyers immediately appreciated the sly humor and directness of "Short Haired Woman": a vain woman, familiar in the black community and a subject of its ridicule, she was liable to spend so much time and money forcing her man to purchase "rats" (artificial hair pieces) and wigs as to make her essentially "nothin' but trouble."

"Few people outside (Lightnin's) race . . . readily grasp the song's deep significance for Negroes," McCormick wrote years later. "A glance at the popular Negro magazines advertising hair straighteners, hair grease, wigs, rats, hair pads, and so on, gives some idea of the energy devoted to overcoming the characteristics of short, kinky hair . . . the pampering attention to hair becomes a ritual in which the men are inevitably caught up and yet manage to regard with disdain. It is a touchy subject, and Lightnin's song has become, for the race itself, the classic comment. The private humor and mockery of 'Short Haired Woman' speaks to the Negro as intimately as does 'Go Down Moses.'"[37]

"Short Haired Woman" must have been a strong regional seller. The Bihari brothers at Modern Records (who had helped make "Jole Blon" a national hit) were quick to reissue it through their better distribution network, but it didn't make the *Billboard* "race" charts (a catchall for African American recordings) on either label. It certainly sold well enough to convince Quinn that he could tap into the market for blues, and while the record was still hot, he started what he called his new 600 series that would be devoted to black music (separate numerical series for different genres—and races—being a then-common habit of the record business). He immediately called Lightnin' back into the studio to record a couple follow-ups: "Shining Moon" and "Mercy." Lightnin' was soon selling enough records to establish a flat fee for the songs he recorded for Quinn, either seventy-five or one hundred dollars (the equivalent value of about seven to eight hundred dollars today), setting a precedent that continued into the late 1960s. The fee was based on expected jukebox and retail sales alone. Neither he nor Quinn had any understanding of the importance of copyrighting a song, which would damage both of them financially. But for the time being, it secured financial independence and local fame for Lightnin'.

The record probably set another, less creditable, precedent in Lightnin's career as well: his refusal to honor exclusive contracts may have started here. No paperwork remains to prove what kind of contract, if any, he had signed with Aladdin the previous November, but it would have been highly unusual if the Mesners had given him anything less than the industry standard, one-to-two-year exclusive contract. His Gold Star session, probably occurring around May 1947, would have been in blatant violation of such an agreement. Eddie Mesner, shocked to find a contracted artist of his with a regional hit on a different label, moved swiftly into action, demanding that Lightnin' return to Los Angeles immediately to rerecord both sides of the Gold Star single for Aladdin.

Which is why, on August 15, 1947, Lightnin' found himself back in California, covering his own record as closely as possible for Aladdin.[38]

When the American Federation of Musicians (AFM), beginning on December 31, 1947, barred its member musicians from making recordings until a settlement concerning rights and payments could be hammered out with the recording industry, Lightnin's ability to record was not impeded. It has often been assumed that sessions dating from 1948, like those Lightnin' recorded that year, must have been bootleg sessions. But there was no union that Lightnin' could have joined at that time, even if he'd wanted to. The Houston local was largely comprised of classical and orchestral musicians—white, well-connected professionals. But this actually worked to the advantage of the small independent labels like Gold Star, for they could pay blues and country musicians whatever they could afford—usually pocket change—rather than the AFM standard scale of $82.50 for leaders and $41.25 for sidemen.[39]

Ultimately, the ban on recording union musicians benefited Lightnin' and over the course of several days in February 1948, he made more than a dozen sides for Aladdin, including an update of Sonny Boy Williamson's 1937 hit "Sugar Mama." He also recorded "Shotgun Blues," which became one of his biggest hits when it was released two years later. "Howling Wolf Blues," a version of J. T. "Funny Paper" Smith's 1931 "Howling Wolf Blues Part 3"; "Moonrise Blues"; and "Abilene" were also recorded. And Hopkins came up with "Whiskey Headed Woman," which was a spoof on "Short Haired Woman":

> Didn't want no woman
> I have to buy liquor for all the time
> Yes, every time you see her
> She lit up like a Nehi sign

Only one or two singles from Hopkins's February 1948 session were actually released in 1948 and had little impact upon Quinn, who continued to record Lightnin' because "Short Haired Woman" had sold so well on Gold Star. Lightnin' was starting to make real money from his music. On May 7, 1948, he signed an "Option on Contract for Unique Services" with Quinn's Gold Star label that referenced an earlier contract (now lost) that was due to end on May 21. This contract could have been with Aladdin, but it's more likely that it had been with Quinn (who recorded "Short Haired Woman" in spring 1947). In either event, upon signing the new agreement with Quinn, Lightnin' was paid $150, to "perform and make recordings . . . as stipulated in the regular artist's contract," which gave Quinn "sole and exclusive" rights. Apparently, Lightnin's contract with Aladdin had already expired, as Aladdin never challenged Quinn and there are no records of lawsuits ever being filed. Aladdin did, however, continue to release Lightnin's records into the early 1950s.

After Lightnin's last recording for Aladdin on February 25, 1948, Quinn produced as many records with him as he could. However, unbeknownst to Quinn, Lightnin' frequently claimed to have written songs that were in fact covers, such as "Baby, Please Don't Go" by Big Joe Williams, who recorded it twice (1935 and 1945) prior to Lightnin's Gold Star release.[40]

Quinn never seemed to question the origins of Lightnin's songs, but instead focused on producing the best possible recordings. According to Texas Johnny Brown, who went to a couple of sessions, "Quinn knew that studio A&R part. He didn't have too many people working with him. Matter of fact, he did most of that set up part himself in his own place. Lightnin' would sing a whole song with all sort of things without you ever knowing what the title of it was. . . . If he come up with a word that matched pretty good and it sound like he could do something with it, he'd start playing and make a song out of it. There was no reworking or rehearsing. Turn your machine on and let him go."[41] Lightnin' played amplified guitar for all his sessions with Quinn, except on Gold Star 634—the guitar in both "Walking Blues" and "Lightnin' Blues," recorded in March 1948, sounds acoustic.

During Lightnin's sessions for Quinn in 1949 and 1950, he recorded more than twenty sides. Of these, "Unsuccessful Blues (Can't Be Successful)" and "Zolo Go" were standouts. "Unsuccessful Blues," Quinn told Chris Strachwitz, was not planned as part of the session, but was made after Lightnin' found out that his wife had already collected money from Quinn as an advance payment for recording it. So, as an afterthought, he went back into the studio and made up this song on the spot, accompanied by the jazz band that was assembling for the next session.[42]

Boy, you know, I went down to my boss man's house

That's where everybody's getting paid

You know, my wife's been down there

Takin' up all in this world that I've made

You know I turned around and went back home

With my mouth all poked out

She had even nerve enough to go ask

"Lightnin', what is all this bull corn about?"

And I told her, "Can't be successful, no matter how I tried"

In the curiously titled song "Zolo Go," Lightnin' made it clear that he was aware of the music of the growing Louisiana Creole population in Houston's Fifth Ward. The word *zologo* was apparently Quinn's misunderstanding of Lightnin's pronunciation of the word *zydeco*, because in his introduction, which was omitted from the 78 rpm record but was included on the original acetate (and appears on the Arhoolie reissue of the song), Lightnin' explained: "Let's zydeco a little while for you folk / You know, young and old likes that." "Zolo Go" is the only recording in which Lightnin' mimicked the sound of the accordion, as he accompanied himself on an electric Hammond organ.

Quinn's recordings of Lightnin' were remarkably well done, given the limitations of recording technology and duplication. Andy Bradley, a recording engineer and co-owner of SugarHill Studios[43] (the current incarnation of Gold Star) speculates, "With the case of Lightnin', Quinn parked one . . . omni-directional microphone in front of him to capture both the guitar and his voice. Probably a foot away from his mouth, and probably a few inches below it that would capture enough of the guitar."[44]

In 1947, "There was no reverb," Bradley points out. "Quinn was recording direct to disk, cutting a master on a lacquer-coated metal disk. And the cutter had a cutting needle that cut grooves in the master acetate. After he cut one song at a time on the acetate disk, the acetate disk went into an electrolyte bath from which would emerge the stamper, which was a negative image of that acetate. [In order to get protection, many places would offer three-step processing, which included not only the master, which could be used as a stamper, but also a "mother" that could then produce any number of stampers.]

And he made a stamper plate for each side, and each plate was then placed on either side of a record pressing machine, and a glob of a warm compound that included shellac [which was generally known as "biscuits"] and that would be placed between the two metal sheets together with the two labels. Basically, the press stamped out the disk and when it was removed, it was put on a turntable and the rough edges were trimmed before it was put in a sleeve."[45] Quinn frequently did not use full three-step protection because it was costly. The complicated part of the process was not the stamping of the actual disks, and he told Chris Strachwitz that several times the acetate master was destroyed in the electrolyte bath. "That accounts for some missing catalogue numbers," Strachwitz explains, "though Quinn said that he sometimes forgot the last release number and for safety would just jump a few numbers ahead."[46]

Quinn struggled to keep his business going, and by the late 1940s the competition between independent record labels in Houston was growing. Eddie's, Macy's, Freedom, and Peacock were all involved in recording local and regional blues musicians, such as Gatemouth Brown, Little Willie Littlefield, L. C. Williams, Goree Carter, Lester Williams, Peppermint Harris, and Big Walter Price.[47] Of these, Don Robey's Peacock label emerged as the most successful, and in time Robey acquired the Duke label and started the Back Beat and Songbird labels.[48]

The differences between the Duke/Peacock sound and the music of Lightnin' Hopkins not only underscored the breadth and complexity of the Houston black music scene, but was also indicative of the social stratification within the African American communities of Houston. Robey favored gospel music and the big band rhythm and blues sound that was popular among an upwardly mobile African American audience, who participated in the social scene of venues like the El Dorado Ballroom and the Club Matinee. For Robey, Lightnin's blues lacked sophistication; there were no orchestrated arrangements. Lightnin' played a gritty, improvised style of blues in the low-income dives of the Third Ward, and many of the people who listened to his music were poor rural blacks looking for work and trying to get a foothold in Houston—the factory workers and day laborers who struggled to support themselves and their families. Although there are no demographic studies about who bought Hopkins's records, there is anecdotal evidence to suggest that his blues did also appeal to some African American professionals, who had either moved to Houston from East Texas or who just simply liked Lightnin's country flair. Dr. Cecil Harold, a respected surgeon in Houston who years later became Hopkins's manager, says that he "always appreciated the way Lightnin' could put into words the mood of the black community—especially a black community that was hit especially hard by the Great Depression."[49]

Lightnin's records were stacked into jukeboxes in cafes and bars in the Third Ward and the low-income black neighborhoods of Houston, but he did also get some airplay. Black groups had been broadcast in Houston since at least the mid 1930s, when Joe Pullum had a program on KTLC. Moreover, on February 3, 1935, a *Houston Chronicle* radio log dated showed both Red Calhoun and Giles Mitchell broadcasting on KXYZ that day. In 1941, the *Informer* mentioned that the gospel quartet the Dixie Four were featured on a local station, and in 1945 the Eddie Taylor Orchestra appeared regularly on KTHT. Lonnie Rochon was the first black disc jockey in Houston (on KNUZ in February 1948). By 1950, there were several black disc jockeys on the air in Texas: Dr. Hepcat on KVET in Austin, Trummie Cain on KLEE in Houston, Bill Harris on KRIC in Beaumont, among others, but white deejays were also starting to play blues and other styles of black music.

Bill "Rascal" McCaskill, a white deejay on KCOH, says he played Lightnin' on his show as early as 1952. "When I first started the 'Harlem Boogie' on KCOH in 1952," McCaskill says, "Lightning Hopkins was one of my most requested singers. He was, in my opinion, a super talented artist who could really make a guitar talk. I also remember that when I was at KLEE that he was one of Trummie Cain's favorite talents, too. Perhaps it was the advent of rhythm and blues and rock music that outdated his numbers as the requests for his songs dwindled down a great deal, but he was still one of the top music makers in the Houston area. I met him one time at the Club Matinee in late 1952."[50] In the summer of 1953 a group of black businessmen headed by Robert C. Meeker bought KCOH, making it the first black-owned station in Texas and the first station in Houston to target black listeners. KCOH was followed in late 1954 by KYOK. According to Texas Johnny Brown, once KCOH became a black-owned station, they rarely "aired any of Lightnin's music. They were much more geared to the mainstream rhythm and blues of the day, which featured the Duke/Peacock sound."[51]

Despite the limited airplay that Lightnin' got on Houston radio stations after the mid-1950s, he had already become well known, especially in the segregated Third Ward where he lived and worked most of the time. Lightnin's music had an edge that he had honed in the gritty juke joints of the Third Ward, and he had built his reputation by giving voice to the downtrodden. In fact, his first song to make it to a national chart was a very unlikely hit. The Gold Star release of Hopkins's song "Tim Moore's Farm" on February 12, 1949, went to #13 for one week on *Billboard* magazine's "Most Played Juke Box Race Records."[52] Within weeks, Quinn had leased the record, called "a sleeper in the South" by *Billboard*, to the Modern label for national distribution.[53] His strategy worked, and in many ways its success was unprecedented. It was a protest song unique to Texas and was one of the only unambiguous black protest songs to ever become commercially viable. Like his decision to release "Jole Blon," Quinn was not guided by the usual commercial ideas that drove the record business, and this unpredictability is what makes Gold Star and other small regional labels like it especially interesting. A more experienced A&R man may have rejected "Tim Moore's Farm" on the basis that few would know who "Tim Moore" was, or what exactly Lightnin' was singing about, making it unfit for commercial release. Quinn was unintentionally oblivious to such considerations.

"Tim Moore's Farm" was about the infamous *Tom* Moore, who owned a plantation in Grimes County, Texas, and was known for his cruelty to the blacks who toiled there. The song itself was traditional with as many as twenty-seven distinct verses that were added by the different singers who performed it. According to Mack McCormick, the song originated in the mid-1930s with a field hand named Yank Thornton who worked on the Moore plantation. McCormick first collected the song with Chris Strachwitz in 1960 from Mance Lipscomb, who at the time wished to remain anonymous on record because he feared reprisal from Moore. Lipscomb sang: "Tom Moore'll whip you, dare you not to tell." He believed that if Moore found out that "I put out a song like that I couldn't live here no more. . . . 'Goddam, you put out a song about me and you made a record of it—I'm gonna kill you!' Or if he didn't do it, he'd have it done."

The song, McCormick wrote, was "a brutally truthful characterization of one particular hardened opportunist who has taken advantage and mistreated his laborers. It is a protest against 'them bad farm' where a farmer can get started with only a borrowed five or ten dollar bill, the ease of which dupes him into working against an ever increasing debt, his life circumscribed by fear of the big boss, and the bells which call him from the field to meals and then call him back to the field where the landlord stands with 'spurs in his horse's flank' and 'the whip in his hand.'"[54]

Lightnin' said he had heard Texas Alexander sing a version of the song, and when he recorded it, he thinly disguised the subject by changing the name from Tom to Tim. But anyone black in East Texas knew whom he was singing about.

> Yes, you know, I got a telegram this morning, boy,
> > it say, "Your wife is dead."
> I show it to Mr. Moore, he said, "Go ahead, nigger,
> > you know you got to plow a ridge."
> That white man said, "It's been raining, yes, and I'm way behind
> I may let you bury that woman one of these dinner times"
> I told him, "No, Mr. Moore, somebody's got to go"
> He says, "If you ain't able to plow, Sam, stay up there and grab you a hoe"

While Lightnin' never worked for Tom Moore, he inserted himself into the song, personalizing it and identifying himself with the hardships of those who did. For listeners in 1949, many of whom had already migrated from the country to the city, "Tim Moore's Farm" epitomized the plight of black sharecroppers and the inhumane conditions to which they were subjected.

After the success of "Tim Moore's Farm," Lightnin' wanted to get back in the studio at Gold Star as quickly as possible. On August 13, 1949, *Billboard* reviewed Lightnin's recording of "Jail House Blues," which was based on Bessie Smith's song by the same title. He was accompanied on it by the steel guitar of Hop Wilson, not Frankie Lee Sims, as has been written for decades. The review doomed its potential by calling it "an old-style, sorrowful blues, warbled and guitared in the ancient manner. Staple fare for the Deep South market." Still, on October 8, 1949, Lightnin's song "'T' Model Blues" made it to #8 on the *Billboard* R & B jukebox charts for one week, even though when it was reviewed with "Jail House Blues" it was called "a provocative double entendre slow blues in the same authentic manner."[55]

A year later, in September 1950, Lightnin's "Shotgun Blues," which he had recorded for Aladdin in 1948, was a hit for four weeks on *Billboard's* "Best-Selling Retail Race Records" chart and peaked at #5. Hopkins was more popular than ever, and Quinn, probably because "Shotgun Blues" had sold so well, thought he might be able to boost his revenues with the sales of Lightnin's records. On December 16, 1950, Quinn entered into another contract with Lightnin' that gave him a two-hundred-dollar advance at each recording session at which four sides are recorded and a royalty of one and a half cents for each side of the record used for recordings. [56]

A two-hundred-dollar advance at *every* recording session was generous of Quinn, particularly at a time when even bigger labels were paying less to similar blues artists, such as John Lee Hooker and Muddy Waters, but it also points out how well Lightnin's records were actually selling, or perhaps, how Quinn expected them to perform in the marketplace. In fact, it was highly unusual for a label to give an artist an advance on every single release, much less an advance of two hundred dollars. How much money Quinn ultimately made from these releases is unknown, and there are no records to indicate whether or not Lightnin' was ever paid any royalties.

By the early 1950s, Lightnin' was nationally known and was firmly part of the R & B mainstream that updated older styles of down-home country blues. In many ways, Hopkins's career paralleled many of his contemporaries. In Texas, Frankie Lee Sims, one of Lightnin's cousins, had two acoustic releases on Blue Bonnet around 1948, but then was discovered in Dallas in 1953 by Specialty, which recorded him with electric guitar, bass, and drums. L. C. Williams, Lightnin's friend in Houston, who was sometimes billed as Lightnin' Jr. on his Gold Star releases, had a national hit with "Ethel Mae" on Freedom. Lil' Son Jackson, who probably had little or no direct contact with Lightnin', was also recorded by Gold Star and then Imperial. Decca discovered Andrew "Smokey" Hogg with B. K. "Black Ace" Turner and brought him to Chicago to record in 1937, and during or right after World War II, he recorded for Modern: his rendition of Big Bill Broonzy's "Little School Girl" went to #9 on the *Billboard* R & B charts in 1950. Lightnin', however, was the most successful of his generation of down-home blues singers from Texas, and the arc of his achievement was comparable to those of both Muddy Waters and John Lee Hooker.

Like Hopkins, Waters and Hooker came from rural farming backgrounds in the South and had ambiguous dates of birth; Waters was born in 1913, but always told people it was 1915, and Hooker's birth has been variously reported as 1915, 1917, 1920, and 1923. All three had limited educations and moved to the city as soon as they were able. All three switched from acoustic guitar to electric, and in time, put together small bands that included bass and drums. Waters, of course, added the harmonica, and Hooker the saxophone, and their fuller and tighter band sounds certainly propelled them forward. However, during the late 1940s Hopkins was getting paid more than twice the union rate ($82.50) per session that Waters was likely earning, making him almost certainly the best-paid country blues singer of that era. By the early 1950s, Hopkins, Waters, and Hooker were competing with each other on the *Billboard* charts, and Waters ultimately became more famous, with sixteen charting hits between 1948 and 1958.

What hurt Lightnin' the most during the early years of his career with Gold Star was that he didn't want to go out on the road with the so-called Chitlin' Circuit tours. These concerts at black-owned venues were organized by the Theater Owners Booking Association and promoted the records of those blues artists who were part of the touring package shows.[57] Lightnin' wanted to stay close to home and didn't seem to understand that touring with his records would have made him considerably more money. Consequently, his records did not sell as well as they might have to the people who listened to them on jukeboxes and radios around the country. The early 1950s were the beginning of one of the most lucrative eras for blues, if the performers were willing and able to travel and promote their records.

By late 1950, Quinn was finding it increasingly difficult to sustain his label. His wife was dying of cancer. Harry Choates had left him for his rival Macy's early in the year, and his country and blues series were selling poorly. Despite several national hits, Quinn had refused to aggressively market his label, and it remained, by all appearances, more of a personal hobby than a commercial firm. It must have come as a shock to him, then, when he received a fine from the Internal Revenue Service in early 1951 totaling an astonishing twenty-six thousand dollars. A 10 percent federal excise tax had long been established on the sale of records, but Quinn either didn't know about the tax or had ignored it on his tax returns since forming the label five years earlier.[58] The penalty probably represented the government's account of the taxable percentage on the total number of records sold on Gold Star from 1946 to 1950. Quinn couldn't pay the fine, and Gold Star was soon to be another casualty in the indie record business.[59]

On September 22, 1951, *Billboard* reported that the Modern label had "shelled out $2,500 for 32 unreleased Lightning Hopkins and L'il Son Jackson masters and the disk contract of the former. Deal was made thru' Bill Quinn, Gold Star Records' topper, who this week shut down his Houston diskery. Hopkins' sides will be issued on Modern's subsidiary. . . . Diskery will release two sides on each artist 1 October."[60]

Relatively speaking, $2,500 was a fair sum to pay for thirty-two masters in 1951; Lightnin' was still perceived as having commercial potential. Modern was quick to release Lightnin's unissued masters on its subsidiary RPM label, including "Begging You to Stay," "Jake Head Boogie," and "Some Day Baby." A standout in the RPM releases was the single "Black Cat," for which Lightnin' took the guts out of the Memphis Minnie and Little Son Joe 1942 hit "Black Rat Swing" and transformed the male "rat" in the original song into a female "cat" in his version.

> Well I took you in my home, you ate up all my bread
> I left there this mornin', you tried to mess up in my bed
> Well you're one black cat, some day you'll find your tree
> Then I'll hide my shoe somewhere near your cherry tree

Quinn had tried to salvage his business by issuing one final release from Lightnin', "Jackstropper Blues," but ultimately had to discontinue his blues series.[61] Any hope that his December 1950 contract with Lightnin' would reverse his fortunes and revive Gold Star as a blues label were dashed when he learned that Lightnin' had already recorded with another producer, Bobby Shad. Shad had founded the Sittin' In With label in New York in the late 1940s, and had come to Houston in 1950 to record Peppermint Harris, among others, but also met up with Hopkins. He asked Hopkins if he was under contract to anybody, and Lightnin', as usual, said no. In 1951, Shad brought him to New York and recorded eight sides with him, including "Coffee Blues" and "Give Me Central 209," both of which would become hits. When Quinn found out about this, he was furious and told Shad that Lightnin' was under contract to him and that he had already been paid. To placate Quinn, Shad bought a bunch of old masters from him and proceeded to release them. Quinn was essentially powerless; his business was collapsing. When Quinn shut down operations, Shad seized the opportunity to record Lightnin' in Houston and produced another fourteen sides with him. Some of these recordings were done with portable equipment that Shad brought with him, and others were done at Bill Holford's ACA studio.[62]

Texas Johnny Brown recalled one such session at ACA: "They had a little recording studio out Washington Avenue. . . . And we used to go out there, and he'd sit and play. . . . And I remember Lightnin' used to take a board, put a board down underneath his feet. And if he didn't have a drum, he'd just pat his feet real hard—on that board—and play right along with it. It always amazed me how he did it, because his timing was his own timing as far as rhythm is concerned."[63]

In the session that Brown described, Lightnin' and Shad were clearly trying to emulate John Lee Hooker and his foot-tapping records, which were making the *Billboard* charts. Lightnin' was in his prime, and he knew what he needed to do to compete. He was eager to record so long as he got his money up front. He refused to be paid on a royalty basis. "Itinerant blues singers like Lightning Hopkins," Shad told Arnold Shaw, "used to hop on buses, perform, and then walk around with a cup. When we picked him up and talked a recording date, he wouldn't sign a contract. He wouldn't accept a royalty deal. He had to be paid cash. Not only that, he had to be paid after each cut. . . . Before he started a new one, I'd pay him a hundred dollars. He did another, I gave him another hundred. He refused to work in any other way."[64]

Lightnin' had no management; he knew that he was selling his songs outright, but didn't consider the consequences. Certainly, if one of his records was a hit, it would have made him a lot more than one hundred dollars. As owner of the songs Lightnin' recorded, Shad is listed as the songwriter on most of his recordings, though he often used a pseudonym. While such a practice is, by today's standards, unethical and evidence of scams that record companies foisted on their artists, in the 1950s it was common practice. It was by no means unique to blues singers or to black musicians. Songs were sold as a commodity, and any future revenues that resulted from them were usually unforeseen. Certainly, whether or not musicians sold their songs outright often depended on how stable their financial situation was, or how much they understood the workings of the music business, or how much they trusted the person or company they recorded for. To somebody like Lightnin', who could barely support himself and lived literally from song to song, it made much more sense to simply sell all rights to a particular composition for $100 than wait four to six months for the possibility of a royalty check. In 1951, one hundred dollars, adjusted to inflation, is the equivalent of about eight hundred dollars today.

Shad, in his liner notes to a 1971 reissue of some of Lightnin's 1950s recordings, wrote, "Our finances were completed at the end of every session."[65] Moreover, he said that Hopkins "would carry his money in his shoes or some hidden pocket," and when he came to New York "once to do some sessions, he left the same night for home as the big city scared the devil out of him." At that point in his life, Lightnin' didn't know anyone in New York, and the city was no doubt overwhelming.

Shad, like his contemporaries—the Mesners at Aladdin, the Chesses at Chess, and the Biharis at Modern—marketed his records exclusively for an African American audience, and the competition among them was fierce. For a brief period in the early 1950s, down-home blues was steadily selling on the *Billboard* charts, prompting columnist Hal Webman, on February 2, 1952, to write: "For the first time in many months, the down-home Southern-style blues appears to have taken a solid hold in the current market. Down-home blues had been taking a back seat to the big city blues, good rocking novelties and vocal quartet ballads for quite a good while. However, the Southern blues appears to have opened up to its widest extent in some time, and the lowdown stuff has been cropping up as bestselling of late. . . . Such artists as . . . Sonny Boy Williamson, Lightnin' Hopkins . . . Muddy Waters, etc., have taken fast hold in such market areas as New Orleans, Dallas, Los Angeles, etc. Even the sophisticated big towns, like New York and Chicago, have felt the Southern blues influence in wax tastes."[66]

Within weeks of Webman's "Rhythm and Blues Notes" column, Bobby Shad released Lightnin's "Give Me Central 209" on his Sittin' In With label, and it quickly rose to the *Billboard* charts, where it stayed for six weeks and peaked at #6. "Give Me Central 209" expressed the down-home message of longing and despair that was also found in the music of John Lee Hooker and Muddy Waters, among others, but Lightnin's performance style was distinctive in the marketplace. The words rung out with a deep sincerity that underscored the resonance of his country-tinged electric guitar and that pathos at that moment had great appeal.

"Give Me Central 209" had its origins in "Hello Central, Give Me Heaven," which, according to McCormick, dated back to 1901 and was a sentimental song that "represented a child innocently trying to reach her deceased father." McCormick pointed out that by 1909 Leadbelly was singing 'Hello, Central, Give Me Long Distance 'Phone" around Tell, Texas, and "the telephone idea was becoming a traditional opening gambit with which to link various leaving-blues verses. (Tin Pan Alley returned during World War I with 'Hello, Central, Give Me No Man's Land' and King Oliver produced 'Hello, Central, Give Me Doctor Jazz.') The number most often called is 209, just as in train-blues it is most often 219 that figures."[67] In Lightnin's version, he was trying to reach out to his "baby," but to no avail.

> Hello Central, please give me 209 (x2)
> You know, I want to talk to my baby, oh Lord, she's way on down the line
> Seems like the buses done stop runnin', the trains don't allow me to ride
> no more (x2)
> Ticket agent say my ticket played out, he'll see that I don't ride for sure

What was not said was amplified in the emotions of the stinging call and response he evoked in the plucking of the strings of his amplified guitar with his bare index finger.

Five weeks after "Give Me Central 209" hit the *Billboard* charts, Bobby Shad released Lightnin's "Coffee Blues," which also made it to #6, but was only on the chart for two weeks. The strength of "Coffee Blues" was that it characterized the mundane tension of the day-to-day life of the average worker. It was at once ironic and caustic in the way it described "papa" being mad at "mama" because she didn't bring any coffee home. But the song was probably also helped by the popular familiarity of the chorus, which Lightnin' lifted from the Buddy Johnson Orchestra's early hit "I Ain't Mad With You."

Texas Johnny Brown recalled that after he returned from military service in 1953, he spent more time with Lightnin' and could tell that Lightnin' was more savvy about the record business. He sensed that the record companies were ripping him off, but he didn't trust them to pay him any royalties. Consequently, he demanded his money up front. "He'd be playing places here in Houston," Brown says, "and I'd be playing in different clubs. We had kind of a nighttime thing together. I used to get off my gig and go by his at night on weekends. And afterwards we'd sit there . . . and we'd share a gin bottle together and talk over business, who was playing where and who was getting what. We'd go to a little bar on the corner of Cleburne and Dowling. He didn't talk about one thing in particular. We just be discussin' how gigs went and where we going to be playing next. . . . He played out in The Heights, and then he played out in Acres Homes, and in a place in the Fifth Ward, they used to call Pearl Harbor [so named for the violence that occurred there], and it was just about like they said, Pearl Harbor."[68]

Between 1951 and 1953, Lightnin' recorded ten sides for Mercury, followed by another eight for Decca, and four for TNT. The Mercury and Decca sessions were done for Shad, who worked for both companies in addition to running the Sittin' In With and Jax labels. Lightnin' played acoustic guitar and was accompanied by Donald Cooks on bass for not only the Sittin' In With and Mercury sessions in 1951, but for the Decca session in 1953. Several of the songs Lightnin' recorded during this period were original compositions, and the topical "Sad News from Korea" was especially poignant.

> Well, poor mother run and cryin'
> Wonderin' where could my poor son be (x2)
> Whoa, I just want you to have some of my prayer
> "Please, sir, God, Send my poor child back to me"

For the Decca session on July 29, 1953, Lightnin' was once again accompanied by Donald Cooks on bass, but Connie Kroll was added on drums. The trio sounded tight, suggesting they had been playing together for a while and were not simply thrown together in the studio. Lightnin's song choices were also carefully selected. "The War Is Over" was a topical song at the end of the Korean War. "Policy Game" was the only song Lightnin' ever recorded about policy, or "the numbers," which was essentially an illegal lottery in which individuals bought a betting slip in a cafe or other small business and picked the amount they wanted to gamble and the combination of numbers that they thought would come up when the policy wheel was turned.[69] In Lightnin's song, he reflected on the futility of policy, but also on how the game was a metaphor.

> Everybody winning policy, oh Lord, but poor me (x2)
> I played 72, but I done decided to play 23
> Tell me, sweet baby, somebody gone win for you

In the end, Lightnin' was determined to win, but didn't know when to pull back and quit.

> Played number 10 but God knows I couldn't win (x2)
> I'm gonna keep on bettin' till my bluff comes back again

"I'm Wild About You Baby," "Merry Christmas," "Happy New Year," and "Highway Blues" are all strong, up-tempo numbers that Lightnin' sang and played with a much brighter tone and an enthusiasm rarely heard on his later recordings. "Merry Christmas" and "Happy New Year" were in the great tradition of holiday blues numbers and were likely suggested by the producer because such songs were "evergreens" that could be sold each holiday season.

In "Highway Blues," Lightnin' is exuberant about hitting the road:

> I'm going to take my girl, have some fun
> If my money don't spend, I can shoot my gun
> I'm going, yes, I'm going, yes, I'm going on that highway

About "Highway Blues," *Billboard* wrote, "Another good blues reading from the chanter—and in his usually effective style," and also praised "Cemetery Blues," which backed it on Decca 48312: "Hopkins' tale of Grandpa's death is told via his guitar, singing, and talking passages for a mighty effective side with lots of folk quality. The gimmick of a crying voice thruout [sic] adds appeal."[70] There's no indication of how well the Mercury sides sold; none ever charted.

The next sides Lightnin' recorded were for TNT, a new San Antonio label as small as Decca was large. They were produced by H. M. Crowe in Houston around November 1953, and for these, an amazingly distorted amplifier added to the brooding intensity of the four songs he recorded that were reminiscent of his earlier work: "Late in the Evening," "Lightnin' Jump," "Leaving Blues," and "Moanin' Blues."

It's likely that the Mercury, Decca, and TNT sessions occurred at Bill Holford's ACA studio, but there is nothing in the Holford's logbooks that would provide definitive evidence. The logbooks only document the master discs that ACA made. They do not document sessions, unless ACA mastered them. This is also true for the Lightnin' sessions for the New York–based Herald label (owned by Al Silver, Jack Braverman, and Jack Angel) in or around April 1954. It's quite possible that Holford and Crowe, who had just started their own music publishing company (CHS Music, BMI), recorded these and then shopped them around to different labels.

The twenty-six sides that Lightnin' issued on Herald took his music to a new level. While little is known of what actually transpired during these sessions, the results were phenomenal. Lightnin's amplified guitar had an explosiveness that had not been heard before, but note for note, Donald Cooks on bass and Ben Turner on drums—two session players in Houston—were completely in synch with his every lick. It was the most rehearsed Lightnin' had ever sounded, not necessarily because he had actually practiced the tunes in advance, but more as a result of a sense of familiarity among the players. They were ready, and the chemistry was just right. Not only did Lightnin' update some of his older songs, like "Ida Mae" (which became "Don't Think 'Cause You're Pretty") and "Shine on Moon" (which took on the name "Shining Moon"), but he also introduced powerful new material such as "Sick Feeling Blues (I'm Aching)," "Don't Need No Job," "My Little Kewpie Doll," "Had a Gal Called Sal," and the "Life I Used to Live." He may have repeated riffs from earlier instrumentals, but his attack on "Move On Out Boogie" and "Hopkins' Sky Hop" was faster, louder, and played with more finesse. *Billboard* described "Sky Hop" as a "rompin' instrumental blues played by guitar with rhythm. Could do business in country as well as r & b market, if it gets exposed."[71]

The Herald sessions contain Lightnin's usual mix of boogies, instrumentals, and down-home blues with the recurring themes of unrequited love, longing, and abandonment, but the ferocious drive, flair, and subtlety of his performance on electric guitar surpasses any of his earlier or later recordings. In two of the songs, it sounded as if Lightnin' was still very much stuck on Ida Mae. In "Nothin' But the Blues," after a piercing instrumental introduction, Lightnin' sang:

> I don't see why the blues come in my house every morning before day
> Every time it come in there, just about time it get there
> My little girl, she done gone away, and her name was Ida Mae

And in "Don't Think 'Cause You're Pretty," which is an updated version of his earlier song "Ida Mae," he once again calls out to her after she's left him.

> Well, don't think because you're pretty woman, got every man in town
> You know the blues is a mighty bad feeling
> When you have them 'long about the break of day
> When you look over on the bed where your baby used to lay

The Herald sessions were a watershed in Lightnin's career. The intensity of his singing and the fierceness of his electric guitar single-string runs had never been greater. Whatever he did in his day-to-day life, when he stepped into that studio, he was on fire.

The Herald sessions were almost certainly done at ACA, but the only Hopkins recordings noted by Holford were the mastering for the Ace label of two songs with new titles from the 1954 Herald sessions. "Lightnin' Don't Feel Well" is an edited version of "Wonder What Is Wrong With Me" and "Bad Boogie" is the same as "My Little Kewpie Doll."[72] Clearly the producers wanted to disguise the fact that they were issuing the same songs on different labels.

By the time Lightnin' recorded for Herald in 1954, his records were on jukeboxes across the country, and for a brief period, perhaps unbeknownst to him, he was named "President of the Blues" by WDIA, the fifty-thousand-watt radio station broadcasting out of Memphis. Deejay Moohah Williams, who wore different hats at WDIA, one of which was "Mr. Blues," hosted a down-home blues show called *Wheelin' on Beale* and held mock elections for the title of "President of the Blues, commander-in-chief of the Royal Amalgamated Association of Chitterling Eaters of America, Inc. for the Preservation of Good Country Blues."[73] Ballots appeared in the African American newspaper the *Tri-State Defender*, and Mr. Blues encouraged his listeners to vote. The 1954 contest pitted the incumbent president Lightning Hopkins against Muddy Waters (whom Mr. Blues liked to called the "unclean stream"). About the election, the *Defender* reported, "President Hopkins is campaigning on a platform which says the pure country blues field is being invaded by modernists who will destroy its pure form and solid corn sound."[74] Muddy Waters denied that his blues had been tainted by modernity and campaigned "on a platform of pure popularity because of recent hot releases." Mr. Blues sided with Hopkins and became his campaign manager, and in an interview just before the election, he said, "The forces of destruction are on the march and are boring from within with an insidious deadliness. We must not be caught unaware. Vote now for a true blues ticket. Vote for Lightning Hopkins."[75] In the end, Hopkins won and retained his title as President of the Blues, but Muddy Waters trumped him on the *Billboard* charts with "Hoochie Coochie Man" in 1954 and ultimately surpassed him in sales.

Historian Louis Cantor maintains that "radio formats targeted at the African-American marketplace made a wide range of 'hidden music' suddenly accessible to all Americans," and "more than ever before, white listeners could tune in and vicariously eavesdrop on black culture and music," though the extent to which white listeners tuned into WDIA is unknown.[76] Yet as early as 1943, Hunter Hancock was broadcasting black music on a show called *Harlem Holiday* on KFVD in Los Angeles, and by 1950, Hancock's program had changed its name to *Harlem Matinee* and had expanded to two hours daily with a rapidly evolving play list that was primarily focused on rhythm and blues, with an increasing emphasis on down-home blues. In part, the shift in programming was propelled by the independent record producers who offered records and payola, though, according to Joe Bihari, Hancock never accepted payola.[77] However, KFVD could be heard only in Los Angeles and WDIA could be picked up only in Memphis, while WLAC in Nashville broadcast nationally and quickly became the most famous station for popularizing R & B. Both blues harmonica virtuoso Charlie Musselwhite and rock 'n' roller Elvin Bishop, for example, recall listening to WLAC when they were kids searching the airwaves to hear the latest songs by Lightnin' Hopkins or John Lee Hooker, among others—Musselwhite in Memphis, and Bishop in Tulsa, Oklahoma.[78]

Lightnin's Herald recordings did not make the *Billboard* charts, and by the late 1950s his appeal to record companies declined. Rock 'n' roll dominated the pop charts, using a blues-based song structure and insistent back beat to combine the influences of blues, jazz, rhythm and blues gospel, country, and rockabilly into a music that was fast and danceable. The Herald sessions had anticipated the rock explosion of 1955 and 1956, but Lightnin' had a hard time keeping pace with his contemporaries—Johnny "Guitar" Watson, Bo Diddley, Chuck Berry, and Little Richard, to name a few.

Even without more national hits, Lightnin' continued to have a local following in the little clubs and beer joints in Houston. The people in the Third Ward crowded in to hear him, and the raucous, smoke-filled banter fueled his live performance, but also stifled his career. As much as he was capable of the tight three-piece band sound of his Decca and Herald recordings, when he played locally, he was looser and more idiosyncratic. He played whatever he was in the mood for, and he'd sometimes let people he knew from the neighborhood sit in. Houston bluesman Rayfield Jackson, who grew up in the Third Ward, said he got interested in Lightnin' when he was in high school in the 1950s. "I used to go over to his house," Jackson said, "and we'd play on his guitar and laugh and talk. He would show me all he knowed, and a lot of times on the weekend, I'd go on a gig with him and sit in, play right along with him. . . . Mama knowed where I'd be going, when I'd get out of school, so she didn't fuss at me. . . . I played some gigs with him, sure did. Right here in Sunnyside, up and down Cullen [Blvd.]. . . . And we was playing in little old joints with about three or four tables in them, and when you got five or six people in there, you had a crowd. . . . I'd go in there and play a little while, sit up there and back him up with the guitar, what he taught me how to do. . . . Wouldn't have no drummer, just two guitars—and Lightnin' stomping his feet. That's it. He'd have them big old shoes on and one of them Big Apple hats, big old wide hats with a feather stuck up in it—looked like a peacock."[79]

Why Lightnin' didn't travel more at the height of his popularity in the R & B market raises difficult questions about his deep-seated inhibitions. Certainly, if he had a manager to coordinate his bookings and touring, he could have sold more records and made more money from his performances. It's likely, however, that in many ways, he was unappealing to reputable mangers who knew that he never adhered to the exclusive terms of any record company contract. Lightnin' was fiercely independent and intensely private. He didn't have a telephone, either because he couldn't afford it or he simply didn't want to be easily found. Moreover, he was a heavy drinker and gambler who lived day to day, following his whims without any apparent long-term ambition. Travel was treacherous for any African American during the years of segregation, and for Lightnin', the perceived danger associated with unfamiliar places was no doubt frightening. Clearly, his experiences in jail and on chain gangs had imbued him with a deep distrust of law enforcement, the judicial system, and to some extent the white world in general. Yet his record producers were white and helped him achieve a stature and income that was unprecedented in his life, even if he didn't trust them. Lightnin' knew what it was like to work for white people. Certainly, the landowners in Leon County where he grew up were predominantly white. Lightnin' did what he needed to in order to survive, and once he started earning more than subsistence wages, he was content to not take unnecessary risks by venturing too far from home.

When McCormick asked Lightnin' why he turned down the opportunities for travel that had been presented to him, Lightnin' explained that he stayed in Houston because he was "treated so nice. Everybody know me and I don't have to get acquainted with too many people 'cause they already know me. And in that way, it make me feel like I'm at home. Knowing I'm treated well—not much reason to get up and leave it."[80]

As Lightnin's recording career seemed to be slipping away from him and his income from his music was declining, a new audience of jazz and blues fans, writers and folk music enthusiasts, Europeans and intellectuals, were becoming increasingly aware of him. Lightnin's records had made him a legend, but his whereabouts to people outside of his community in the Third Ward were largely unknown.

4

〜〜〜〜〜

Rediscovery

ightnin' Hopkins first met Mack McCormick around 1950 through
McCormick's mother, who was then working as an X-ray technician at the
Telephone Road office of a doctor whose patients included Bill Quinn of Gold
Star Studios.[1] McCormick supported himself by doing part time and intermit-
tent jobs as an electrician, short-order cook, taxi driver, and record librarian at
KXYZ, but in his free time he was a record collector, playwright, and freelance
writer, who regularly contributed articles to *Down Beat* magazine and other jazz
journals, reviewing Stan Kenton, Frank Sinatra, and Chubby Jackson, among
others. He was also active in the Houston Folklore Group, which had been
founded in 1951 by John A. Lomax Jr. and Howard Porper with the mission "to
sing, collect, and perpetuate the folklore of the people."[2]

In 1958, Sam Charters, a music historian, writer, record producer, musician,
and poet, contacted McCormick. Both Charters (b. 1929) and McCormick
(b. 1930) were originally from Pittsburgh, and their careers had in some ways
paralleled each other, especially in terms of their interest in blues, jazz, and other
styles of folk and traditional music. Both believed blues was the bedrock of jazz,
echoing the thinking that informed such writers as Frederic Ramsey Jr. and

Charles Edward Smith in *Jazzmen* (1939), Hugues Panassie in *Real Jazz* (1942), and Alan Lomax in *Mister Jelly Roll* (1950). Moreover, both McCormick and Charters had written numerous articles for jazz journals, though Charters was also a musician who had been playing and leading his own New Orleans–styled groups since 1948. Charters was also a more accomplished writer. He was college-educated; after being kicked out of Harvard because of his political activism, he attended Sacramento City College and the University of California at Berkeley, where he finally received a bachelor's degree in economics in 1956. Charters had started listening to jazz early on, and when he moved to New Orleans at the age of twenty-one, he began to absorb the history and culture he had only read about, and he studied jazz clarinet with the legendary George Lewis. A year later he and his wife Ann Charters began making field recordings for Folkways Records.

Folkways Records and Service Corporation had been founded by Moses Asch in 1948 to document musical and spoken-word traditions from around the world. Among his earliest releases on ten-inch, 33⅓ rpm records were *Square Dances* with Piute Pete and His Country Cousins, *Who Built America* with Bill Bonyun on guitar, *Darling Corey* with Pete Seeger on five-string banjo, *Take This Hammer* with Leadbelly and his twelve-string guitar, and *Songs to Grow On* with Woody Guthrie. Asch's tastes in music were eclectic and reflected not only the values of the burgeoning folk revival, but also included gospel, traditional jazz, blues, and different musical styles from around the world. Asch had been heavily influenced by John Hammond's 1938 "Spirituals to Swing" concert at Carnegie Hall, which set the stage for Big Bill Broonzy, Brownie McGhee, and others to crossover into playing for white folk/blues audiences. Frederic Ramsey (the producer of Leadbelly's "Last Sessions" for Folkways), introduced Asch to Charters, who was beginning to gain a reputation as a jazz scholar. Charters's first Folkways release was a recording of the Six and Seven-Eighths String Band from New Orleans and was followed by numerous other albums of traditional New Orleans bands, notably the Eureka Brass Band that had been formed in the 1920s.[3]

Shortly after the publication of Charters's first monograph in 1958, *Jazz: New Orleans 1885–1957*, Nat Hentoff interviewed him on a radio show in New York City, and asked him what he wanted to do next.[4] When Charters told him about his deep interest in blues, Hentoff gave him the name of his editor at Rinehart, and within days after dropping off a sample text, Charters had a contract and a five-hundred-dollar advance to write a book on country blues.[5] At this point, there had been numerous articles published on blues in small magazines, but never a full book devoted to the subject.

Charters first learned about Lightnin' Hopkins in 1954 when he heard one of his records, "Contrary Mary," which had been recorded for the Jax label three years earlier. "It was still around town on the jukeboxes," Charters says. "And a musician I knew heard it and got a copy up on Rampart Street." Mistakenly, Charters thought Lightnin' was accompanying himself on an unamplified acoustic guitar, when in fact he was playing electric, but the song made a lasting impression. Lightnin' was singing "a mean, unhappy blues in the long, irregular rhythms of a man who learned his singing in the fields or along dusty southern roads." Charters tried to find Lightnin', but to no avail. Then, one day, a cook overheard Charters talking about Lightnin' in a small restaurant on Bourbon Street and identified himself as Lightnin's cousin. He told Charters that Lightnin' was in Houston, but didn't know how to contact him. "I was in and out of Houston the next five years," Charters wrote, "recording, interviewing musicians, and asking about Lightnin' Hopkins. When I'd come from California to Houston, I'd find out Lightnin' had gone back to California, and when I'd get to California, I'd find out Lightnin' was back in Houston."[6]

On one of Charter's trips to California, he met Chris Strachwitz in Berkeley. Strachwitz (b. 1931), a Silesian German immigrant who listened to blues and jazz on British and American Armed Forces Radio in the years after World War II, came to the United States with his family in 1947. Once in California, Strachwitz began to actively collect records. In 1951 he enrolled at Pomona College, where, he says, "I remember hearing this amazing voice [on Hunter Hancock's radio show in Los Angeles] singing: 'Hello Central, Give me 209/ I want to talk to my baby, She's way on down the line.' . . . I was just totally wigged out. I was a teenager, rebellious, insecure, skinny, couldn't speak English right. I thought this was paradise; this was heaven. And somehow this voice—that guitar style—Lightnin's sound just kind of haunted me and became really my favorite. . . . Certain sounds just grab you; that's all there is to it. I could just tell he must have just made this stuff up on the spot, at least that was my conviction. And I kept being a hound for this music, scrounging up 78s."

After two years at Pomona, Strachwitz transferred to the University of California at Berkeley, where he graduated after serving in the United States Army from 1954 to 1956. He got a job as a high school social studies teacher, but in his free time he read jazz magazines and continued to collect records. "I bought anything I could find that I had heard on the radio—blues, jazz, hillbilly, anything," Strachwitz says. "I very rarely would buy a brand new R & B record because they were expensive. They were seventy-nine cents plus tax. But I had discovered Jack's Record Cellar in San Francisco and the Old Englishman on Eddie Street, also in San Francisco, and the Yerba Buena Music Store in Oakland, which specialized in traditional jazz and blues and several record shops in the black neighborhoods. This was a time when 78s had gone out of style and were being dumped because they were being replaced by 45s. Then there were the jukebox operators like the Tip Top Music Company and I had to go and see what they had to sell. They were real cheap and they would sell you records at ten to twenty-five cents a piece, sometimes only a nickel. There I would pick up anything that said 'blues singer' and 'guitar.' That's how I got to know that stuff. I was listening to KWBR out of Oakland and deejay Jumpin' George Oxford played people like Howlin' Wolf, Muddy Waters, John Lee Hooker, Jimmy Reed, and Lightnin' Hopkins."[7]

In early 1958, Strachwitz met Charters in Berkeley at a club where Charters had performed with a New Orleans–style jazz band; they started talking and realized they were both record collectors. "I would go over to his place, where he had a trunk full of these old 1920s records that he had picked up at junk stores in the South. Sam was primarily interested in prewar blues and New Orleans jazz. And Sam would in turn come to my place and listen to some of the current blues that I liked—Sonny Boy Williamson, and I played him Lightnin' Hopkins's records because he was one of my favorites. We were probably listening to some of Lightnin's Herald recordings."[8]

Charters became more familiar with Lightnin's music, but felt that "something was being lost" as he "turned out more and more records that were simply designed to sell to the teenage rhythm and blues audience. He was using a loud amplified guitar and there were usually a loud bass drummer and bass player to do away with the subtle rhythm that made his earlier records so memorable." [9] At this point, Charters didn't seem to understand that virtually all of Lightnin's recordings had been made with an electric guitar, even those on Aladdin, Gold Star, Sittin' In With, and Jax that he liked the most, because they didn't have bass and drums. As Charters was writing his book *The Country Blues*, he started to feel that Lightnin' was "perhaps the last of the great blues singers," despite the fact that "his professional career was a series of clumsy mistakes." Charters believed that "Lightnin' was one of the roughest singers to come out of the South in years. . . . He was the last singer in the grand style. He sang with sweep and imagination, using his rough voice to reach out and touch someone who listened to him."[10]

During the fall of 1958, Charters heard about McCormick from Frederic Ramsey at Folkways, who suggested that Charters contact McCormick in Houston and Asch in New York about recording Lightnin'. By then, Asch had already issued several blues LPs, featuring Brownie McGhee and Sonny Terry, and was in the process of producing others with Big Bill Broonzy, J. C. Burris, Sticks McGhee, and Memphis Slim.[11]

McCormick was interested in getting to know Charters and invited him to stay at his house in January 1959. Together they went looking for Lightnin'. One lead led to another, but they couldn't find him the first time they went hunting around the Third Ward. "Everyone was very guarded all the time," Charters says. "But you could feel safe. No one was going to do anything to this white boy wandering around. I wasn't looking for drugs and I wasn't looking for sex, and so this meant I wasn't fitting into the categories in which I could easily be placed. I was just the right age and build to be a young cop. I was wearing a knit shirt and chinos. I was not prepossessing."[12]

A pawnbroker who had two of Lightnin's guitars had an address for him in his files. When they got to the house, he wasn't home, though a young boy directed them to Lightnin's sister, who suggested they check two or three bars that Lightnin' was known to frequent, but he wasn't there either. Frustrated, they went back to McCormick's house, and the next morning, while McCormick was busy, Charters went to Dowling Street to look around. "And on that day, he found me," Charters says. "Everyone was aware that I was moving around through the ghetto looking for Lightnin', and everyone was reporting this to Lightnin'. The cab drivers were watching me, and I'm sure they all knew where he was. But who was I? And finally the word was passed onto Lightnin'. So I was stopped at a red light in my coupe and a car pulled up beside me and there was a man with sunglasses saying, 'You lookin' for me?' And I said, 'Are you Lightnin' Hopkins?' And Lightnin' said, 'Yeah.' So he found me. I had been checked out and the decision was that I was safe."[13]

They both pulled over, and Charters told Lightnin' that he wanted to record him. Lightnin' was interested, but he had pawned his guitars, a fact that implied that he wasn't playing music at the time. "Lightnin' was wearing Salvation Army clothes, baggy, grey, no color at all," Charters says. "He was poor."[14] When they got to the pawnshop, Lightnin' wanted his electric guitar, but Charters picked the acoustic because he knew that was what the white folk audience wanted to hear. As much as Lightnin' may have preferred the electric, he didn't object. He needed the money and certainly knew that he could play either instrument well. But the acoustic wasn't in very good shape, and apparently Lightnin' hadn't played it in some time. "I had to get him some strings," Charters recalls, "but as we passed some school kids, Lightnin' began playing with the five strings, playing more guitar than I'd ever heard, playing 'Good Morning Little School Girl.'" Finally, after getting some guitar strings, they went to Lightnin's rented room at 2803 Hadley Street, where Charters recorded him with a single Electrovoice microphone and his portable Ampex tape recorder.

"Lightnin' had a room in the back. It was a quiet street. The room was small, it had a bed, one chair, and it was in the back of the house. . . . I sat on the bed holding the microphone while Lightnin' sat in the chair in the room, and we made the record that afternoon." Charters says that Lightnin' introduced him to his "wife," named Ida Mae, but she didn't say much. She was "watchful, and very aware that it was a complicated situation, and she made nice, as simple as that."[15] No one had ever come to Lightnin's residence to record him. He had always gone to a studio, and the presence of this equipment crowded into Lightnin's bedroom, with a white man holding a microphone in front of him while he played and sang, must have seemed very strange. Charters had had fieldwork experience, but for Lightnin' and Ida Mae, the circumstances were completely new.

After a couple of songs, Lightnin' thought he was done. "I had not only asked Lightnin' to play the acoustic guitar," Charters remembers, "but I was consistently asking him to play the old songs. This was new to him, and with that I could only give him three hundred dollars [the equivalent of about $2,100 today] to make a record, and the fact that I was doing an LP was just not in his comprehension. He was used to doing two songs for two hundred dollars, and I kept asking for more songs . . . but then I started asking him about people like Blind Lemon and he became interested. It was the first time anyone had ever asked him about these things. So he really went back into his memory. So finally we got what I thought was an extraordinary session. I did it all with a hand-held microphone. I could do the vocal and move it down to get the guitar solos, and keep him from popping the mike as he always did and could get a sense of balance. And as an old folkie myself, I kept insisting that he tune the guitar. . . . But we did have two or three hours of quiet time, and concentration."[16]

The session was over by about four o'clock in the afternoon. Charters paid Lightnin' the agreed-upon three hundred dollars in cash, and Hopkins signed a simple release. A hand-written memo by Charters to Asch described the difficulties he encountered: "This was a hard, mean session; so I had to be content with what I could get. 'Lightning' is used to much more than $300 for 9 tunes and he's worth more than $300 for 9 tunes to a house like Atlantic or Riverside. To us, he's worth $300. But it was a long, rough afternoon. I got him because I thought he could do us some good. I'm sorry I couldn't get more or that I couldn't have had some selection. For sure, we'll never get him again at this price."[17] Lightnin' consented to the recordings because he needed the cash. At that point in his life, given the opportunity to make money from his music, he couldn't refuse, but he could hold back.

Lightnin's recordings for Charters were a mix of a few up-tempo boogies— "She's Mine," "Come Go With Me," and "Fan It"—and covers of tunes he'd already recorded earlier in his career, like "Bad Luck and Trouble," "Tell Me Baby," "Penitentiary Blues" ("Groesbeck Blues"), and the Blind Lemon Jefferson song "See That My Grave Is Kept Clean" ("One Kind Favor"). One track is an excerpt from Charters's interview with him, called "Reminiscences of Blind Lemon," in which Lightnin' talked about hearing Jefferson for the first time, meeting him, and playing with him in Buffalo, Texas.

Overall, the guitar playing is solid but rough and is evidence that Lightnin' had not played an acoustic instrument in some time. The lyrics reiterated Hopkins's established themes of unrequited love and how hard work and tough times were at the root of his blues. In "Goin' Back to Florida," one of his most poignant lyrics evoked the futility of the plight of the sharecropper:

> I was gettin' forty cents a hundred, pickin' for me and wife too
> When I learned my lesson, you don't know what I had to do
> And I couldn't do nothin', whoa, man, keep that sack on the scale

Charters was looking for Lightnin's songs that evoked his rural past and what he perceived as the core of his country blues. But when Charters returned to McCormick's house and played the recordings he had made earlier that day, McCormick was disappointed. "He just thought it was terrible," Charters says. "He really said, 'It doesn't sound like Leadbelly.'"[18]

Soon after completing his recordings, Charters sent Strachwitz a postcard saying, "I found Lightnin' Hopkins; he lives in Houston, Texas. A guy named Mack McCormick is trying to be his agent. Here's Mack's address." Strachwitz quickly contacted McCormick and made plans to visit Houston in the summer. "That was like the Holy Grail to me," Strachwitz recalls. "Nobody knew where Lightnin' was or even if he was still alive."[19]

Once Charters left Houston, McCormick went and recorded Hopkins himself. Although he didn't admit it at the time, the recordings that Charters played for McCormick must have given him a different perspective on Lightnin'. Like Charters, McCormick felt that Lightnin's commercial recordings obscured his "true identity" as a bluesman. Both McCormick and Charters wanted to record Lightnin's "old" songs, the ones that he remembered from his early years growing up in Leon County. These songs, McCormick and Charters believed, were the wellspring of the blues form.

Between February 16 and July 20, 1959, McCormick, somehow overcoming the difficulty Charters had encountered, recorded forty-six songs with Lightnin' in six different informal sessions. In a discography by Strachwitz in *Jazz Monthly*, McCormick commented that the sessions were "held in either Lightnin's bedroom or mine. No time limitations were imposed and selections range from one to six minutes in length, most averaging four or more. Many begin with Lightnin's speaking some explanation or comment, talking himself into the song. He was encouraged to choose material he felt inclined toward. . . . His choice of material strides from unique impressions of jukebox records he's vaguely heard to the intensely autobiographical narrative-blues."[20]

McCormick enjoyed corresponding with Strachwitz, and when Strachwitz got to Houston in June 1959, he took him to see Lightnin' play. "I had taken a bus to Texas," Strachwitz recalls, "and was staying at the YMCA when Mack took me to meet Po' Lightnin' that afternoon. Po' Lightnin' always lived in this boarding house; it had a room he rented." For Strachwitz, Lightnin' had "a neat existence; he didn't give a shit about what was going to happen. If he needed a few dollars, he'd go play that night."[21]

Once Strachwitz heard Lightnin' perform, he was even more entranced. "I remember very vividly us walking in there to Pop's Place that night," Strachwitz says. "It was a little tiny joint, and when we came in, Lightnin' was standing to the left of the door about twenty feet away. He was just moaning some blues. He was playing a highly amplified electric guitar, with Spider [Joe "Spider" Kilpatrick] on drums. . . . Well, Lightnin' was singing about how his shoulder was aching that day and how he hardly got to the job that night because of the water. It had been raining, and the rain covered the chuckholes in the road and his car would hit these holes, and he needed a BC pill [an over-the-counter medication for muscle pain]. But I thought he would be doing songs that he had recorded, but that wasn't the case at all. What he was singing was a wonderful mishmash of totally improvised material and lines from his records. And since he'd seen us walking in, he suddenly pointed his long finger in our direction and sang, 'Whoa, this man come all the way from California just to hear Po' Lightnin' sing,' and then he went on singing to some gal who was standing in front of him. And he'd be hollering at her and I mean I had never seen anything like that. I was just in blues heaven. This was just ferocious, and the whole scene was something I had never really experienced before." Strachwitz was from a "fairly upper-middle class" background in Europe and hearing Lightnin' in what was ostensibly a low-income black neighborhood was illuminating: "To me, this was better than any books I could ever read, because it was right there, living.

"One night, after he had finished a job, Lightnin' said, 'You guys, wanna come with me? Po' Lightnin's gonna wanna do some gambling.' So we went to this house, totally dark. I forget which ward it was in and Po' Lightnin' banged on the door and sooner or later the lights went on inside. And this sleepy black man appeared at the door in a bathrobe. 'What you all want?'

"And Lightnin' said, 'Man, you know what I want.'

"So, they sat down at a table and they played dice. And I thought the other man was half asleep, but as soon as Lightnin' would roll those dice, this man's eyes would just pop open and he would focus in on those dice and a couple of times Lightnin' tried to grab them: 'That's me! That's mine! I gots that.'

"But his eyes were just on it. 'You muthafucka, that ain't yours!'

"It was really something. The cockroaches were this big [three inches long] out there in Texas. I'd never seen creatures like that. They were wandering up and down planks on the side of the room, and it was hot. You know, the only time you could ever live was in the nighttime. There was no air conditioning in many places. By then, I was staying at Mack's place and he had a fan, and you went to sleep and you woke up feeling just as tired in the morning. It was humid! I had never experienced anything like it. But I thought this was just great and I decided at that time that I wanted to start—literally started a record label because I thought I wanted to capture Lightnin' Hopkins in his beer joints. And a year later, that's exactly what I did. That was the beginning of Arhoolie Records."[22]

While Strachwitz was enthusiastic about the raw power of Lightnin's performance on electric guitar accompanied by bass and drums, that sound didn't interest McCormick or Charters, who both knew that the folk revival audience wanted to hear the unaccompanied, unamplified solo blues. McCormick, of course, had seen Lightnin' perform in the gritty juke joints of the Third Ward on numerous occasions, but Charters had not and had based his opinions about Lightnin' largely on his interpretation of his records and his single meeting with him.

McCormick, in addition to recording Lightnin', started promoting him in Houston and elsewhere. By the late 1950s, McCormick had become the chairman of the Houston Folklore Group, and had helped to organize a program called Hootenanny at the Alley at the Alley Theater in Houston on July 20, 1959, that was modeled after the hootenannies that musician, singer, songwriter, folklorist, and labor activist Pete Seeger and the impresario Harold Leventhal had organized for more than a decade in New York City.[23] John Lomax Jr. performed on the same bill with Lightnin', as well as with Howard Porper, Jim Lyday, Kyla Bynum, Jimmie Lee Grubbs, and Ed Badeaux, who were all folk revivalists. For the hootenanny, they each took turns singing traditional ballads and songs like "The Yellow Rose of Texas," "Midnight Special," and "Wayfaring Stranger," accompanying themselves on guitar, autoharp, and banjo, interspersed with a choreographed script on folk music narrated by Ben Ramey. They were all active on the Houston folk scene, frequenting the Jewish Community Center when it was located at Hermann Park, and later, in the 1960s, the Jester (a small club off Westheimer), both of which featured local and nationally touring folk revival acts.

Bynum was a classically trained violist who performed with the Houston Symphony Orchestra, but was an active participant in the Houston Folklore Group. Her father played guitar and banjo and taught her traditional music as a child. "When I got to Houston from Oklahoma," Bynum says, "my husband, Jim Lyday, and I went to the Unitarian Church and they had a program on folk songs that was presented by the Houston Folk Group [in the mid-1950s]. And we got involved. Jim was a banjo player. He worked for the Army Corps of Engineers. And I had studied the songs of Appalachia, the ballads collected by Cecil Sharp. I'd been singing ballads for a long time. I sang for the Kiwanis Club, the Rotary Club."[24]

Bynum didn't know McCormick, though she did have a vivid memory of the event. "This was the old Alley [on Berry Street, not the current theatre in downtown Houston]," Bynum says. "It used to be a barrel factory, and there were four entrances, four ways to come in. It was theater-in-the-round; people were all around you. We had to use their set that had been built for a production of *The Iceman Cometh* and we couldn't change anything. So we just had our hootenanny on top of *The Iceman Cometh* set. We all came in with our guitars and banjos strapped to our shoulders, singing, 'Father and I went down to camp . . . ' Lightnin' Hopkins came out later."[25]

McCormick introduced Lightnin' to the Alley audience, but didn't know what to expect. "I was apprehensive," McCormick wrote, "because I knew the audience had come to hear the familiar ballads and songs popularized by book-trained singers. Here, in its habitat, there has never been any interest in the blues."[26] Clearly McCormick was expressing his feelings about the local folk crowd vis-à-vis local blues, even though Leadbelly, Big Bill Broonzy, Brownie

McGhee, and Sonny Terry were by then relatively well known among folk revival audiences across the country and abroad. In Houston, McCormick understood the limitations of his audience.

For Lightnin', the Alley Theatre hootenanny was a completely new experience. While he had recorded for white producers, he had never performed for a predominantly white audience in a formal concert. "Yet," McCormick remembered, "within seconds of the time he came out to prop his foot by me and begin 'That Mean Old Twister,' he'd begun to steal the show. By the time he sang [the verse] 'the shack where I was living really rocked but it never fell' the audience was hanging on every nuance of his voice. When his face stretched in pain, the guitar ringing bitterly, as he cried, 'Lord! . . . turn your twister the other way!' the theater filled with the taut gasp of an audience caught and held in the grasp of a single man."[27] McCormick said that he encouraged Lightnin' to re-create the way he played on the streets of the Third Ward.[28] The two-hundred-seat theatre was sold out, and when Lightnin' sang John Lee Hooker's "Hobo Blues," the audience went quiet out of respect for the performance.[29] But Lightnin' was confused, and at one point in the middle of a song, McCormick recalled that Lightnin' said, "'Well, a preacher don't get no amen in this corner,' meaning people are clapping, but they're not saying anything during the song."[30] Lightnin' didn't hear any of the banter he was accustomed to when he played in the little joints in the Third Ward, which may have made it more difficult for him to improvise, as so much of the improvisation in blues stems from a call-and-response exchange with the listener. In the case of Lightnin's performance of "Hobo Blues," there was, however, an added level of irony, in that it was probably the same song he had recorded as "Freight Train Blues" for Sittin' In With in 1951, but also represented some stagecraft on the part of McCormick to have him sing a song that implied he was a hobo who rides trains, when in fact he only once rode a train as a hobo, decades before.

The day after the Alley performance, two articles appeared in the Houston press, and were likely the first in a Houston paper to ever mention Lightnin'. Frank Stack of the *Houston Post* reported, "Lightning Hopkins, a Dowling Street Negro folksinger who makes up his own songs, in the grand old ballad tradition from his own experience, overshadowed everybody else on the program with an easy personable style."[31]

In the *Houston Chronicle*, Bill Byers was more evenhanded in his review, but he was especially moved by Lightnin', who appeared on stage "with dark glasses, shined shoes to reflect his broad grin . . . to sing some folk songs of today's woes and smiles. Unlike the others in the 'Hootenanny' program, Lightnin' concentrated on his own anxieties in life—the trouble with a short-haired woman ["Short Haired Woman"] and the miseries of tornados ["That Mean Old Twister"] sweeping into East Texas. His personality electrified the overflow audience . . . which had thought it was going to hear only songs which detailed the bitter laughter and travail of the past. But Hopkins's surprise was only one of the many given by members of the Houston Folklore Group."[32] Byers praised Ben Ramey, who narrated the evening program, "as a relaxed comfortable storyteller, with the authority of a friendly professor and the warmth of a good friend . . . introducing chapters from American history to be told in song." Each of the performers received positive notice, as did the entire event: "The audience particularly enjoyed the times when it was asked to sing, and often joined in when Ramey least expected. It's hoped it won't be long before the Alley stages another 'Hootenanny' so more people can participate in the spirit and fun found in this one."

For his performance, the Folklore Group paid Hopkins twenty dollars, which was his share of the $425 box office take.[33] While twenty dollars doesn't seem like much pay, McCormick reassured him that he could make more money doing these type of shows. McCormick became the point person for queries about Hopkins and began negotiating performance dates on his behalf as his manager.

In August 1959, Charters's recordings of Lightnin' were released on the Folkways label. In John S. Wilson's three-column review in the *New York Times*, McCormick was never mentioned because, apparently, Charters did not talk about him in the interview, though he did acknowledge him in his liner notes to the LP. Wilson reported that Charters had "gained pre-eminence for his invaluable series of disks for the Folkways label called 'The Music of New Orleans.'" In his praise of Charters's recordings of Hopkins, Wilson wrote that they were "technically . . . the best of his disks and in some ways, one of his most important," documenting "some stirring examples of undiluted, close-to-the-earth blues by an unusually talented and balanced singer."[34] However, Wilson's article perpetuated a myth of "rediscovery" in the way he described how Charters "rescued from obscurity a singer who seemed to have committed professional suicide by trying to adapt to rock 'n' roll standards. . . . He attempted to shift his ground, and by changing from unamplified guitar to a clangorously amplified one and supplementing its heavy beat with a loud drum and bass . . . he not only failed to catch on in rock 'n' roll but also lost his blues following and soon dropped out of sight. . . . On the basis of these recordings, Mr. Hopkins must be counted as one of the best (possibly *the* best) of unalloyed country blues men still singing." While Wilson's review in the *New York Times* was a major boost to Lightnin's career, it also demonstrated a gross misunderstanding of Lightnin's work up to that point. Lightnin', in his mid-1950s recordings, was not "trying to adapt to rock 'n' roll standards." Blues was the lifeblood of rock 'n' roll, and Lightnin' was trying to sustain his own popularity with black audiences.

On the same day that Wilson's article appeared in the *New York Times*—August 23, 1959—Charlotte Phelan published an article in the *Houston Post* that never mentioned Charters's recordings. Aside from the fact that Phelan's knowledge of Hopkins's career prior to his involvement with McCormick was very limited, her interview with Lightnin' was revealing. Lightnin' told her that playing at the Alley was "wonderful," and that he "wouldn't mind doing that again. A lot of people see those faces, turn around, and go back. I just love people. I don't care if it's 50,000. I ain't never scared, but I'm just kind of particular."

Phelan noted that Hopkins, when he wasn't performing, was a "quiet, self-contained man with deep-seated dignity," but that he could also be "pensive, remote, reluctantly responsive, even after his regular breakfast of two bottles of beer, which are always supported during the day with similar sustenance." By most accounts, Hopkins often appeared on stage with a flask of gin, which he liked to pull out of his pocket and take a sip from in between songs. Kyla Bynum described Lightnin' as a "lush," and said that on the day of his performance at the Alley Theatre, "somebody had to stay with him all day and keep him sober or he wouldn't show up for the show. Ed Badeaux [a folk revival singer who worked for Folkways] might have helped us out with that because it was a matter of just sort of babysitting him, talking to him, keeping him happy until the eight o'clock show time came. . . . It was well known he had a real drinking problem as we say these days."[35]

When Phelan followed Lightnin' into the "magic milieu of one of his dance halls [in Houston's Third Ward] where he is surrounded by a crush of intense and voluble admirers," she observed that he rejected an acoustic guitar in favor of an electrically amplified instrument, ignoring "the expressed objections of McCormick and other purists. Lightning makes his point about needing amplification: 'It gets so noisy, my sound is taken away from me. I can't hear myself.'"

Apparently McCormick never mentioned Charters to Phelan, because neither Charters nor his recordings for Folkways are discussed in the article. McCormick, as Lightnin's new manager, was interested in getting his own publicity, and was careful about what he told Phelan. But McCormick also promoted himself by announcing his own recordings and the discography he was compiling, adding that he had received a letter from Harold Leventhal, the impresario and manager of the folk revival group the Weavers, who was interested in possibly bringing Lightnin' to New York to perform at Town Hall or Carnegie Hall. [36] Overall McCormick wanted to emphasize and secure his role in Lightnin's "rediscovery."

Despite the fact that Lightnin' lived in a segregated, urban neighborhood in Houston and had pursued a commercial career for more than a decade, McCormick focused on his rural and oral culture roots as the basis for his authenticity. In keeping with John Lomax Sr.'s pastoral ideal of black folk singers, McCormick believed that Lightnin' was a "genuine folk artist," whose "roots are not the motley impressions of phonograph records but the distinct heritage of his birthplace." [37] For McCormick, Hopkins was a "strangely innocent man, isolated and oblivious to much of contemporary life, and ignorant in some astounding ways." [38] In his liner notes and articles, McCormick liked to quote Hopkins's stories of cotton picking, singing in church, and playing blues in East Texas to bolster his argument that "beneath the sharp urban manners," Lightnin' was "pure country" and that East Texas "is a magic spring from which the great blues minstrels have flowed in an unbroken line."

Folklorist Patrick Mullen suggests that while the dichotomy that McCormick set up between the modern world of recordings and other technological developments on one side and the traditional oral world of the isolated, rural folk community on the other was widely accepted by folklorists and folk revivalists of that period, it was ultimately flawed. Mullen maintains that "the traditional and the modern, oral and media transmission, are not isolated entities, they have always interacted with one another because tradition is a concept of the past that is always constructed in the present."[39] Lightnin' may have personally interacted with Blind Lemon Jefferson and Texas Alexander, for example, but he also heard their recordings and the recordings of others like John Lee Hooker, John Lee "Sonny Boy" Williamson, Big Bill Broonzy, Tampa Red, Big Joe Williams, and others who were performing rhythm and blues and had nationally known commercial hits.

McCormick, as historian Benjamin Filene points out, was one of several mid-century researchers who responded to "what they perceived as bourgeois culture's corrupt materialisms and constraining standards of propriety," and depicted "bluesmen as the embodiments of an anti-modern ethos."[40] Even Charters, in his book *The Country Blues* published in November 1959, had a highly romanticized view of African American blues singers and described Hopkins as "one of the last of his kind, a lonely, bitter man who brings to the blues the intensity and pain of hours in the hot sun, scraping at the earth, singing to make the hours pass. The blues will go on, but the country blues . . . will pass with men like this thin, intense singer from Centerville, Texas."[41] McCormick, writing in *Jazz Journal*, reiterated this perspective, but even went further in his portrayal of Hopkins as a counterpoint to what Filene has called "the emptiness of contemporary society." Hopkins, McCormick wrote, "is a fascinatingly complete man: even the least of his routine actions seem in tune with the earthy cynicism that characterizes his songs. A man with a tribal sense of belonging to his culture, he is outside the modern dilemma."[42]

Certainly McCormick was aware that racism and discrimination in Houston were rampant. While the white liberal-minded audience at the Alley Theatre appreciated Lightnin', the reality of life in Houston during the 1950s imposed definite limitations. Isabelle Ganz, a classically trained mezzo-soprano, composer, conductor, and teacher who moved to Houston after living in New York City and was active in the Houston Folk Group, says that the hootenannies in Houston emulated those in New York City, and tried to be as inclusive as possible. "I got interested in folk music singing union songs in high school," she recalls, and as she got older she started listening to Pete Seeger and going to folk shows in New York. But in Houston, she says, "it was different because it was strictly segregated. Blacks and whites did not mix. I was shocked by the colored-only water fountains in Foley's department store, and in other places around town. I'd never seen anything like it."[43] Kyla Bynum concurs: "Houston was pure McCarthyism. Absolute bigotry. Houston was a god-awful place."[44]

The NAACP had been fighting for decades in Houston against racism and discrimination against African Americans. By 1945 it was looking for a plaintiff to challenge Texas's segregated university system and targeted the policy that excluded blacks from the University of Texas law school. The resulting case of *Sweatt v. Painter* was finally resolved in 1950 when the U.S. Supreme Court ruled in favor of the plaintiff, Heman Sweatt.[45] While this was a landmark decision, the dismantling of the Jim Crow system in Houston proceeded slowly. In the 1950s and 1960s African Americans there fought hard in the courts to gain the right to sit on juries, to eliminate segregation in housing and education, and to obtain equal pay for equal work and equal access to social services and public transportation. In 1958, Hattie Mae White won a seat on the Houston School Board and became the first African American elected to public office in Texas since Reconstruction. White, in a coordinated effort with the NAACP and African American community leaders, mounted a sustained effort to force members of the school board to implement court-ordered desegregation.

Opposition persisted, however, and racial tensions intensified. In March 1960, four masked white youths followed Felton Turner, an unemployed awning installer who had participated in a sit-in with Texas Southern University students, and abducted him at gunpoint as he walked through the Heights section of the city. They took him to a deserted wooded area not far from downtown Houston and strung him up in a tree, beat him with chains, and carved two sets of KKK initials on his abdomen with a pocket knife.[46]

In an article in the *Houston Post* on April 24, 1960, columnist Jim Mousner noted that "the city's Negro population is increasing at the rate of 3 percent a year from immigration—mostly from East Texas, Louisiana, and Arkansas. . . . More than half of Houston's Negro population lives in three sections of the city, the Fourth Ward, the oldest Negro area, located west of downtown; the Fifth Ward in the north part of town; and the Third Ward, south of the downtown area."[47] Of these, Mousner noted that the Fourth Ward, "the poorest of the three areas economically, is touched by every segment of the city's freeway system, making it a highly unstable place to live." The Third Ward, Mousner observed, was the middle-class residential area for Houston's African American population and afforded a "more desirable environment except in the north portion [where Lightnin' lived] where a heavy traffic flow and a 65 per cent increase in small businesses in the last decade have contributed to instability." Moreover, statistics gathered by Dr. Henry Allen Bullock, director of graduate research at Texas Southern University, showed that "these blighted areas with their decaying buildings, unsanitary living conditions and drab atmosphere produce a high mortality rate, crime and juvenile delinquency. Most of Houston's homicides, two-thirds of which involve Negroes, occur in or near these areas." But "profound changes," Mousner maintained, were being made, as Carter Wesley, an attorney and publisher of the African American newspaper the *Houston Informer* pointed out: "Ten years ago we couldn't have had a headline about a Negro woman being elected to the school board. Mrs. White was not elected by Negroes but all of the Houston community. The Negro has won the right to serve on juries. The Negro has won a Supreme Court decision on schools. . . . Changes are going on but we need a new approach."

The 1960s were turbulent years, and while there weren't riots in Houston, there were sit-ins and protest marches that confronted racism and discrimination.[48] Desegregation in Houston proceeded slowly and came as a result of bitterly fought legal battles. Thurgood Marshall, Martin Luther King Jr., and other civil rights leaders came to the city and helped to propel civic change.

In Lightin' Hopkins's blues, there were few direct references to social protest, though his "Tim Moore's Farm" was a scathing indictment of plantation owner Tom Moore and his cruelty to sharecroppers. Throughout his career Lightnin' largely stayed away from racial themes, which made his recording of "Tim Moore's Farm" even more striking, considering it was released in 1949.

While McCormick was impressed by Lightnin's commercial recording of "Tim Moore's Farm," he wanted to probe deeper into Lightnin's repertory in his own recordings to establish the roots of his blues. He carefully constructed field sessions that were relaxed and imposed no time limits. Lightnin' was free to essentially do as he wished, talking and singing, so long as he played acoustic guitar and restrained from the rocking material he'd recorded for Herald. The resulting blues were both personal and reflective. McCormick's recordings, when first released in 1960 (or late 1959) helped to establish Lightnin's credibility as a living connection to the work songs that were a basis of country blues and to the music of Blind Lemon Jefferson, Texas Alexander, Leadbelly, and others. Though production values were low, and the overall sound quality was poor, given the technical limitations of the microphone and tape recorder that he used, McCormick was able to get Lightnin' to open up and to perform some of the oldest songs that he remembered.

In early 1960, Doug Dobell, who had a record shop in London and operated a small label, issued some of McCormick's field recordings on the LP titled *The Rooster Crowed in England.*[49] This may have been the first album from the McCormick sessions to hit the market—but only in the United Kingdom, as it probably coincided with the release of the LP *Country Blues* in the United States. The strongest selections on the *The Rooster Crowed in England* LP are the intensely autobiographical "Beggin' Up and Down the Streets," the highly emotive "Have You Ever Seen a One-Eyed Woman Cry?" and "Children's Boogie," about which McCormick wrote, "His imagination chuckles to itself."[50] In "Back to Arkansas," Lightnin' alluded to Ray Charles's recent hit "What'd I Say," and "Met the Blues on the Corner" and "Goin' to Galveston" are sourced from a 1954 acetate that McCormick acquired from Bill Holford at ACA, and featured Lightnin' on piano.

One of the most talked-about songs on this LP was "Blues for Queen Elizabeth," a rambling blues, which Lightnin' actually introduced before he started singing. "This is a song I'm goin' to make up for the Queen in England," he said. "I think that it would be all right. My wife brought home a picture and she was very, very upset over it because she looked so good to her. She said she looked like a rose that just bloomed in May. So I got a little idea. And I'm makin' this song for the Queen and her husband, which I don't know. And I'm hopin' some day I get to come over in England and play some blues for them."

Lightnin's explanation of why he wrote the song seems contrived, and one has to wonder if he was prompted by McCormick. And when he finally got around to singing, the lyrics were disjointed.

> Whoa, you know the rooster crowed in England
> Man, they heard him way over in France

You know, I'm prayin' to the good Lord in heaven
Oh Lord, please give these people a chance

Finally, after a long interlude, with bluesy guitar runs answering each verse, Lightnin' finally got back to the point of the song: "I'm gonna take my wife to England, tell me she was in Chicago a few days ago." While Lightnin's mixing of time periods between what is apparently a reference to World War II in France and the present of 1959 seemed random and disjointed, it was nonetheless representative of how he, and many other traditional singers, put together blues. As McCormick pointed out, "Many of his songs are spontaneous improvisations, made and forgotten in the time he takes to sing them," and "Blues for Queen Elizabeth" was certainly one of those songs which, by the time he finishing singing it, barely made sense.[51] Yet the song attracted immediate attention in the press. Phelan wrote in the *Houston Post*: "Lightning's incredible spontaneity is equal to any occasion, it seems. Told that Queen Elizabeth II was in Chicago, the minstrel immediately composed 'Blues for Queen Elizabeth,' but when chided because he called the Queen of England 'baby,' Lightning flashed his gold teeth in a sheepish grin. 'I wasn't talking just to her,' he said."[52]

Around the same time that Dobell released *The Rooster Crowed in England*, McCormick leased Diane Guggenheim (a.k.a. Diane Hamilton) and her Tradition label enough material for two Lightnin' LPs that were released in late 1959 or early 1960: *Country Blues*, followed by *Autobiography in Blues*.[53] Musically, the recordings that McCormick was producing did effectively document the breadth of Lightnin's traditional repertoire on acoustic guitar, even if he was in fact re-recording some songs, like "Short Haired Woman," that had already been commercially released. Lightnin's versions of such songs as "See, See Rider," "Bunion Stew," "Hear My Black Dog Bark," and "When the Saints Go Marching In," evoke a bygone era.

Country Blues received far greater attention than *The Rooster Crowed in England* had. About *Country Blues*, Robert Shelton wrote in the *New York Times*: "Despite a poor job of taping, it is a record of great interest. Although there are occasional flashes of wit, Hopkins' mood here is generally more introverted and somber than it was on his Folkways release of a few months ago. One gets the feeling of listening to a sensitive man reflecting on a hard life with pathos, not sentimentalism, and meaning every word he says, an attribute rarely found in the rhythm and blues style."[54] Of particular interest to Shelton was the song "Go Down Ol' Hannah," in which Hopkins took a traditional work song and reshaped it into a blues.

During McCormick's 1959 field sessions with Lightnin', in addition to collecting blues, he unexpectedly recorded one selection, "The Dirty Dozens," that he felt at the time would "never be placed on the open market."[55] But McCormick ultimately changed his mind and entered into an agreement with Chris Strachwitz to release it in December 1963 on an LP titled *The Unexpurgated Folk Songs of Men*, for which he provided no artist credits because of the salaciousness of the lyrics.[56] There was, however, a sixteen-page insert authored by McCormick, who wrote that the anthology was "an informal song-swapping session with a group of Texans, New Yorkers and Englishmen exchanging bawdy songs and lore." McCormick traced the origins of the dozens in African American folklore as a cycle of ritual insults in which "the players strive to bury one another with vituperation. In the play, the opponent's mother is especially slandered and thus the male asserts himself through the rejection of the feminine and by the skill with which he manages the abuse. The appropriate reply is not to deny the assault, but to return even the greater evil-speaking hurled at the other person's mother."[57] In Lightnin's version of "The Dirty Dozens," there is no verbal battle; it is instead a diatribe that strings together a series of insults that are at once vile and offensive:

> What the hell you trying to play the dozens with me?
> I don't play the dozens with nobody.
> Now, hell, I don't like the way you talkin' no how.
> Talkin' about my mama, your mammy, and all that kind of junk. . . .
> You got a crooked ass hole, nigger, and you can't shit straight. . . .
> You old black son of a bitch, you were born with a rag in your ass . . .
> Your mama had the shingles around her bloody cock, you big black
> bastard, now get out of here![58]

Clearly it was impossible for McCormick to credit Lightnin' as the singer of "The Dirty Dozens," as it no doubt would have identified him as obscene and would have made it very difficult to get him booked in "respectable" venues. It remains one of Lightnin's least-known recordings.

McCormick was building a reputation for himself as a folklorist, and 1960 was a Watershed year. In addition to the release of his recordings of Hopkins, he issued a two-LP set A *Treasury of Field Recordings*, a compilation of blues, zydeco, country, and folk materials recorded from 1951 to 1960 by the Houston Folk Group.[59] McCormick had made a majority of the recordings himself. At the same time that McCormick was working on these projects, he also sought to undermine Charters and create problems at Folkways.

On November 26, 1959, Antoinette Charles, apparently with McCormick's guidance, handwrote a letter on behalf of Lightnin' to Folkways. Lightnin' usually referred to Antoinette as his wife, though in fact they were never married. "Nette," as Lightnin' often called her, had a husband and children and a separate residence in Houston's Fifth Ward. How Lightnin' met her is unknown, but in 1948 they started having an affair that continued until his death. According to Strachwitz, Antoinette was originally from southwestern Louisiana. She was related to Clifton and Cleveland Chenier, and it may have been through them that she and Hopkins got to know each other. In time they developed a romantic liaison, and at some point during the 1950s, Antoinette became involved in Lightnin's business affairs. In her letter to Folkways, she complained about the terms that he had agreed to with Charters: [All spellings *sic*] "I was thinking I was going to get a share of the money that was made, and that would right I think any that sell your records they are suppose to give you part of the money made. If you dont agree I ask you to stop the records. This company doesn't have the contrack to be selling my songs & my singing on records. they didn't send me a copy of my records I did think they would send me one. I have a nother record coming out that is paying me Roaltes so I see no reason for not getting a shere from you all."[60]

Lightnin' had never wanted royalties before—even though Quinn had included a provision for royalties in one of his contracts with him—but instead had insisted upon cash payments. When Charters had recorded Hopkins, he had paid him three hundred dollars in cash and explained that it was payment in full.[61] But once Charters was gone, McCormick seized the opportunity to challenge Charters and the business practices of Folkways. To his credit, McCormick helped to make Hopkins more aware of the pitfalls of the record business, but he had an ulterior motive—he wanted to prevent Folkways from producing any more of Lightnin's albums.

Asch responded to Hopkins's letter by stating that Folkways was not "a large company and the $300 represents a lot of money to us. We could have made this money part of a royalty agreement if you had received $100 advance and the balance to be paid at the rate of 25 cents per record sold. However, you did receive the $300 and we think this covers the lifetime of the record."[62]

Hopkins answered Asch in a typed letter, dated December 12, 1959, which sounded as if it had been written by McCormick, asking that Folkways remove the record from sale. Hopkins also explained that prior to recording for Charters, he was paid $350 for recording four songs for the San Antonio–based TNT label: "It was my original idea that I was to receive my standard fee which would have been $200 for two songs. I was trapped into thinking this and did not find out otherwise until the recording had already begun. You got 9 songs altogether and I was only paid a part of the money down and my understanding was that royalties would be paid to make up the rest."[63] In addition, the letter mentioned that he was paid $120 for the lease of a selection of his recordings to be issued in a limited edition of ninety-nine copies and to be sold only by mail order from England (*The Blues in East Texas* LP on Heritage). Moreover, it stated that Hopkins was "protected by the fact that my original songs are not copyrighted (and so are not subject to the compulsory license provision of the copyright law) and so are still my property and cannot be used without my agreement."[64] Hopkins (McCormick) then reiterated his fundamental point that he would agree to Asch's "making an album" only if he was given a "fair royalty payment," and went on to detail what he thought was fair: "That would be 7%-of-the-retail price on all copies sold after the first 100; the first 100 copies would be paid for at $100. This is the same agreement as I have made with the English company. I will give you the same opportunity if you sent [sic] out the contract immediately." However, Hopkins (McCormick) also insisted that Asch's contract include "some bond with a $100 penalty" to be paid if he did not receive his royalties on time. In addition, he alluded to the royalty problems that John Lomax Jr. had been having with Folkways and the grievances articulated in McCormick's December 5, 1959, letter to Ed Badeaux, written on behalf of the Houston Folklore Group, John Lomax Jr., and Lightnin' Hopkins.[65]

Charters says Asch had told him that he was going to be sued by McCormick on behalf of Hopkins, but he never heard what ultimately transpired to settle the dispute, and there are no written records in Asch's files that indicate that the suit was ever filed or brought to court. In a letter Charters wrote to Asch, dated January 13, 1960, he complained, "I am much disturbed that McCormick is bothering you about Hopkins. As I've told you, McCormick is simply a leech on Hopkins' side. I'm sorry I even gave him Hopkins' address," implying that McCormick didn't even know where Hopkins lived until Charters told him.[66] Charters, in an effort to bolster Asch's position, wrote, "If it will be of any help to you in dealing with him—my English contact has written that McCormick sold an LP of Hopkins material to an English company for the total sum of $70. No royalty. I really fail to see where McCormick can involve himself. Especially after we took all the chances and presented him on LP."[67]

Over the next several months, the tension surrounding Hopkins's Folkways album intensified. An unsigned memo, dated May 6, 1960, apparently from Marian Distler to Asch, stated that McCormick had not really been interested in recording Lightnin', even though he claimed through a letter written for Hopkins, dated December 12, 1959, that he had wanted to make an album two years earlier. In the end, after months of heated exchange, Lightnin' did sign a contract with Folkways, dated October 21, 1960, in which he was promised a "royalty of 25 cents per record album and/or tape album sold," a percentage that exceeded the standard commercial contract of that time. However, it's difficult to determine the extent to which Hopkins ever received royalties, or how many copies of the Folkways album sold.[68] Asch's accounting records are inexact.

While McCormick wanted to help Lightnin', he was not completely altruistic. Like Asch, McCormick was a complex individual who, though he may have shared Asch's mission to "record folk music and people's expression of their wants, needs and experiences," also saw the potential for personal gain. By acting as Lightnin's manager and promoter, McCormick probably didn't make much money, but he was able to enhance his own reputation as a folklorist through his articles and liner notes that espoused the values of the folk revival. McCormick was smart to cultivate his own relationship with Lightnin' and

Antoinette, but as hard as he tried, he was not able to control them. As time went on, Antoinette was to become a much more important influence upon Lightnin' than McCormick probably ever realized.

While McCormick and Charters celebrated Lightnin's "country" roots, they minimized the influence of the urban reality in which he lived and ignored the inherent social stratification within the African American community. Lola Cullum, for example, and to some extent Antoinette were from more financially stable backgrounds than Lightnin', though the people who frequented the little dives where he played in the Third Ward were more like him, farm workers and day laborers who migrated away from the country hoping to find a better life in the city. Among African Americans, the appreciation of Lightnin's music, whether for its expressive qualities or finesse, was rooted in a shared cultural experience, and in this way was significantly different from the perceptions of those associated with the folk revival.

Charters, McCormick, John Wilson of the *New York Times*, and many others writing during this period all denigrated Lightnin's use of the electric guitar, yet it was this instrument that had propelled his commercial hits and contributed to his vitality in Houston's Third Ward. By championing the acoustic sound, the folk revival perpetuated a misunderstanding of not only Lightnin's earlier recordings, but the history of blues in general. Yet, at the same time, the folk revival created a context in which Lightnin' and many of his contemporaries could reach new audiences and earn more from their performances and records than had ever seemed possible.

5

~~~~~~~~~

The Blues Revival Heats Up

While the blues revival overlapped with the folk revival, it had been incubating for years. Record collectors were among the first researchers of blues in the 1930s, if not earlier, compiling discographies to piece together the history of the music. However, for a long time blues was thought of as a basic building block of jazz. Sam Charters, Mack McCormick, and Chris Strachwitz first learned about blues from 78-rpm records, and like their colleagues in the United States and Europe, were arriving at an understanding of the blues from a jazz background.

Prior to the publication of Charters's book *The Country Blues*, accompanied by the release of his Folkways recordings of Lightnin' Hopkins in 1959, little had been written about the subject. Certainly McCormick's research paralleled Charters's quest, as did the pioneering record work of Paul Oliver, among others, in England and throughout Europe. The first attempt at a Lightnin' Hopkins discography was compiled by New Yorker Anthony Rotante and published in the British magazine *Discophile* in 1955.[1] Building on Rotante's work, Strachwitz published a Hopkins discography in the British *Jazz Monthly* in 1959, with explanatory comments by McCormick.[2] These discographies were crucial to the blues revival, which was propelled by an orientation to records and the record-listening experience that became the basis of new documentation and interpretation.

As the blues revival evolved, it became a kind of romantic movement, as Jeff Todd Titon suggests, among "idealists of all ages, involving a love for blues as a stylized revolt against bourgeois values."[3] Blues revivalists idealized African American life and music, especially as it related to the apparent rejection of the conventions of work, family, worship, and sexual propriety. The blues singer appeared to embody what many blues revivalists lacked—the confidence to express his or her innermost feelings and desires in music without reproach.

In the context of the early years of the blues revival, Lightnin' became a focal point of discussion, documentation, recording, and, to some extent, controversy among those who sought to advance their own careers by championing his. McCormick was trying to manage all of Lightnin's affairs. However, concurrent with McCormick's promotional efforts, John A. Lomax Jr. also tried to help Hopkins advance his career. Lomax Jr. was not a professional musician, though he did like performing and sometimes appeared on stage with Lightnin'. McCormick disapproved, and, in an interview with researcher Andrew Brown years later, commented, "John and he [Lightnin'] started playing a game that can best be described as 'The Nigger and the White Man.' And that really started getting to me, because it was like old times have come again. Lightning was perfectly willing to play it. And they ended up with some dialogue on stage, little set routines, that were like Amos 'n' Andy, and even worse. Just patronizing little exchanges: 'Yeah, boss, yeah.' So some of the Lightning Hopkins/ John Lomax Jr. concerts I was hearing about—and a few I attended—turned into these essentially offensive exchanges. That aggravated me."[4] At the time, however, McCormick also imposed his views about how Lightnin' should perform, though he did not appear with him on stage in such a patronizing fashion. Both McCormick and Lomax wanted Lightnin' to recreate his past for an audience hungry for what they thought was a "pure" sound, though in fact it was contrived. During this period, Lightnin' was changing sharply. He was more self-conscious and aware of himself as an entertainer. He played along with the wishes of McCormick and Lomax because the money was good, but he also held out for more. "Lightning had this habit of doing as little as possible musically on stage," McCormick said, "and talking as much as possible. The story that led into 'Mr. Charlie' got up to twenty minutes at one point. If you're on stage and you got an hour-and-a-half, two hours, you get a restless audience pretty quickly that way."[5]

Lightnin' liked to perform the song "Mr. Charlie" about the man he remembered who ran the mill in Centerville. "See, that child, little old boy," Lightnin' recalled, "he couldn't talk, he stuttered. He went to Mr. Charlie . . . but Mr. Charlie didn't figure that he could work." But one Sunday, he "run on up to Mr. Charlie's house. . . . He tried to tell Mr. Charlie that his mill was on fire. . . . He tried to tell him but he stuttered so. Mr. Charlie said, 'You back again, boy, I got my work to do.' And the boy kept trying, but couldn't get the words out, 'Y. . .Y . . .Y . . .' And Mr. Charlie said, 'If you can't talk it, just sing it.' And the little boy sang, 'Ohhhh, Mr. Charlie, your rollin' mill is burnin' down.'"[6] Lightnin' loved to tell this story, and it became a kind of prologue, which varied in length, before Lightnin' started singing.

Lomax didn't want to interfere with Lightnin's performance on stage and tended to let him ramble on for as long as he wanted to. Despite the criticism leveled against him, Lomax was not deterred in his efforts to bring Lightnin' to a wider audience, and he didn't want any financial compensation for helping him. Lomax was a successful builder and real estate developer who headed a construction company in Houston and participated in the activities of the Houston Folklore Group when he had the time. After the 1959 Alley Theatre hootenanny, Lomax corresponded with Barry Olivier and his staff at the Berkeley Folk Festival, to be held on the University of California campus in July 1960, and was able to get Lightnin' booked for four hundred dollars, a fee that exceeded that for any of his previous public performances. However, Lomax did have some reservations. In a letter to B. J. Connors, secretary of the Committee for Arts and Lectures at the University of California, Lomax wrote: "If Lightning's presence adds to the rich flavor to the Festival, as I believe it can, I wish you know that I will be due at least a large pink rosette for my extra curricular duties with him. Largely, he lives each day to itself. . . . You might be surprised at the number of conversations and meetings I have already had with him to get the proceedings to this point. I had to agree to stay with him at all times throughout the trip; this includes his performance too."[7]

Lightnin' was high maintenance, and although McCormick had a fairly good working relationship with him, he knew that he could be difficult. "Lightning behaved like he was some great star who should have champagne cooling in his hotel suite when he arrived," McCormick told Andrew Brown. "He didn't demand those kinds of things, but he *did* demand an awful lot of care and protection in terms of arrangements, getting to places, this and that. Otherwise, he just suddenly wasn't there. So you couldn't just call a university and say, 'Would you like Lightning Hopkins to appear?' You better be prepared to deliver him—to take him personally, to go get him up, buy his beer, carry his guitar, and all of that. And he had the people that would do that around town, all these young guitar players that wanted to learn from him, and people who treated him like a celebrity. So that was his existence here. He had an entourage; he went around like a prizefighter. Why should he, because he's going to a university, be this lonely person propelled into this world he really didn't want?"[8] Although Lightnin' seemed content to simply be a "star" in the Third Ward, shying away from the audiences McCormick was dragging him toward, he was nonetheless beginning to earn more than he ever had before.

In the summer of 1960, Chris Strachwitz came back to Houston with his portable Roberts tape recorder and Electrovoice 664 microphone, hoping to record Lightnin'. But Lightnin' was in no position to record because he was getting ready to leave for California.[9] On June 30, 1960, Lomax flew to San Francisco with Lightnin', who performed at the Berkeley Folk Festival on July 3 and 4 to great success. Alfred Frankenstein of the *San Francisco Chronicle* called Lightnin' a "great, authentic folk artist . . . whose gorgeous bass voice, colossal rhythm, and subtly shaded delicacy in guitar-playing provided the festival with one of its most distinguished moments."[10]

Lightnin', when asked about the Berkeley Folk Festival the following week in a radio interview, said, "I liked it so well I just can't tell you. I had a wonderful time. I could go up on top of those hills and see the beautiful lights, cool breeze, just look down. . . . It was my first time up there which I hope it don't be the last time. I enjoyed it so, I want to go back again."[11]

From San Francisco, Lomax took Lightnin' to Los Angeles, where his sister Bess Lomax Hawes helped to arrange a couple of dates at the Ash Grove, a folk club owned by Ed Pearl. Hawes was a folklorist and musician who was

Pearl's guitar teacher, and when Lightnin' and Lomax got to Los Angeles, she hosted a "welcoming party." In attendance were lots of people from the L.A. folk scene who had heard Lightnin's records but had never met him, including the singer, songwriter, and radio host Barbara Dane, a regular at the Ash Grove who was eager to meet Lightnin'. But she was shocked when she saw that Lomax had dressed Lightnin' as "a country bumpkin" in a flannel shirt and dungarees, because apparently that was his impression of what the folk scene was. "It was completely the wrong approach," Dane says. "Ed was very sophisticated about these things and had plenty of the old timers, like Reverend Gary Davis, Jesse Fuller, a whole range of people coming to sing there. So it was not necessary to go through this charade."[12] Finally, after watching Lightnin' from afar, Dane moved closer to him. "I could see that he was uncomfortable," Dane recalls, "so I wanted to give him a chance to be a little more relaxed, and just walk around with him a little bit in a blues manner. And he kind of let his hair down to me about the whole situation. He said, 'You know, Mr. Lomax wanted me to dress like this.' And then he said he wasn't going to have his electric box, he was going to have a natural box. He was very uncomfortable in all of that, and so having said that to me, I said, 'Don't worry about it. He [Ed] will see it through. He knows quality when he sees it and relax.' And he was fine with all that. And Ed did; he would have booked him sight unseen because, the thing is, Lightnin' had actually been very popular in the black cultural arena in years past. . . . So it was ridiculous to think you had to present him in some other way."[13]

The afternoon before the show at the Ash Grove, Lightnin' got in touch with his old friend Luke "Long Gone" Miles, who was then in Los Angeles with his wife, Hazel.[14] "Luke Miles was somebody who appeared on Lightnin's doorstep some time a long while back in Houston," Pearl says. "He was very tall and very skinny and very gangly. And he just appeared on Lightnin's doorstep, and Lightnin' wanted to close the door on him, and Luke proceeded to just go to sleep on the door stoop. And he just stayed around. He was a real country guy. So, finally, Lightnin' took a fancy to him and let him hang around. . . . He was a good singer. And he'd do anything for Lightnin'. He'd carry his guitar if he needed it."[15]

In the dressing room of the Ash Grove, Lightnin' was uncomfortable, not so much because of the clothes Lomax Jr. had provided for him but because his hair was a mess. He wanted to get his hair conked (processed and straightened), and Pearl didn't know where to find the chemicals. Lightnin' and Long Gone piled into Pearl's car and drove around Los Angeles, stopping at different drug stores, but they couldn't find the right product. Finally Pearl remembered that beneath his mother's apartment on West Adams was a black beauty salon. When he went inside, the beautician remembered him and gave him the chemicals. From the beauty salon, Long Gone took them to the home of Joe Chambers (of the gospel group the Chambers Brothers) and he conked Lightnin's hair. Lightnin' was pleased, and the show at the Ash Grove was a hit.

In a radio interview with Dane, Lomax talked about what he was hoping to accomplish by taking Lightnin' to California. While he didn't explain why he dressed him as he did, he was well intentioned, even if he didn't fully understand the expectations of the audience. Clearly he had been influenced by his father, John Lomax Sr., who had dressed Leadbelly for one of his first concerts on January 4, 1935, in a rough blue work shirt over a yellow one, and old-fashioned high-bib overalls and red bandanna around his neck.[16] To Dane, Lomax Jr. said, "I was very happy to have made this trip. Lightnin' has been with me all the time. I just want to say that I've had a lot of personal enjoyment out of it, from my own singin' in a small part, and from helpin' Lightnin' to make this trip. I thought that he would be of great interest to all the people he could sing to and that could hear him because he has a big appeal to me. I felt that certainly . . . he was bound to find some spark with anybody who would take time and be quiet enough to hear him here."[17]

At the Ash Grove on July 6 and 7, Lightnin' performed as part a program that included Big Joe Williams, Sonny Terry, and Brownie McGhee. "Lightnin' simply created a sensation," Pearl says, "because the audience seemed so ready for it. I had had Brownie and Sonny and a couple of other traditional blues players before Lightnin'. But Brownie and Sonny had been playing for decades variations of their original music, but it had been adapted to the wishes of a white audience, but Lightnin' wasn't that. Brownie knew what songs people wanted to hear."[18] It was the first time Lightnin' met McGhee, Terry, and Williams, whose 1935 recording of "Baby, Please Don't Go" was undoubtedly an influence upon him. However, Lightnin' had relatively little experience playing for white audiences, so when he came on stage, no matter how much Lomax Jr. may have tried to coach him, he could only be himself. There was no pretense. Lightnin' was still trying to figure out what white audiences really wanted, so he played whatever came to mind, and his songs rambled on in the style he was accustomed to.

The World Pacific label worked out a deal with Lightnin' and the other musicians to make an LP together. [19] Pearl says, "*Down South Summit Meetin'* was recorded entirely in the studios of World Pacific studio, by Ed Michel, with me there as holding it together, kibbitzing and making suggestions. [Applause was added to the LP master to make it sound as if it was recorded live at the Ash Grove.] It was initially called *First Meeting* as it was the first time Lightnin', Brownie, and Sonny had appeared on an LP together. Surprised the hell out of me, but there it was. . . . I bought a huge bottle of whiskey at the request of the guys as we drove to World Pacific. Big Joe drank half of it in the first couple of hours and not so gradually slipped through incoherence into dreamland. An historic error by yours truly."[20]

Essentially the LP was a loosely structured jam session, with the four performers trading licks in songs that extended longer than five minutes each. Lightnin's vocals and acoustic guitar picking were impressive because he was able to quickly improvise as he played along, but it was the banter that propelled the session forward.[21] "Big Joe Williams, he got over there," Lightnin' said, "he told me, 'You can steal my chicken, Lightnin', but can you make her lay?' I told him I had roosters all over my cabin, and I make any hen lay when the times get hard. I think it was great. . . . I guess we all felt good, and we all went along with it."[22]

Billboard wrote, "A meeting of minds and voices is the accomplished fact of this unusually entertaining folk-blues album by four top names in the current folk-blues revival. All four share playing and singing improvisations on four of the tracks. Two others are shared by Hopkins and McGhee and Hopkins alone. Extremely entertaining fare."[23]

After Lightnin' returned to Houston, he went back to work in the little joints in the Third Ward, though it was clear that he was rapidly gaining an expanding white audience, primarily as a result of the efforts of Lomax and McCormick, who were vying for his favor. McCormick was more ambitious, and in addition to trying to get bookings for Lightnin', he continued trying to find other blues musicians to record.

While Lightnin' was in California, McCormick and Strachwitz went to Navasota, Texas. "We drove out towards Washington County," Strachwitz says. "And I literally just got out of the car and I saw people working in the fields and asked them, 'Have you heard of any guitar pickers out here?' And they said, 'You better go to Navasota for that.' Mack recalled a Hopkins song 'Tim Moore's Farm.' . . . Mack had a feeling that Tom Moore might have a plantation in the area because he knew Lightnin' was from that part of the country, and thought the best place to start inquiring would be a feed store. We walked into the feed store and Mack just walked up to one of the employees and said, 'Does Tom Moore live here in town?' And he directed us to his office over the bank building in Navasota. And Mack acted very police-like. 'Can we visit your plantation?' 'Well, you have to make an appointment. I don't have time right now.' And then Mack asked something to the effect of 'Do you know of any hands who play music for your workers?' And Mr. Moore said, 'There's a fellow here they seem to like him. I don't know his name but you need to go to the railroad station and ask Peg Leg. He can tell you.' So, we went to the railroad station and Peg Leg told us his name was Mance Lipscomb and that he was probably cutting grass out on the highway, but he also told us where he lived. So, we couldn't find him on the highway and we turned up at his house that evening and those recordings became the first release on Arhoolie Records."[24] Lipscomb subsequently enjoyed a starring role in the folk-blues revival, often paralleling Lightnin's experiences and occasionally sharing the bill with him. While Lightnin' and Lipscomb are often grouped together as exemplars of Texas country blues, their music was significantly different. Lipscomb was a songster and played finger-style guitar; his repertoire included folk songs, ballads, and dance tunes. Lightnin' developed an emotive, single-string guitar style that reflected the commercially recorded blues artists of the 1920s and '30s.

After recording Mance Lipscomb on August 11, 1960, Strachwitz went to Memphis to meet up with Paul Oliver, who was traveling with his wife, Valerie, across the United States, supported by grants from the Foreign Specialists Program of the Bureau of Educational and Cultural Affairs of the United States and the Council of Leaders and Specialists of the American Council of Education. Oliver, in addition to expanding his research of blues, was also conducting interviews for BBC Radio. "A past student of mine happened to have been made a program director," Oliver says, "so we got in touch. He helped to arrange for me to have the equipment, which was difficult in those days . . . the one [tape recorder] I had belonged to the army, and the BBC had gotten it from the army. It was entirely in a khaki bag that was made to fit it. So I never did get to see what kind of tape recorder it was. It was all very concealed, being a military thing."[25]

Oliver had corresponded with Strachwitz after reading his early article on Lightnin', and together they went back to Texas, where Strachwitz introduced him to Lipscomb. But Oliver was especially interested in Lightnin' because he was familiar with his records and wanted to interview him for his radio series and for the book he was then developing, titled *Conversation with the Blues*.[26] "The interview was in the Third Ward," Oliver says, "on the front door step basically of his house. We met there socially and independently with a couple of his friends. One of them, L. C. Williams, died very shortly after, a very nice young singer, and Long Gone Miles and Spider Kilpatrick.[27] . . . I interviewed him [Lightnin'] I suppose for twenty minutes of actual time. But the amount of text from him was very limited. He was a kind of slow speaker. He'd just give an answer to a question, and then I'd have to reshape another question, and get another one sentence answer, and so on and so on. It wasn't really flowing. My wife Val was there, and I think that seemed to reassure him in a sense. He was feeling safe without stress and so on. His wife brought us some coffee. It was very relaxed actually."[28]

When Oliver completed the interview, he asked Lightnin' to sign a release for the BBC, and then paid twenty-five dollars. Oliver says that he didn't "want to tell him at the start that he was going to be paid, because I wanted him to speak honestly rather than because he was going to get some money." On each of the next three days, Oliver met up with Lightnin' and also went to see him perform at both Irene's and the Sputnik, Third Ward bars where Lightnin' was a regular. Oliver was amazed by Lightnin's inventiveness and his ability to not only play both acoustic and electric guitars, but to "come up with different words and different themes. He seemed to have the capacity to improvise on the spot. He was great. He was playing acoustic at Irene's, but he was playing electric at the Sputnik bar. Irene's was a very little place. Sputnik bar was more a cafe-bar with tables. Irene's was a bit cozier. You asked for a drink at Irene's, whereas at the Sputnik, you could be served."[29]

Although McCormick didn't accompany Oliver and was not present at his interview with Lightnin', he had corresponded with him and was eager to work with him. McCormick had a grand plan for a book on Texas blues, and Oliver, impressed by McCormick's research and liner notes, agreed to collaborate with him. The two worked together throughout the 1960s, but they ultimately had a falling out after Oliver had completed thirty-four chapters, and the book was never finished.[30]

In the early 1960s, McCormick was extremely busy as Lightnin's manager, promoter, and agent, in addition to "a number of other roles" that included picking him up, taking him to gigs, and bringing him home. As early as 1959, McCormick had been contacted by Harold Leventhal, a New York folk music impresario, who was the manager of Pete Seeger and the Weavers and wanted to present Lightnin' in New York.

Leventhal had been "a song-plugger for Irving Berlin," Seeger recalls, "and then he decided to take a job with his brother, who was a clothing manufacturer, but he met the Weavers and was interested. And he suggested to a friend of his that his friend become our manager. However, when the Weavers were finally blacklisted out of work [by McCarthy and the House Committee for Un-American Activities], we took a sabbatical, and as Lee Hayes said, it turned into a Mondical and Tuesdical."[31]

Blacklisted as communists by McCarthy and the House Committee for Un-American Activities, the Weavers were forced to disband in 1952, but Leventhal persisted in trying to find them an audience, and in 1955 he organized a reunion concert at Carnegie Hall. "Town Hall had turned him down," Seeger says, "unless we would sign anti-Communist oaths, but he went to Carnegie Hall and they said, 'We'll rent to you. Just give us the money.' And to everyone's surprise, it was standing room only."[32] The success of this concert in 1955 led to others, and for the Hootenanny on October 14, 1960, at Carnegie Hall, organized as a benefit for the folk music magazine *Sing Out!*, Leventhal booked Lightnin' as part of a program that included Pete Seeger, Joan Baez, the Clancy Brothers with Tommy Makem, Bill McAdoo, Elizabeth Knight, Jerry Silverman, and the Harvesters.

John Lomax Jr. had corresponded with Irwin Silber at *Sing Out!*, and negotiated the terms for both Lightnin' and him to perform not only at Carnegie Hall, but as part of another Pete Seeger concert in Philadelphia, as well as a Sunday afternoon show at Art D'Lugoff's Village Gate. The fees agreed upon were: $250 for a 20 minute set at Carnegie Hall, $200 in Philadelphia, and $150 against 50 percent of the gross at the Village Gate.[33]

Leventhal worked with Silber to promote the shows, and in a letter dated September 23, 1960, to George Hoefer at *Down Beat*, wrote: "I am bringing Sam 'Lightnin'' Hopkins to New York for a limited period to do concerts and club work in the New York and Boston areas. This is the first time that Lightnin' Hopkins will be appearing [in public] in the north, and should you be interested in interviewing him or getting a story, I would be glad to arrange this."[34]

Leventhal's promotion attracted considerable attention, and Robert Shelton devoted most of his concert review in the *New York Times* to Lightnin', stating: "Although Carnegie Hall is hardly the ideal forum for this sort of musician, Mr. Hopkins was surprisingly effective in surmounting the size and impersonality of the auditorium. His voice is dark, supple and intense. In a half-dozen surging blues songs, derived and adapted from his own experience as field hand and rambler, he demonstrated some of the pain and some of the release that make the country blues such a strong vehicle. . . . His highly imaginative guitar work was impressive throughout."[35]

For Shelton, the highlight of the evening was Lightnin's "relaxed, verse-swapping number with Pete Seeger, the master of ceremonies, and Bill McAdoo, a 23-year-old folk singer from Detroit, [in which] Mr. Hopkins began to show those gifts of wit and flair and improvisatory skill on which part of his justifiable reputation rests."[36] Years later even Seeger commented that what impressed him the most about Lightnin' was his ability to improvise lyrics on the spot. "Lightnin' would look over," Seeger says, "and see someone: 'Oh that man with a big moustache, he's met a woman with red hair,' and it would become a song."[37]

Nat Hentoff, writing in the *Reporter*, described the Carnegie Hall show and its audience in greater detail: "At most 'folk' events, the audience was predominantly young, very young. They looked like—and some were—the intense questioners at meetings of the Young People's Socialist League and the Saturday picketers at Woolworth's. The folk music they prefer consists largely of ballads and novelty songs they've learned from records by Pete Seeger and the Weavers. They are most moved by traditional songs with new lyrics that condemn Jim Crow and the Bomb."[38] Hentoff went on to praise Hopkins as "the only real folk

singer on the program as distinguished from singers who 'interpret' folk material," noting that he made "some contact with audience . . . avoiding his harshest
songs and focusing instead on women, those lost and those invited back. The
applause was loud but dutiful."[39]

Lightnin' impressed the audience with his authenticity; he was an intrinsic
part of the African American culture that he sang about, and in this sense he
was a true folk singer, not a singer of folk songs, like the members of the Weavers,
who were revivalists. Yet his performance at Carnegie Hall was still staged and
lacked the direct interaction with the audience that he was accustomed to in
Houston. In the little joints of the Third Ward, Lightnin' engaged in a kind of
running dialogue with his audience, who sometimes shouted out to him and
interrupted his singing so that he could respond in kind. At Carnegie Hall, the
audience was much more polite, applauding after each song.

Pete Welding, writing in *Coda*, also praised Lightnin' and pointed out that
he had already released over two hundred sides on a variety of labels, but his
recent recordings, made by McCormick on both American and British labels,
have "served to introduce Lightnin' to a wider audience and to establish his reputation as the finest of the unalloyed blues singers still performing."[40] However,
Welding also voiced the concern of many writers "as to whether Lightnin' will
be able to weather the adulation of the 'folkniks' who now comprise the bulk
of his audience. . . . Will success spoil Lightnin'?" Welding didn't think so, and
acknowledged that Lightnin' was actually quite sophisticated in his understanding of his different audiences. "Lightnin' is aware of the sharp dichotomy that
exists between the fare he offers his concert audiences and the powerful, impas-
sioned and fiercely introspective blues he sings for his friends on Houston's
Dowling Street. 'I stay with my own people,' he says. 'I have all my fun and I
have my trouble with them.' Since his songs reflect this situation, he reserves
the full force of his artistry for them—and they'll always serve as a touchstone
for him."[41]

Welding was essentially right, though what he didn't seem to fully understand was that even in his own community, Lightnin' catered to his different
audiences. McCormick had observed, "In his finest moments Lightnin' becomes
a dramatist with an incredible knack for spontaneous rhyme and crisp, scene-
setting narratives. He'll state an experience in the first-person present-tense,

picking some intimate memory and bringing it completely forward to the moment—while the guitar suggests shifts of mood and underlines the action."[42]

In performance, Hopkins might slump back, rambling on about his day until he found an up-tempo boogie to suggest coming awake, and then fade into a more religious tone that evoked a different mood, singing "When the Saints Go Marching In." While these shifts kept the audience engaged, they also reflected a sensitivity to what the people listening might be feeling, though Lightnin' usually did exactly what he wanted to and expected those around him to keep up with him.

After Carnegie Hall, Lightnin' appeared on October 23, in his first full concert at Art D'Lugoff's Village Gate at 185 Thompson Street in Greenwich Village. The show time was 3:30 P.M., and once again, it attracted an enthusiastic audience and the attention of Robert Shelton, who, in his review in the *New York Times*, commented that Lightnin' was more relaxed than in his Carnegie Hall appearance. "Although Mr. Hopkins' sentiments are primitive," Shelton wrote, "their expression is not. Trouble was treated sardonically, with broad humor and pathos. The blues form may seem simple and limiting, but at the hands of a master, they burgeoned into a subtle expression of moods."[43]

Three days after playing at the Village Gate, Lightnin' went to Englewood Cliffs, New Jersey on October 26, 1960, to record at Rudy Van Gelder's studio (famous as the site for many Prestige and Blue Note jazz recordings). Ozzie Cadena, who had worked for the Savoy label as an in-house producer and A&R scout in the 1950s, produced the session, and Bluesville later issued the recordings. Bluesville was a subsidiary of the jazz label Prestige, which was founded in 1959 to focus primarily on older "classic" blues artists.[44] Lightnin' was a perfect fit for the Bluesville catalogue, and this album titled *Last Night Blues* featured him accompanied by Sonny Terry on harmonica and two New York area sidemen, Leonard Gaskin on bass and Belton Evans on drums. Both Gaskin and Evans were veterans of the jazz scene; Gaskin's musical associations included Miles Davis, Dizzy Gillespie, Charlie Parker, and Eddie Condon, and Lovelle had worked with Earl Hines, Arnett Cobb, Teddy Wilson, and Buck Clayton.

For *Last Night Blues*, McCormick wrote the liner notes and discussed the parallels in the artists' rural upbringings and their respective developments as individual stylists.[45] McCormick posited that Hopkins and Terry eventually became aware of each other through their recordings: "Sam sat in front of Houston juke-boxes hearing about [Terry's] 'Hot Headed Woman' and Saunders [Sonny's given name] heard about a nappy-headed [Hopkins's] 'Short Haired Woman' from one end of Lenox Avenue to the other."[46] While some of McCormick's comparisons were a stretch, his fundamental premise was sound in that both were part of the same generation, born six months apart, and their music expressed the plight of their fellow African Americans, moving to the city to work as "mill hands, freight loaders, porters, and yardmen." Moreover, both Hopkins and Terry were itinerant before they settled in urban areas, though "for all their similarities of heritage and experience, the men are direct opposites. Where Lightnin' is leery of strange situations, dependent and suspicious, and the victim of his handicaps, Sonny is the strong one, a man on casual terms with his handicap—blindness—and one capable of warm, binding affection for the men he plays with." Ultimately, however, McCormick saw their differences as deeply reflective of their personalities—"These personal qualities are reflected in the music heard here: Lightnin's sly charms and innocence set against Sonny's warm-hearted joy of life."[47]

Musically, Terry's harmonica was well suited as accompaniment for Hopkins; the production values were much more polished than the field recordings of Charters and McCormick. In a new version of "Rocky Mountain," one of Lightnin's first Aladdin recordings, Hopkins's guitar and vocals were matched by Terry's heartfelt response on harp. According to McCormick, the song was based on Lightnin's travel to Arizona in the 1930s on a cotton-picking contract, though this contradicted what Hopkins had told Charters about how he wrote the song when traveling to Los Angeles with Lola Cullum. In any event, in this version, Lightnin' did sing about going through Arizona. In one verse, he even expressed his contempt for the federal prohibition law and his compassion for the American Indians, who, McCormick said, Lightnin' met when he got involved in bootlegging Mexican wine and whiskey into the Papago and Gila Indian Reservations.

> If you ever go out in Rocky Mountains
> Boy, will you please stop by Arizona town (x2)

You know they won't sell them Indians nothing to drink
And they don't hardly allow them around

In "Got to Move Your Baby," Lightnin' sang about a sixteen-year-old girl who apparently found him irresistible, warning "if you got a young girl/ you better keep her away from me." In the end, the implication was ambiguous:

Just one more time before you leave me here
Baby, I know you love me somethin'
But you still in mama and papa's care

Then, in "So Sorry to Leave You," he complained about being homesick and his longing to be back home:

If I had wings like an angel
I want to tell you where I would fly
Whoa, I'd fly to the heart of Antoinette
That's where poor Lightnin' would give up to die

This was Lightnin's first mention of Antoinette in a song, and while Lightnin' was devoted to her, he was certainly known to have affairs with other women.

Perhaps the most moving song on the *Last Night Blues* LP was "Conversation Blues," in which Terry sang, "Junior, I want you to tell old Sonny something to make him see," to which Lightnin' responded:

Well, you ask Po' Junior to give you something
Whoa Lord, to make poor Sonny Terry see
You know I only got two eyes and I offer you one
Whoa, now yes, don't you think well of me

On November 9, 1960, Hopkins recorded another LP for Prestige/Bluesville, produced by Cadena, titled *Lightnin'*, with accompaniment again by Gaskin and Evans and liner notes by Joe Goldberg.[48] Highlights on this LP included Lightnin's version of Big Boy Crudup's "Mean Old Frisco" with a loose and fast swing in the guitar; a remake of "Shinin' Moon" that he recorded for Gold Star and Herald; the slow and melancholy blues "Thinkin' 'Bout an Old Friend" about love "way out in the West somewhere"; and "Automobile Blues" (also an update of a Gold Star single) in which he pleaded with a kind of sexual innuendo: "Yes, your car so pretty, baby, please will you let me drive some time." *Billboard,* in its review of this album, wrote, "Lightnin' Hopkns is one of the great blues artists of the decade. Prestige's recording of him captures his driving intensity and individualism."[49]

On November 13, 1960, CBS Television Workshop taped Lightnin' for his first television appearance in its production of A *Pattern of Words,* a program produced by Robert Herridge and advertised as a "lyrical entertainment" that was "an experiment in four elements of expression, all of which deal with basic experiences of human life—joy, love, birth and death."[50] Broadcast on Sunday, November 20, the program featured the "contrasting techniques" of four individuals: the talking blues of Lightinin' Hopkins; the harmonica of John Sebastian, performing the works of Bach and his own original compositions; and the folk songs of nineteen-year-old Joan Baez.[51] Little is known about how this television program took shape, but it is likely that Harold Leventhal was in part behind it, given the involvement of Hopkins and Baez, who had both performed at the Carnegie Hall hootenanny.

Two days after the taping of A *Pattern of Works and Music,* Nat Hentoff brought Lightnin' to Nola Penthouse Studios in New York to record an LP for Candid, founded by Archie Bleyer, the owner of the Cadence label, who wanted another label to record the jazz and blues that he loved. Bleyer had approached Hentoff, and together they produced LPs until the label went out of business in 1962, not long after the release of the *Lightnin' in New York* recordings.[52] It's surprising that Lightnin' recorded for Candid, especially since he was under contract to Prestige/Bluesville, though apparently some kind of arrangement was made, given there is no evidence of any complaints or lawsuits.

In his liner notes, Hentoff said that Lightnin' was relaxed during the session: "He had found out that Carnegie Hall was not all of New York and that maybe there were a few more whites than he'd imagined who relate to more of his hurting songs."[53] For the LP, Hopkins recorded seven guitar blues, and one on the piano, though at one point in the session for "Take It Easy," he briefly played both piano and guitar while singing.

In "Lightnin's Piano Boogie," he demonstrated his prowess as a pianist, playing a hard-driving instrumental, mixing tempos with a resolve and humor reminiscent of the barrelhouse sound he might have heard back in the 1930s. In "Mighty Crazy," Lightnin' struck a humorous chord. The song was up-tempo, combining a fast shuffle on his guitar with a foot-tapping rhythm and talking blues about the foibles of doing laundry, where each verse ends with the line: "It's crazy to keep rubbin' at that . . ." punctuated by a high-pitched, single-string run.

> Yeah . . . sister got a rub board, mother got a tub
> They gonna around doin' the rub, the rub, ain't they crazy
> Get up in the morning, take a little toddy
> Take in washin' for each and everybody, ain't they crazy

Billboard heaped praise on the *Lightnin' in New York* album, giving it a four-star rating for strong sales potential: "This is an in-depth musical portrait of Lightnin' Hopkins, not as a popular blues singer, which he has been for many years, but as a serious singer of serious songs."[54]

After completing the Candid session, Lightnin' went to Massachusetts to perform at a date booked by another folk revival promoter, Manny Greenhill, at the Agassi Theatre on the campus of Harvard University, where he appeared on a bill with Cisco Houston. Harold Leventhal had been in touch with Greenhill and helped to facilitate Hopkins's work in the Boston area.[55] The Harvard show was a joint presentation of Manny's Folklore Productions and the student group Radcliffe Harvard Liberal Union, and was the beginning of an ongoing relationship with Greenhill, who managed and booked Lightnin' until about 1966. "I couldn't say how long my dad represented him," Mitch Greenhill, Manny's son, says. "I think it might be hard to pin down. My dad was always extremely loyal to the people he represented, and if they went off and found what seemed like a better deal and come back a couple of years later, he'd always take them back."[56]

Mitch recalls that when Hopkins came to Massachusetts, he stayed with him and his parents at their house in Dorchester. "My dad liked him more than my mom did," Mitch says. "My mom found him kind of a prickly house guest, because one time she made him some eggs for breakfast, I guess they were scrambled eggs, and they were too soft or too hard, or something, and he spit them out all over a wall in the kitchen. It didn't endear him to her."[57]

Then, when Mitch went to see Lightnin' perform, it was not what he had expected. "He was such a showman," Mitch says, "He had this big smile, and he would do what I would call gimmicky show things. One of the things that got me interested in traditional music was I wanted things to be more real. I kind of maybe expected him to show up in work clothes, or something like that. He was dapper and natty." During intermission Mitch saw the singer/songwriter Eric von Schmidt, and when he started to tell him how he was surprised by Lightnin's presence on stage, "Eric kind of wringed me out and said, 'You're missing the whole point. Listen closer to what he's doing. It's a very brave performance he's putting on here.' And I listened and he was right."[58] Lightnin' was an entertainer, and he had learned how to engage a white audience.

From his concert date at Agassi Theatre, Lightnin' went back to New York City, where he met the African American producer Bobby Robinson of the Fire label. "Well, I looked him up," Robinson told John Broven in an interview. "He was playing at a little club in the Village somewhere. I went out to the club. I asked him to record. 'All right,' he said, 'I'll do it, give me $400, I don't want anything else in my life,' he said. 'It's your record, you got it. . . . I don't want no royalties, I don't want nothing, it's your record.'"[59] Lightnin' knew he was violating the contract McCormick had negotiated with Candid, but it didn't seem to matter to him. Apparently Lightnin' was never faithful to any contract, a fact that makes his later complaints about record companies extremely compromised.

Robinson had a record shop in Harlem called Bobby's Happy House, which he opened in 1946 at the corner of Frederick Douglass Boulevard and 125th Street, and over the years he began to produce his own records. He established several different record labels, some in partnership with his brother: Red Robin Records (1952), Whirlin' Disc Records (1956), Fury Records and Everlast Records (1957), Fire Records (1959), and Enjoy Records (1962).[60] By the time

Robinson met Lightnin', he had had considerable success with his recordings of Buster Brown, Wilbert Harrison, and Elmore James, among others.

When Robinson brought Lightnin' into the studio, he recorded him solo, but he wasn't sure what to do next. He felt he needed to have a band sound to make the recordings more commercial, but he knew Lightnin' was "so unortho-dox, you never knew which way he was gonna go." So he decided to bring in a drummer named Delmar Donnell, who "was one of those little local guys" and wasn't a professional. In the studio Robinson told Donnell, "Listen, all I want you to do, wherever this guy goes you follow . . . just keep the beat going and follow whatever he does." And once the session was underway, Donnell "got the feel of it, he put a book on his drums for a muffled sound and played with the brushes." Lightnin' sat down, Robinson said, "cigar stuck in his mouth, crossed his legs, and I set a mike on his acoustic guitar and another mike for him to sing. I sat him on a tall stool so that his vocal mike was above the other one. We didn't have an amplifier so I had to set the mike at an angle right near the box, that way we could divide it with the drums, and we ran it down and I put it out, it was like an instant [hit] record."[61] By the time they were done, Lightnin' had recorded enough material for an LP, which Robinson called *Mojo Hand* after the title song, though the album was not released until after the single "Mojo Hand" scored big in the marketplace, charting in *Cashbox* magazine's "Top 50 in R&B Locations" for five weeks.[62] While the "Mojo Hand" single didn't make the *Billboard* charts, it was a "Pick Hit" and did get a positive review: "Hopkins is at his very best with these two monumental efforts. Top side ["Mojo Hand"] is up-tempo blues—a story of women, love and superstition. Flip ["Glory Be"] is a slow dirge-like blues also spotlighting drums and the singer's own guitar. Two great sides."[63]

Strachwitz recalls that when McCormick found out about the session with Bobby Robinson, he was furious, even more so after "Mojo Hand" became a hit when it was released as a single in 1961. "Mack called," Strachwitz says, "and he asked me, 'Chris, do you have any idea how and where that was made?' And I told him, 'That's a New York label. Bobby Robinson runs that,' And so, he finally confronted Lightnin', 'When did you . . . I hear you recorded for . . .' And Lightnin' said, 'Well, lookie here, I needed to make me some money, and this boy come up and said, 'We'll make you some records.'"

Lightnin's "Mojo Hand" built on the success of Muddy Waters's cover of the song "I've Got My Mojo Working," written by Preston Foster, though it also may have taken its inspiration from the numerous blues songs that had used the line "I'm going to Louisiana to get me a Mojo hand." These include Ida Cox's "Mojo Hand Blues" (1927), Texas Alexander's "Tell Me Woman Blues" (1928), Little Hat Jones's "Two Strings Blues" (1929), Tampa Red's "Anna Lou Blues" (1940), Muddy Waters's "Louisiana Blues" (1950), and Junior Wells's "Hoodoo Man Blues" (1953). Mojo hand refers to a magical charm used in hoodoo, but also to sexual potency. According to Strachwitz, "Lightnin' apparently believed it. His 'wife' [Antoinette] was a Creole from southwest Louisiana and was probably very aware of those cultural traditions."[64] However, prior to "Mojo Hand," Lightnin' had only recorded one song on the subject, "Black Cat Bone."

Lightnin' had made a name for himself in New York, and judging from the response to "Mojo Hand," he still had an audience among urban blacks to whom Robinson's Fire label was primarily marketed. But his appeal among the folk and blues revivalists was growing, and he was often featured with an eclectic mix of performing artists. On November 26, 1960, he appeared in a program called "Folk Songs, Country & Blues," presented by Harold Leventhal, at the Ethical Society Auditorium. Leventhal advertised the show as Lightnin's "Last Performance in New York," but also included the New Lost City Ramblers with John Cohen, Mike Seeger, Tom Paley, Cisco Houston, and Zarefah Story.

By the time Lightnin' returned to Houston, he had spent about six weeks in New York City. How he traveled to and from New York is unknown, though Strachwitz speculates that he probably went by train or bus, because Lightnin' hated to fly. However, Art D'Lugoff at the Village Gate remembers that he sometimes used to pick Lightnin' up at the airport and take him to his hotel, but he wasn't sure exactly when. Lightnin' played the Village Gate numerous times during the 1960s because he was paid well and one gig led to another.[65]

Lightnin' had stayed in Harlem the first time he traveled to New York in 1951 to record for Bobby Shad's Sittin' In With label and had seemed to like it, not only because of the money he made there. In one of his interviews with McCormick, he said, "That time I went to New York to make records . . . I stayed across the street from where Count Basie was. Count Basie, Joe Turner, Preacher Williams, they was all there. I had me some fun dancing there two–

three nights." But when Lightnin' got to New York City in 1960, the room that was booked for him was, according to Hentoff, in a "depressing, run-down Harlem hotel." Hopkins asked to be moved and was taken to "an even grimmer, gloomier hotel in the Village." Lightnin' told Hentoff, "There's no light down there," and during his first morning in the room the darkness made it hard for him to wake up, and he was late for an appointment. "There's no sun," Hopkins said, "so I didn't know what time it was. I just sat down on the bed and played my box a while."[66]

Lightnin', however, didn't stay in that hotel very long. Hentoff reported that he moved into the apartment of Martha Ledbetter, the widow of Huddie "Leadbelly" Ledbetter, and that "was one warm place in the city." How Lightnin' met Martha is unclear, though it's possible that she attended the Carnegie Hall concert. Leadbelly had performed on different occasions with Pete Seeger as part of hootenannies and labor union rallies. In any event, according to David Benson, who traveled as a road manager for Lightnin' in the 1970s, Martha Ledbetter gave Lightnin' a ring that he showed off to people he met—"A gold ring with a black face with a gold S on it. He wore it all the time."[67] After 1947, Lightnin' was far better known among black audiences than Leadbelly ever was.

Lightnin' had now firmly established himself on the folk and blues revival scene, but to say that he had been "rediscovered," as John S. Wilson did in the New York Times in 1959, is misleading. His career was continuous, and to some extent he straddled both white and black audiences, though his popularity ebbed and swelled on the Billboard and Cashbox jukebox and retail charts. He may have stopped recording between 1954 and 1959, but his music was not only available, it was also re-packaged and promoted during those years. Herald issued 45 rpm singles of Lightnin's recordings every year from 1955 to 1960, and the Mesners produced a compilation of Aladdin singles intended for the growing LP market on the Score label in 1958.[68] However, for the Score LP, called Lightnin' Hopkins Strums the Blues, their marketing strategy catered to the folk audience. The unsigned liner notes on the back of the LP reads: "Lightnin' Hopkins is a true folk singer. His songs are the heart of the South, the very essence of his people, their joys, their triumphs, their difficulties, their oppression. But Lightnin's music too, like that of every great artist, has a universal quality. . . . Like all great folk artists . . . Hopkins improvises easily. . . . All turn his talent into a quick, fluent, outpouring of feeling."[69] Twelve years earlier, in 1946, many of the songs—like the hit "Katie Mae Blues"—on this LP were released for the "race" market, but with the burgeoning folk revival, the Mesners recognized a new opportunity.

In 1960, Herald also compiled twelve of Lightnin's recordings from 1954, which had been released only as singles over the years, and issued them on an LP titled *Lightnin' and the Blues*, though rather than trying to appeal to the folk audience, "J.S." in the liner notes tried to exploit Lightnin's mystique by stating that "nothing much is known about Sam Hopkins, and he is not one to venture any information. . . . The session and two bottles of gin were finished and Lightnin' just shuffled away counting his money. We have not seen or heard from him since, but every time the phone rings we somehow hope we'll hear his voice sayin', 'Man, I wrote a mess o' new tunes for you.'"[70]

The response to *Lightnin' and the Blues* among jazz and blues purists was negative. In the *Saturday Review*, critic (and coauthor of the book *Jazzmen*) Charles Edward Smith wrote: "No doubt he could do something with the electric guitar; he uses one here sometimes with deftness, though the overall impression is one of blatant sound. This impression is reinforced by added bass and drums and a souped-up juke box sound, leaving little room to hear what Lightnin' could do, assuming he wanted to."[71]

Also in 1960, Bobby Shad decided to issue recordings he made with Lightnin' during the period from 1951 to 1953 on the Time label, including two of his biggest hits, "Hello Central" and "Coffee Blues." But Shad decided to take a much more intellectual approach to contextualizing Hopkins's music and was able to get Nat Hentoff, who was then coeditor of the *Jazz Review*, to write the liner notes. The LP, taking its title from Sam Charters's book *The Country Blues*, is called *Lightning Hopkins: Last of the Great Blues Singers*. Shad, like the Mesners, was trying to capitalize on the new folk market and wanted to appeal to a young white audience looking to understand the blues.

Hentoff quoted heavily from McCormick's article on Hopkins in the *Jazz Review*, in which he explained: "The essence of Lightning's art is a specialized form of autobiography. . . . A line can have the blunt stab of T. S. Elliot [as McCormick pointed out] . . . 'you ever see a one-eyed woman cry.'"[72] But to

McCormick's assessment of Hopkins, Hentoff added, "It's not all tragedy though. Lightning continues the blues tradition using irony as a weapon of survival as well as getting whatever peace of mind is possible under the circumstances. . . . In addition to the warm but cutting quality of his voice . . . is the extent to which he talk-sings his music. The result is the impression of completely spontaneous autobiography—a man talking about what he feels so that the natural phrasing of his speech blends easily and flowingly into his singing."[73] Then, in describing Lightnin' performance style, Hentoff quoted from the Belgian critic Yannick Bruynoghe, who wrote that Hopkins's guitar playing "is adapted to his speech as intimately as a second voice would be. . . . When he starts a chorus one can never tell where he's aiming, how the phrases will be developed, and what sudden and abrupt changes he may introduce and bring to their logical conclusion."[74]

The growing interest in Lightnin's music made him reassess his attitude toward traveling. He liked playing for white audiences because he was getting paid more than he ever could in the Third Ward. Lomax Jr. had set a high standard for what Lightnin' began to expect. He wanted someone to make his airplane arrangements, carry his guitar and suitcase, get him checked into the hotel, take him to the gig, take him back to the hotel, and make sure he had the beer and booze that he wanted. When he played the white club dates, there were always young, white guitar players, among others, who wanted to follow him around, buy him drinks, and provide for his needs and wishes.

As much as McCormick wanted to manage his career, Lighntin' often resisted. However, on May 19, 1961, Lightnin' signed a contract with Prestige, negotiated by McCormick, for "a minimum of 10 LPs," for which he was to be paid an advance of five hundred dollars for each album and a royalty of twenty cents "per doubled faced 12" LP record." In this agreement Lightnin' also appointed McCormick, "according to the terms of a pre-existing agreement . . . as his sole authorized agent . . . to collect and receive all monies due him."[75]

On July 26, 1961, Lightnin' recorded a solo LP for Prestige/Bluesville, titled *Blues in My Bottle* and produced by the folklorist Kenneth S. Goldstein and McCormick at ACA Studios in Houston. Surprisingly the guitar is poorly recorded, but Lightnin' seemed completely at ease in the studio, judging from the way he was joking around at the session in his version of Stick McGhee's 1949 R & B hit "Drinkin' Wine Spodee-O-Dee," calling out the names of his friends who were there: "Why if you a got a nickel, Mary, I got a dime/ 'Nette [Antoinette], let's get together, Mack, and bring a little wine." In "Buddy Brown's Blues," he ended with an old melody he learned from Texas Alexander, and in "DC-7" he sang about the crash of a Braniff Airline DC-7 that exploded in the air above his mother's home in Centerville in 1959.

> I want to tell you the first time I taken a notion
> To let the airplane take me off this earth (x2)
> Look like the first time I begin to ride that DC-7
> I remember the first day I was birthed

This particular plane crash haunted Lightnin', especially since his mother and others he knew in Centerville were witnesses to the disaster. According to Joe Kessler, who years later acquired three of Lightnin's guitars, Antoinette said that Lightnin' kept a mental record of airplane disasters. "If someone asked him to travel somewhere," Kessler says, "he often refused by saying on such and such a day, airline 'x' crashed."[76]

Carroll Peery, an African American who managed the kitchen and bar at the Ash Grove in the early 1960s, recalls that Lightnin' talked often about how much he hated flying. "He only flew if he had to," Peery says, "and then he'd have to get drunk to do that. He liked to take the train. I met him at the train station several times. I was kind of amazed about how little, or how small his suitcases were, because he really packed a lot in them."[77]

Peery and Lightnin' became good friends at the Ash Grove and spent a lot of time together not only in Los Angeles, but also in the Bay Area, where Peery later moved to work at the Cabale. "The more we talked the more we saw how much we had common ground," Peery says. "He was an extremely complicated man. He had very little formal education, but he had what they call 'mother wit' to a great degree. I remember laughing a lot. He could really turn a phrase."[78]

One night, when Lightnin' wasn't working, Peery told him he wanted to take him to a quiet place, where everything would be relaxed so he could enjoy his time off. But as it turned out, the evening was anything but relaxed: "I took him to this coffee house called the Xanadu and . . . there was a big fight. . . . I was trying to keep everybody away from Lightnin' and his guitar and so on.

And this one guy started cursing at Lightnin'. So I had to grab him and take him outside, and we got into a fight. And the guy had a knife and cut me, but I didn't know it. He was a black guy. And Lightnin' just sat there, and I'm really glad he did. But I didn't know I had been cut until later when somebody asked, 'Is that blood on the back of your pants?' So I had to go to the emergency room and they fixed me up there. And when I came back, Lightnin' says, 'Little as you are, you don't need but one ass hole.' He could come up with things like that all the time."[79]

On another occasion, Peery says he and Lightnin' stayed up after hours with an Israeli dance group: "They were at UCLA, and Lightnin' was at the Ash Grove. And so they thought, 'Soon as we get off the show, we got to get over to the Ash Grove to see if we can see this guy,' because they had all of his recordings back in Israel. So they came over there. I was just locking the Ash Grove up and me and Lightnin' were the only two people there, and this huge limousine pulled up and all of these half-naked girls get out. I says to Lightnin', 'Do you think you might wanna give them a private concert?' And he says, 'Well, it looks like I ought to.' So I took some wine and stuff from the cooler and we went across the street to where he was stayin' at the time . . . and he sang and they danced all night long. Next thing you knew the sun was comin' up."[80]

Other than traveling to New York and California, most of Lightnin's performance dates in 1961 were local and around Texas; he played the Rainbow Room and the Shriner's Auditorium in Dallas, though he did go on the road with Clifton Chenier and his Zydeco band. Clifton was related to Antoinette, and Lightnin' sometimes had Clifton's brother Cleveland accompany him on rub board.

Back in Houston, Lightnin' (with or without McCormick's knowledge) made a largely acoustic folk-blues album that was issued the following year on Vee-Jay as *Lightnin' Strikes*. It was an effective album, presenting some songs that he'd never recorded before, like the utterly rural "Coon Is Hard to Catch" and a rare nod to gospel music, "Devil Is Watching You." The writer's credit on all but two of the album's songs went to Bill Quinn and Lola Cullum, who probably produced the album along with Houston country music kingpin H. W. "Pappy" Daily.[81] (Daily released two of the songs as a single on his Dart label prior to the Vee-Jay album.) Andrew Brown speculates that both Quinn and Cullum "must have wanted to do something to re-establish themselves as Lightnin's discover-ers after he started to become famous again. Perhaps they both read articles or album liner notes that only mentioned Charters and McCormick and were miffed about not being credited for the major roles they played in Lightnin's career. So they pooled their money together and paid him $100 a song, just like old times, and Lightnin' did this for them as an expression of gratitude." It was the last time Lightnin' worked with Cullum, though he did apparently continue to have some contact with Quinn, whom Brown speculates probably engineered his *Goin' Away* album in 1963.[82]

During the summer of 1961, Chris Strachwitz returned to Texas hoping to produce his own recordings, but it didn't work out. "Well, I tried one night to record Lightnin' [at a live club date]," Strachwitz says. "It was horrible sound. . . . The tape recorder was apparently overmodulating without indicating that this was happening. I used one of those little volume controls with two microphones, one for the singer and that electric guitar and the other for the drummer . . . but what I found out later was that the two microphones were out of phase with each other. That one night we tried to record Lightnin', he got really pissed, 'I gotta have my money, you know!' Mack [McCormick] tried to explain to him that I had to see if this [the test recording] was any good or not, and Lightnin' didn't like that one bit. He said that anything he does is good. But he didn't think about my being technically incompetent. You see, the previous guys he'd encountered, they all had good recording machines and they knew what the hell they were doing. I didn't know nothing. So they almost started a fight outside this beer joint; I'll never forget that. Mack and Lightnin' were yelling at each other, and they were ready to punch each other in the nose, except there was both of us. So that didn't really come about and then he left."[83]

Frustrated, Strachwitz returned to California, and finally got the opportu-nity to record Hopkins in Berkeley on November 26, 1961, at Sierra Sound Lab. "He was already in California for a program," Strachwitz recalls. "On October 20, Lightnin' had appeared with Jack Elliott at the Ash Grove in Los Angeles. While he may have gone back to Texas, it's possible he stayed in California and went on to Oakland, where he had two cousins. He was probably booked at the Cabale."[84] The Cabale was opened in 1961 by Debbie Green and Rolf Cahn with the help of Bay Area "proto-hippie" Howard Ziehm. Green and Cahn had moved from Cambridge, Massachusetts, to Berkeley a year earlier, but were both quite familiar with the Bay Area folk scene as performers and promoters. "It was a real hippie, folkie-dokie club," Strachwitz says. "They were selling coffee and cookies. All these folkies would come by. Lightnin' didn't draw any huge crowd. He never said if he liked it or not. It was just part of the day."

When Strachwitz recorded Hopkins, he wanted him to play the instrument of his choice. "The whole business of electric and acoustic never entered my head. People played what they had. . . . If I thought about it, I wanted the electric sound that he had on those later records. . . . The stuff being played on the radio then [the early to mid-1950s] were the Mercury and Herald records, especially the Herald ones. They got the ferocious electric guitar, also the Decca— 'Merry Christmas' and 'Happy New Year'—That's just gorgeous stuff. So that's what I wanted."[85]

In his contract with Lightnin', Strachwitz agreed to pay "the total of $400 ("$300 to be paid . . . at the time of the session—$100 to be paid to Mr. Harold Leventhal [who was then acting as Hopkins's "super-agent" in association with McCormick and as the representative of the music publishing company Sanga Music] for commission earnings as an advance royalty of 5 percent of the retail price of the records if in the LP form, 1 cent per side in the case of 45s or similar singles."[86]

Lightnin' came to the session prepared. "He had the numbers kind of figured out of what he wanted to do," Strachwitz says, "But he really wasn't into this idea of making albums at all. He was still on the trip of making a couple of songs now and then. And that's how he would make all his singles down there [in Texas]. Because ideas would come to him, a few at a time." Strachwitz asked him to play some of his "older stuff" because he knew that was easier for him, and he did manage to record him playing the piano singing "Jesus, Won't You Come By Here" ("Needy Time"), an old religious song that Lightnin' recorded several times under different titles.

While Strachwitz was certainly a part of the folk revival, he was still trying, at that time, to reach an African American audience. "I was trying to make those 45s for the black market. [The DJ] Rockin' Lucky would actually play them on KSAN-AM [in San Francisco] at that time. And he had a record shop, and you had to give him a hundred free ones otherwise he wouldn't play them, because he sold them in the store. I was all for it. That's the way that stuff got on the air. He was funny. He was from Orange, Texas, and he would have this little rap, 'All right, baby, Come on, Say shake or break it. You want me to shake or break this damn thing.'" But after Lightnin's first session, Strachwitz didn't feel any of the songs were strong enough to stand alone as a single release. "I was working with the black distributor, Olin Harrison," Strachwitz says. "He had the Acme Sales Company in San Francisco. It was difficult to get LPs distributed on the radio and the little mom and pop record shops. They wanted 45s with a big sound. That's why I got the Bay Area drummer Victor Leonard for Lightnin', but it wasn't enough and I never released a 45 of any of those first recordings."[87]

However, Strachwitz was not deterred in his efforts to reconnect Lightnin' with a black audience. Lightnin' had never had a black promoter in California, and Strachwitz wanted to get him booked into a couple of black venues: the Continental Club in West Oakland and the Savoy Club in North Richmond. Lightnin' liked the idea of going to the Continental Club, and the people there definitely responded to his music. Many had bought his records, or heard them on jukeboxes in the 1950s. But after Lightnin' got off stage, a well-known, local black R & B promoter approached Strachwitz, when Lightnin' was in earshot, and said, "I could use that boy." Lightnin' recoiled. He left the club soon afterwards with Strachwitz, insulted that he was called a "boy" by the black promoter. When he went to play at the Savoy Club, he was even more warmly received; one woman going in the front door at the same time as him looked over and asked, "Are you the real Lightnin' Hopkins?" And he replied, "You better believe it, baby." Lightnin's presence made people gravitate to him, though he could rebuff them in an instant. "He never seemed to lose his cool," Strachwitz says, "and moving around the black world of the Bay Area, he was amused that he was still so well known. He'd been selling records for all these years. But no one had ever seen him, because he wouldn't travel behind his records, and as much as he liked the black club scene, he was starting to realize he could make more money playing for white folkies."[88]

To finish his first LP with Lightnin', Strachwitz recorded him performing the song "California Showers" in his apartment in Berkeley, but he still needed more to round out the release. So after Lightnin' returned to Houston, Strachwitz asked him to go with his drummer Spider Kilpatrick to Bill Holford's ACA studio to record four more songs.[89] Lightnin' was used to going over to ACA Studio, and Holford sent Strachwitz the tapes.

ACA Studio was highly regarded, not only because of Holford's technical expertise but because he could work well with Lightnin'. In 1962, McCormick supervised the recordings at ACA Studio of three more of Lightnin's LPs for Prestige/Bluesville: *Walkin' This Road by Myself*, *Lightnin' and Co.*, and *Smokes Like Lightning*. For these LPs, McCormick wanted a bigger band sound, probably because he or his producers thought it might sell better, and he brought in Billy Bizor on harmonica, Buster Pickens on piano, Donald Cooks on bass, and Spider Kilpatrick on drums. They were all friends of Lightnin's who had played with him at different times over the years. *Walkin' This Road by Myself* contained one of Lightnin's most well-known songs, "Happy Blues for John Glenn," which, according to McCormick, he composed after watching John Glenn make the first American orbital space flight on his landlady's TV on February 20, 1962. In his session notes, McCormick wrote, "He arrived at the studio an hour early, in itself a rare event presaging things to come. As members of his entourage unloaded instruments and ran his errands, he sat out back in his car. At one point he asked for a piece of paper, and with a nod at the Gettysburg address legend, a torn envelope was provided. His making notes for the song was essentially a symbolic act, for a half-hour later the envelope contained only three marks resembling hex signs." But when he sat down to record, he "insisted on propping it up in front of him as he took his place beneath the microphone. In some way the cryptic marks identified for him the incidents he wished to touch upon, and with it in place he was ready to extemporize. He called for a last-minute reference to confirm Glenn's first name and whispered his question because, child-like, he intended to surprise those present (including the musicians who accompany him) with his song's subject."[90]

Despite all the preparations, a short in the guitar amplifier ruined the first take. "It had been a moody blues set to the same tune as the bitter protest 'Tim Moore's Farm,'" McCormick said, but while the repairs were being made to the amplifier, Lightnin' saw a newspaper account of Glenn's flight and changed his tone: "some detail there seems to have altered his concept, for when he launched into the song again it was definitely a happy blues."[91]

In the song "Happy Blues for John Glenn," Lightnin' played a melodic pattern that was less familiar than what he usually did, and while performing he apparently couldn't remember the chord sequence and the band got confused, but in the end were able move into a strong, grooving rhythm. And while the lyrics were some of Lightnin's most imaginative, they bordered on nonsense.

> People all was sittin' this morning with this on their minds
> There ain't no man living can go around the world three times
> But John Glenn done it. Yes, he did! He did it, I'm talkin' about it
> Only he did it just for fun
> Half a million dollars made him feel so well
> He got to eatin' his lunch, he could hardly tell

The other songs on the LP were more typical to Lightnin's repertoire, but the band had difficulty following him. Lightnin' did play an up-tempo version of Sonny Boy Williamson's standard "Good Morning Little School Girl," in which he quipped, "Lightnin' is a school boy, too."[92]

On *Smokes Like Lightning* the band sound was a little tighter, and the solos by Hopkins were the highlights. But in McCormick's notes, it became clear that his relationship with Hopkins was deteriorating. McCormick began the notes by responding to a question he was then being asked about how Lightnin' had changed since he met him: "No, he has not changed. He is just the same as he has been his adult life, a natural born easman, consumed by self-pity and everlastingly trying to persuade the world that it is his valet." McCormick then ridiculed Lightnin' further, maintaining, "We might almost imagine Lightnin' the most purely dedicated of all artists for he goes to astonishing lengths to maintain himself in a pathetic, blues-producing state. He is, for example, an incorrigible gambler who will take advantage of simple-minded friends with the crudest of dice tricks. . . . He is a joke to the gamblers of Houston's Third Ward."

McCormick's tone was at once angry and illuminating about Hopkins's personal life: "Lightnin' sings endlessly of mistreating women though in fact he has been the pampered daytime pet of a married woman [Antoinette Charles] for 14 years. She often accompanies him on trips out of town and is then introduced as his wife, but in Houston, a triangle is maintained with everyone keeping carefully to their own corner. He has no personal relationships that are not severely limited. He spends most of his time surrounded by a coterie of 'helpers,' restless young men who envy him on one hand and on the other answer his incessant demands for attention, accept his drunken tongue lashing, and let him maneuver them into humiliating positions (ie. [sic] Clearing a path to the men's room for him). He is lovable and yet tyrannical in the same sad way of a very spoiled child."[93]

The details about Lightnin's daily life are revealing, though it is surprising that they were published as liner notes, especially given the ranting tone of McCormick's text. McCormick, instead of discussing the music on the LP, continued his diatribe against Hopkins and described how Lightnin' left Houston to avoid his sister's funeral, leaving the harmonica player Billy Bizor to make the necessary arrangements. Reportedly, Bizor drove Lightnin's brother Joel and their mother, Frances Hopkins, who was eighty-eight years old at the time, back to Centerville after the funeral and discovered that the gas and electricity had been turned off because the bills had not been paid. Resigned, Mrs. Hopkins, "resting herself on the steps of the rickety two-room cabin," McCormick wrote, "mused by herself: 'I had five children and they could each play music, but the baby couldn't do nothing else but. And he never has been no help to nobody except when you wanted to hear music.' She turned her head to the west, as if seeing the Hollywood nightclub where Lightnin' had gone, and firmly answered the question the fans had been asking: 'I guess he never will change.'"[94]

Lightnin' had pushed McCormick to the limits of what he was able to endure. While the tone of his text is harsh, it is likely a realistic portrayal of what McCormick observed and experienced. Lightnin' was not easy to work with, but on the other hand, McCormick had been telling him what to do for years, and Lightnin' was no doubt fed up. In other places and with other people, Lightnin' was perceived differently. Ed Pearl from the Ash Grove describes him as a "gentle person," as did Barbara Dane. But neither of them had tried to be Lightnin's manager as McCormick had; they might not have thought of him as "gentle" if they had.

Especially insulting to Lightnin' was the way McCormick characterized his relationship with his mother and implied that he had neglected her needs. Lightnin' was devoted to his mother and did his best to help her. Years later,

Lorine Washington, a 105-year-old woman in Centerville who had been friends with Lightnin's mother, remembers, "Sam used to come back to Centerville and bring money for his mother and his aunt."[95] Mabel Milton, another friend of Frances Hopkins, concurs, "He'd come with Nette. She was a beautiful woman. Lightnin' liked good-lookin' women. And they'd bring things to his mother."[96]

In a 1960 interview with Dane on KPFK-FM in Los Angeles, Lightnin' talked at length of the importance of his mother in his life. "She raised all us kids. . . . She's a mother and father, because my father got killed when I was three years old. . . . So I think it's my duty to stick around and do the very best I can for her until something else happens. That's the way I feel about it."[97]

In this context McCormick's liner notes were likely intolerable to Lightnin', who, from his point of view, had given to McCormick more than he ever received in return, though McCormick didn't see it this way. McCormick's frustration with Hopkins had been building over the years of his association with him. To Andrew Brown, McCormick said, "He became a lot less vigorous about what he was doing as he made more money. . . . He took a glee in giving the least of himself and still collecting greater sums of money than he'd made earlier. . . . I think he kind of felt like he was scamming people. 'Here I come, I'm supposed to sing, I do mostly talking, and the people laugh,' but it was often a slightly embarrassed laugh, because he was doing things that made people uncomfortable."[98]

As much as McCormick blamed Lightnin' for the problems that ensued, he nonetheless did what he could to control his affairs. As he pointed out in an undated letter to Prestige in 1963, "Lightnin' Hopkins has been under comprehensive contract to me since 1959," and acknowledged that Lightnin' had signed a ten-record deal with Prestige, of which only four of the LPs had been completed with him as producer. McCormick complained that Prestige had not contacted him for nineteen months and had moved forward to continue recording Lightnin' "in violation of the agreement." Moreover, McCormick said that he was willing to "supervise what ever final sessions they should desire," but they needed to be done quickly because "Hopkins's poor health and arthritis" was "growing more serious." This letter prompted an exchange of correspondence between McCormick, Prestige attorney M. Richard Asher, and Sam Charters, who was then working as recording director for Prestige in Englewood Cliffs, New Jersey.[99] A deal was finally hammered out in November, and Prestige agreed to pay Lightnin' through McCormick for "at least 50 strong potential selections" with an advance payment of twelve hundred dollars and a balance of eight hundred dollars to be paid out in eight monthly installments. However, McCormick never produced the recordings, and on December 18, Prestige stopped payment on the second one-hundred-dollar installment check to McCormick.

On January 24, 1964, Charters made arrangements for funds to be transferred to the Homestead State Bank in Houston for the purpose of Lightnin' being paid five hundred dollars for each LP recorded at "the studios of Mr. J. L. Patterson, Jr." (who had purchased Gold Star Studios from Bill Quinn).[100] Lightnin's last three Prestige albums, starting with *Goin' Away* from June 1963, were recorded at Gold Star and overdubbed with bass and drums in Englewood Cliffs, New Jersey.[101] Prestige severed their working relationship with McCormick, who had disappeared and appeared to have taken the advance payments sent to him. McCormick later wrote to Charters from Jocotepec, Mexico, where he had gone to get away from "Houston's dampness and cold for health reasons," stating that Lightnin' had received no royalty payments and questioned whether or not the check sent had in fact ever been cashed.[102] Charters, who had long held a grudge against McCormick, angrily replied on February 27, 1964: "Your letter reached me in time to delay the issuing of a warrant for your arrest in Houston; however, if I don't hear from you concerning the money you have received for the Lightning Hopkins sessions I will have to consider some kind of action . . . . Lightning Hopkins, for whom the money was sent to you as agent, has stated verbally . . . that he did not see you at any time before you left the country and that the money sent on to you was not turned over to him. He also stated that he knew nothing about a pending exclusive contract with a major label and denied that poor health is interfering with his playing."[103] Moreover, Charters says that he had researched the Prestige files on Lightnin' to confirm that he had been sent regular statements, both as artist and composer, and that "all checks had been cashed."

In a letter to Charters, received by Prestige on March 16, McCormick denied any wrongdoing. He claimed that he had made all the necessary arrangements before leaving for Mexico and had given the advance payment, after it had cleared the bank, to Lightnin' via a personal check, though this has never been confirmed. There are no copies of McCormick's canceled check to Lightnin' in the Prestige files. McCormick did not want to accept any responsibility for the missing money, nor did Lightnin'.[104] It is possible that Lightnin' owed McCormick money, and that McCormick kept the advance as a means of collecting what was due to him. Lightnin' could be extremely demanding and irresponsible, but McCormick had nonetheless worked hard to record, manage, and promote his career. McCormick was a major figure in introducing Lightnin' to a white audience, but this incident with Prestige pushed their already strained relationship to the breaking point. Needless to say, McCormick never worked with Hopkins again.

When Charters saw Lightnin' a few months after McCormick had run off, he felt "Lightning didn't seem to mind what had happened that much. . . . He shrugged his shoulders and said, 'You can manage me for a while—if you got any jobs.'"[105] Lightnin' realized that he needed help to get the best recording deals and bookings in the white blues revival scene. He was making more money than he ever had in his life, and he was enjoying himself. He particularly liked the West Coast, where he was able to visit with family and friends. Antoinette had relatives in the Los Angeles area, and Lightnin' could spend time with her there without the pressures of her "other family" in Houston. The blues revival had untold benefits that Lightnin' was only just beginning to realize.

6

The Touring Intensifies

In 1962, Peter Gardner, the adult activities director for Houston's Jewish Community Center, started a Folk Song Series that featured a mix of revivalists and traditional musicians. Lightnin's first show at the Jewish Community Center on March 15, 1962, was a big hit, though he was initially skeptical. To perform for an enthusiastic audience of white, mostly middle- and upper-middle-class Jews, some of whom spoke Yiddish among themselves, must have made Lightnin' a little uncomfortable, yet more acutely aware of how his life and career were changing. His concert there typified the expanding folk and blues revival scene that was taking hold across the country, and the opportunities for new bookings had never been greater. But at this point, Lightnin' also had a following in the juke joints and cafes of the Third Ward, where he liked to gamble and carouse. As much as he was able to cross between black and white audiences, he did so with caution. He had a deep-seated distrust for some white producers and concert promoters, but he was learning how to get what he wanted and was loyal to those who treated him fairly.

Less than a week later Lightnin' returned to New York City, where he stayed for several weeks, presumably with Martha Ledbetter, and performed at the Village Gate seven times in a month-long period, appearing on bills with flamenco guitarist Sabicas, Roy Haynes, the John Coltrane Quartet, the Modern Jazz Quartet, Nina Simone, and Don Sherman.

On March 31, 1962, Robert Shelton, in his *New York Times* review of Lightnin' and Sabicas at the Village Gate, alluded to the comparisons "many have drawn between the flamenco music of the Spanish gypsies and the Southern Negro folk blues for their emotional content, personal expressivity, and rhythmic vitality," but pointed out that "there is really more to contrast between these two leaders in their fields."[1] Most notably, Sabicas played a seven-hundred-dollar Velasquez guitar with "an ordered consciousness of technique," while Lightnin' accompanied his "moody subjective songs" on a sixty-five-dollar Harmony. Moreover, Shelton observed that Hopkins's demeanor on stage had changed since he appeared in three New York concerts in the fall of 1960. "Aware that his fame has spread far from his home in Houston," Shelton commented, "Mr. Hopkins seems more expansive on stage, and the audience seems more receptive to his subtle showmanship and wry humor."[2]

About three weeks later, on May 17, 1962, Shel Kagen supervised a live recording of Lightnin' at the Second Fret, a folk club in Philadelphia. The resulting LP was called *Hootin' the Blues* and was issued two years later by Prestige, which timed its releases in an effort to not oversaturate the marketplace with Lightnin's recordings. Lawrence Cohn wrote the liner notes and recounted his meeting with Lightnin' when he came to New York City to perform at Carnegie Hall in 1960. "A man of many, many moods (some of which must baffle even Lightnin' himself)," Cohn wrote, "he can be sullen and brooding, pompous and sarcastic and yet, in his own way and to his own personal desire and satisfaction, charming and coy—possessed of an unbelievable naiveté in respect to many worldly considerations and matters." Yet Cohn maintained the coffee-house setting of the Second Fret enhanced Lightnin's music: "His sharpness and magnificent delivery have never been presented in better light and quite possibly, the atmosphere created by the live audience to which Lightnin' can work is responsible."[3]

Bobby Robinson, when he issued his LP *Mojo Hand* on his Fire label in 1962 with the recordings he had made with Lightnin' two years earlier, took a different approach. In his liner notes Robinson wrote, seemingly in response to the intellectualism of folk and blues revival writers: "With so much having been said about the man, Samuel 'Lightnin' Hopkins . . . has been probed, by every important committee on un-musical activities, even an attempt at assassination by the Mafia'd of Snobdom, and each time came out completely exonerated—there is no room or need for additional dissertation on the great personable career of this titan of the blues. Lightnin' stands today, as he has for more than a decade, a giant in the field of focus."[4] Robinson then went on to tout, tongue-in-cheek, the fidelity of his album and its presentation of "a new dimension in recorded sound . . . the aroma of his cigar, the open flask and the odors incident to and usually manifested as a result of the proximity of instruments and bodies, is evident and oozes up and out from every groove."[5] Robinson, based in Harlem for decades, understood his audience, and while the records he released had crossover appeal, judging from the charting success of not only Hopkins but Elmore James, Buster Brown, and others, he had a solid following in the African American community.

By the end of 1962, Lightnin's recording career was going strong, and his recordings on the Fire label combined with those on Arhoolie, Bluesville, and Vee-Jay were garnering considerable sales and attention. He had demonstrated his vitality among white college-age audiences, who were part of the burgeoning blues revival scene. Lightnin' even won the 1962 *Down Beat* International Jazz Critics Poll as "New Star, Male Singer," probably as a result of his appearances at the Village Gate.

On March 21, 1963, the German filmmaker Dietrich Wawrzyn and his wife, Anna Marie, documented Lightnin' in the Third Ward as part of a two-month tour around the country that Chris Strachwitz had been hired to arrange for them. "They wanted me to lead them to some of the most interesting vernacular musicians I had encountered," Strachwitz said, "and to help them by doing sound recording and some lighting. We started in the Bay Area by filming Barbara Dane, Jesse Fuller, and Lowell Fulson, among others, and then set off to Los Angeles and went through Arizona, where we recorded Indians and Reverend Louis Overstreet. From Arizona, we traveled to Texas, and in Dallas we filmed Alex Moore and Black Ace, in Navasota, Mance Lipscomb, and in Houston, we met up with Lightnin' Hopkins before going on to Louisiana, Tennessee, and North Carolina."[6]

For the filming, Lightnin' played "Lonesome Road" and "Lightnin's Blues," which was actually a version of "Green Onions," the recent hit by Booker T. and the MGs.[7] For "Lonesome Road" he accompanied himself on acoustic guitar and was shown outside sitting on a chair in the middle of a sidewalk. He was wearing a plaid shirt, creased slacks, a Mexican *chaleco* [blanket vest], sunglasses, and a pork-pie hat, and had a towel slung over his shoulder. The footage was intercut with four domino players sitting at a table in a beer joint that was apparently the setting for "Lightnin's Blues," an instrumental on a Harmony guitar with an electric pickup. Lightnin' was sitting in a chair with a group of men, sipping beers, looking on, listening, but very much aware of the camera.

In 1963 the enthusiasm for Lightnin's music continued to grow, and he began touring more than he had ever before, returning to the Second Fret, and working the Retort Club in Detroit, the Cabale in Berkeley, the Continental Club in Oakland, and Ash Grove in Los Angeles. He became a regular at the Village Gate, and was invited back from May 14 to May 31, playing on the same bill as Valentine Pringle, as well as the great Herbie Mann (May 28 to 30) and the Jimmie Smith Trio.

On June 4, 1963, Lightnin' recorded again for Prestige/Bluesville for an album titled *Goin' Away*. Once again Lightnin' recorded his tracks at Gold Star in Houston. They were then overdubbed with bass and drums at Rudy Van Gelder's studio in Englewood Cliffs, New Jersey, under the supervision of jazz and gospel producer Ozzie Cadena, who had considerable experience recording blues artists such as Brownie McGhee and Sonny Terry.

Dan Morgenstern, who was then the editor of *Jazz Magazine*, wrote the liner notes, and instead of defining Lightnin' simply as an artifice of the musical past, he saw him in the context of jazz history. Morgenstern had seen Lightnin' perform live a couple of times at the Village Gate. "Lightnin' Hopkins would come in between acts," Morgenstern says. "There he was, just a guy with a guitar, sometimes he'd have a rhythm section [bass and drums] with him, but most of the time, he was by himself. And he was able to engage that audience which was not necessarily a blues audience. He was there and he would grab them. He was so direct. One of the things about Lightnin' that was not true of all blues performers was that although he had a very natural diction, it was very clear. It was easy to understand what he was singing about. . . . He had a great sense of humor. Some of his stuff is very funny. It's sarcastic. . . . He was an engaging performer and human being. He seemed to be very much at ease with different people. Lightnin's thing was much more intimate than say Muddy Waters, because Muddy would have a band."[8]

At the Village Gate, Lightnin' appeared at ease. "It was a very ecumenical club that was an epicenter for blues and other styles of music," Morgenstern recalls. "Art D'Lugoff was a real village guy in the sense that he liked a lot of different stuff. He would have jazz, different kinds of jazz, and you had blues, and at the time, political stuff. It was like a cabaret. It was a big cavernous place. It was downstairs, and there were long tables. It was like what you had in a cafeteria or something. It was congenial."[9] At the Village Gate, Lightnin' could interact with his audience through his talking blues. He was comfortable, and because he played there fairly often, he got to know some of the people, not necessarily in a personal way but as a performer who recognized the faces of those who frequented his performances.

"Blues in New York City came into the picture through the [white] folkniks," Morgenstern says. "New York hadn't really had a blues scene. Harlem was not a blues center. In Harlem, it was jazz. Even in the 1920s when Ma Rainey came to New York, she was not a hit. And she was a tremendous hit down south. People like Pete Seeger, Oscar Brand, and so on brought the blues to New York. But it was the folk thing, it was very much a left-wing thing. . . . There was a consciousness about the plight of black people."[10] Politically, many of those who came to hear Lightnin' were supporters of the civil rights movement and were active in protest marches and even traveled to the South to help the Freedom Riders. Lightnin's blues were not good-time dance music; his lyrics focused on his failed relationships with women and the hardships he and other African Americans of his generation endured. The white people who came to hear Lightnin' were looking for a meaningful alternative to the superficialities of pop music.

When Lightnin' went to California in the fall of 1963, he had just as much appeal, if not more than he had had in New York. Radio broadcast specials in Los Angeles—first on September 2 on KRHM-FM 94.7 with a show called "Blues with Lightnin' Hopkins"; and second on October 13 on KCBH-FM 88.7 with "Walking This Blues Road by Myself"—aired to a folk-oriented audience. The following week Strachwitz booked Hopkins for performances at the Berkeley Community Theater (October 18) and at Jenny Lind Hall in Oakland, where he was accompanied by the great jazz bassist Pops Foster. From the Bay Area,

Lightnin' went back to Los Angeles to appear (October 29 to November 10) at the Ash Grove before returning to the Cabale in Berkeley (November 11 to 14) and the Continental Club in Oakland (November 15 to 17).

In Texas, Lightnin' still played the local joints in Houston, but not as much, and was more willing to leave when opportunities were presented to him. According to music critic Joe Nick Patoski, "If you gave him enough money, he'd play in your apartment living room, as he did for [concert promoter] Angus Wynne III at his pad in Dallas in 1963."[11] Lightnin' was even invited to perform at an afternoon party at a University of Texas fraternity's lake house. Gordon Dougherty, who was then a senior and a member of a different chapter of the fraternity, went to the party thinking there was going to be some kind of jam session, but when he got there, his "heart sank." There wasn't a jam session. "It was your standard 1963 college scene," Dougherty said. "Sorority goddesses with bouffant hair, guys in regulation BMOC casual, not an authentic folkie in the bunch. Everyone was out on a large patio and Lightnin' was over in a corner, together with a bass player and drummer. . . . He had this beat-up guitar with a cheap pickup jammed into the sound hole and connected to a small speaker."

Dougherty had been familiar with Lightnin's music and thought he looked like the pictures on his albums, but up close he saw that "he had a wizened, wrinkled face and was sitting on a chair with a mike in front of him. He was skinny and his clothes were loose and baggy," and "to those who didn't know who he was, he probably looked completely out of place."[12]

As the afternoon progressed, the party went from bad to worse. The bass player and drummer hired for Lightnin' couldn't keep up with him. "The bass man bravely trying to follow standard 12-bar form was constantly behind chord changes that came too early or too late," Dougherty said, "and both he and the drummer were often off-beat . . . endings were a catastrophe . . . several people complained they didn't like his music . . . lacking a steady beat at the right tempo, the kids couldn't dance to Lightnin'. They were constantly off step, speeding up and slowing down, finding themselves still dancing with the music suddenly absent." After about forty-five minutes, Dougherty decided to leave the party, disgusted that the people there didn't understand they were listening to "one of the most famous bluesmen in the country."[13]

There are no accounts of Lightntin' ever having played other fraternity parties, and it's likely after the experience that Dougherty described, if anyone presented the idea again to him, he would have declined. Nonetheless, in the folk world, Lightnin' was more in demand than ever. Wherever he went, it seemed people wanted to hear him play and to record him. The word was out: he'd record for anyone who paid him a hundred dollars a song. There was no exclusivity; even if he signed contracts, he had no regard for them. Lightnin' was his own man and he did whatever he pleased whenever it pleased him.

In February 1964, Strachwitz returned to Texas to meet Horst Lippmann from the Frankfurt-based Lippmann and Rau Company, who had come to Houston because his French promoter had said that he would not take on the American Folk Blues Festival again if he did not get Lightnin' Hopkins to perform. Lippmann had started the American Folk Blues Festival in 1962 with Fritz Rau as an outgrowth of the jazz shows they had been promoting for more than a decade. They learned about Lightnin' from his records and saw Strachwitz as a vehicle to booking him.[14] "Horst had heard that I was the only guy he should deal with," Strachwitz says, "and apparently it helped that I was German. And when I got there, we met with Lightnin', who said he wouldn't fly to Europe if I didn't go with him. So Horst said he'd pay for my whole trip, hotel and all, to tour with Lightnin' in October."[15]

After Lippmann left, Strachwitz stayed in Houston for a while, and one day Lightnin' told him that his oldest brother, John Henry Hopkins, had recently been released from the penitentiary, where he had been serving time for murder. "Lightnin' said he was the best songster in the family," Strachwitz recalls. "So I asked Lightnin' if he wanted to make a family record that would include not only John Henry, but also his brother Joel, and he agreed." At first Lightnin' didn't know the whereabouts of John Henry, but finally he located him in Waxahachie, Texas. They left Houston in two cars; Strachwitz, Joel Hopkins, and a folk singer from New Orleans (whose name Strachwitz could not remember) in one, and Lightnin' and his mother in the other. Lightnin' led the way, and eventually he found the shack where John Henry lived.

Once they got to Waxahachie, Strachwitz set up his equipment and managed to record about twenty songs, but it was difficult and frenzied. "It was horrible," Strachwitz says. "We always had to get some little drink thing. 'Got to get some toddie,' Lightnin' would say. So we took some along and got to the shack, and first it was real nice and friendly, 'I haven't seen you in many years,' you know, all this kind of stuff, and it was going good, but they could never agree who was playing behind who. They were all not very good at playing together. None of them were quite in the same tuning."[16]

The resulting LP that Strachwitz produced with the Hopkins brothers is intriguing; Lightnin' hadn't recorded with Joel since he accompanied him on "Short Haired Woman" in 1947, and he had never recorded with John Henry. John Henry hadn't played guitar or performed in a long time, though the traditional lyrics he peppers into his songs evoke a strong sense of the rural tradition out of which the Hopkins brothers came. To Blind Lemon's "Matchbox Blues," for example, John Henry added the traditional verse:

> I got the blues so bad, it hurts my feet to walk
> I got the blues so bad, baby, it hurts my feet to walk
> You know what it's done on my brain, that it hurts my tongue to talk

In "Black Hannah," Lightnin' traded traditional verses with John Henry, but John Henry's guitar playing was so weak that the song barely hung together with lyrics that were traditional, but only tangentially connected by the improvisation with which they were performed. One of the most interesting recordings on the LP was Lightnin's story about a dice game that he had gone to with John Henry when they were boys. Lightnin' had won about four dollars, but the "fella who lost" got angry, grabbed a piece of wood, and smacked Lightnin' across the head. John Henry pulled a gun, and the man backed off.

As the session progressed Strachwitz says it got "very chaotic, and towards the end they all got pretty drunk and Lightnin' got really ugly. When I paid them their little money, maybe a $150 each, and Lightnin' went up to John Henry, 'Lookie here, brother, you owe me that from 1930,' And John Henry got so pissed he threw the money at Lightnin'. It was just horrible. You knew the guy didn't have a pot to piss in. I don't think Lightnin's mother said but peep. Not that I remember. She was totally quiet; when they got into it about the money, she just sat there. She wasn't going to get between them drunk brothers."[17]

On an unspecified date in 1964, presumably after Strachwitz's Arhoolie recordings of the Hopkins brothers, Lightnin' recorded an LP for the Guest Star label, a budget record line, at the Bird Lounge, a small jazz/blues club in Houston. The fidelity was poor, and the songs offered nothing new despite the claim in the liner notes that the live recordings "captured Lightnin' seldom heard." According to blues fan George Lyon, Lightnin' played often at the Bird Lounge in the mid-1960s, sometimes with Cleveland Chenier and once with Elmore Nixon. Located on Shepherd Drive on the outskirts of the wealthy River Oaks, and not far from "one of the wilder Houston ghettoes [the Fourth Ward]," it was later known as Lu's Ricksha Lounge (in 1966), and was a place that Lyon thought was a "beat hangout" when he was growing up in Houston. "Houston was a minor oasis for beats stranded away from either coast," Lyons wrote in the British *Blues Unlimited*. "It was suitably trashy and regularly raided (the reason, I'm sure, it became the Bird). The clientele was lily white, almost exclusively. It really wasn't a folky place . . . they were mostly, I think, white trash and frat boys."[18]

One night, Lyons recalled, "Hopkins was between songs, and some asshole in the back yelled out, 'Sing, nigger!' Hopkins ignored him. He repeated himself, somewhat louder. After a bit, Hopkins looked back and adjusted his glasses and said, 'What chew [sic] want?' The drunk yelled out again and Hopkins said, 'What?' He straightened his glasses with irritation. By now the guy was really yelling and looked like a real fool. Finally Hopkins said, 'Well, I can't play the song for you if I can't hear what you're asking for,' and continued his set, cool to his toes."[19]

By 1964, Lightnin' had had considerable experience performing in white clubs, though the Bird Lounge was a much tougher scene than the Jester on Westheimer in Houston, which was more like the folk clubs of New York, Los Angeles, and the Bay Area. Lightnin' was on the road a lot during this period, and he traveled often between Houston, the West Coast, and New York City, though he still avoided airplanes and took the bus and train as often as he could. On May 4 and 5, he recorded enough material for two LPs—*Soul Blues* and *Down Home Blues*—for Prestige/Bluesville, probably at Gold Star in Houston with overdubbing by Gaskin and Lovelle at Rudy Van Gelder's studio in New Jersey. The recordings were technically well produced and were essentially free form improvisations by Lightnin' on songs, ranging from "I Like to Boogie" to "Just a Wristwatch on My Arm." But again, musically, there was little new.

After Lightnin' returned from the East Coast, he headed off to California to play at the Cabale, where Strachwitz recorded him with Barbara Dane. The session wasn't planned, but emerged somewhat spontaneously. Strachwitz was recording Dane on Thursday afternoon, June 18, 1964. When Lightnin' walked in with his guitar and saw Dane on stage, he wanted to join in. "I was making a folk music style record by myself with a guitar," Dane says. "Chris [Strachwitz] had his machine set up in there, and I had invited Carroll Peery and a few friends to come by so I'd have an audience recording it. And Carroll knew that Lightning was in town and brought him over. And of course, when Lightning saw me with a guitar, you know, up on the stage with a microphone, well, he just had friends there. It was the afternoon, and he assumed it was just a jam. And he pulled out a guitar and started playing along, and then we started to improvise lyrics at each other. That's all. There was no plan to it at all. It was not a normal recording session, and you can see how well he adapted to the situation and just, it's great. It's a wonderful example of how artists on the same wavelength can work together with their own idiosyncrasies. Every solo artist has little special things that they do. If they're really artists, they can sacrifice some of those in the spirit of doing something new together. So he was able to do that."[20]

Dane had performed with Hopkins at different times, both at the Ash Grove and the Cabale. "Whenever I was in the Bay Area," Dane says, "I would play the Cabale with Lightnin' or opposite Lightnin'." For Dane, performing with Lightnin' was "always a surprise and a joy. The guy was a great team player. . . . I'm not anywhere in the league of a guitar player as he was. I'm playing rhythm guitar, and all of the idiosyncrasies that he has in terms of rhythm and meter and everything when he's playing with me . . . he's right there with me. . . . It's all improvised."[21]

By the time Dane and Hopkins recorded together, they had already become good friends. "I had a personal relationship with him . . . hanging out back stage, or he'd come by my house. There's a lot of that stuff in the songs. We're jivin' about one time he came over to my house all dressed up, and his cousin drove him over there. He knew I had to split from my husband. I guess he was hoping to see if there was any action there, whatever . . . it was natural for a musician, a guy on the road, to see how long the reception was; how can I put it? So he came by around dinnertime . . . I had three children, and . . . I was getting dinner ready, getting the kids ready for school. . . . So I kind of welcomed him in and he sat in the parlor. I use the word *parlor* because that's exactly how it was treated, very formally, sitting on the edge of a chair, just paying a social call. And I told him I'm really busy. So he said, 'That's okay. My cousin's waiting in the car for me anyway.' So it was one of those situations where both parties were protecting their options and protecting their dignity. And he left appropriately."[22]

Jesse Cahn, Dane's son, remembered Lightnin' coming to their house whenever he was in the Bay Area. "I don't know how young I was when I first met him. I just remember Lightnin' being around, but by the time I was about fifteen, he was staying at Carroll Peery's house in Berkeley and so was I. And some situation had come up, as a crazy fifteen-year-old, I had hit a wall and broken a hole in the door. One of those jilted girlfriend situations or something like that, a typical thing. So I'll never forget . . . Lightnin' said, 'When I gets like that, I hit the pillow,' meaning a number of things behaviorally that are pretty obvious, but he was also saying if you want to play guitar, you better take better care of your hands."[23]

Cahn described Hopkins as a "complete gentleman," who liked to dress well: "Lightnin' had sweaters and that Mexican *chaleco* that he liked to wear. He wore dapper slacks, really nice shoes, polished Stacy Adams, classic, shined."[24] On stage, Cahn felt that Lightnin' played the role of a kind of "jester," and was sometimes self-deprecating when he called himself "Po' Lightnin'," but musically, he was much more versatile than he usually let on. "I remember one time," Cahn says, "I don't know if it was during a sound check, but he was on stage. I was about fifteen years old and I used to clean the bathrooms and sweep up the inside of the Cabale. And I'm watching him, and he's playing his usual blues thing, and I turn away and remember hearing these jazz chords, and I turn around and he's playing these jazz chords and he's looking dead pan right at me and then he goes back to his blues thing."[25]

On the Arhoolie release, titled *Sometimes I Believe She Loves Me*, Dane and Hopkins engaged in a kind of blues dialogue, and "made up stuff, taking it [their relationship] to a further degree, acting like there was really some kind of thing going on there, which there wasn't."[26] The lyrics are suggestive, humorous, teasing, and sometimes silly.

In the LP's title song, Lightnin' begins by singing:

> Sometimes I believe she loves me
> And then again Poor Lightnin' believe she don't
> When I say can I go home with you
> She won't, won't let me

And Dane answered:

> Well, I said come over Lightnin', I'm gonna cook you some hash
> But when you come there, daddy, you done got smashed
> Now, if that's the way you want to do, I say that's all right, that's all right
> I'll just keep waiting on you

Lightnin' replied:

> You know I come to your house, I come that eve
> But what you had cooked for Lightnin'
> Do you know I had to eat it out on the streets

Overall, Dane and Hopkins's blues dialogue is entertaining; the guitar work is tight, but at times rambling, and the lyrics have a drive that evokes the spirit of improvisation and the joy of swapping words and music on a Thursday afternoon for a small audience of friends and family.

When Lightnin' got back to Texas, he mostly played around Houston, though he did perform as part of the KHFI festival at Zilker Park in Austin on July 13, 1964, with Mance Lipscomb, Carolyn Hester, John Lomax Jr., and Mickey and Marty. Over the course of the summer, Lightnin' didn't travel much, though he was no doubt thinking about the American Folk Blues Festival that he had agreed to earlier that year. His dread of air travel meant he was even more apprehensive by the time Strachwitz arrived in Houston to fly with him to Germany. "We took a United or American plane from Houston to New York, New York to Frankfurt," Strachwitz says, "In those days, it was a charter flight, it wasn't the system they've got now. Air India was one of the ones that had one plane a day flying around. I think the whole fleet had three planes. And if one got stuck some place, then you got stuck. Anyway, we got on this Air India plane. I think it was one of those back loading ones where you crawl in on the back, and I remember Lightnin' and I were already sitting in our seats and the crew walks in. And Lightnin' turns to me, 'Chris, these people are going to fly this airplane?' I said, 'Ya, they're good, you know.' And it only dawned on me later on that he had never encountered these East Indians, except as 'hoodoo' people down in Louisiana."[27]

When they finally landed in Frankfurt, Lightnin' was a wreck: "He was just sickened. He couldn't play. We called a doctor and they couldn't find anything wrong with him. And thank God, we had a whole week in Baden-Baden for the television program that Joachim Berendt had arranged for and had apparently paid for much of the whole tour. So they put him on the last day of the week. By that time, he sort of regained his ability to play. I think he had a nervous breakdown."[28]

During the TV recordings, the German photographer Stephanie Wiesand took an interest in Lightnin' and realized his mysterious illness was psychosomatic. "I was looking after Lightnin'," she recalled; he "spent quite some time at my kitchen table and on a sun chair on my balcony [located in Baden-Baden]. Lightnin' recovered under my supervision, after providing him with his beloved soul food (steaks, etc.)."[29] Lightnin' was very grateful to Wiesand, and the following spring, on March 17, 1965, enshrined his memories of her in a song he recorded with his brother Joel Hopkins for Chris Strachwitz, who simply called the loosely structured tune "Two Brothers Playing (Going Back to Baden-Baden)."[30]

Strachwitz felt Hopkins "must have been scared shitless that these damn hoodoo people were going to fly that airplane. That was his big thing. 'I'm gonna get me a mojo hand, so I can fix my woman so that she can have no other man,' and all this stuff. He really believed in that."[31] In any event, once Lightnin' got better, he was able to perform and by all accounts was well received during the tour that included Sonny Boy Williamson, Hubert Sumlin, Willie Dixon, Clifton James, Sunnyland Slim, Sleepy John Estes, Hammie Nixon, John Henry Barbee, Sugar Pie DeSanto, and Howlin' Wolf.

After playing for German TV in Baden-Baden, the American Folk Blues Festival went to Strasbourg, where it was featured at the Palais des Fêtes. Francis

Hofstein, who was then a student at the University of Strasbourg, was at the performance, and after the show he got a chance to meet Hopkins. Like many in Europe at that time, Hofstein was excited to see Lightnin' because he viewed him as a kind of myth or legend, but ultimately he didn't get much of a response. "He was detached, but present," Hofstein says. "I asked him some questions: How is it to be in France? And he wasn't very interested, but then I asked him when we were leaving together if he would come again to France or to Europe and he said, 'No.' Like that. And I asked him why. And he just answered, 'I don't want to die wet.' And that was it."[32]

From Strasbourg, the festival toured to Denmark, Sweden, Norway, Germany, Belgium, Switzerland, and back to France for one date in Paris before leaving for Great Britain. Derek Stewart-Baxter in *Jazz Journal* described the festival as the "most important blues event of the year" in England, where there were five dates, presented in association with the National Jazz Federation.

British blues fan Alan Balfour recalled going backstage before Lightnin's show at Croydon's Fairfield Hall concert and asking him to sign an album sleeve. Lightnin' looked at Balfour "over the top of his dark glasses and said rather testily (people were plaguing him like mad for interviews and discographical information) 'Boy, everybody's bin asking me one damn thing or another. I'll sing you something from that record when I get out there. You're here to hear me sing, ain't ya?'"[33]

In reviewing the concert, Stewart-Baxter wrote: "Good as all this was, it was not until Lightnin' Hopkins ambled on stage that things really began to happen, for he, in his own quiet way, proceeded to take the Fairfield Hall apart. Like all really great performers, Hopkins has the ability to cast a spell over his audience even before uttering a word; and when he commenced to sing and play his guitar the effect was electric. It was a most memorable experience and was to be repeated at every concert. Everything he sang was magnificent from his well-known "Short Haired Woman" to a semi-improvised blues on his fears of air travel. The latter a good example of how Lightnin's music is influenced by every-day events. My only criticism was that his spot was far too short. This man is quite capable of carrying a whole show on his own."[34]

Paul Oliver concurred with Stewart-Baxter in *Jazz Monthly* and wrote: "In the completeness of his performance Lightnin's appearance was the peak spot of the concerts." Oliver described Hopkins's performance with exacting detail: "Lightnin' came on with the slow tread which earned him his ironic nick-name. He looked sleek and slick, his gold-edged teeth flashing and his newly straightened and brushed-up hair dyed with a positive hair-line. Lightnin' settled down at the chair, picked the strings with elaborate casualness and played as he talked. To the large audience he spoke conversationally as if they were just a handful of people around him. His easy-going manner hardly alters on stage or in club; it is the secret of his success in these unlikely circumstances. Many of his conversational asides must have been virtually incomprehensible to all save a very few collectors . . . like that 'one-eyed woman when she cry. . .' he commented, making reference to a small incident that occurred several years ago and affected him deeply. Hardly a soul could have known what he was talking about but they were happy to be taken into his confidence. 'Two old women in a foldin' bed . . .' he sang; then stopped and said, 'Y'know, it's bad when there's two people in one foldin' bed . . . 'specially if they both mens. . .' The audience picked that up all right. Lightnin' talked about his trip over to Europe. He was still shaken by one air trip and apprehensive of the flight back, for he is very frightened by aircraft. He talked about it and sang 'Airplane Blues'. . . 'Mister Airplane driver, you got po' Lightnin' in your hand . . .' which was a version of 'DC-7.' It was indicative of his lack of any self-consciousness or even any real awareness of usual delicacies . . . that he sang:

> I'm gonna tell my woman like that Dago told the Jew
> Yes, gonna tell my woman like the Dago told that Jew
> You don't lika me, and I sure God, don't lika you
> They both had plenty money, that's why they couldn't get along[35]

The British photographer and critic Val Wilmer wrote in *Jazz Beat*: "Lipmann and the NJF [National Jazz Federation], assisted by the good judgment of Willie Dixon, put on the best balanced package shows blues enthusiasts could hope for. This one was no exception." About Hopkins, Wilmer focused on his performance style: "He walked on stage, cool, assured, slid into a chair and just went into a blues about a little girl. . . . His splendid eerie guitar made him the hit of the show for this reviewer and a partisan section of the audience screamed their approval to show they felt the same. He did 'Baby Please Don't

Go,' sang some more about air transport, imitating jet noises with his instrument and then he was gone."[36] Wilmer hoped that a "single tour" could be arranged for Hopkins, but commented that "apparently his price is prohibitive." While many American blues singers regularly included England in their tour itineraries, the 1964 tour was the only time Lightnin' ever played there.

A film clip from an unspecified date during the American Folk Blues Festival in the United Kingdom shows Lightnin' on stage, decked out in a black tuxedo and bow tie, with processed hair, sunglasses, and a neatly folded white handkerchief in his breast pocket. His introduction to the song "Come On, Baby, Come Home with Me" was awkward—he stumbled on his words and explained, "It's not exactly the blues right now"—but his playing was sharp on amplified guitar and his vocals shuffled forward with confidence.

When Lightnin' got back to Texas, Kay Pope interviewed him about his trip for the *Houston Chronicle* Sunday magazine. "Lightnin' Sam Hopkins leaned back and talked about what he'd seen in Europe," Pope wrote. "Next to the bed the TV carried on its own conversation and down below his little wife, Antoinette, applied determination and a dust mop to the stairs of their boarding house." In the article Pope not only recounted Hopkins's impressions of his travels, but also evoked a sense of his home life with Antoinette, who rummaged around their living quarters, looking for the list of tour dates and a packet of photographs. Even though Lightnin' and Antoinette were not legally married, they were very much living as a couple.

Highlights of the trip for Lightnin' included "good German beer," eight bottles of which he bought for himself and carried with him. "They're good folk over there," Lightnin' said. "But their bread's too hard. When I'd finally find some food I liked, I'd a whoppin' of it. I found some chicken in one or two places, I'd order a whole chicken. Wrap the rest in paper and take it with me." Overall, Lightnin' was pleased with the way the audience responded to him. "I talked to a few people over there," he said, "them that spoke English who wanted my autograph. A few, not many. But I make my guitar talk just like I talk. They could understand. They all jump, shout, jaw, and grab me at the end. They wouldn't be happy like that if they didn't like me."[37]

While Lightnin's acclaim was growing in England and throughout Europe, his recordings were garnering strong reviews in the United States. On October 3,

1964, *Billboard*, in its review of Lightnin's "Down Home Blues" (Prestige 1086), wrote: "The appeal of real blues is growing. It is part of America's contribution to musical culture. Lightnin' Hopkins is an outstanding purveyor of the blues as blues should be sung. His guitar and vocal work are a perfect marriage of instrument and talent."[38]

Lightnin' was in demand, and although he often was reluctant to travel, some gigs were too good to refuse. On November 7, 1964, he was featured in another show at Carnegie Hall, which by then had become a major venue for folk and blues shows. Lightnin' appeared on the same bill as Mississippi John Hurt, Phil Ochs, Dave Van Ronk, and Doc Watson. Barbara Dane, who by then had moved from Berkeley to New York, attended the concert but was disappointed: "Lightnin' walked on stage and put his shades on and started to do his thing, and it was totally, how should we say it, contained. He was not giving anything, not giving anything emotionally to it that was visible. He wasn't attempting to communicate or do the kind of thing he would have done at the Cabale or the Ash Grove where he's sitting face to face with people, basically talking to them through his music. In this case, in the Carnegie Hall setting, I was really studying it carefully, and saw how different his demeanor was. My take on it was, he was saying, 'Okay, you know, this is a hot shit place and everything. I'm not giving you anything because you don't understand it. It's not for you. I'll just do what I gotta do. You all love me if I do something great or not because you're into this sort of gotta really love the black artist, that kind of thing, and I'll just do and get off of here.' And that's what he did. Then, of course, the audience went wild."[39]

While Dane sensed that Lightnin' felt contempt for the audience at Carnegie Hall, other factors may have been at play. She wasn't with him backstage, and what she observed may have simply been an indication that he had had too much to drink, as he sometimes did, before he got on stage. Lightnin' was very much aware of the fact that he was revered by white audiences no matter what or how he performed. Mitch Greenhill said that he once asked him "whether he preferred performing to white audiences or black audiences. And he said that white audiences were much more attentive and respectful. He was really happy to have found this little niche and he was working it."[40] In other words, he didn't have to work very hard for the money he earned from such performances. Lightnin' was a star, but he was loyal to his longtime supporters, and when he returned to Houston, he performed at the Jewish Community Center on November 19 as part of its folk song series, a gig that no doubt paid considerably less than what he got from appearing at Carnegie Hall.

On December 2, 1964, Lightnin' made his last LP for Prestige/Bluesville; it was produced by Sam Charters, who featured six song tracks and eight tracks of interviews that he did with Lightnin'. These interviews constitute the only recorded autobiography that Lightnin' ever did. However, they contained little new material. By the time these recordings were made, Lightnin' had done countless interviews, and the stories related to his childhood, his meeting with Blind Lemon Jefferson, travels with Texas Alexander, move to Houston, discovery by Lola Cullum, getting his nickname, and thoughts on the blues had appeared in liner notes and articles by Mack McCormick and others. What's particularly striking, however, is Lightnin's tone and awareness that he was shaping his own legacy, even if the facts were skewed and somewhat vague.

In addition to recording for Bluesville in December 1964, Nashville producer Aubrey Mayhew (who may have been responsible for the Bird Lounge LP) brought Lightnin' into a studio in Houston and recorded a solo album with him for the Pickwick label. The overall quality of the session was poor; Lightnin' rehashed old material, drawing upon previously recorded songs and reiterating themes and lyrics that had become the staples of his concert performances.

For the first few months in 1965, Lightnin's touring slowed down, whether it was by choice, fear of flying, or a saturated market. On March 18, Strachwitz recorded Lightnin' in Houston, accompanied by drummer Harold "Frenchy" Joseph, whom he had heard play with Lightnin' in the Third Ward. "He was a tough drummer," Strachwitz says, "and he really grooved with Lightnin'. Spider [Kilpatrick, one of Lightnin's primary Houston drummers] was always sort of raggedy. He didn't put that solid beat behind him. Spider drummed in the Holiness Church and was Lightnin's usual cat because he would play for very little, I think. He was from Houston. Frenchy was also in Houston. . . . He was a total wine head, but he could sure play drums. That's when we did 'Money Taker' and 'My Little Woman,' which has got a sort of racist tone: 'My little woman, she ain't no Mexican. You better believe she ain't no Jew, but she's my Frenchman little girl.'"[41]

In April, Lightnin' traveled to Chicago, where Willie Dixon had helped to arrange some dates for him. Dixon and Hopkins had become friends during the American Folk Blues Festival tour. "Dixon was a great diplomat," Strachwitz says. "He always talking. . . . He helped Lippmann and Rau get all these musicians for the festival tour. And when Lightnin' came to Chicago, he would have arranged for him to stay some place, or maybe with him."[42]

Lightnin' stayed in Chicago and played Western Hall on April 17, Peppers Lounge on April 18, and then went to Gary, Indiana, before returning to Western Hall on April 24 and 25, and a club in Joliet, Illinois, on April 26. While he was playing largely for white audiences in other cities, all of his Chicago dates were in black venues, except for perhaps the booking in Joliet. "The black world still loved him," Strachwitz recalls. "The black world finally met him. He had never gone anywhere, because he didn't travel in those days [in the 1950s]. He was a country boy, and when he was in the big city, he found his way around there by knowing these people, you know, that came from the country."[43]

In July, Strachwitz took Lightnin' to the Newport Folk Festival, which by then was well known for presenting legendary blues singers from around the country, including Reverend Gary Davis, Brownie McGhee, Sonny Terry, Mississippi John Hurt, John Lee Hooker, Fred McDowell, Sleepy John Estes, Son House, and Skip James, among others.[44] Strachwitz was excited to bring Lightnin' to Newport, but it was more chaotic than he had expected. "I remember staying in this dormitory, kind of a bunk house," Strachwitz recalled, "it was like army barracks, and we were sleeping in these double bunks. Anyway, I was driving around, and Lightnin' said, 'I got to get something to drink,' and so he got his little gin and I decided to get some plum brandy. I got fuckin' drunk on that shit, and the next day, I remember, they all left, Dixon and everybody. 'We got to go to work. C'mon, Chris.' I said, 'Man, I can't get out of bed,' and I just laid there sick as a dog. And I remember them coming back. Willie Dixon said, 'Chris, you missed a big fight' [he used to be a boxer]. Oh, man, this guy [Alan] Lomax, him and this Dylan manager [Albert Grossman], they got into a fistfight. Dylan had plugged in [July 25, 1965], and Mr. Lomax didn't like it. Grossman had said, 'No, that boy stays plugged in.' I forget exactly what they said, but he said they had an all-out fight there. God, I felt so bad missing that fight. That was my entire memory of the festival."[45]

On stage, Lightnin'—who appeared July 24, the day before Dylan—played an amplified acoustic guitar and was backed by drummer Sam Lay on four of eleven songs.[46] Lay, who toured with the Paul Butterfield Blues Band, remembered that Hopkins had already heard of him, and "they [the festival organizers] knew I was capable of following any kind of traditional blues like that, that is my kind of music. And he stated that he'd never heard a drummer could play like that, and follow his timing and all. It was just that simple to me. That type of stuff I've heard so much on recordings and things. There really wasn't any time [for rehearsing], but neither of us needed rehearsing with the other one. He knew what he was going to do, and I knew what to do with what he was doing."

Near the end of Lightnin's set, Willie Dixon came up on stage and jammed with him and Lay. "Willie came up to bandstand and played bass," Lay says, "and there was no stumbling around." The response to Lightnin' was enthusiastic, and his set was tight and dynamic, as evidenced by the recordings that were finally released on the Vanguard label in 2002.[47] About Lay, Strachwitz commented, "He was a real pro. To him, Lightnin' was a real, individualistic guy, but he knew what to do. It was a black community thing."[48] Lay knew how to follow Lightnin's lead. He was more familiar with his music than most sidemen. Lay, like Hopkins, had southern roots. He had come to Chicago in 1960 with Little Walter, and decided to stay.

From Newport both Hopkins and Lay went to New York City, where Lightnin' was booked solo at the Gaslight Cafe on August 4, 5, and 6, 1965, and Lay was appearing at the Village Gate. "We stayed in the same hotel," Lay says. "It was the Hotel Albert. It wasn't one of the big hotels. It was where a lot of us stayed. And went out in the daytime together, myself, him, and my wife. We'd go up me and him, and walk down through the park, Washington Square Park, down through the Village and go on to one of these places called Chicken in a Basket. We walk out there and get some chicken. He would pay for it."[49] After his gig, Lay would go over to the Gas Light to hang out with Hopkins. The Gaslight was a coffee house at 116 MacDougal Street, and Lightnin' was on a bill that included the singer/songwriter Eric Andersen and the comedian Flip Wilson, and it was an easy walk from there to the hotel. The shows at the Gaslight were much like those at the Village Gate, and often featured an unexpected mix of performers, who alternated sets.

Lightnin's travel schedule was intense; the offers were too good to turn down, and during the summer of 1965 he was in and out of California. On October 4 and 5, the Verve label, in association with Folkways, recorded him in Los Angeles for an LP called *Lightnin' Strikes*.[50] The sessions were tough, but Lightnin' was actually to record three albums worth of material. The sidemen, Jimmy Bond on bass and Earl Palmer on drums, had some trouble keeping up with him, and the producers decided to overdub Don Crawford on harmonica to fill out the sound on yet another version of "Mojo Hand," as well as on "Little Wail," "Hurricane Betsy," and "Shake Yourself." Overall, the production was sloppy, and when *Lightnin' Strikes* was released a year later, it mistakenly had a photograph of Reverend Gary Davis on the cover on the first pressing.

Lightnin' wasn't picky about his recordings. He accepted every opportunity that came his way, and when he was approached by Stan Lewis of the Jewel label, he was ready to go. Lewis, based in Shreveport, had been one of the biggest distributors of R & B records in the South since the 1940s and had started Jewel Records in 1963. He recorded such artists as John Fred and His Playboy Band, John Lee Hooker, Justin Wilson, Memphis Slim, and Little Johnny Taylor for Jewel and two subsidiary labels, Paula and Ronn. Bill Holford had told Lewis about Lightnin' when he was recording Justin Wilson for him at his studio. "Bill said Lightnin' came in there all the time," Lewis recalled, "and asked me if I would like to do a session on him. I said, 'Yeah.'"[51] Lightnin' was easy to work with: "He insisted being paid a flat fee at the date. In cash. He wouldn't work any other way. He wouldn't take a contract and didn't want royalties. He'd say, 'You pay me right now, and I'll do one take.'"[52]

The first Jewel session included Elmore Nixon on piano and two unidentified sidemen on drums and bass. At one point, Lightnin' stopped in the middle of a song, Lewis says, and scolded the drummer, "'If you don't get that beat right, I'm gonna fire your ass.' But he never did that."[53] It isn't clear where this session actually occurred, though it may have been at Robin Hood Brians's studio in Tyler, Texas, where Lewis claimed years later to have recorded Lightnin'. The engineer's voice heard on the Westside reissue of this album is definitely not Bill Holford in Houston.

A song that Lewis called "Fishing Clothes" was actually a misnomer because he misunderstood the line "ain't got sufficient clothes." The tune was hardly a blues at all and had a country tempo, refashioning the melody of "Midnight Special," though some of the lyrics draw from the traditional "Doggone My Good Luck Soul." Lightnin' twisted the core lyric and sang, "Dog gone my bad luck soul, this old world down here is a big bad luck to me." In many ways, the song typified the problems with the recordings. Lightnin' was doing whatever he wanted, and his accompanists could barely keep up.

Lewis described Hopkins as a "real humble, nice guy . . . a man of his own in the way he wanted to record and more or less, wanted to do his own thing."[54] Apparently Lewis didn't know much about Lightnin's earlier recordings, given the mish-mash of songs he produced, including yet another version of "Short-Haired Woman" that he called "Wig Wearing Woman." The last verse of "Wig Wearing Woman," however, was updated with a strange, though disjointed, comment on topical events:

> She seed the Beatles, they liked to run her blind
> That the reason she keep on asking me for that little money of mine
> You know, I don't want no woman I got to buy wigs all the time[55]

In the end, the most successful single to be released from the first Jewel session was "(Letter to My) Back Door Friend," which Lewis says sold "fairly well." More interesting, however, is the Demon Music (Westside) reissue, which included a strong sense of what it must have been like trying to record Lightnin' and included the banter between presumably Robin Hood Brians and Hopkins before the song was recorded. At the beginning of the track, Hopkins shouted, "What?" And the engineer replied, "I had to get out there and set your mike up on your guitar," to which Lightnin' answered, "Oh, you should have told me, man." "Ah, you see we would have been able to get it straight," the engineer said, "When you started playing, I thought you were just practicing. You never did stop," to which Hopkins muttered, "But you come out here and set up ah . . . go ahead . . . I ain't tell you nothin' now. I'm gonna play it different all the way now." "All right, it's rollin'," the engineer said, and Hopkins began playing.[56] The song itself hung together musically, but the lyrics were highly repetitive.

> What you going to do with a married woman
> When she got a back door friend

> She prayin' all the time for you to move out
> So her back door friend he can move in[57]

Other tracks on the Jewel LP were more problematic. "Move on Out," for example, was a weak revival of an instrumental he had recorded with much greater authority and drive during the Herald sessions.

While Lightnin's first Jewel session was at times messy, he may have been paid more than what he'd been getting from the folk revival labels. Lewis says that he gave Lightnin' $2,500 for eight songs, a figure that seems unlikely given how much he was paid by others. At that point, Lewis was a relatively small independent producer, and was working to build his catalogue.

In the fall of 1966, Prestige released Lightnin's *Soul Blues* LP, which had been recorded more than a year earlier and showcased a more polished side of his music than what Lewis was able to record. On this LP, Lightnin' sang a tribute to "The Howling Wolf" and covered Big Bill Broonzy's "Too Many Drivers," but also performed one of his own more poignantly ironic songs, titled "I'm Going to Build Me a Heaven of My Own." It began with a spoken word dedication to "the whole world" and "the womens especially" that was followed by a talking blues about how he was going to build a heaven of his own (albeit a small one) so that he could provide "all these loving womens" a place to live. But then he implied that he might not be able to follow through: "I ain't gonna call myself Jesus, poor Lightnin' ain't gonna call himself God" and concluded with a plea: "If you're J.C., baby, will you please give poor Lightnin' the key? Mr. J.C., will you please help poor me?"[58] In this song, Lightnin' demonstrated his capacity to turn a phrase and improvise at will with his characteristic wry humor and pathos.

For blues revivalists, the music of Lightnin' Hopkins, like that of his contemporaries, Muddy Waters and John Lee Hooker, needed to be preserved and documented. In London, John Holt helped to found the Lightnin' Hopkins Appreciation Society with "its aims to publish articles, photographs, etc. and to promote record sales." In a letter to Folkways Records, dated June 13, 1965, Holt requested details concerning recording dates, personnel, localities, and matrix numbers for not only the first Folkways release, but "any other items released, and of any unissued materials."[59] Six months later, the newly formed Texas Blues Society published a special issue devoted to Hopkins with a discography compiled by Holt and essays by Frank Scott and Paul Oliver.

Holt's discography was the most thorough to date, and provided a detailed catalogue of about four hundred of Hopkins's recordings. In so doing, Holt drew from Anthony Rotante's groundbreaking work published in the December 1955 issue of *Discophile*, Serge Tonneau's discography that appeared in the December 1964 French *R & B Panorama*, as well as the efforts of Simon Napier-Bell of the British *Blues Unlimited* magazine and numerous collectors, including Tony Russell and Mike Rowe, among others. While these discographies may not have directly benefited Hopkins, they did serve to boost record sales and fuel the interest of concert promoters who sought to book Lightnin' for live shows.

The general disarray of his contracts and the lack of a royalty structure, other than with Prestige and Arhoolie, were complicated further by the fact that he sold most of his songs outright, and thus was not entitled to any royalties. Lightnin's approach hadn't changed since the start of his career; in other words, since he received one hundred dollars a song from Bill Quinn, he used that as his fee whenever making new albums. Lightnin's newest records on Prestige, Jewel, and Arhoolie were competing with reissues on labels like Imperial and Time that were packaged like they were new (but were in fact just re-releases of 1947–1953 material, often with reverb added to make them sound more modern). Essentially, Lightnin's style hadn't changed, so many buyers probably thought they were indeed new albums by him.

Paul Oliver, in his essay in Holt's compilation, made clear that even though Lightnin' was by then "known throughout the United States and in Europe, too," what mattered most to him was Dowling Street and the grid of narrow streets that spoke out from it: "He lives himself in a pleasant house just off the street. It has a ubiquitous wooden porch but the roof that shades it is supported by brick piers. . . . Lightnin' sits out on the porch most of the time, talking with friends who gather around him or sit on the steps. . . . The clubs where Lightnin' plays are small places, 'juke joints,' hardly advertising their character from outside. . . . They are wooden frame affairs, white painted once and furnished with metal chairs and tables . . . the clubs are noisy, the crowd comes and goes, sits and talks and drinks. . . . Every so often a few couples get up to dance, and many men dance alone to the music."[60] It was in this environment that Lightnin' honed his skills and to which, as Oliver suggested, he "thankfully returns" when he has finished a tour. While Oliver made it sound like it was the music that kept Lightnin' going back to the Third Ward, at this time in his life, the allure of Houston likely stemmed more from his affair with Antoinette Charles, who had occasionally traveled with him. McCormick had written in the notes to the *Smokes Like Lightnin'* LP that he believed their relationship may have started as early as 1948, but the details are sketchy and the extent to which they were spending time together at this point remains in question.

By 1965 the quality of Lightnin's life had improved, and as much as he balked at traveling, he flourished on the festival and concert circuit. While there are few records of how much he was actually paid, he seemed to be doing well, relatively speaking. His promoters took care of him, finding him a decent place to stay, driving him around, and getting him food and booze when he wanted them. And when he got back to Houston, he loved to cruise the streets of the Third Ward in his black-and-white Dodge, making his rounds, shouting out to his friends, and sitting in for a card game or rambling into a back alley to shoot dice.

Yet even though he had more cash to throw around, he still complained about being broke much of the time. Mansel Rubinstein, who operated Mansel's Loan Office on Dowling Street, saw Lightnin' often during the 1960s and says, "When he'd get back from out of town, he liked to get out there and play cards and gamble and drink, and when he needed quick money he'd come see me. He'd pawn one of his guitars, and I give him a short-term loan, of maybe fifty or a hundred dollars, and then when he needed the guitar, he come back and pay off the loan plus the interest, which back then was probably about 10 percent." Mansel had grown up in the Third Ward, and operated his pawnshop and loan office in the back of Rubenstein's Dry Goods, one of his father's three stores on Dowling Street.[61] Rubenstein says that Lightnin' came to his father's store often, not just to shop or pawn his guitar, but to talk, and they eventually became friends. "Lightnin' trusted me, but he wanted me to travel with him and help manage his affairs, but I didn't want to. I also had a small record label, called Whiz Records, but I never recorded Lightnin'. But if he was doing something locally, I might go with him to be sure he got his money."

As much as Lightnin' was earning more than he ever had before, he spent his money fast. His habits and vices hadn't changed. He was still a voracious gambler who was known to lose huge sums in a single game. And he was a heavy drinker, though Strachwitz says Lightnin' once told him that "Antoinette had saved his life" by getting him off the rotgut wine that had "nearly killed him" in the 1950s. "He may have switched to gin," Strachwitz says, "but he still liked to drink."[62]

7

Mojo Hand: An Orphic Tale

I n 1966, Trident Press, a division of Simon & Schuster, published J. J. Phillips's novel, *Mojo Hand* (later reprinted as *Mojo Hand: An Orphic Tale*), which is loosely based on an affair she was in the midst of with Lightnin' Hopkins. While the book is fiction, many readers have assumed the biographical fallacy and interpreted the book as thinly disguised autobiography, with Phillips as the character Eunice, and Lightnin' as the blues singer Blacksnake Brown, with whom she was obsessed. In fact, the novel is significantly different than the actual affair. Unraveling the facts of the relationship is revealing as a means to illuminate the life of the man behind the music. Little is known about Hopkins's private life and the experiences that informed the self-styled autobiography of his blues.

Phillips's story elucidates some of the social and cultural dynamics surrounding Lightnin's career and life that are much more complex than had been previously thought. While a close examination of Hopkins's discography and the continuous stream of record releases serves to debunk the myth of "rediscovery," his day-to-day life experiences, as recounted by Phillips, offer a window into his currency and vitality among African Americans.

Phillips was born April 2, 1944, and grew up in a progressive African American family in Los Angeles. "My immediate family was assimilated, atheist, and were for all intents and purposes indistinguishable from Caucasians in visage and speech. My immediate family was also neither 'color struck' nor class bound. My mother's family came to Los Angeles from Austin, Texas, and the Kansas prairies in the 1880s. My mother attended UCLA, and taught elementary school for 60 years in the public school system. My father was a claims examiner for the State Department of Employment. His father, who knew Classical Greek and Latin, had been a professor of Belles Lettres and Modern Languages around the turn of the twentieth century at Virginia Normal and Collegiate Institute, a historically black college, where he received his education. In the early 1920s, he moved his family to Pasadena, California, and became that city's first African American attorney and real estate developer, and he was active in the early civil rights community. I grew up in a neighborhood that was quite diverse as to ethnicity and class, and consequently, from early on I was exposed to varieties of cultural expression, including dress, food, music, languages, dialects, idiolects, ways of looking at the world and inhabiting it."[1]

Phillips became interested in black roots music while she was a freshman at Immaculate Heart College in Los Angeles in 1962: "That year, the musicologist Peter Yates came to the Art Department to give a series of lectures on American music. In addition to introducing us to the music of Charles Ives, John Cage, Harry Partch, and other avant-garde American composers, Yates played old Southern music, white and black, including African American work and prison chants and shouts, as well as the music of Leadbelly, and other kinds of music that predated the blues. I loved it all, but was especially drawn to the chants and to Leadbelly's music. It grabbed me. I was living in the dorm. The folk music scene was burgeoning at that time; we all listened to Baez and Dylan, Odetta, old country bands, wailing women from the hollows of Appalachia. Several of us got guitars and tried to play along, I among them. I took a few lessons in basic folk guitar and tried my hand at various styles."[2]

That summer after completing her freshman year, Phillips traveled to Raleigh, North Carolina, to join the civil rights movement. She worked on a voter registration campaign administered by the National Students Association, and later joined a CORE-sponsored sit-in at a Howard Johnson's restaurant.

She was arrested and sentenced to thirty days in the county jail. Once she was released, she flew back to California, and as the fall semester geared up, the nuns at Immaculate Heart College saw her as a problem. "My life had not been consciously touched by racism," Phillips says, "until I came to Immaculate Heart, and I was ill-equipped to handle it. Even then, the school prided itself on being liberal and progressive; and I could not compass the fact that I'd gone to Raleigh to help eradicate racism, I'd gone to jail *and* I'd been a passenger in a car that was chased by the Klan—I literally put my life on the line for my convictions, only to return to Los Angeles to be done in by the very beast I had gone South to slay—at the very institution I had naively put my trust in. In despairing rage and frustration, I was driven to repudiate everything I had previously known and aspired to."[3]

In reaction to what had happened to her, Phillips says, "I consciously began to explore African American culture, and as I delved more into black roots music, I came across Samuel Charters's book, *The Country Blues*. I cannot remember whether or not this was the first time I had ever heard of Lightnin' Hopkins, but it was the first time he caught my attention, and after reading Charters's description of him, I was immediately captivated, both by the man Charters described and by what his music seemed to promise. I bought a couple of Lightnin's albums and was extremely put off by his music when I first listened to him.[4] I don't know just what I'd expected, but what I heard was so raw and direct that I couldn't handle it, neither the blues nor the boogies. The more I listened, the more I came to like it, and soon I was hooked."[5]

The elusive Lightnin' that Charters depicted in his book also intrigued Phillips, and she wanted to go to Houston to see if she could track him down as Charters had done. "I and one of my roommates, Krista Balatony, who was very blond and from Austria (now clinical professor of law emerita at the University of Wisconsin), decided we were going to find Lightnin'. Krista and I went to Houston over Thanksgiving break [1962], telling our parents that we were going to spend the holiday at a friend's home in Montecito. We took the Sunset Limited, hoboing in coach by keeping one step away from the conductor." They were worried that they were too light skinned and that Lightnin' might reject them for this reason, even though Phillips was in fact African American: "As the train neared Houston, we slathered ourselves with Man Tan [an early sun-less tanning cream] so we'd look darker and less conspicuous, but instead of imparting the desired degree of brownness to our skin, we turned a ghastly yellow ochre, as if we were jaundiced and in the terminal stages of liver disease. We couldn't wash it off; it took several days to fade. We felt so foolish. That was my brilliant idea."[6]

When they got to Houston, they checked into a hotel on Dowling Street and asked around for Lightnin'. "Krista recalls that we met a fellow who told us he knew where Lightnin' lived, but said that he wouldn't be at home until much later that night. The three of us then went to our hotel and waited around, it seemed interminably, until about two in the morning, when the man declared that Lightnin' would now be at home. He walked us over to Mama's Place on Hadley Street, just a few blocks from the hotel, where we found Lightnin' in his room, and we introduced ourselves. He told us he'd be playing the next night at a honky tonk called the Snowboat Lounge, and we could see him play there. The meeting was brief; we bid him adieu, ditched our new friend, and returned to the hotel to get some much needed sleep.

"Sometime the next day, I got a call from one of Lightnin's minions, perhaps Billy Bizor, instructing me to repair to a particular alley nearby and wait for Lightnin' to meet me there. It was all very cloak and dagger, but I followed his instructions. I don't remember what time of day it was, but I did meet Lightnin', who was in his car, with his shades on. He wanted to know who we were. He and I exchanged a few words. He seemed very enigmatic, and soon he was gone, crunching gravel as he slowly drove away. I don't know what he said to me or what I said—or more probably stammered—to him in that encounter. I might well have said something very brash and outrageous, such as 'Hey, I like your music and I want to be your woman.'

"That night, we showed up at the Snowboat Lounge and immediately became the cynosure of all eyes in this rather raucous juke joint—especially blond, vivacious Krista, whom everyone called 'Crystal.' I was fairly oblivious to the stir we caused in the club and on Dowling Street because my objective was to meet Lightnin'. I was surprised that people did not simply sit quietly and listen, then applaud demurely when a song or a set was over. They drank and ate and talked while the music was playing, and sometimes whooped and hollered. But it was nothing akin to a supper or folk club atmosphere, either. There was no raised stage or special lighting. Lightnin' was just a few feet away from the audience, and frequently directly interacted and bantered with them, as individuals and as a group, drawing them in, weaving them into his performance, cracking jokes, making up timely verses on the spot, directing songs or lines of songs to specific people, who would counter with wisecracks and perhaps get up and dance.

"We returned the next night as well. Krista says that there was an after-hours room at the rear of the club, where people continued partying into the wee hours, while Lightnin' played and sang. I had my guitar and jammed with him in the after-hours room both nights, though I have only a very dim memory of this. I could barely play the guitar at this time, and cringe at the thought that I could have had that much chutzpa."[7]

Back in California, Phillips and Balatony returned to school, and when the spring semester began in January 1963, Phillips was expelled. "I was extremely distraught. I wanted to be in school, but clearly the nuns didn't want me there. And soon after that I came up with the idea to write a book that combined my fascination with Lightnin' with my abiding interest in herpetology, especially the blacksnake, which became the first name of the blues singer in *Mojo Hand*. My first decision was to use the folklore and natural history of *coluber constrictor*, the American blacksnake, as a structural component, and trope this into a story of one person's journey from a non-racialized state to the racialized real world, as was happening to me. But I had no idea how to use it to create a fictional narrative until I realized that the perfect vehicle for effecting this was my own bluesy Orphic quest, which developed after I had seen Marcel Camus's classic film *Black Orpheus* several times, and which led me to Lightnin'. The movie is a version of the story of Orpheus and Eurydice set in the black *favelas* of Rio during Mardi Gras. Classical mythology and herpetology were two things I'd been keenly interested in for as long as I can remember. In addition, I'd come under the influence of the existentialists and outlaw writers, such as Henry Miller, Genet, Sartre, Camus, as well as Richard Wright, and I was irresistibly drawn to the idea of the anti-hero and the bad boy in literature and life. So when I contemplated an Orpheus, I didn't think of a sunny, conventionally handsome Breno Mello [who portrayed Orpheus in the film], but rather a chthonic and Dionysian Orpheus. Further, Orpheus is a bucolic figure who played a stringed instrument and sang, and the country blues is for me the *locus classicus* of the blues, so no other African American music would fit the bill. Then, in walked Lightnin', a musical sorcerer, beautifully dark-skinned, thin as a snake, who sometimes moved like a snake about to strike when he played guitar. He was elusive, an enigmatic trickster just like the blacksnake, with a frisson of danger about him that I found alluring."[8]

By the time Phillips went back to Houston in the spring of 1964, she had a plan. She brought her guitar and hoped that Lightnin' might teach her to play. This time she didn't try to darken her skin, and when she finally met up with Hopkins, he "just couldn't figure it out. . . . I don't know if he knew I was black then. At that time, I don't think so. At some point, he did. . . . I think he probably thought I was white when I first met him."[9]

Phillips moved into a rooming house in the Third Ward and went to see Lightnin' perform whenever she could at Irene's, the Sputnik Bar, and the other little joints that he frequented. However, she confined her activities primarily to the Third Ward and never went to the Fifth Ward, because she had heard that he had a deep relationship with a French (Creole) woman named Antoinette, who lived there and who had a powerful hold on him. At the time, Lightnin' stayed most of the time in a rooming house informally known as "Mama's Place" (which was where Charters had recorded him in 1959) on Hadley Street, though Phillips recalled that he also had an apartment on Gray Street. "Antoinette was married," Phillips says, "but Lightnin' usually referred to her as his wife, and he sang to her as his wife. When Antoinette traveled with him, she traveled as his wife. There are people who will swear up and down that they were married. They weren't. I knew that and everybody down there knew that. She was married to another man. She had a family of her own on the other side of town."[10]

In Houston, Phillips says, "I adopted the name Skinny Minnie, a rather outré persona to accompany it partly in tribute to an inimitable woman I met while doing voter registration in Raleigh, who called herself "Miss Skinny Minnie." It was the perfect *nom de funk*, or 'pigmeat name,' as Lightnin' termed colorful, evocative African American names in a recitative in one of his boogies, when he asks an imaginary woman: 'What's your name? Suzanne? Oh, I don't like no Suzanne. Give me Lyra or Vera. Give me a pigmeat name.' Acting under the rubric of 'When in Rome . . .' plain Jane wouldn't do. I needed a pigmeat name.

Lightnin' later changed it to 'Jicky Minnie,' and in 1964, he recorded a song 'Leave Jike Mary Alone' [on the LP titled *Live at the Bird Lounge*] and changed 'Minnie' to 'Mary' in a rather lame attempt to conceal the subject of the song from Antoinette."[11]

In the song Lightnin' made it clear that Antoinette knew he had another woman, but tried in vain to explain that his relationship wasn't serious while at the same time admitting feelings for Jike Mary.

> My wife told me, 'Babe, I believe you're going crazy' (x2)
> I know you got a little woman, they call her Jike Mary
> Hush your mouth, baby, take your time (x2)
> I say I ain't bought Jike Mary nothin' but one fifth of wine
> Goin' to be trouble if Jike Mary don't come home (x2)
> Everything I ever did is telling me, leave Jike Mary alone[12]

Phillips was touched and amused by the song, but said she never drank wine with Lightnin'. She shared his beverage of choice, Gordon's Gin. "It's true that he consumed liquor on a daily basis (again part of a larger Texas ethos). Yet I never saw anybody drunk or not in control of their faculties."[13]

How often Phillips got together with Lightnin' varied: "I would see him a lot at Shorty Calloway's garage. Sometimes I spent time at Mama's on Hadley Street when Lightnin' was elsewhere. Mama owned the rooming house and her kitchen was a lively gathering place, but for the most part, I went to Shorty's. Lightnin's cronies congregated there, and though it was a male environment, Shorty welcomed my presence, and I had a lot of fun hanging with these older men. Though Lightnin' lived within easy walking distance to Shorty's, he frequently drove his car over. At that time, he had a black-and-white Dodge."[14]

Shorty's had several chairs at the front of the garage, where people would sit around and drink: "They'd shuck and jive, tell lies and stories, while Shorty worked on a car. There was an alcove in the back where people would shoot craps on a fuzzy blanket with peewee dice. Lightnin' was often found kneeling at the edge of the blanket, completely absorbed in the ritual and litanies of spinning the dice. And when Lightnin' didn't want Antoinette to know he was at Shorty's, he'd walk over. She checked on him frequently. People told me that she'd drive around town looking for his car to ascertain his whereabouts. He was forever trying to move his car so she wouldn't know where he was. However, sometimes he wanted her to think he was at Shorty's, so he'd park his car in front of the garage and leave with someone in another car."[15]

Once, Antoinette discovered Lightnin's car parked outside another woman's house at night, and had someone steal it: "So, Lightnin' comes out and there's no car. And he's going crazy, running around telling everyone that his beloved, black and white Dodge had been stolen, but not revealing his specific where-abouts when the supposed theft occurred. However, Antoinette had already told Mama what she'd done and why, and Mama told everybody else who hung out at Hadley Street. Word spread to Shorty's, so all of us knew what had happened. When he came into Mama's kitchen with his lament, our mock expressions of shock and outrage for Po' Lightnin' turned to hoots of laughter as soon as he left the room. At times, he was made the butt of jokes because at times, he did silly things which deserved to make him the butt of jokes, but the joking was done with good humor, and he bore it with good humor, often laughing at himself, as he did when he finally learned just who stole his car and that he was the last to know."[16]

Shorty's was a good ole boys' hang out, a "spit and argue" club, where Phillips would "sit around, have a beer, and try to write down as much conversation" as she could, but these notes didn't survive. Phillips loved to listen to the stories in and of themselves, but knew how important they were to writing her book. Matters of regional speech and dialect were frequently puzzling to Phillips, espe-cially as it related to Lightnin'. "For instance, it took me awhile to understand Lightnin's use of the word *bullcorn*, which he tended to say instead of *bullshit*. What precisely was the 'corn,' I wondered—did it refer to the excrement itself, or to undigested kernels in the dung of cattle fed on corn, or perhaps simply corn as fodder? And *mollytrotter*—did that refer to a mule? A swiftly trotting mule? A homosexual? A swiftly trotting homosexual? Creole expressions, which filtered into the local black dialect because of the Creole population in East Texas were particularly opaque to me, though I had taken some French in school.

"When Lightnin' wrote, he sometimes used the obsolete formal *thou* and *thy*. And once in awhile, he used words so archaic that I had to resort to the dictionary. One particular word stands out: his use of the word *fain*. I had never heard this word used in conversation, and don't recall anyone else using it when I was in Texas. It was a word like *lief* that I knew only from reading the likes of Shakespeare and Spencer, and didn't completely understand its usage in those contexts. I later concluded that this must be one of those old Scots-Irish lexical retentions present in the regional Southern Englishes of both whites and blacks alike."

The only time Phillips recalls that Lightnin' became completely exasperated with her was due to a misunderstanding of regional speech, when he asked her to go to the local grocery store to buy "Arsh taters" and she returned empty-handed: "I told him that the store had plenty of potatoes, but I couldn't find any of the 'Arsh' variety. I assumed that they were a special, regional variety of potato, hitherto unknown to me. 'Arsh taters, Arsh taters,' he repeated in consternation. 'Every grocery has Arsh taters. How come you can't find none?' Finally, a light bulb lit up in my head and I realized that he must be referring to Irish potatoes, which I knew as Russets or Idahoes. We both got a good laugh out of my linguistic incompetence, and Lightnin' got his Arsh taters."[17]

Early on, Phillips and Lightnin' became intimate: "We had a sexual relationship," Phillips says, "and it went on for about five years, though when we first got together in Houston, I was there for maybe two months. Not a very long time." Lightnin' would come to see Phillips in the rooming house where she was staying. For a very brief time, Phillips worked at a cafe and beer parlor off of Dowling Street, and "this woman, her name was Mrs. Cash, ran the place with her husband, but she was the one who held the reins. I rented a room in a house she owned behind the cafe."[18]

Phillips says that while she was in Houston, Lightnin' would "play music three, sometimes four times a week; and sometimes on weekends in one day he'd play two gigs at different places." Phillips wouldn't always go with him. "Mostly," she says, "because of Antoinette. He had his own things to do, and I was enough of an intrusion, but I didn't go everywhere because I didn't want to. It wasn't just because of Antoinette. He had his own life. I spent more time with him at Shorty's than anywhere, where we were all just hanging out together. It was a way to be near him, and be part of the gang."[19]

Lightnin' would let Phillips know when he was going to come to her rooming house after gigs. "Either Billy Bizor, or somebody, would tell me," Phillips says. "I didn't have a phone. Billy would relay a message from Lightnin' letting me know when he was going to come over or where he'd be playing and if it was safe for me to drop by."[20]

Phillips and Bizor became friends. "He protected me and helped me navigate the terrain; and when I was really strung out from the situation—love as disease—I would lose my appetite and was prostrate half the time, and Billy would make sure I ate. He would take me places and talk to me about Lightnin'. . . . He liked Lightnin' in his way as much as I did. Both men and women were drawn to Lightnin' in powerful ways."[21]

For Phillips, Lightnin' was "a wonderful person to be around, a lot of fun to hang with, and do things with. . . . He loved to 'ride and look,' as he called it. He'd drive his own car, or have someone, such as Billy, drive him around. He could drink a little bit and relax. And there were always his cronies to do things for him."[22]

As much as Lightnin' liked cruising around Houston, he was always on guard. Phillips remembered riding with Lightnin' in his Dodge when, she says, "he showed me a large pearl-handled revolver, which I'm certain was loaded." But Phillips saw it as "a continuation of the Texas country/cowboy culture— white as well as black, and a phenomenon that extends across class as well—a culture which had fused the ethos of the Wild West with that of the old South into that brash, inimitable Texas 'thang,' which encompasses just about every aspect of one's behavior. . . . Lightnin' and his friends even used the word *desperado*, which they pronounced 'desperator,' when they referred to those who used or threatened violence in the commission of their crimes."[23]

Lightnin', however, rarely dressed in Western styled clothes, though he did wear a straw cowboy hat in hot weather: "He usually wore lightly starched short-sleeved sport shirts—sometimes unbuttoned so that his undershirt was visible, though I remember him always wearing pleated slacks, never jeans or work pants . . . he wore a pair of cut-off pants underneath—he was *so* thin, that gave him some bulk."[24]

Despite Lightnin's urban appearance, he retained a country sense of humor with long, rambling anecdotes, which Phillips found very appealing. Once, Lightnin' took Phillips and his brother Joel to a chapel to view the body of a friend of theirs. "We went inside and two open coffins were on display," Phillips says. "They walked up to one, peered into it, shook their heads, then went over to the other casket and saw that in it was the man they knew. They stood around it making droll, *sotto voce* comments about the deceased, which I wish I could remember (one had something to do with remarking that their friend appeared considerably whiter in death than he had been when he was alive. Well, yeah, because whitish powder had been applied to his face, and it looked positively ghostly and kind of Kabuki). After awhile, they strolled over to the other coffin and began making more droll comments about the body of the woman who reposed therein. The things they were saying were so hilarious (not cruel or ghoulish, just terribly irreverent), that I had to stumble outside because I was choking with suppressed laughter. After about half an hour, they decided they'd spent enough time paying their respects to the deceased, and we departed."[25]

The first time Phillips met Antoinette was unexpected, but nonetheless unsettling. She tried her best to stay out of Antoinette's way, but inevitably, one day their paths crossed. "I'd been down there awhile and was at Shorty's garage," Phillips says, "when Lightnin's car pulled up outside and stopped in the street, with the driver's side facing the garage (I'm nearsighted and didn't have my glasses on), I assumed it was Hops (as we often called him). I got up from my chair and walked to the car to say hi, but when I got close to the driver's side, I saw it wasn't Lightnin', it was Antoinette. Oops! I think she was as startled as I was. I backed away into the garage, and I'm sure I must have asked for a stiff shot because that rattled the heck out of me."[26]

That day, Antoinette was driving Lightnin's black and white Dodge on one of her patrols. "Who knows where he was," Phillips recalled, "but she was checking out all his haunts, and then some. . . . Her patrols were very funny. Lightnin' trying to sneak around and get away from her was funny. And that didn't mean he was necessarily up to anything nefarious. He could simply have gone fishing or 'ridin' and lookin'" with Joel or Spider or Billy, or he could have been at a card or craps game in another part of town. No matter, Antoinette kept her eagle eye out for him at all times."[27]

After this incident with Lightnin's car, Phillips realized that she needed to make herself more scarce and began visiting Hattie's tailoring shop, a few doors down from Shorty's. "Hattie was probably in her forties, a seamstress, a stone Texas cowgirl who went to rodeos, was crazy about catfish, and said that she had once killed a no-good boyfriend. I got to know the people who dropped by her shop.[28] I didn't see much of Lightnin' during this period, though he occasionally dropped by just to say hi. He and Hattie knew each other through Shorty, but didn't run in the same circles.

"Hattie began calling Lightnin' 'Turkey Neck' (though never to his face), not so much because of his neck, which was a bit long but not exceedingly so; but because when he wore a certain pair of boots which apparently didn't fit very snugly, he'd be overly careful when he walked. He would tip forward a bit and his head would bob up and down, which reminded Hattie of a barnyard fowl searching for kernels of grain on the ground. Whenever she saw him stepping past her shop going toward Shorty's, she would exclaim 'Yonder go Turkey Neck, yonder he go!'"[29]

After Phillips had been in Houston for a while she "settled into a routine and lost the sense of there being any other life." But she was running out of money, and while she liked spending time at Hattie's place, she had been exiled from Shorty's garage (because Antoinette had discovered her there), and was isolated from the action. Moreover, she recognized that her presence in Houston was disrupting the lives of the people around her. "I realized that it was a situation realistically impossible to sustain. It wasn't right," Phillips says, "no matter how much I tried to ignore that fact," and her "adventure came to a swift end" when she "learned two alarming pieces of news: the first was a warning that I should watch my back because Antoinette was tired of me poaching her man and was going to put some Louisiana hoodoo on me or shoot me, or both; and the second, truly humiliating news was that my parents were apparently planning to come to Houston to bring me home. Whether Antoinette's alleged threat was real or a scare tactic, I'll never know—I didn't wait to find out. But I especially did not want to suffer the ultimate mortification of being ignominiously carted home by my parents, so I went back to L.A."[30]

Phillips moved home, got a job as a fry cook, and began writing *Mojo Hand*, which she finished in 1965. "I told no one that I was writing the book, but after I'd completed the manuscript, I showed it to lay professor Fallon Evans at Immaculate Heart," Phillips says, "because I hoped he would tell the nuns that I could actually accomplish something even though they'd expelled me from college. That was *all* I wanted. But Fallon, who had published a series of detective novels, sent it to his agent without telling me, and Trident bought the rights almost immediately. However, my editor, Bucklin Moon, insisted that the name Orpheus be taken out of the book because he denied that it had any relevance to the story."[31] Phillips wasn't prepared for the book to be published because she had no intention of becoming a novelist. She had written the book for personal reasons.

Phillips's novel fictionalized her relationship with Lightnin', and when she completed the book she was still very involved with him. Whenever Lightnin' came to California between 1964 and 1966, Phillips tried to meet up with him. "The liaison continued for a number of years after I left Houston—when he would come to town," Phillips says, "either to L.A. or San Francisco. Not always, but frequently, I would stay with him." On these occasions, Phillips was able to spend concentrated periods of time with him. "We'd get up together. You know, he always had a nip in the morning. And then he would have eggs and grits." During the day, they'd drive around, do errands, and Phillips would usually go to his gigs at night.

Phillips had hoped that Lightnin' would teach her to play guitar, but he was fairly protective of his musicianship and guitar picking moves. "He did not go off somewhere to rehearse, nor did he rehearse his repertoire at all *per se*, but he was extremely open in allowing me simply to be present during his private music-making times. When he had some song, or verse, or guitar riff that he wanted to develop and fix in his mind and fingers, he would pick up his guitar and work on it completely unselfconsciously, while I would kick back and listen. Sometimes he would sing a line or verse directly to me as an ironic way of commenting on my mood or actions, or to express affection. Sometimes I had my guitar and we'd play a game with a succession of increasingly intricate riffs, and even though he would frequently show me his fingering, I was invariably left in the dust . . . and he was genuinely tickled when I studied his picking and fingering, and tried to copy his licks, though I was by no means a quick study."[32]

Once in Los Angeles, Phillips says, "Lightnin' and I were in Schwab's drugstore on Sunset Boulevard. He was searching the shelves for a laxative; the food wasn't agreeing with him because he wasn't in Texas or the black part of L.A. and who should we look up and see but John Lee Hooker—looking for a laxative too. They both said, 'Oh, the food here, man.' They started groaning and commiserating about their indisposition."[33]

Sometimes when Lightnin' came to L.A. to play at the Ash Grove, he'd stay with two sisters, Jimmie and Tee, who "lived way down in south L.A. They had a soul food cafe downtown, 'Jimmie and Tee's' near Seventh and Grand across the street from J. W. Robinson's, and their clientele consisted of white professionals who worked downtown, as well as blacks. They were superb cooks from Mississippi. I don't know when he met them, perhaps during his first trip to L.A. back in 1946, but they were old friends, and I'm sure that's all they were. Jimmie and Tee were very conservative women, modest, soft-spoken, all about cooking, a bit plump and plain in dress, they wore white uniforms when they cooked and served in their restaurant. They were very traditional in a Southern sense; I liked them a lot."[34]

When Lightnin' was in town, Phillips would go over to Jimmie and Tee's house to see him. "We'd sit around watching TV and eating food they brought home from the restaurant, or they'd cook just for us." Surprisingly, "Lightnin's favorite TV fare seemed to be old Amos and Andy shows, old B-grade westerns with Stepin Fetchit, and other stereotypical black sidekicks hamming it up to the hilt, and Charlie Chan movies. This, of course," Phillips says, "will be extremely controversial to many, but I spent many a night, into the wee hours of the morning, sitting in their living room watching the worst old film and TV *dreck* imaginable (which I adore), including these racist films, and I'd be rolling on the floor at Lightnin's comments. Jimmie and Tee didn't like him to watch the films, but soon they'd be weeping with laughter, as well. I wish I could recall some of the cracks he made. I think that he had a keen sense of stereotype and the way in which it was deployed by African American actors in many but not all of these films as a transgressive weapon. And I appreciated that."[35]

From the first week of April to the third week of October 1966, Lightnin' played more than a dozen dates in California, dividing his time between the Matrix, the Fillmore, the Cabale, the Berkeley Folk Festival in the Bay Area, and the Ash Grove in Los Angeles. The crowds at the Ash Grove were diverse and sometimes included celebrities, some of whom would stop backstage to meet Lightnin', but he wasn't necessarily welcoming. "Once when I was with Lightnin' in the dressing room at the Ash Grove," Phillips says, "Bobby Darin knocked on the door and asked to come in; he wanted to tell Lightnin' how much he admired his music. I'm not sure that Lightnin' really knew who Darin was as a pop icon, though he certainly knew his name. My jaw dropped when Darin came in, but I tried to play it cool. Here was one of my teen heart-throbs . . . come to pay his respects to a man *he* considered a master of music."[36]

Phillips loved spending time with Lightnin', but after Antoinette found out about their trysts, she did her best to stop them. Antoinette began to travel with Lightnin' to California, but instead of attacking Phillips, she tried to befriend her. Antoinette realized that if she got to know Phillips, she could keep better track of Lightnin', so when she saw Phillips she approached her and they began to talk. When Phillips eventually returned to Houston in late 1966, Antoinette even asked her to go on a road trip with her to Opelousas, Louisiana. "She invited me to hear her cousins Clifton and Cleveland Chenier," Phillips says. "We drove there and she took me to her family home, a fairly large, well-maintained farm just outside Opelousas. . . . People in the Third Ward made a point of telling me that she was educated and had gone to Catholic school."[37]

When the two women were together, they didn't talk about Lightnin'. Antoinette focused on explaining aspects of Creole culture to Phillips, which, Phillips says, "was wonderful. She would tell me about the food, the language, peculiar habits of place. We didn't talk about personal matters. Half the time she was translating from Creole for me." And when they got to the club where Clifton and Cleveland were performing, Phillips was surprised by how old fashioned everything was. "A man came over and wanted to know where my father was so that he could ask permission to dance with me. 'Whoa!' I couldn't believe it. They were dancing the two-step. It wasn't at all like Texas [where they'd just say], 'Hey baby, come on over here and shake your booty.'"[38]

After traveling with Antoinette to Louisiana, Phillips says they "became wary friends," and her relationship with Lightnin' underwent a shift. While Phillips was primed to dislike Antoinette, she did eventually gain respect for her. She understood that Lightnin' loved Antoinette, and that Antoinette, in turn, cared for him in complex ways. But as Phillips pointed out, "Antoinette was cuckolding her husband . . . and part of my thing was: 'Lady, don't get all uptight about me; I wasn't going to run off with him, and it wouldn't happen if I tried because he was tied to *you*.' I was obsessed with Lightnin' and had come to Houston specifically to follow my obsession, to embody my personal Orphic fantasy, and to gather material to write the book, but *l'amour fou* does not make for enduring love, and I knew that, so, it was a strange kind of thing."[39]

Most of what Phillips knew about Lightnin's relationship with Antoinette, she learned from other people, "both down there and also from blues aficionados elsewhere. Many people told me that she saved him from probably dying an untimely death."[40]

As Phillips and Antoinette got to know each other, they started spending more time together when Lightnin' was in town. "Antoinette was reserved and demure," Phillips recalled, "but she definitely had a presence. At the Ash Grove, sometimes Antoinette and I would be in the dressing room when Lightnin' was on stage, she'd giggle and say 'Let's have a little juggalo', then she and I would conspiratorially pour drinks from his stash. *Juggalo* was her name for a drink. She never drank much, and always maintained her composure. When she began traveling with him, my romantic involvement with Lightnin' had essentially ended. I'd drive to the Ash Grove, spend the evening, and go home. I'd drive them to and from the airport, and just be a running buddy."[41]

On one occasion Lightnin' was booked to play in San Francisco and Antoinette was with him, but someone had "reserved a room for them in a filthy, reeking, crime-ridden Tenderloin hotel on Eddy Street. There was a bed with dirty sheets on it, I think; the room was littered with rotting garbage and trash. Completely appalling." Phillips says she had picked them up from the airport and was with them at the time. "When they got there, they were beside themselves with anger, bewilderment, and frustration. Antoinette was furious and disgusted, she began cursing and dumping the bags of garbage and trash out a window that opened onto one of those inner shafts or wells of the building. Then somebody threatened to call the police on *them* and have them arrested for disturbing the peace and vandalism, which put them into a complete tizzy. I don't think they even sat down on anything. Turned out the person who had booked the room for them, I can't remember who it was, said he thought they'd be 'more comfortable.' More comfortable with what: ensconced in filth and squalor, as some Neanderthal, stereotype-riddled (even highly educated, liberal) whites to this day simply assume blacks are 'comfortable' with? After contacting Chris [Strachwitz], within a very short time they were booked into a room at a clean, decent place, *not* in the Tenderloin. Profuse and profound apologies were tendered, but the outrage of such a crude and offensive assumption, you can imagine cut them deeply. I don't know how they maintained their dignity through it all, but they did."[42]

Over the years that Phillips knew Lightnin', she never saw him lose his temper, as Blacksnake Brown in *Mojo Hand* did when he slapped Eunice. "While readers have the right to *interpret* this or any scene any way they choose," Phillips says, "it is completely unwarranted to extrapolate from this, as some literalists do, that Lightnin' ever struck me, because he did not; nor did he ever threaten to, nor was he verbally abusive or otherwise aggressive or domineering. And I did not see him behaving that way toward others. True, Lightnin' had a violent past, but I was not clearly aware of that when I first became involved with him. Whatever the source of his transformation—and I think that in good part it was due to the presence of Antoinette in his life—the change, I contend, was genuine. I bogarted my way into Lightnin's life and indeed, he bore my intrusion, excesses, and inanities with amazing equanimity—far more equanimity than I could have mustered had some crazed, lovesick, fool fan fetched up on my doorstep out of the blue. But that is not to say that he'd become an angel or a pushover. By no means was this the case."[43]

When *Mojo Hand* was published in 1966, it got enthusiastic reviews. The *Charlotte Observer* wrote: "*Mojo Hand* is as sophisticated as primitive sculpture, and has the same element of magic. The characters move along invisible threads, as if under a spell. . . . The language is racy and rough, so if you're easily offended pass over *Mojo Hand*. You'll be missing an odd, startling experience."[44] The *Los Angeles Times* described Phillips as "an impressive talent," who "must surely write and write," and the *Dallas Times Herald* stated, "This book should mark the entrance of a contributing talent of superb dimensions to the American literary scene."[45] Henry Miller loved the book. He invited Phillips to meet him, and they became friends. She even appeared briefly in *The Henry Miller Odyssey*, a biographical documentary made by Robert Snyder.

There was negative criticism as well, which came from different quarters, including a particularly scathing diatribe written by the black critic Albert Murray, who called *Mojo Hand* "a fiasco from the very outset and can be dismissed and forgotten as if it never happened."[46] Murray considered the book poorly written, patently inauthentic, and perpetuating racist stereotypes. And once, when Phillips gave a lecture at a college in Los Angeles, she was almost set upon by irate members of the emergent black power movement, who accused her of writing about retrograde aspects of African American culture and music. Ironically, it was Julius Lester, author of *Look Out Whitey!: Black Power's Gon' Get Your Mama*, who in 1999 placed *Mojo Hand* on the Los Angeles Times's list of books considered as "Forgotten Treasures of the 20th Century."

To Phillips's knowledge, Lightnin' never read *Mojo Hand*, though she was fairly certain that Antoinette did. But Antoinette didn't say anything about it, and Phillips never discussed it with Lightnin'. However, Lightnin' did once mention in passing that he knew the book had been published.[47]

While *Mojo Hand* was considered by some to be a significant literary accomplishment, Phillips's backstory related to its creation is the most lucid document that exists of Lightnin's personal life in the 1960s. It also gives a strong sense of the contradictions of the man behind the myth—impetuous, selfish, brash, boisterous, witty, and loving. Phillips's memories humanize Lightnin' and provide a vivid sense of his personal life and his community, which not only bought his records, but helped to energize his music.

8

An Expanding Audience

By the mid-1960s, Lightnin's audience was growing to include rock 'n' roll fans. The folk revival was fading, while the blues scene among white audiences was gaining strength. However, the enthusiasm for bluesmen like Lightnin' among rock 'n' rollers wasn't completely new. Ringo Starr of the Beatles, for example, recalled that as a teenager in the late 1950s, he was "trying to immigrate to Houston, Texas, because Lightnin' Hopkins, the blues player, lived there," and that he was still into the blues: "Lightnin' is still my hero. . . . We just wanted to be around Lightnin'. . . . It would have been interesting if that ever happened."[1]

Lightnin's recordings with electric guitar, bass, and drums, particularly the Herald sessions, intrigued young white rockers. But it wasn't only his music that made him an icon. His lanky, mysterious appearance, his sunglasses, and the way he presented himself as a bluesman made him especially appealing. Lightnin' was never a hippie, but hippies were fascinated by him.

From September 21 to 26, 1965, Lightnin' was the headliner at the Matrix in San Francisco, which had opened about a month earlier with the Jefferson Airplane as its house band. Initially the Matrix was a folk and blues club, but it soon became synonymous with "The San Francisco Sound" in psychedelic rock music. Once again Lightnin' was in unfamiliar territory, but he was treated as a star, and apparently adapted well to an ever-changing audience. Lightnin' was invited back the next month to perform with Jean Ball and J. C. Burris, and over the next two years, he shuttled back and forth to San Francisco, appearing at the Matrix and the Fillmore, where he even appeared on October 21 and 22, 1966, with the Grateful Dead and Loading Zone. During this period, Lightnin' was greeted with anticipation wherever he performed, whether it was at the Matrix, the Fillmore, or the Berkeley Blues Festival, Sylvio's in Chicago, the Longhorn Jazz Festival in Austin, or the Ash Grove, where he was a regular, appearing with groups as diverse as the Nitty Gritty Dirt Band and the Lydia E. Pinksham Superior Orchestra.

In the mid-1960s, aspiring filmmaker Les Blank frequented the Ash Grove in Los Angeles, where he heard Lightnin' for the first time and got the idea to make a documentary about him.[2] Blank was making a living doing industrial and corporate films, and one of his clients, the Gulf States Tube Company, sent him to Texas. At the time Blank was thirty-three years old; he was originally from Tampa, Florida, where he grew up in an upper-middle-class family. He attended Tulane University, where he received a BA in English literature and an MFA in theatre. Then, in 1967, after two years in a PhD film program at the University of Southern California, he left college and began doing freelance work. In Texas, Blank met Skip Gerson, the son of a ladies shoe manufacturer who had grown up on Long Island, outside of New York City. Gerson was in his early twenties and was also trying to figure out how to become a filmmaker. Blank told him if he came to Los Angeles he would hire him as an assistant; he had finished his first short independent film on Dizzy Gillespie in 1965 and was starting a new film on the hippie love-ins in Los Angeles.[3] Gerson had been working as a "hippie clown" on a television station in Houston, but was looking for something "more meaningful" to do with his life.

"For me," Blank says, "it was the cohesion of what they called the alternative movement, or the hippies, or the love children, the flower children. There was something definitely happening in American culture that had never happened before, and I got a sense there was an important movie to be made. Well, around the time I was completing the film,[4] I was at the Ash Grove listening to Lightnin' and Skip told me, 'If you want to do a film on Lightnin' Hopkins,

I think I could get some money from my dad.' And that's exactly what he did, and his father came through with five thousand dollars in 1967. It was a lot of money."[5]

To get started, Blank and Gerson got in touch with John Lomax Jr., whom they had heard was the "only white man" Lightnin' trusted, and Blank sent him his short film on Dizzy Gillespie that he had finished in 1965 as a kind of sample of what he wanted to do. Lomax was impressed and agreed to help. He then arranged for Blank and Gerson to meet Lightnin'. "We approached Lightnin'," Blank says, "with a 16mm projector in hand and a copy of the Gillespie film and we asked him if we could do a film on him and he said, 'Uh . . .' And we said, 'We could show you some stuff I had done in the past, to give you an idea what I can do with musicians and film.' So we showed the film on the wall of his dressing room at the Ash Grove in between sets. And he thought it was pretty interesting. And he said, 'How much money you boys got for Po' Lightnin'?' And we told him we had five thousand dollars. And he replied, 'That'll do.' Well, we said, 'That's all we have, and we need some of that for film stock and food and we got to get to Texas.' So we knocked some figures around and he agreed to accepting about a third of it, or fifteen hundred dollars, and we offered him five hundred dollars in advance and then promised to give him another five hundred dollars half way through and then another five hundred dollars when we were all wrapped up. And he agreed, and John Lomax Jr. suggested that we give him the money in dollar bills, which sounds kind of weird now, but it looks like a lot of money when you see 500 one-dollar bills all stacked up together."[6]

To make the film on Lightnin', Blank borrowed a 16mm Éclair NPR camera, a tripod, and a Nagra II recorder and headed off to Houston. But the first day of filming was not very successful. "The very first day we showed up we were very eager to film," Blank says, "and he was friendly and we hung around at his feet and tried to film everything he did. He had an apartment. I think there was a Naugahyde [vinyl] couch, a big chair, and then there was a little dining area beyond that. Somewhere there was a bedroom. I wouldn't say he was that well off, but it wasn't a slum, that's for sure. It was a decent place. And a woman was there named Antoinette, whom he referred to as his wife. Antoinette was quiet and pretty and kind and generous. And we got some stuff with Lightnin' sitting on the front porch overlooking the street. We tried to get him to sing some songs, but there was a telephone going in the background. This was 16mm so the film would only run for eleven minutes at a time. We'd run out of film and have to change the magazine. And it was pretty rough going, and we were all drinking with him because that's what he wanted. And we weren't very good at what we were doing, trying to get synchronous sound recordings."[7]

Lightnin' didn't fully understand the filmmaking process, and at the end of the day, he thought he was done. "He announced to us that he had recorded ten songs that day," Blank says, "and when he did an LP album, ten songs was all he ever did, and he wanted us to pay him the rest of the money we owed him and clear out and not come back. And we tried to plead with him to get him to change his mind, and he wouldn't hear of it. And so, as we were packing up, we were very depressed because we had fucked up all day long trying to get this equipment to perform for us. He had played in a little club and we tried to film him there, and we had sound problems. We got lots of songs he performed all the way through, and we tried to film them but we couldn't. We didn't get any of them in their entirety. We just got snatches here and there. He felt he'd done his ten songs and he definitely felt he'd had enough of us for impeding his normal enjoyment of his life."[8]

Just as they were leaving, Blank noticed that Lightnin' was dealing cards and gambling, and for lack of anything else to say, Blank asked him what game he was playing. "Lightnin' said, 'It's called Pitty Pat . . .You want to learn how to play it?' And I said, 'Yeah.' Anything to stay around there. I learned the rules. . . . It's like playing Go Fish, trying to figure out what's in the other person's hand. You need to fill a pair. It's called Pitty Pat or Pitty Pair. It's a pity if you don't have a pair. So I had like forty dollars in my wallet and he won all forty of my dollars and I got upset. I was losing all the money we had tied up in the film, and my whole future was down the drain. I didn't have money to buy breakfast in the morning. And he found it amusing. He chuckled and said, 'If you can find some more money and come back tomorrow and I'll play you some more.' So I borrowed some money and came back the next day, and he played me again, and this time I was sober and looking very carefully to see how he could be cheating me. . . . I checked the cards to see if they were marked. But he knew what I had and took all my money. This time I got really upset and he got really delighted. And said, 'Well, maybe you guys aren't so bad after all.' But he was sober by now,

The house where Lightnin' Hopkins' stayed when visiting his mother in the early 1950s, Centerville, Texas.
PHOTOGRAPH BY ALAN GOVENAR

Leon County Courthouse, Centerville, Texas, 2008.
PHOTOGRAPH BY ALAN GOVENAR

Warren's Bottom, Leon County, Texas, 2008.
PHOTOGRAPH BY ALAN GOVENAR

The house where Lightnin' Hopkins lived in the 1930s, Leon County, Texas, 2008. PHOTOGRAPH BY ALAN GOVENAR

Bill Quinn, Houston, Texas, ca. 1960. © CHRIS STRACHWITZ

Lightnin' Hopkins's Gold Star promotional
photograph, 1948. COURTESY OF ARHOOLIE RECORDS

Ray Dawkins, Centerville, Texas, 2008. PHOTOGRAPH BY ALAN GOVENAR

Lorine Washington, Centerville, Texas, 2008.

PHOTOGRAPH BY ALAN GOVENAR

Lightnin's daughter Anna Mae Box, Crockett, Texas, 2002.

PHOTOGRAPH BY ALAN GOVENAR

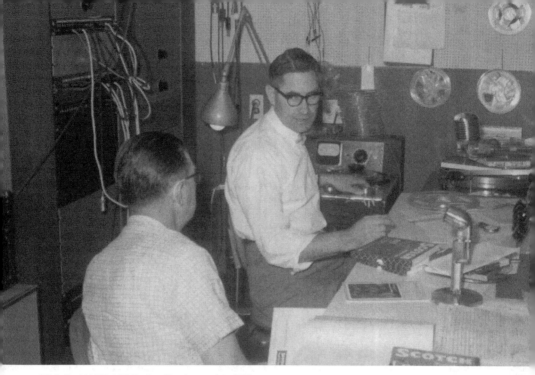

Bill Holford (right), ACA Studios, Houston, ca. late 1950s. COURTESY OF RICH PATZ/ANDREW BROWN

Lightnin' Hopkins at the Sputnik Bar, Houston, Texas, 1961. © CHRIS STRACHWITZ

Lightnin' Hopkins, Houston, Texas, 1959. COURTESY OF THE ESTATE OF ANDREW A. HANSON

Texian Boys members (L–R) Ed Badeaux, John A. Lomax Jr., and Howard Porper jamming at the Houston Folklore Society. PHOTOGRAPH BY MARGARET LOMAX, CA. MID-1950S. COURTESY OF JOHN LOMAX III

Lightnin' Hopkins, Houston, Texas, 1959. COURTESY OF THE ESTATE OF ANDREW A. HANSON

clockwise from top: Long Gone Miles, LC Williams, Spider Kilpatrick, and Lightnin' Hopkins, Houston, Texas, 1960; Paul Oliver interviewing Lightnin' Hopkins, Houston, Texas, 1960; An unidentified friend, Long Gone Miles, Lightnin' Hopkins, and Chris Strachwitz, Houston, Texas, 1960. © CHRIS STRACHWITZ

(left) Lightnin' Hopkins at Sierra
Sound, Berkeley, California.
PHOTOGRAPH BY WILLIAM CARTER, 1961. COURTESY OF
ARHOOLIE RECORDS

(below) Lightnin' Hopkins and
Barbara Dane, Berkeley, California.
PHOTOGRAPH BY WILLIAM CARTER, 1961. COURTESY OF
ARHOOLIE RECORDS

Lightnin' Hopkins and Long Gone Miles, Houston, Texas, 1960. © CHRIS STRACHWITZ

Dietrich Wawzyn and his wife, Anna Marie, filming in the Third Ward, Houston, Texas, 1963. © CHRIS STRACHWITZ

Joel, Lightnin', and John Henry Hopkins with their mother, Frances Hopkins, Waxahachie, Texas, 1964. © CHRIS STRACHWITZ

Joel, Lightnin', and John Henry Hopkins, Waxahachie, Texas. © CHRIS STRACHWITZ

Lightnin' Hopkins, Berkeley, California, ca. mid-1960s. © CHRIS STRACHWITZ

Lightnin' Hopkins and Antoinette Charles, Berkeley, California, ca. mid-1960s. © CHRIS STRACHWITZ

FAIRFIELD HALL, CROYDON

General Manager: T. J. Pyper, M.I.M.E.H.

MONDAY 19th OCTOBER

at 6.45 p.m. and 9.00 p.m.

"A DOCUMENTARY OF THE AUTHENTIC BLUES"

THE NATIONAL JAZZ FEDERATION

in association with HORST LIPPMANN presents the THIRD

AMERICAN NEGRO BLUES FESTIVAL

LIGHTNING HOPKINS	★	HOWLING WOLF
SLEEPY JOHN ESTES	★	HUBERT SUMLIN
JOHN HENRY BARBEE	★	HAMMIE NIXON
SUGAR PIE DESANTO	★	CLIFTON JAMES
SUNNYLAND SLIM	★	WILLIE DIXON

SONNY BOY WILLIAMSON

TICKETS : 6/- 8/- 10/6 12/6 15/- 17/6 21/-

Available from FAIRFIELD HALL BOX OFFICE (CRO. 9291); NATIONAL JAZZ FEDERATION
MARQUEE, 90 Wardour Street, London, W.1 (GER. 8923) and usual Agents

clockwise from top left: American Negro Blues Festival poster, Fairfield Hall, Croydon, England, October 19, 1964.
COURTESY OF DOCUMENTARY ARTS; Lightnin' Hopkins, Munich, Germany. PHOTOGRAPH BY STEPHANIE WIESAND, 1964. COURTESY OF ARHOOLIE
RECORDS; Stephanie Wiesand, Lightnin' Hopkins, and Evelyn Parth, Munich, Germany, 1964. © CHRIS STRACHWITZ

(above) Lightnin' Hopkins at the Newport Folk Festival, 1965. © CHRIS STRACHWITZ

(right) Les Blank during the production of
Blues According to Lightnin' Hopkins, 1967.
PHOTOGRAPH BY SKIP GERSON, COURTESY OF LES BLANK.

J. J. Phillips (left) in her dormitory at Immaculate Heart College, Los Angeles, California, 1962. COURTESY OF J. J. PHILLIPS

J. J. Phillips, El Cerrito, California, 2009. PHOTOGRAPH BY ALAN GOVENAR

Lightnin' Hopkins, Navasota, Texas, 1967. © LES BLANK

Lightnin' Hopkins, Houston, Texas, 1967. © LES BLANK

Lightnin' Hopkins, Houston, Texas, 1964. © CHRIS STRACHWITZ, 1964

Billy Bizor and Lightnin' Hopkins in front
of ACA Studios, Houston, Texas, 1968.
COURTESY OF ANDREW BROWN

(L–R) Townes Van Zandt, Margaret Lomax, Antoinette Charles, and Lightnin' Hopkins in the Lomax family backyard, Houston, Texas, ca. 1968.

John Lomax Jr. and Lightnin' Hopkins, Houston, Texas, 1968.

Poster for the Lightnin' Hopkins appearances at Fillmore Auditorium, San Francisco, California, October 21–22, 1966. COURTESY OF ALAN GOVENAR

Berkeley Blues Festival poster, April 15, 1966.
COURTESY OF CHRIS STRACHWITZ

Boogie n' Blues poster, Carnegie Hall, April 10, 1979.
COURTESY OF ANTON J. MIKOFSKY

Lightnin' Hopkins at the New Orleans Jazz and Heritage Festival, 1974. © MICHAEL P. SMITH

Cleveland Chenier (above) and Clifton Chenier (below) with Lightnin' Hopkins at the New Orleans Jazz and Heritage Festival, 1974. © CHRIS STRACHWITZ

Lightnin' Hopkins, Houston, Texas, 1972. © BENNY JOSEPH

Lightnin' Hopkins and Antoinette Charles (seated), Gothenburg, Sweden, 1977. © PHOTOGRAPH BY ERIK LINDAHL

Lightnin' Hopkins, Rotterdam, The Netherlands, 1977. COURTESY OF HANS KRAMER

Lightnin' Hopkins memorial by Jim Jeffries, Crockett, Texas, 2007. PHOTOGRAPH BY ALAN GOVENAR

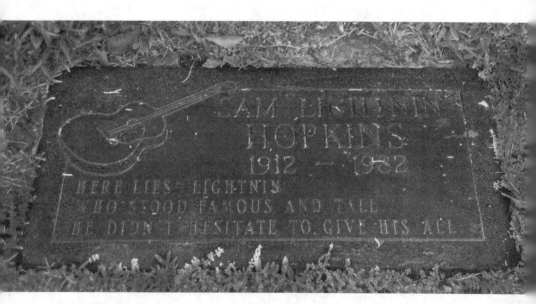

Lightnin' Hopkins grave marker, Forest Park Cemetery, Houston, Texas, 2007. PHOTOGRAPH BY ALAN GOVENAR

too, and more rested, and said, 'You can get your camera out now if you want.' So we did some shooting and this time we were very careful about pushing him. If we saw him getting tired or irritated, just the slightest sign of this, we'd excuse ourselves and disappear for a day or two, and then drop by, and see how he was feeling, and if he was in a good mood, we'd get the camera out and shoot. If he was in a bad mood, we just keep on going."[9]

Blank and Gerson spent six weeks shooting the documentary during the spring of 1967. He lived on the floor of a hippie crash pad in Houston, but the filming proceeded very slowly. The shooting ratio was six or eight to one, and it just took a long time to get the footage they needed. During the making of the film, Blank says he "was amazed by Lightnin'. He had kind of an otherworldly quality about him. He was a shaman of some sort. He could know what people were thinking. He could read into the way people walked, or just their body language. He could talk on about this person or that person and make up stories about their lives."[10]

Blank recalls how Lightnin' told so many stories during the filming that not all of them could be recorded. For example, when Lightnin' showed his ankle scars and talked about the chain gang, he or "someone close to him" explained that he had been put in jail because "he had an affair with a white woman," but there are no other interviews that confirm this as ever actually having occurred. In another story he told Blank, he said that he had once been a "cop," as evidenced by the long aerial in the back of his car that was pulled over and tied down from the front. "It's a long aerial," Blank remembers Lightnin' telling him, "that the cops used to use in the days of radio communication. You had to have a tall aerial like that to receive such a signal. He had such a radio and he liked to keep the antenna on his car to remind people and him that he used to be a cop."[11]

Whether or not all of Lightnin's stories were true was in a sense irrelevant, Blank says. "He had a take on life and things that was always enchanting, the way he saw the world. Like a pure poet, he was constantly being fed sensations and stimulations from the world around him that he poured through his sensitivity and it came out creative." But Lightnin' was impatient and impulsive: "There's a lot of times when he used to get angry, especially when he was hitting the bottle too much. He drank constantly and started first thing in the morning. . . . He always had his little half-pint in his back pocket. And when he could get pretty mean, irascible, he would feel like he was being taken advantage of."[12] This was especially apparent at the end of the film where he looked disheveled. Apparently Antoinette's cousin had been staying with them in their apartment and had forgotten to lock the door when he left. When Lightnin' got home, he was furious; he had some valuable guitars in the apartment, which could have been stolen. He cussed out the cousin, and the cousin took offense, and they "had some words and Lightnin' threatened to shoot him, and the cousin packed a loaded gun and threatened to shoot Lightnin'." And when Blank showed up to film Lightnin' that night, he told him the story and said that "his wife Antoinette had gotten so mad at him for badmouthing her cousin that she went home to her mother. And that's the occasion at the end of the film where his hair's messed up, singing a song . . . the closing song for the film. It was that night, and he was drunk and angry. . . . Lightnin' had a long 38 revolver tucked in the front of his pants the whole time he's singing that song, it's stuck inside his belt."

Months later, however, Blank had a rough-cut of the film and wanted to show it to Lightnin' to see how he responded. "And he liked everything," Blank said, "but the scene that I described before where he was improvising a song on film right before our eyes. . . . He had his hair messed up. And when I finished showing him the film, he said that I had to take out that scene because his hair was messed up. He didn't like the way he looked. And I tried to tell him that it was an important scene, maybe one of the best scenes in the whole film, and he said he wanted it out. I had to struggle with his wishes and with my gut feeling that this song needed to be in the film. And then finally, I decided to go with it and finish the film with the scene with his hair messed up. And when I finally showed him [the completed documentary] I dreaded to see his reaction to the film with that scene still in there. And I showed it to him, and when it got to the part with Billy Bizor, who has a scene early in the film where he plays on the harmonica and sings and cries into a pillow, Lightnin' got very moved, said, 'Oh, there's Billy,' because Billy had died since the filming . . . and he was so happy to see Billy Bizor alive on the screen that he totally overlooked the scene at the end with his hair messed up."[13]

The Blues According to Lightnin' Hopkins is not a documentary in a conventional sense, and as such it has been both praised and criticized. The viewer learns few specifics, but instead is left with an impression of Lightnin' as a rural blues singer, when in fact he had been living in Houston for more than twenty years. The film opens with a shot of farmland and cows before the camera shifts to Lightnin', blues singer Mance Lipscomb, and harmonica player Billy Bizor, playing together on a dirt road. The scene is intercut with shots of chickens and a rooster, and there is little sense of the urban world of Houston and the Third Ward neighborhood where Lightnin' lived and worked. Most of the film was shot in Centerville and is structured as a kind of homecoming, where Lightnin' jokes around with people in town, rambles on about his life and music, and wanders off by himself to an empty, weather-beaten church in the middle of a field. The only recognizable Houston scenes, aside from his apartment, are some of the facades of small businesses, from the office of the NAACP in the Third Ward to Wesley & West Beauty Salon and Leroy's Tavern in the Fifth Ward and a rodeo at the Diamond L Ranch on South Main Street on the outskirts of the city. But there is no indication of the relationship of these places to the freeways that divide the black neighborhoods from the skyscrapers downtown.

The English blues writer Mike Leadbitter happened to be in Houston at the time of the filming and wrote vividly about his impressions. He appeared for a second in the film, sitting behind Lightnin' at the rodeo, and recalled: "We pulled in to the rodeo, which was an exclusively Negro affair, and were pleased to see the imposing figure of John Lomax Jr., standing by the arena. Clutching beer cans we climbed up to the very familiar sight of Lightnin' sitting behind dark glasses high in the stands. After much hand shaking and cries of recognition, we sat to watch the show and talk. I was introduced to Skipper and Les, the Flower Films men, who were busy shooting the rodeo and Lightnin' from every conceivable position. . . . To a lad from Sussex, the whole scene was almost too fascinating to keep up with. I have a vivid recollection of a thrown rider lying in a wheelbarrow with a broken ankle, a game of Georgia Skin behind the toilets, endless cans of beer being passed around and the steady stream of jive between Lightnin' and just about everyone."[14]

Particularly striking in *The Blues According to Lightnin' Hopkins* is the cinematography and the roving camera that provides a visual bed for Lightnin's stories and excerpts from his songs that are performed by him, accompanied by Bizor, and in one scene by rub board player Cleveland Chenier. The blues is rough and headstrong, and some of the most powerful moments are intercut with wild harmonica solos by Billy Bizor, who, at one point, breaks down and falls to his knees. As Roger Greenspun pointed out in his review of the film in the *New York Times*, "Hopkins himself controls the film's moods. Not so much in his exposition of the meaning of the blues as in what he makes of them when he sings and plays his guitar. In this he is very fine—with wit, virtuosity, and the immersion in his medium that is a music maker's true exemplary magic."[15] While *The Blues According to Lightnin' Hopkins* is in the end a romanticized portrait, it is at once poetic and poignant, which is remarkable, given the experience Blank and Gerson had with Lightnin' in the making of the film.

Soon after Blank and Gerson completed production of the film, the *Houston Chronicle* published the longest article about Lightnin' to run in a local paper in his lifetime. Titled "The Day Lightnin' Hopkins Went Home" and featured as the cover story of the *Chronicle* Sunday magazine on July 30, 1967, writer Jeff Millar, after recounting an overview of Lightnin's career, commented: "An astounding number of people in Houston, Hopkins' adopted city, haven't the slightest idea who he is or why we're devoting a considerable amount of energy to telling you about him. It's one of the quiet ironies of Hopkins' life that he's uncelebrated, except by a few, in his hometown [Houston] and rather a famous person in areas of the West Coast and in New York City. His celebrity is such that a team of California filmmakers, Les Blank and Skip Gerson, followed him around for a couple of weeks during the spring." While Millar pointed out the irony of Lightnin's "uncelebrated" life in Houston, Leadbitter had a completely different perception and wrote that in the Third Ward, Lightnin' "called himself 'The King of Dowling Street' and got away with it."[16]

In 1969, Blank finished a short sequel to *The Blues According to Lightnin' Hopkins* titled *The Sun's Gonna Shine*, which combines some of the same footage with new material, featuring the young Wendell Anderson to recreate Lightnin's decision at age eight to stop chopping cotton and start singing for a living. Years later, Blank also edited together his outtakes into a short piece, in which Lightnin' sings a version of "Mr. Charlie, Your Rollin' Mill is Burnin' Down."

The difficulties that Blank and Gerson encountered struggling to film Lightnin' were in part a result of the fact that in the mid-1960s his career was going full tilt. Lightnin' could pick and choose what he wanted to do. When it came to recording and performing outside the Third Ward, he would only work if the money was right, and once he showed up, he was usually demanding. If there was a technical problem, or he rambled on too long during his performance, or he rerecorded one of his old songs, it didn't matter to him, but it did apparently impact the labels that had been producing his albums.

In 1966 it does not appear that Lightnin' was recorded at all, aside from the live recordings that Chris Strachwitz made with him at the Second Annual Berkeley Blues Festival on April 15. He didn't have another session until December 18, 1967, and when Strachwitz recorded him at his apartment in Houston, he was completely engaged: "Lightnin' didn't want to go to a studio, and he asked me to bring my stuff to his place. By that time, I had a two-channel Magnacord tape recorder and two mikes, one for his voice and one on the guitar amp. I made some suggestions, especially about 'Bud Russell Blues.' I had a copy of Lowell Fulson's recording of 'Penitentiary Blues,' but I wanted Lightnin' to do something like that. I also wanted him to do 'Tom Moore' because I had heard all of these different versions of it with lots of verses, by him on Gold Star and by Mance Lipscomb and Marcellus Thomas, who had been Big Joe Williams's chauffeur back in 1960. 'Tom Moore' was the last song. He was getting ready to quit. But overall, there were no hassles during the sessions. He was at home and had no audience to act for."[17]

After the session was completed, Strachwitz took him outside and photographed him in front of Johnnie Lee's grocery store. Overall, the session was a great success and produced some of Lightnin's finest recordings on Arhoolie, including the haunting "Slavery," which was his ultimate statement on race in America and was never recorded again. In "Slavery," Hopkins attacked the deference forced upon African Americans:

> Thousands years my people was a slave
> When I was born they teach me this way
> One thousand years my people was a slave
> When I was born they teach me this a way
> Tip your hat to the peoples, be careful about what you say

As Lightnin' sang, the counterpoint between the guitar and lyrics intensified:

> I'm gonna get me a shotgun
> And I won't be a slave no more

"Slavery" may be Lightnin's most powerful song in that it expressed the frustration and anger that he and his generation of African Americans must have felt, given the conditions of racism and discrimination they were subjected to. In addition to "Slavery," Lightnin's new versions of "Tim Moore's Farm" (called on this LP "Tom Moore Blues") and "Penitentiary Blues" (titled here "Bud Russell Blues") had a freshness that underscored their strength.

"Bud Russell Blues" was a talking blues about a legendary lawman who worked as a transfer agent for the Texas prison system for thirty-nine years, beginning in 1905, and was known for his roughness and cruelty. When Russell retired in 1944, the *Dallas Morning News* reported that he had delivered 115,000 persons to prisons around the state and had handled many noted Texas criminals, including Clyde and Buck Barrow and Raymond Hamilton: "He told tough guys, 'You're just forty years too late if you think you're tougher than I am.'"[18]

In "Bud Russell Blues" Lightnin's voice was filled with the disdain of a convict sentenced to a prison farm in 1910. "Sure is hot out here," he began, punctuating his words with a piercing guitar run, "Bud Russell don't care. . . . You know, Bud Russell drove them pretty women just like he did them ugly men." And in the end, he pleaded, "Please take care of my wife and child, I may not turn back to my home life," warning, "You know, the next time the boss man hits me I'm gonna give him a big surprise, And I ain't jokin' neither."

In contrast to the harshness of "Bud Russell Blues," "Little Antoinette" was more sentimental as Lightnin' expressed his deep affection for the woman he loved, but it was also tainted with a sense of remorse once she was gone from his bed.

> You know, I looks over on the pillow where Little Antoinette used to lay
> Felt on my pillow, yes pillow felt warm (x 2)
> You know, you could tell by that dear friend
> Poor Antoinette hadn't been very long gone
> She used to cook my breakfast, fix my table like it should [19]

Carroll Peery, who had worked at the Cabale in Berkeley, recalls that when Lightnin' stayed with him, he'd talk about his wife Antoinette, but then bring "dates" back to his apartment: "Lightnin' liked his women, but he was cool. He never acted like low life. His style was if he met somebody, white or black, and he was attracted to her, he'd get to know her well before he'd bring her home. He was very careful; on one hand he totally understood white society, but on the other hand he was scared to death of it, especially when he was by himself. Antoinette didn't travel much with him, but one time she showed up when he wasn't expecting her. This was in 1967, after I had left the Cabale. I had arranged for him to perform at the Forum on Telegraph Avenue and the place was big and full of hippies and students who really liked folk and blues. So the darndest thing happened. He was on stage performing, and Antoinette walked through the door. Never gave him any warning. She wanted to catch him, and afterwards, they had a big flap about that, but when I saw it, I knew I better get a certain person [with whom Lightnin' was having a little fling] out of there. Antoinette and Lightnin' were shouting. But he didn't shout very much. She was doing most of the shouting. And he was criticizing her for showing up. Usually Antoinette was very careful with what she said and did. But there was a lot of fire in that woman."[20]

At some point in 1968, Dr. Cecil Harold, an African American surgeon in Houston (who retired in 1994), started to act as Lightnin's manager. Harold, who was considerably younger than Lightnin', said he started to work with Hopkins because Lightnin' needed help. Having listened to his music for years, Harold wanted to meet Hopkins, and in 1967, he saw that Lightnin' was playing at the Jewish Community Center and went to see him. The two men met and talked and struck up a friendship.[21] About a year later, Lightnin' told Harold that he was getting ripped off by the people who were booking and recording him and that he needed help in keeping up with his scheduled dates. "He never was completely sure where he was supposed to play," Harold said. "He'd tell someone he was to play at this place Saturday, and then he might tell someone else the same thing. I just organized things for him, took his calls and made sure he got a fair deal. I never got any money out of it. I did it because I loved his music and him."[22] The extent to which Harold was involved with Lightnin's bookings is unclear. As many have observed, Lightnin' was his own man, and as he became more well known, he was able to do essentially whatever he wanted and get paid. Still he often needed help in getting what was promised to him, and Harold was invaluable in his role as a buffer and manager of his business affairs.

During the first four months of 1968, Lightnin' had five sessions in rapid succession, but none compared to the intensity and focus of his *Texas Blues Man* album on Arhoolie. On January 3 and 4, Lightnin' recorded one of the strangest albums of his career that was given the pretentiously psychedelic title *Free Form Patterns* for the local International Artists label at the old Gold Star studios in Houston. For the session Lightnin' was accompanied by his longtime friend, Billy Bizor, on harmonica, as well as by Duke Davis on bass and Danny Thomas on drums, who were both members of the psychedelic rock band The 13th Floor Elevators. Overall, the recordings were raggedy and mixed badly: "Fox Chase" had a pop country beat with Billy Bizor on harmonica and vocals performing a sloppy version of a traditional tune; "Give Me Time to Think" had a fuller R & B sound; "Mr. Charlie" rehashed old material and rambled on. "Mini Skirt" was a humorous commentary on 1960s fashion, but the mixing muddies the song; when the piano comes in, it drowns out all the other instruments.

Mansel Rubinstein, who had the pawnshop in the Third Ward that Lightnin' frequented, proposed the idea for an LP to Lelan Rogers, who was the chief A&R man at International Artists.[23] "Lelan and I would see each other at different places around town," Rubenstein says, "and one conversation led to another. So Lelan came by to see me one day, and I told Lightnin' about it and he said okay so long as he was paid his one hundred dollars a song in cash."[24] Davis and Thomas were already quite familiar with Lightnin' and were excited by the idea. "We were thrilled," Davis recalled, and after Rogers presented the terms to Noble Ginther, one of the owners of International Artists, the session was planned.

The stories surrounding the session are legendary but muddled, and much of what's been published or told about the session is false: from Johnny Winter sitting in and Paul McCartney and John Lennon calling and asking if they could come to the studio to Lightnin' being paid one thousand dollars a song. Lightnin' was never interviewed about what actually transpired, but during the session, Davis and Thomas were doing psychedelic drugs, and by all accounts, Lightnin' was drinking heavily.

John David Bartlett, who had been signed by International Artists right out of high school, says he picked Lightnin' up at his apartment on Gray Street in the Third Ward to take him to the session. "Noble Ginther asked me," Bartlett says, "and I told him sure, 'Absolutely wonderful, I'd love to do it.' He gave me an address and I went over there to the Third Ward . . . with a bottle of whiskey that he handed me to take to Lightnin'. . . . And I knocked on the door and went into the house . . . it was a very tense, very weird atmosphere. It felt like I was definitely not the most welcome human in the world. Lightnin' was in the kitchen, and he was trying to decide whether or not he wanted to go or not, and finally I talked him into going along."[25]

Thomas, however, said he went with Lightnin' to pick up Billy Bizor "in the ghetto from a one-room apartment with a cot and basin hanging off the wall. And there were lots of people [at the studio], many of whom were musicians, and the scene was at times chaotic. Danny and I were the rhythm section on all the tracks on *Free Form Patterns*. The other players were Billy Bizor on harmonica and Elmo [Elmore Nixon] on piano. Lelan was there for most of the session and Fred Carroll engineered. Lelan was in his usual state and most interestingly, Danny and I both were on psychedelics of some sort, but Lightnin' made a comment, 'I don't have nothin' against playin' with white boys but we're gonna drink first!' Whereupon he pulled out some homemade 'shine' and we passed the bottle. Interesting mix with drugs, to say the least. Fred would put a roll of tape on and we'd just play. Lightnin' would say, 'Here's one that goes like this' and just kick it off. No explanation of key or arrangement, just play the blues. It was mostly 16-bar blues but occasionally it would be 15-bar, or 17-bar and no one would know it was comin'. That was just the way Lightnin' did it. Lightnin' wouldn't say, 'Here's what happens here,' or anything like that, he'd just say, 'Well, here's one that goes like this' and kick off another song instead of trying to explain the previous debacle. Fred actually left the control booth periodically since there wasn't much engineering to do. He'd come in now and then and just throw on a clean roll of tape and we'd keep pickin'."[26]

Despite the unevenness of the recordings, Lightnin' liked Thomas and Davis and asked them to accompany him on other gigs over the next two months, when they weren't touring with the Elevators. "Lightnin' used Duke and me for live performances," Thomas said, "at Love Street Light Circus in Houston and at Vulcan Gas Co. in Austin.[27] I spent about the next two months as his drummer for live shows because the Elevators were doing studio work and weren't doing live gigs. There was a soup kitchen/cafe in the Montrose/Westheimer area where we all used to hang out for good soul food and jam sessions at night called Cleveland's. Lightnin' would bring his wife [Antoinette]. They were stylishly dressed and Lightnin' was always a gentleman."[28] Lightnin' even appeared in a show with the 13th Floor Elevators at Rice University on March 7, 1968.

For Bartlett, Lightnin' was a major influence. "He even taught me songs," Bartlett says. "I was particularly drawn to the song 'Mr. Charlie.' He showed me an E minor thing that he did, and I played 'Mr. Charlie' for him, and he said, 'You played that pretty good, and you have my permission to sing that song.' And I made it part of my repertory."[29]

Within weeks after Lightnin' recorded for International Artists, Stan Lewis decided to bring him back into the studio for his Jewel label. He made the necessary arrangements with Lightnin' and sent Don Logan, who had previously worked as a deejay on KEEL-AM, a top forty station in Shreveport, to produce the LP in Houston at Bill Holford's studio on January 17, 1968. Logan had started work that year as vice president of Lewis's recording company, which by then included three different labels: Jewel Records, Paula Records, and Ronn Records.

"Stan set the session [with Lightnin'] up," Logan says, "As far as I know, Lightnin' did not have a phone number that he gave out to anybody to where they could just call him. As far as I know, there was just a pay phone number that Stan would call. . . . Lightnin' liked to handle his own business." But when Logan got to Houston, finding Lightnin' was more complicated than he anticipated. "It was one of the largest ghettos that I had ever seen," Logan recalls, "and I'd been to Washington and Detroit. . . . I flew down to Houston by myself and got a rental car. And then a guy named Wild Child Butler, he was a blues singer and harp player who had recorded for Jewel, he was one of our artists; he helped me locate Lightnin'. I spent two days looking and finally we saw him in his Chrysler with his big whip CB antenna on the back, waved at him. Wild Child and I had been to every dive in the ghetto there. 'Hey have you seen Lightnin'?' Finally Wild Child went into a grocery store and asked if anyone had seen Lightnin' around . . . and the people there knew him."[30]

For the session, Lightnin' put together a small band with Butler on harmonica, Elmore Nixon on piano, and two other sidemen on bass and drums, whose names were not written down. However, once the session was underway, Logan realized that the drummer was a problem. "He would slow up and get fast, and then slow down and get fast. And I said, 'Well, Lightnin' this is never going to see the light of day, and I got money in my pocket and I'm not going to give it to you if we don't get a good cut on these things.' And I told him the drummer would have to go."[31]

Finally Lightnin' gave in; he dismissed the drummer who was there and called another one. While they waited for him to arrive, Holford said, "You know, I'm going to have to charge you for the time while we're waitin' for the drummer to get here." So Logan tried to get Lightnin' to record a song he had written, but he wouldn't do that and Logan decided to record an interview with him. The interview has never been released and, according to Lewis, it's "buried away" in an off-site storage facility he rented. In the interview, Lightnin' rambled on about playing at Carnegie Hall years before and retold the stories he'd been telling interviewers for years. "He even talked about playing for the Queen [of England]," Logan says, unaware that this was yet another "myth" that Lightnin' sought to perpetuate. Interestingly enough, he had told the same story to Lelan Rogers during the International Artists session, and it appeared on the back cover notes of *Free Form Patterns*.

When the new drummer arrived, the session proceeded quickly; Lightnin' recorded eleven songs and was finished in about four hours. Overall, however, the recordings were rough; the band was unrehearsed, and the recordings rehashed old material. The stand-out on this LP is "Vietnam War," which he had never recorded before and had an ominous, though enigmatic, tone.

> Mama says, "Son, how can you be happy
> When your brother's way over in Viet Nam?"
> I told her, "He may get lucky and win some money
> Before he die, he may bring some money home"

Logan was relieved to finish the session, though he realized he might need to do some overdubbing before the LP was released. But when he prepared to leave the studio, he saw the drummer who had been fired waiting near the door. "We were standing shoulder to shoulder, and Lightnin' stepped in between us . . . and Wild Child said later, 'Man, you almost bought the farm there because the guy had a knife.' I never saw a knife . . . but Lightnin' soothed him over."[32]

In addition to the problems getting the drummer right, Logan also had difficulty getting Lightnin' to sign a contract. "I had publishing contracts and recording contracts for Lightnin' to sign," Logan remembers, "and I said, 'Look, man, I got the money, but I'm not going to give it to you unless you're going to sign this contract.' So what he did, he gave me the contract and he signed it with an X. Well I knew what to do when somebody signed it with an X, I had my witnesses sign and say that's his signature." But then Logan noticed that he carried a notebook around with him. "He had a list of songs written down, and in there he told me was every song that he had ever recorded since he first started recording. And who he recorded it for. And he had everything that he had recorded for us."[33] While Lightnin' may have written down his songs in the notebook he was carrying, it seems likely that someone else, perhaps Antoinette or Harold, had helped him. He certainly was able to sign his name if he wanted to, as evidenced by other documents that exist from years earlier. By signing with an X he was simply expressing his refusal to abide by any contracts presented to him.

After Lightnin's session with Logan, he spent much of his time during 1968 in Houston, though he did play at the Vulcan Gas Company in Austin on February 23 and 24, and in Los Angeles at the Ash Grove on April 4 and July 24–28. He was also invited to participate in the Smithsonian Institution's Second Annual Festival of American Folklife, held on the Mall from July 3 to July 7, and for which Mack McCormick was hired as fieldworker and was likely the main coordinator of Texas talent. By this time, Lightnin' had little, if anything, to do with McCormick, though McCormick was responsible for Lightnin's booking at the Festival. Lightnin' appeared on a program on Sunday night, July 7, that also showcased two of McCormick's other main discoveries, Mance Lipscomb and barrelhouse pianist Robert Shaw, in addition to the Baca Orchestra, a group of Czech-Americans from Fayetteville, Texas.[34]

The scope of Lightnin's touring expanded in 1969. The Dallas Museum of Fine Arts presented him in a program with John Lomax Jr. on March 7 and 8, and in May he traveled to California, where he recorded an album for the

Vault label in Los Angeles that was produced by Bruce Bromberg. At the time, Bromberg was working in sales for California Record Distributors, a company that was owned by Ralph Kaffel and Jack Lewerke, who also started Vault as their own independent label.

Bromberg had seen Lightnin' at the Ash Grove, and finally met him through Long Gone Miles, who most people considered his protégé. According to Ed Pearl, "Luke 'Long Gone' Miles [a young black singer] appeared on Lightnin's doorstep in Houston a long while back, and Lightnin' wanted to close the door. And Luke proceeded to just go to sleep on his doorstep. . . . He was a real country guy. So Lightnin' took a fancy to him and let him hang around and he was a good singer, and Lightnin' sometimes let him perform with him on stage. And when Lightnin' came to L.A. by himself, he often stayed at Long Gone's house."[35]

Bromberg got to know Long Gone because he admired his singing and wanted him to join his own band. "One time," Bromberg said, "me and my friend Walker were rehearsing at Long Gone's house and Lightnin' was there. That was kind of scary. Mostly he was sleeping. He was sleeping on a couch. He had his hat over his eyes and we were clunking along there. We played every song in the same key, E. And he raised his head up and just said in his great voice, 'Your E string is a little out of tune there.' And put his hat back on and went back to sleep."[36]

For the Vault LP, "Lightnin' recorded live [with his Gibson guitar and electric pickup], no overdubs. He sang and he played what he wanted, but I had some songs that I really liked by him. I'd say you know that one . . . you got one sorta like that? And he'd do it. He was a pleasure, he was a prince."[37]

For the Vault LP title song, Lightnin' made up "California Mudslide (and Earthquake)" on the spot, in which he bemoaned the torrential rains and the wrath of God. He reflected on his own life as a sinner: "Why you know I must be born by the devil, Po' Lightnin' don't wanna be baptized," but then asked for forgiveness:

> You know, please, please, please, forgive me for my mistake
> But after all that flood come in California, do you know
> The good Lord's ground begin to shake

When Lightnin' finished recording, Tony Joe White of "Polk Salad Annie" fame, who listened in during the session, picked up his guitar and the two jammed for a while. "Tony really knew his blues," Bromberg says, "and Lightnin' really enjoyed it, but he wouldn't let us record. Tony wrote the liner notes." But instead of providing any contextual information about the session, White was descriptive, personal, and almost trite: "And his boots were from Mexico with silver caps on the toes and brown baggy pants tucked inside . . . he was a soulful sight . . . it's hard to say anything . . . as I'd much rather sit, be quiet, and listen to him. I've dug him since I was 12, and met him when I am 25. He can make chills run over you when he sings about 'The California Mud Slide' or anything."[38]

From Los Angeles, Lightnin' went to Berkeley and recorded an album on May 19, 1969, for Poppy, an independent label that had also recorded the singer/songwriter Townes Van Zandt, who had championed Lightnin's music in Houston and had hung out with him whenever he got the chance. Van Zandt's girlfriend Fran Petters Lohr recalled that one time, "it was announced in the paper that Lightnin' Hopkins had died," and Van Zandt got "real upset." Together they drove over to Lightnin's apartment and they knocked on the door. "Lightnin' always had these bodyguards, these people around, so they opened the door and Townes said, 'Oh, my God, Lightnin'. They said you were dead.' And Lightnin' just says, 'I don't think so.' So we sat there and they played guitars and talked for hours."[39]

For Lightnin's session on Poppy, produced by Strachwitz, he was accompanied by Jeff Carp on harmonica, Johnny "Big Moose" Walker on piano, Paul Asbell on rhythm guitar, Gino Skaggs on bass, and Francis Clay on drums. Lightnin' had flown up to the Bay Area for an appearance at Zellerbach Hall with Mance Lipscomb, Bukka White, and Son House. Concert organizer Joe Garrett, who greeted Lightnin' at the airport, said that when he got off the plane, "he pulled out a bottle of whiskey and he drank it like you would drink a Coca Cola on a hot day, just to get his nerves back. . . . He was really shaken up by that."[40]

About the Poppy session, Strachwitz says, "Kevin Eggers from Poppy got in touch with me and asked me to supervise Lightnin's recordings. He wasn't particularly interested in new material. He wanted his hits. I thought the whole thing was so-so, and he probably could have gotten one good LP out of it, but he made it into a two-volume set."[41]

Often times, when Lightnin' went to California, Strachwitz says he took the bus, but by the late 1960s, with his ever-expanding audience, he was forced to fly more often.

Strachwitz recorded Lightnin' twice in 1969, once on May 20 for Poppy and again on December 8 for Arhoolie. Francis Clay accompanied Hopkins on drums, and with his solid backing, Lightnin's sound was tight and yielded a few songs that were at once fresh and revealing. "Sellin' Wine in Arizona" was autobiographical:

> I was tryin' to make a living, I even taken a quart of wine, sold it to a
>   chile (x2)
> They picked me up right then and put me on that rock pile
> Breakin' rocks all day long, that's the reason if you ever go to Arizona
> You better leave them Indians alone

While "Sellin' Wine in Arizona" had the character of many of Lightnin's songs in which he cast himself as a victim, "Up On Telegraph" is both topical and funny as he commented on the hippies he encountered on a walk on that famous avenue:

> I looked at them little pretty hippies
> The dress so short, I says, "Whoo, look at that little girl walk"
> I liked her a little better when I heard her, she begin to talk
> She says, "Sam, ain't this a pretty sight to see?"
> I says, "Yeah," She says, "Just lookie here, take a hip on me"

Clearly, Lightnin' was enjoying himself, and his guitar playing was light and ironic to underscore the good-natured humor of the moment. Lightnin' had made a number of friends in Berkeley, and he liked spending time there. He'd see Barbara Dane, or stay with relatives in Oakland, or visit with Carroll Peery from the Cabale, or go around town with Strachwitz. On this trip, from Berkeley he headed back to southern California to play in a show on May 30 that included the rock band Canned Heat and Albert Collins, who said his mother was "kin to all the Hopkins family."[42]

When Lightnin' got back to Houston, Stan Lewis contacted him again, and Don Logan took him to ACA studio (not Muscle Shoals, as has been written since the album was new) to record an LP called *The Great Electric Show and Dance*. During the session, Logan said he "got along all right" with Lightnin' and the recording proceeded smoothly. "I knew that what would sell was Lightnin' and his guitar," Logan says, "but I had this weird idea that if I put some electric-type fuzz guitar in the background, we could reach the college kids. At that time, we were one of the few record companies sending out samples to the small-power college radio stations, and that was at Stan's insistence. So Jewel came out with the album *The Great Electric Show and Dance* [which was in many ways like Muddy Waters's *Electric Mud* LP] and the [Lightnin'] fans did not like it. . . . But it still got a lot of play on college campuses around the country. . . . And over the years, the fans have said that it would have been better if I'd taken out all that shit [overdubbed effects] I'd put in there and just came out with the album."[43]

In the end, Logan recognized that Lightnin's strength was not in the background accompaniment. "You just have Lightnin' singing the song and you have him playing his guitar licks. He was an unorthodox singer, but musician-wise on the guitar, he played some licks that made all of the white groups buy his stuff. . . . So, every little band out there probably bought Lightnin' Hopkins just to hear his licks, which were simple, but they made a lot of sense in his music."[44]

Ultimately Lightnin' was not a big seller for Jewel, but Logan worked hard on sales and promotion. "I pretty much did everything," Logan says, "I'd even call the mom and pop shops and say, 'Man, I got a great new blues.' It wouldn't be big orders, but it'd be small ones. That's the kind of artist Lightnin' was."[45]

During the summer of 1969, Lightnin' began to venture out and travel to festivals and cities where he had never been before. On August 3, at the Ann Arbor Blues Festival in Michigan, Dan Morgenstern described Lightnin's performance as "anything but eclectic. His style both vocally and on guitar, his demeanor, and his material (though he also dips into the traditional well) are genuinely original, and he was a joy to behold. *Sharp* from dark glasses to yellow shoes, he seemed determined to have a good time and take the audience with him. 'It's good out here in the prairie like this,' he told them, launching into 'Mojo Hand.' Among the things that followed in a set that seemed to end too soon (Lightnin' knows how to pace himself), the standouts were 'Don't Wanna Be Baptized' and a long anecdote about a girl who stole his brand new Cadillac."[46]

Backstage at the Ann Arbor Blues Festival, writer and photographer Dick Waterman recalled that Son House's wife Evie approached him and asked, "Dick, do you know that Lightning Hopkins man?" Waterman was in a way shocked by the question; Evie was known to go to church three or four times a week and read the Bible at home. But she genuinely wanted to meet Lightnin', who was "holding court . . . with processed hair and sunglasses, he was dressed in a shark-skin suit and held a cigar in one hand and a plastic cup of whiskey in the other." And when introduced to Evie, Lightnin' dropped his cigar and "drew her to his side and looked up at her: 'Hello, sweet thing,' he whispered. 'What's a young girl like you doing here all alone?'" Evie, Waterman wrote, "put her hand to her face and started to giggle," and after a few minutes came over to him and said, "That Lightning, he sure does say some pretty things to the ladies."[47]

Waterman had known Lightnin' for a number of years, and sometimes took him to festivals and concert dates. On one road trip going to a gig in Santa Monica, Lightnin' pointed to a liquor store in front of them. Waterman dutifully stopped the car, but when he asked for some money, Lightnin' replied, "Aw, now Dick, I ain't got nothing but a hundred dollar bill." Waterman replied, "They'll change it," and Lightnin' countered, "Dick, now you take a look at how Lightning is dressed tonight. Ain't I looking sharp?" Hopkins was wearing a "white suit, black shirt with a bolo tie, and black and white saddle shoes." Then Lightnin' stroked himself from his ribs down to his knee, and said, "They goin' to give me some big mess of dirty one dollar bills and five dollar bills. . . . See how smooth ol' Lightning is lookin'? I can't be having it, Dick. I can't let them give me some big ball of dirty money because it would just mess up my line." Waterman looked at Lightnin' with amazement and went in and bought "the damn bottle again."[48]

From Ann Arbor, Hopkins went to the Blossom Music Center in Cleveland, Ohio, where he appeared on a bill with B. B. King and the Staple Singers on August 8, and was featured at the Chicago Blues Festival on August 30. In the fall, he played dates mostly around Houston before going back out to the West

Coast, where he recorded in Berkeley on December 8, and appeared at the Ash Grove from Christmas Day to January 4, 1970, on a program that included Firesign Theatre as well as Taj Mahal on New Year's Eve.

On January 27, 1970, Lightnin' was in a bad car wreck; the car in which he was a passenger was nearly totaled and he injured his neck. He was driving back from Austin or Dallas, and the person at the wheel didn't see a barricade in front of him and drove off the road. Lightnin' cracked a vertebrae in his neck and was lucky he wasn't paralyzed, but he had to wear a neck brace for some time that restricted his traveling.[49] In June, however, he did go to California, playing at Lincoln School Auditorium with Ramblin' Jack Elliott and Sandy Bull in San Francisco, and then went back to the Ash Grove, June 18 to 28. "He started coming back whenever he wanted to or whenever I wanted him to," Ed Pearl says. "One of us would call the other. I didn't work with anyone. There were no agents. When Lightnin' came to the Ash Grove, he just introduced a whole new aspect of the blues, and people flocked to it. And he just set a standard and kept on top of it. His draw was as big as Muddy Waters or Howlin' Wolf. But to the Ash Grove crowd, Lightnin' was there a lot and was never second to anyone."[50]

While Lightnin' was in Los Angeles, Pearl took care of him. Pearl had an apartment across the street from the Ash Grove where Lightnin' sometimes stayed, but on other occasions, he'd go to a hotel or visit with his or Antoinette's relatives. "My impression was that they [Lightnin' and Antoinette] were married," Pearl says. "I enjoyed being with Antoinette. She was shy, nice, gentle, and he treated her beautifully. And we'd have different social interactions. We had dinner together, and sometimes just sat around and talked."[51]

The subjects of conversation varied, from Lightnin's gigs and his travels, and once in a while they even talked about politics. "He knew his limitations," Pearl said, "and he was happy to be part of his community, but he knew there was a bigger world out there. He thought people should be equal and he thought, you know, poor people should have more. And everyone is a child of God. He was against the Vietnam war."[52]

Bernie Pearl, Ed's brother, also got to know Lightnin' when he came to the Ash Grove. "He was charming, but he was also dramatic," Bernie says. "He was immaculate. . . . He had sharp creases, he had patent leather shoes. He had bling on his fingers. He had that gold tooth. He had sunglasses, he had that hat. He had that towel around his neck. . . . And his words, you really had to listen to it. To me, he was charismatic. And he could play the guitar like hell. . . . He fit less into the idea of what a folk performer was, to my thinking. It was more theatrical; it was not phony. His gestures, how he would be expressive with the guitar, with his hands on and off, and the way he would explain things to people in that deep baritone, very Southern humor, kind of like he knew he was coming from a place different than the audience that was there."[53]

Bernie was then a student at UCLA and had a varied schedule, making it possible for him to meet Lightnin' when he got to Los Angeles. Lightnin' usually came on a Greyhound bus, and Bernie would take him from the station to wherever he wanted to go. "Always see him with half a pint of Gordon's gin," Bernie says, "That was his drink, and we'd sit down and talk, and I'd drive him around to see family around here."[54]

Once, Bernie and two of his friends, David Cohen and Barry Hansen (who later became known as Dr. Demento), made arrangements with Lightnin' for a formal guitar lesson. "We each paid him twenty dollars," Bernie says, "and he actually showed us this is this. He told us what the riffs were. Of course, we were looking mostly at the left hand, and not at the right. David was a much quicker study, and he got the thing immediately, and I had just spent years figuring this stuff out, and then realized how crucial the right hand was in getting the sound and the feel. But it was this is this lick, and I suppose we asked questions, like could you slow it down? He was not practiced in giving lessons."[55]

Bernie liked hanging around Lightnin', and one night Lightnin' asked if he wanted to join him on stage at the Ash Grove. "I really kind of attached myself to Lightnin'," Bernie says. "I never demanded to play, but he asked me to come and play with him, which I did regularly throughout his tenure at the Ash Grove. What I played was back up. I never played a solo. I was there to support him. What I learned to do was play what he played on the treble. I learned to play an octave lower on the bass, and I would hit chords with him. He changed chords when he wanted to, and his measures never had to complete their full four counts. There was a basic coffee house thing that he did. He repeated a lot of the same material. Mostly he played in E. Typically, the B7, following the turnaround would be in some form abbreviated. It would not be a complete B7 chord. Just E, but not the standard E, A7, and B7 chords. I love the songs he played in A, 10 or 20 percent of the time, E was most of the time."

In contrast to Lightnin's coffee house style, Ed Pearl recalls, was the way he played in black clubs. Ed had never really understood the difference until Lightnin' asked him if he would drive him to a gig in South Central after the Ash Grove closed. "We went there," Pearl recalls, "and the place was full with people waiting to see Lightnin'. And he had played the Ash Grove so many times, but the electricity, what he was playing for the people there [for a black audience], was something different. He would make a gesture, or he would say five words and the audience would respond in a way that I didn't understand. But what I realized very quickly once he started was that he was expressing things in ways they may not have been able to express. He evoked deep feelings in every person there. Most of the people were middle-aged and had moved to Los Angeles from the South. He was somebody who spoke for them, and also was one of them."[56]

Lightnin' liked working in Los Angeles. He had his black friends and his white friends, and to some extent, they mixed. In fact, Ed Pearl said that when Lightnin' wasn't working, he'd sometimes come to the Ash Grove just to hear some of the other styles of music. "He had a broad view. Lightnin' liked Bill Monroe. He came in to see Bill's show. He came in to see Doc Watson's show."

Over the years, Lightnin' wrote several songs about California. In "California Showers," he identified with the plight of the farm worker:

> Tell me why do it rain, why it storm in California all the time
> I don't want the rain, but you still have plenty sunshine
> You know it keeps on rainin', you know this poor man can't make no
>   time (x2)
> You know if I can't go to my job, how I'm gonna feed this family of mine?

In "Burnin' in L.A." he sang about the devastation of the fire in Los Angeles and the plea of one girl who wanted to get away:

> You know a little sixteen-year-old girl come to me talked and said
> Lightnin', would you take me for your souvenir?

You know they had a big fire down in L.A.
All them buildings is burnin' down

Lightnin' returned to Los Angeles often between 1965 and 1973, when the Ash Grove closed, though Ed and Bernie Pearl continued to see Lightnin' whenever they got a chance. Bernie even traveled to Houston to visit with Lightnin' and Antoinette. "I took a Greyhound to Navasota," Bernie says, "I spent Christmas with Mance [Lipscomb], and stayed three or four days and then I took the bus to Houston. And when I got off the bus in Houston, I hailed a cab and there was a black woman cab driver. And I gave her the address, she said, 'No, you don't want to go there.' I said, 'Yes I do.' 'Oh, yeah that's in the Third Ward.' 'I'm gonna see Lightnin' Hopkins,' and she just about flipped out. 'You're going to see Lightnin' Hopkins.' So she delivered me there and got an autograph from him."[57]

Over the years, Bernie became close friends with both Lightnin' and Antoinette, and one time, he traveled with them to the Bay Area. But when they got to Berkeley, there were no rooms left in the motel. "Antoinette was with him," Bernie says, "and I didn't have a place to stay. So they invited me. They said, 'Well, come stay in our room,' . . . and the three of us ended sleeping in the same bed because there was no couch, and they didn't want me to sleep on the floor. And needless to say, it was a very warm and generous thing. . . . It kind of shows the nature of the friendship."[58]

In the mid-1970s, Bernie played backup for Lightnin' when he appeared at the Lighthouse in Hermosa Beach. For Bernie, Lightnin' was a mentor who taught him not only how to play some of his licks on the guitar, but who also helped him to define himself. "There was one point where I might have been with his family and I might have been acting white or nervous. And he looked at me and said, 'Be yourself.' And I've taken that to be the watchword of how I approach this music. It was like *boing* somebody dropped a life message on me."[59]

The Ash Grove had been an anchor for Lightnin' on the West Coast. It was a base from which he could plan other gigs, both in Southern California and the Bay Area, where Strachwitz was eager to record him and help him find jobs. Ed Pearl would book Lightnin' whenever he wanted, and the combination of family and friends made Los Angeles one of his favorite destinations, even as he began to get offers for larger concerts as a headliner. Lightnin' was loyal to Pearl and to Strachwitz because they treated him well and paid fairly.

In 1972, Lightnin' received his one and only Grammy nomination for Best Ethnic or Traditional Recording for *Lightnin' Strikes*, a reissue on the Tradition/ Everest label of his 1965 album of the same title for Verve-Folkways. Muddy Waters, however, won the award for his LP *The London Muddy Waters Session.*[60] Even though Lightnin' didn't win, interest in his music continued to swell, and whether or not he played electric or acoustic guitar became irrelevant. However, it became more difficult for him to assess the opportunities that were presented to him and to organize the logistics of touring. Dr. Harold worked with him to manage his contracts, but only on a volunteer basis, and he didn't really have the time to go out on the road with him. After Lightnin's car wreck, he became more cautious about whom he traveled with, but he was still drinking heavily. As time went on, his needs intensified; the invitations to play festivals and concert dates had never been greater.

9

The Last Decade

In Houston, the Third Ward of the 1970s was in many ways more dangerous than it was in the 1940s or '50s, when the neighborhood was flourishing and Dowling Street was a main thoroughfare of African American life and culture. During the years of desegregation and integration, many of the black-owned businesses in the Third Ward closed or moved, and the problems of drugs and violence were exacerbated by urban decay and neglect. In music, the Third Ward had gone from the jazz-oriented big bands of Milton Larkin, I. H. Smalley, Conrad Johnson, and the rhythm and blues of the Duke/Peacock era to the popular soul/funk of the TSU Tornados, Oscar Perry, and John Roberts and the Hurricanes. Archie Bell and the Drells had a #1 hit with "Tighten Up" in 1968 and continued to have a strong presence in the Houston scene of the 1970s. Guitar-based blues in Houston was declining. Young African Americans were after a sound that reflected the world in which they were coming of age and most were not interested in down-home blues.

In this context, though Lightnin' may still have been known among older African Americans in his community of the Third Ward, he had become a legend for white blues and rock audiences. He rarely played in the bars and nightclubs in the Third Ward anymore, and even he viewed his neighborhood as threatening. Lightnin' always carried a loaded gun and had been known to drive around with a shotgun on the back seat of his car. He lived in a culture of violence, where he knew people who had been killed, beginning at an early age when he learned about the murder of his father. And as he got older, there were others. According to McCormick, Buster Pickens, who had accompanied Lightnin' on piano, was "senselessly shot to death in a West Dallas Street bar on November 24, 1964."[1] Moreover, Leadbitter wrote that Thunder Smith had been "murdered in 1965 after a drunken argument."[2]

David Benson, a twenty-three-year-old African American from the small town of Waycross, Georgia, met Lightnin' in the fall of 1970 while he was a student at the University of Houston. A classmate, Alfie Naifeh, who was then accompanying Lightnin' as a drummer on some local gigs, asked him if he wanted to go over to Lightnin's apartment on Gray Street. Benson had played alto saxophone when he was younger and had grown up playing the blues: "So I knew about these old bluesmen already, though I had never known a bluesman. I knew the validity and the history of that music because my uncles lived in that world."[3]

Going into Lightnin's apartment for the first time, Benson felt that he "was walking into the presence of greatness." He wanted to get to know Lightnin' and went to visit him as often as he could. He also got to know Antoinette, because they were often together. "I had been around older people as a younger boy," Benson says, "so I knew how to say, 'Yes, Ma'am,' and 'No, Ma'am,' and keep my mouth shut and be properly respectful and polite and that's how I got in there."[4]

In time Benson met Dr. Harold, who realized that Benson could help Lightnin' in ways that he could not. Dr. Harold began asking him to drive for Lightnin' and to accompany him as a kind of road manager, ensuring that he was paid properly and that his lodging and per diem needs were adequately met. Benson respected Dr. Harold and worked in coordination with him to manage Lightnin's business dealings. "From the start," Benson says, "we were part of that shifting of gears in Lightnin's career. . . . He considered me and considered Dr. Harold . . . to be intelligent African American men that he could trust and depend on to change that whole exploitative sort of cycle that he had been in for so long."[5]

While there is little question that Lightnin' had been manipulated and exploited by various club owners, promoters, and record producers both white and black over the course of his career, this was not uniformly true. Arhoolie and Prestige/Bluesville had been paying advances and royalties with timely statements since the early 1960s. In other instances, where no royalties were paid and the fees may have seemed low, Lightnin' consented to the terms when he wanted the money. To simply say, for example, that white producer Bobby Shad and black producer Bobby Robinson exploited him is not fair to them; they paid Lightnin' the flat fee that he asked for, and while they knew that he might eventually earn royalties, Lightnin' insisted on getting paid in full up front. Moreover, Lightnin's flagrant disregard for the "exclusive" contracts he signed, his propensity for recording the same song for different labels, and his reluctance to record more than one take of any given song made him difficult to work with, though from his point of view he likely felt that he was getting back at those who were already taking advantage of him.

Undoubtedly, Lightnin's heavy drinking and gambling impeded his ability to keep up with his business affairs, and even when Harold and Benson worked to manage his interests, he did not always follow their advice. Harold recalled, for example, that Lightnin' liked to buy a new used car every Labor Day because the banks were closed and it was impossible to check his credit rating. Lightnin' would keep the car for as long as he could without making payments, knowing that it would in time be repossessed.[6]

By the time Benson met Lightnin', he wasn't performing very much locally around the Third Ward. "He was playing college gigs and predominantly young, white nightclubs. And he would say, sometimes, off the mike . . . it was my job to really be that buffer between him and club owners, at places like Liberty Hall in Houston, because it was a pretty alienating environment for him in comparison to what he had come up in and what he was used to—and what he preferred."[7]

Benson liked socializing with Lightnin', but getting to know him on a personal level was a gradual process. "He would reveal himself in pieces to me," Benson says. "What you didn't see [for example] is that he was a tremendous tap dancer and buck dancer. I mean, beyond, a Sammy Davis Jr. type dancer. But he would only do it behind closed doors. And I never knew it, and then, one day, all of a sudden, we were sitting in the dressing room passing time, and he got up and he just started dancing."[8]

Benson traveled with Lightnin' as often as was possible, even after he graduated from the University of Houston and enrolled in a PhD program at Michigan State University in East Lansing. He continued to work with Harold, who tried to coordinate Lightnin's performance dates with Benson's vacations and days off. One time Lightnin' was invited to perform at the student coffee house at Michigan State and Benson made arrangements for Lightnin' to stay with him. Benson cooked for him and helped him get around. "Lightnin' had very particular dietary tastes," Benson says, "and being a student, I made some kind of chicken stew." And when Benson came back to Houston on vacation, Antoinette wanted the recipe because Lightnin' had told her how good his cooking was. Antoinette, Benson recalls, did most of the cooking for Lightnin', and it wasn't long before they all became close friends. Lightnin' called Benson "Babe," and often referred to him as Antoinette's boy, and Antoinette treated him like a son, though in fact she was still living with her own children and husband in the Fifth Ward. "She had two separate lives, and I never met her other family," Benson said, "except for her daughter, who sometimes came over to Lightnin's. But Antoinette never spent the night at Lightnin's apartment in the Third Ward. She'd stock the refrigerator with food for Lightnin' and for me. His favorite food was chicken and dumplings, and so was mine."[9]

The Houston city directories indicated that Lightnin' lived by himself in unit 14 at 3124 Gray Street in 1967 and 1968, but shared a residence with Antoinette from 1969 on. While it is clear that Lightnin' and Antoinette were never married, there is a Houston court record dated November 19, 1973, granting a divorce to Antoinette Stout Charles from Leonard Charles. However, Benson could not confirm whether or not this was the same Antoinette. When he was with Lightnin', there was never any discussion of divorce, though it was clear that Antoinette had a family in the Fifth Ward.

Benson sometimes spent the night in a guest room at Lightnin's, though when he finally moved back to Houston after finishing his doctorate in social work, he got his own place. "Lightnin' pretty much seemed like an uncle to me," Benson says, and "Miss Nette would say, 'Oh, that's such a nice boy, Lightnin'.' And she kind of became my play mother. . . . And every time he would play, I would go with him; he always wanted somebody to drive his car for him, so I'd drive for him. And he started trusting me to collect the money. I became kind of the enforcer, so to speak. He'd always say, 'Anything that have to do with business,' he'd say, 'go talk to David.'"[10]

Even though they often traveled together, Lightnin' was still his own man, and if he wanted to play a gig and Benson was not available, he'd find someone else to drive him. During the 1970s, Lightnin's recording tapered off. The market was saturated with his records, but people still wanted to see him perform live. He toured less but got paid more. In 1972 he played club dates in Chicago, as well as a benefit sponsored by the River City Blues Project at Municipal Auditorium in New Orleans. In 1973 he was booked for a five-night gig at the Egress Nightclub in Vancouver from February 19 to 23, then he jetted off to Carnegie Hall for a concert on March 4 that also featured Bonnie Raitt and Muddy Waters. And in the fall he taped a television special for broadcast on Channel 31 in New York City. "Everywhere Lightnin' went," Benson says, "people crowded in to see him. How much money he was making at this point is difficult to say, but it was definitely a lot more than he had ever earned before." According to Harold, his minimum fee for a club date was six hundred dollars for two forty-five-minute sets, though for concerts in bigger venues, he asked for more and usually got it.[11]

Sam Charters returned to Houston in 1974 to record Lightnin' for Volume 12 of the *Legacy of the Blues* series he was producing for the Sonet label in Stockholm, and found that Lightnin's musicianship had declined. "His singing and guitarwork was more sloppy, " Charters says. "I did the best I could. I knew . . . it was not going to add one iota to what had been done, or hadn't been done over and over again."

Given the dispute of money and royalties surrounding Charters's first recording for Folkways in 1959, Lightnin' was suspicious, even though he had dealt with Charters since then when he was working with Prestige/Bluesville in the 1960s. To make matters worse, Harold was extremely difficult. "He started with the point of view that I was a white motherfucker," Charters says, "that I was going to rip off every black man that I met. . . . And how much money was I going to pay? I will temper my language, but he insisted, because of his distrust for whites, that he had to be paid in cash a five-thousand-dollar advance, but I wasn't going to pay him until I did the recording. So as the session wore down in the studio we were using in the ghetto, we began to attract the usual people, and various gang members were hanging around outside. And I really had had enough, and as we were leaving, people were looking in the window, I said quite loudly, 'Here's the $5,000 you asked me for' and I handed him the $5,000 in small bills. And he and Lightnin' looked at each other; they weren't sure how they were going to get out to the car with all this cash. Dr. Harold was a very trim, very well dressed dude. He enjoyed his role of giving people like me a hard time. And so to see him and Lightnin' figuring out ways to hide the $5,000, stuffing it in their socks, literally, gave me a certain kind of pleasure."[12]

Charters and Lightnin' had not communicated with each other in years, and the animosity during this session was a potent indicator of not only how their relationship had deteriorated but also how they both had changed since their first meeting in 1959. Charters had definitely grown more cynical, and Lightnin's resentment toward him built on the antipathy he already felt toward Folkways and other record producers. However, the five-thousand-dollar advance that Charters paid for the Sonet recordings not only exceeded the rates for most blues artists at that time but was also a sum that the LP could never earn back. In the end, the Sonet album turned out poorly. The songs contained bits and pieces of previously recorded material that were rehashed haphazardly and never seemed to gel like the lyrics he improvised years earlier. Lightnin' played an acoustic guitar with an electric pickup, and was accompanied by drums and bass. Lightnin' did play slide guitar on "Please Help Poor Me" and "The Hearse is Backed Up to the Door," demonstrating some versatility, but ultimately the songs themselves sound fragmented. When the album was released in 1975, it didn't sell very well.[13]

Despite Lightnin's erratic performances, by the mid-1970s, he was a legend and he attracted a following. This audience likely knew relatively little about his early recordings or that his blues had become rote and predictable. Blues had arrived and was covered heavily in the popular media. Aging bluesmen like Lightnin', John Lee Hooker, and Muddy Waters were more revered than ever. Benson says he even once saw the renowned French American art collector and philanthropist Dominique De Menil, who lived in Houston, come to Lightnin's house. "We'd played the New Orleans Jazz and Heritage Festival [1976] and the weather was bad, so we couldn't get back to Houston until late. We were going to meet Mrs. De Menil and her daughter, Christophe, who was very fond of Lightnin' and wanted to find a way to sponsor him through some kind of arts grant. Well, by the time we got back, Mrs. De Menil was sitting in the parking lot in front of Lightnin's apartment building, waiting for him to come home. And he asked her to come inside, where she sat around awhile, and then said she was tired. He told her, said, 'Well, you can use the extra bedroom,' and she went in and took a nap. So, think about it, Dominique De Menil, the empress of art of Houston, in the Third Ward, sleeping in Lightnin's bedroom.'"[14]

While many of Lightnin's performances during the 1970s were uneven, he still had the capacity to be completely engaging. Robert Palmer, in his review in *The New York Times* of Lightnin's show at the Palladium on May 13, 1977, wrote that even though Lightnin' was on stage for a little over thirty minutes, he "turned in a superb performance." Palmer commented that Hopkins's lyrics were largely unoriginal, drawing from "the common pool of folk and commercial blues lyrics," and that neither his singing nor his guitar playing was virtuosic. However, Palmer felt "putting over the blues has always been a matter of timing and timbre, and these Mr. Hopkins handles with the assurance of a master. He doubles rhythms back upon themselves, drops bars of music for dramatic emphasis, and draws a stinging, acerbic sound from his guitar which is the essence of the blues." Moreover, Palmer praised Lightnin's accompanists, Charles Calamese and Willie Smith, bassist and drummer with James Cotton's band, who had probably never played with Hopkins before, but who "followed his deviations from formal symmetry with unerring accuracy."[15]

Lightnin's reputation in New York was well established, and he could pretty much get booked there whenever he wanted. This was also true in California and in Texas, where he was now celebrated as a major figure in the history of the blues. In 1977, he was a headliner for the first Juneteenth Blues Festival, founded by local jazzman, educator, and promoter Lanny Steele.[16] The Juneteenth Blues Festival provided Lightnin' with the opportunity to not only play on the same stage as John Lee Hooker, Muddy Waters, and the other giants of postwar country blues, but to interact with them backstage, to swap stories and joke around. In fact, he got to talk to Muddy Waters about his upcoming travel to Canada the following day. "So we were sitting around drinking champagne," Benson recalls, "and Lightnin' told Muddy, 'We're going to Montreal tomorrow.' And Muddy says, 'Doudou [Boicel], that's the man you need to go see.' So, the next day, we get ready to go to Montreal. We're going through customs at Toronto, which Lightnin' called 'Doronto,' and the man at the desk asks for our work visa. And out of the clear blue, and loud in the airport, Lightnin' says, 'Doudou, motherfucker, Doudou.' And the guy says, 'What?' He says, 'Doudou, goddamit, don't you know Doudou?' He says, 'Everybody knows Doudou.' Out of context. Everybody in the airport was looking. Needless to say, we were in customs three hours."[17]

Once they got to Montreal, they discovered that Doudou was in fact "a top-notch impresario in Canada," and that he was more than generous. "He had a reputation for overpaying you," Benson says. "If he made money that night, he'd give a $500 bonus or a $1,000 bonus. He always put us up in the best hotels. So all of the musicians really appreciated Doudou because the guy treated them so well."[18] In addition to presenting Lightnin' at the Rising Sun Celebrity Jazz Club on June 23, 1977, Doudou recorded the performances, but they were not released until 1996.[19]

Lightnin' liked Canada, Benson says, especially Montreal, because there was "a French and Acadian influence. . . . So every time that Lightnin' played 'Mojo Hand' with that kind of zydeco beat that he would do sometimes, they were lined around the block in thirty-below-zero weather."

When Benson and Lightnin' traveled together, they generally shared the same room. "He didn't want me to sleep any place else," Benson says, "but he was an old man, and he'd wake my ass up, two or three times a night, man. He'd make noises and clear his throat. He'd ask, 'You asleep, baby, you asleep?' And I'd say, 'Well, I was sleepin' until you woke me up.' And then we'd pick up guitars and he would think of some old song he hadn't sung in a long time and he'd say he was going to sing it that night or something, and we'd sit there and we'd play guitars. And he would tell me stories about all these things that went down when he was a younger man. Tricks they would play on people and all kinds of stuff like that."[20]

Sometimes, however, Lightnin' and Benson would get into arguments with each other. Lightnin' didn't approve of Benson running around with girls he'd meet in the clubs, but that was what Benson looked forward to when they were traveling. "Me, being a young man . . . part and parcel of being in that business is to hook with somebody that night, mostly white girls. And he didn't like for me to leave him. So, we would get into little spats, I'd collect the money, take care of business, leave the money with him, and take off with some little girl, and then he would get upset, because I wouldn't come back. I might spend the night out."[21]

One time, in Montreal, Benson bought some yogurt and Lightnin' said, "What in the fuck are you buying that shit for?" So, Benson put it in the refrigerator in the hotel room to save it for later, but then after the gig, he went out with "some little girl" and stayed too long. "I came back the next day, and he had eaten the yogurt. . . . And he'd started bitching, 'You been gone and I had nothin' to eat, and I had to eat that shit in the refrigerator.'"[22]

Sometimes, Lightnin' would push Benson too far, and Benson would get angry, and then back off. "He'd say something like, 'You eat too goddamn much. If I had a goddamn dog, it would be better than you, because at least I could feed the dog when I want to, but you gonna eat when you want to.' And then the next day, he'd say, 'I dreamed last night you and me had a fight,' and I'd say, 'Yeah, it wasn't a dream. It was for real, and I kicked your ass.' And then he'd back out and say, 'Oh, baby, you know I'm just kidding.'"[23]

Benson felt Lightnin' became cantankerous because he didn't like being away from Antoinette, and he wanted to be at home. But when he got home, Antoinette advised Benson to 'give him a little room, and he'll look for you again.' She'd say, 'Lightnin's the kind of guy that if he wants you and needs you first, he's going to treat you better than if he's got you under his thumb.'"[24]

Lightnin's mood swings bothered Benson, but in part he attributed his behavior to his drinking. Lightnin' often had a "nip" in the morning and continued drinking throughout the day, sipping Pearl beer, and consuming untold amounts of gin or whisky from his pocket flask. Whenever possible, Lightnin' avoided driving and preferred to have Benson and others take him to and from his gigs. But on October 8, 1977, Lightnin' was arrested for speeding, driving under the influence, and carrying a loaded gun in Centerville, Texas. "So, when his court date came up," Benson says, "we went to this courthouse and it was a real throwback to the past. You could almost hear the ghosts of people [who] had gone through there and been tried. It was kind of an eerie thing. But everyone knew who he was of course, so the judge told him, 'You had a weapon on you, from now on, leave your gun at home, and stop drinkin','" and they gave him probation and we went on back to Houston."[25] Times had really changed; had Lightnin' been arrested for the same offenses when he lived in Centerville in the 1930s, he would have been sentenced to a chain gang or prison.

Whenever anyone mentioned going to Europe, Lightnin' was skeptical, especially about the air travel. He preferred driving, but he liked the "idea of Europe," Benson says. "He liked the reception that he got, because there was a tremendous reception. But he always complained there wasn't enough to eat."

Norbert Hess, a German blues aficionado and concert promoter, contacted Harold about organizing a European tour for Lightnin' in the fall of 1977, but had some difficulty convincing him. However, when they agreed to pay him several thousand dollars, Lightnin' finally agreed. Benson wasn't able to go, but his friend Ron Wilson (the future Texas congressman) was available to travel with Lightnin'. They left Houston first for the Netherlands, where Lightnin' appeared at the Rotterdam Jazz Festival on November 12. From there they went to the Dortmund Jazz Festival, headlined a concert in Berlin with Duke Ellington's Orchestra and James Booker on the bill, and then traveled to Sweden, where he played four concerts at the Gothenburg University Students' House.

In Dortmund the concert was taped for television for a program called *Homage à Lightnin' Hopkins*, and according to Hess, "Several modern jazz groups paid tribute to the old master. James Booker played a short solo set and backed Hopkins for three numbers. Hopkins was accompanied by George Green on drums and Ewald Warning on bass, two black musicians who lived in Munich and had only ever played modern jazz. They knew nothing about Lightnin' Hopkins. So, as an homage, it was one of the worst concerts I'd ever attended. As road manager for Lightnin', I must say I enjoyed him very much but he was hampered by the bass player and drummer, who didn't really understand his blues."[26]

In 1978, Benson traveled with Lightnin' to Japan and toured six cities in thirteen days, but once again he had some trouble persuading Lightnin' to go. "Some guy got in the car one day in the Third Ward," Benson says, "and told him that they had dropped an atomic bomb in Japan and there was no food. So Lightnin' said he wouldn't go to Japan. So I told him that was during World War II; that was thirty years ago. They've rebuilt and everything since then." But Lightnin' wouldn't listen. He was adamant about not going, and he and Harold had such a big falling out about him refusing to honor what was already an existing contract that Dr. Harold turned over all of Lightnin's records to Benson. "He said, 'You're the manager now. You go do it. I'm tired of messing with him.' And I had to deal with it," Benson remembers. "So around February, Miss Nette and Lightnin' came over to my house, and I received a call from [the promoter] J. J. Jackson in California who said Lightnin' had to go. He'd already signed the contract, and if he didn't go, he was going to be sued for breach of contract. So I told Lightnin' that and he said he didn't really care, because he wasn't going. . . . But then this Russian promoter and this woman showed up in the middle of the night in the rain over to Lightnin's place on Gray, and brought a substantial down payment for the trip, and Lightnin' just sat there when he saw the money. He didn't say anything, so I just proceeded to negotiate it as if he was going. This is probably a Tuesday or Wednesday night, and they said they wanted us to be in L.A. on Friday. So I took the guy and the woman to a nearby motel that night, met him the next day and went to the Japanese consulate, and he arranged for us to get a work permit and all the paperwork that needed to be done. I just proceeded to talk to Lightnin' as if we were going, and he gave in. He said he would go if I took three cases of Pearl beer and some sardines and some saltine crackers, so he could be assured that he would have at least something to eat while he was there."[27] Lightnin' was always careful about what he ate and how his food was served. Benson says that Lightnin' believed that his father had been poisoned, and throughout his life he worried that the same might happen to him.

The overall contract for the Japanese tour was for fifty thousand dollars, which was by far the most Lightnin' had ever been paid, and the organizers also provided first-class air travel and a fifty-dollar per diem. En route, Lightnin' asked Benson a very curious question about whether or not the world would end. Benson says, "I thought he was kind of waxing apocalyptic and answered, 'You know, Lightnin', the Bible says, the world will end and Jesus will come back,' and he said, 'No, if we keep flyin' in this motherfucka, will we go off the end of the earth.' And I said, 'No, the earth is not flat. Wherever we take off from, if we keep going, we come back to where we started.' That was a real sweet moment [though it was also kind of sad that Lightnin' seemed to lack such basic knowledge]."[28]

Lightnin' and Benson left Houston on February 10, 1978, and arrived the next day in Tokyo, where they had a rehearsal at TOA Attractions studio. On

February 13, Lightnin' performed in Tokyo, followed by Yokohama on February 15, Osaka on February 17, Nagoya on February 18, Sapporo on February 21, and Sendai on February 22. Also on the bill were Sonny Terry and Brownie McGhee, both of whom Lightnin' had known for nearly two decades.

Overall, the tour to Japan went well, but Benson says he always had to be on guard. "The language and the customs made it difficult to sort everything out. They'd want us to come to the studio. And they'd kind of play like they were just kind of rehearsing for the gig. And then, next thing you know, they got a couple of tracks out that he's recorded. So we decided that we didn't give them anything that they could use unless they really wanted to sit down and talk."[29]

In Sapporo, Lightnin' ran out of sardines, crackers, and beer, and he had to go to the hotel restaurant. He was reluctant, but he had no choice, and when he got to the restaurant, he heard Sonny Terry complaining, "Can you see that waiter anywhere? I ordered some pancakes." And Lightnin' was amused and chimed in, "Get your order, man!" Finally, the waiter came and brought Sonny his pancakes, and Benson says, "They were these little silver dollar pancakes and when Sonny felt them on his plate, he yelled out as loud as he could, 'Hey, motherfucka! I ordered some pancakes, I didn't order no biscuits!' And Lightnin' kept eggin' him on to give the people hell. I was embarrassed as hell in that situation."[30]

From then on, Benson either got Lightnin' room service or brought food to him. "Lightnin' pretty much stayed in the hotel. He didn't like Brownie, and Sonny and Brownie hadn't talked, other than on stage, for twenty-five years. Lightnin' was more on Sonny's side and they were better friends, and they hung together."

On stage Lightnin' was accompanied by Donald Bailey, a drummer and studio musician who also worked with Sonny and Brownie. The other sidemen were Japanese, and according to Benson, "They were perfect mimics of Lightnin's sound." The concert venues were huge and sat four to five thousand people and they were lined up around the block.

After Lightnin' got back to Texas, he didn't do too much traveling. He mainly played around Houston, where a new generation of white blues rockers connected with his music. Lightnin' would let just about anyone get up on stage and sit in, and if he didn't like what they were playing, he'd brush them off. As early as 1971, Jimmie Vaughan and his band Storm had appeared on the same bill with him at Liberty Hall and Fitzgerald's, and in the years that followed, he played numerous dates at Liberty Hall with musicians as diverse as Tracy Nelson and Jimmy Reed. He also went often to Austin, where he was booked with Stevie Ray Vaughan and Double Trouble in 1978 at the Armadillo, and was even featured on the *Austin City Limits* television show in 1979 in a program that included the Neville Brothers and barrelhouse blues pianist Robert Shaw.[31]

Michael Hall, writing in *Texas Monthly*, described Hopkins's appearance on *Austin City Limits* as "one of the all-time great Lightnin' moments. . . . He was wearing a bright-blue leisure suit with rhinestones that sparkled in the TV lights and a beige fedora cocked at a 45-degree angle on the side of his head. He looked like a fabulous old pimp. He played a Fender Stratocaster in front of a rhythm section that included bass player Ron Wilson [who had been elected to the Texas House of Representatives]." While the performance was uneven, combining "flashes of brilliance competing with the age-related tendency toward sloth and crankiness," Lightnin' was nonetheless captivating and halfway through his song "Ain't No Cadillac," his soloing took an unexpected direction: "For some reason he had a wah-wah pedal, and he either stomped it too hard or it had been turned up way too high, because his amplifier let out a high-pitched squeal—a loud, intense, and not unpleasant sound that lasted about three seconds. At first he appeared taken aback, but he kept playing, and a satisfied smile crossed his face. . . . He may not have planned that particular outburst, but like all the other notes he played and noises he plucked, he was proud of it. 'That's what I'm talkin' about,' he said, and jammed the pedal down again. Then he went on to craft a solo that began quietly and cascaded through a fall of bad notes, bringing the song to an early crashing end, dragging his rhythm section down with him, as he'd been doing for years."[32]

As much as Lightnin' might have enjoyed the attention he got from his white fans, Benson felt he was always suspicious of their motives. "I think all of us Southern boys have inculcated into us a certain amount of cultural paranoia that I call the 'Emmett Till complex.' And that is, white people will be straightforward with you as long as it behooves them, but they can turn on you in an instant. So if it comes down, especially, to white womanhood, then you had to be super-careful in terms of how you stepped. So all of these young guys who came along, who I felt were less prejudiced, he still saw them pretty much as being unpredictable; there was a possibility they could turn any minute and become very hateful. What he would say to me is that, 'David, you're going to get killed. These white folks are going to kill you because you talk to these white folks like they're niggers.' I was part of a different generation. I didn't have any problem going haggling for his money or negotiating with [a] club owner."[33]

One time Benson and Alfie Naifeh were driving with Lightnin' to Dallas, and they ran into an unexpected problem. "We were going to the club Mother Blues, and we were on Interstate 45. Well, he never would use a restroom anywhere. He had this paranoia about those things. He would always have a Spam can, a very long Spam can in the trunk of his car, and that's what he would urinate in. So we stopped on the side of the road, so he could get his Spam can out, and he began to urinate. And a white woman in a car by herself drove past him on the highway, and he said, 'Oh, my God, she looks like she'll tell a lie.' He thought she was going to stop and report him, accuse him of exposing himself. He was that paranoid. But he was standing on the side of the car. There was no way she could see what he was doing. But, for him, having been raised in segregated, hateful America, this was how people got lynched. And that fear never did leave his bones."[34]

When Lightnin' finally got to Mother Blues, Benson says, his demeanor changed. If anything, he exuded a sense of confidence and cool. Mark Pollock, a white blues guitarist from Irving, Texas, said when he saw Lightnin' live at Mother Blues, he felt he "looked exactly like he stepped off the album cover, the half-pint in the back pocket, or shoved down his boot. He had those dark sunglasses . . . he played that old Gibson, or a Stella, or a black Stratocaster . . . he wore a cowboy hat and he was the first blues guy I saw wearing cowboy boots."[35]

Anson Funderburgh, another aspiring white blues guitarist, saw Lightnin' for the first time in 1974 at Mother Blues when he was about nineteen years old. "I was awestruck. Lightnin' had on a brown suit and a brown hat and had a fifth of whiskey in his coat pocket wrapped up in a brown paper bag. He had like a big gold-colored medallion around his neck with a lightning bolt on it." On stage, Lightnin' was in complete control, but it was obvious that he hadn't rehearsed with his sidemen, or perhaps even met them, until he showed up at the gig. "He had a bass player and a drummer playing with him," Funderburgh says, "and by the second set, the bass player was gone. He fired the bass player. Both of them were white. But the drummer stayed. Lightnin' made his music go where his vocals were going, and where his singing was going. Lightnin' went right where he wanted to go, and he expected anyone that was with him to follow him. . . . He was the one who was making the rules."[36]

Three years later, Funderburgh understood even more clearly what it was like to play with Hopkins when he was invited to perform with him on stage at the Granada Theatre in Dallas on August 27 and 28, 1977. "I was scared to death," Funderburgh says, "because I was such a big fan." For the show, the promoter Danny Brown put together a group of musicians to accompany Lightnin' on stage that included Funderburgh and Marc Benno playing rhythm guitar, Doyle Bramhall on drums, and Larry Rogers on bass. "At the rehearsal," Funderburgh recalls, "we were set up, and they had a piano on stage, because evidently he had requested a piano. Well, we were just sittin' around talkin' and the piano tuner came and he got it all tuned up. And after a while, they brought Lightnin' in and he hit one chord on the piano and he said, 'That goddamn piano's out of tune, I can't use it.' And he didn't play it all night."[37]

Prior to the show, the band had very little interaction with Lightnin', who seemed to be reserved and a little withdrawn before he went on stage. Funderburgh, Benno, Bramhall, and Rogers were the opening act, and at the appointed time, they started a song. Lightnin' came on, and "evidently," Funderburgh says, "we weren't doing it exactly the way he wanted to, and I remember him turning to Marc Benno and saying, 'I told you, you were going to do this to me.' Well, I was nervous as a cat. But he always seemed to like what I did. I just turned down really quiet. I just listened to him and tried to follow him. I know I made mistakes. I really wasn't trying to be loud or anything. I think maybe that's what he liked about me . . . I wasn't trying to play all over him."[38]

Funderburgh learned quickly what he needed to do. "He was very difficult to follow because he kind of changed chords whenever he wanted to change chords. It was a slow blues, so it was built around a three-chord slow blues thing, but he may play an extra measure of the one chord and then switch real quick down to the four, and then back to the one. The whole key to following Lightnin' Hopkins was to really listen to where his vocals were going. He didn't follow a hard pattern."[39]

Doyle Bramhall concurs, "He [Lightnin'] was a tough bird. There weren't any rehearsals or sound checks or anything like that. You just showed up, and you immediately jumped in the deep end. He made you pay attention, so my deal was to just stay in the groove, in the pocket. But he would stop the whole show with a packed show at the Granada and say, 'Man, this bass player just got to get it together.' He never did it to Anson, and he never did it to me. But he gave bass players a hard time. He used to say, 'Lightnin' change when Lightnin' change,' as far as his chord playing went."[40]

After the first set, the band went backstage and Lightnin' held court, Bramhall says. "When Lightnin' came into a room, he was the center of attention, and he was that way without ever trying. Here we were, a bunch of white kids, just soaking up everything he had to say."[41]

"He was like a hero," Funderburgh adds, "I was just kind of hanging on to every word that he said. And we were all backstage, and he looked over at me, and I guess I had done a pretty good job because I felt like he kind of took to me somehow. I was surprised because he remembered my name. He said, 'Anson, go get Lightnin' a beer,' And so I just hopped right up and ran over and got him a can of Pearl. And right when I leaned down to give it to him, I popped the top. And it was like I was froze in time. I'm sure it wasn't very long, but it seemed like hours had gone by. I'm standing there holding this beer and he would never take it from me. And finally he looked up at me and goes, 'Anson, don't ever drink from something someone opened for you. Now, go get Lightnin' a Pearl.' So, I just jumped on over there and got him another Pearl and let him open it. And he drank it right down."[42]

Funderburgh was needless to say a little embarrassed, but Lightnin' didn't rub it in. He just wanted his needs to be met on his terms. "Lightnin' knew what he was doing," Bramhall says, "Him being the teacher and all of us being his students. He would be backstage: Would you get ole Lightnin' a cigarette, or would you get ole Lightnin' his guitar or whatever. We didn't mind doing it because he was Lightnin'."[43]

Yet Lightnin' and his sidemen were worlds apart, not only in terms of their musical backgrounds and worldview, but most noticeably in appearance. "We were hippies," Funderburgh says. "I had hair down to probably the middle of my back and a feathered earring in my left ear with bell-bottom blue jeans and house slippers called Jiffy's that I wore all the time. They [Bramhall, Benno, and Rogers] looked about the same."[44] And Hopkins wore suits: "He was a slick dresser with a lot of gold," Bramhall adds, "and he was very articulate. He always had a tie. He always dressed really sharp. His shoes were shined so bright you could see your face in them."[45]

Tim "Mit" Schuller in his *Living Blues* review of the Granada show was far more critical than the musicians themselves, describing the opening act as a "miserable four man aggregation introduced as the Lightnin' Hopkins warm-up band. No more need be said about them except to point out that their rhythm guitarist was Marc Benno and their lead guitarist was of the type who have given white blues musicians a bad name."[46]

According to Schuller, when Lightnin' finally took the stage in a "highly theatrical walk-on," he took "an absurdly long time to tune his guitar . . . and just when things were rolling tolerably, he'd stop and begin reprimanding an errant sideman." To be fair, Schuller pointed out that the sidemen actually made few "really drastic mistakes," but that Hopkins's songs "emerged as rambling inconglomerates, made of disjointed fragments from any of his countless recordings. Little real music surfaced . . . the irritating part of this whole trip is that Lightnin' is quite able to play well but simply chooses not to do so." The highlights of the evening for Schuller were the performance of "Mojo Hand" and his playing of "My Babe" for two verses until the drummer "blew a cue (one that most bluesmen could have covered easily) and the music stopped while Lightnin' chewed him out, griped, philosophized, and drank from a Pearl beer can." Schuller concluded his review by stating that "one hesitates to criticize a legend, but Lightnin' has done this bit before in Dallas and I have seen him do it in Cleveland's Music Hall. That Lightnin' deserves respect is indisputable; he is an irrevocable part of the musical history of this nation. But the legend has become a caricature of itself."[47]

During this period, Benson says, Lightnin' became more selective about the touring dates he accepted because he "didn't really want to go out that much on the road." However, he did continue to play at venues that he liked in Dallas, Houston, Austin, and New York City, where he might get three or four dates a year at the Village Gate. In the summer of 1978, he returned to Canada to play at the Rising Sun in Montreal and the New Yorker Theater in Toronto on the same bill with John Hammond, whom Benson heard criticize Lightnin' in a radio interview in Houston. "I was listening to KPFT and the DJ was talking to John Hammond, who was playing at Liberty Hall, and he was kind of defaming Lightnin' and Juke Boy Bonner. . . . He was talking about how Lightnin' never made it big and how he would never make it big because he didn't play according to meter. So I heard it on the radio, so I went to Liberty Hall and I went straight to the dressing room. And I confronted John Hammond and he and I were there for a couple of hours talking music theory and that kind of thing. We were talking about meter being something that actually had been introduced later. Because meter is to the blues what grammar is to language. The music existed before."[48] Benson was defensive about Lightnin', but clearly by the late 1970s, he was declining. "I thought something might be wrong with his health, but I couldn't be sure. And he didn't say much about it."

With Harold and Benson managing Lightnin's bookings, he was much more selective, and he enjoyed spending more time with Antoinette in Houston. On Friday nights, Benson says, Lightnin' and Antoinette had a steady date night, and went to some friends' house where they played the card game Pitty Pat. On other nights, Lightnin' loved to gamble and shoot dice. "He would take me with him to Fifth Ward and to Third Ward," Benson remembers, "different places where he would shoot all night. He would want me to go with him. I'm a pretty big guy, so he would want me to go with him to hold his money, and then we'd go in there, and he'd always have a couple of guns."[49]

In the Third Ward, there was a man by the name of Mr. Blackwell that Lightnin' liked. "He owned a walk-up barbecue stand at the corner of McGowen and Dowling," Benson said, "and he and Lightnin' would shoot dice at Lightnin's place. They would take a bathroom rug and turn it upside down, and they would shoot head to head dice all night. Sometimes Mr. Blackwell would lose fifteen thousand dollars, and maybe Lightnin' might lose. And they'd bullshit each other. Lightnin' would say, 'Mr. Blackwell, you need to go sell some barbecue and c'mon back.' They were good friends."[50]

On Sundays, Lightnin' liked to get in his car and cruise past the churches in the black neighborhoods of Houston, but never go inside. "We would get in the car," Benson recalls, "and at twenty miles per hour we'd cruise Third Ward, and Fourth Ward, and Acres Home, but we would still have some cold Pearl and CC

[Canadian Club] and he would cruise and yell at people and say little things like, 'Hey, baby, where you goin' with them groceries?'"[51]

When he wasn't cruising the neighborhoods or shooting dice, Lightnin' hung out in front of Johnny Lee's, a Chinese grocery in the Third Ward. "He sat in his car at his corner," Benson says, "and he would make loans to people in the community, and he would sit there with a couple of pistols in the car and a half pint of Canadian Club. So whenever I wanted to find him, I'd get in my pick-up truck and I would cruise and usually catch up with him there. . . . And I would go sit in the car with him and we'd sit and drink Canadian Club until both of us would get drunker than shit and then he would say, 'Let's go get something to eat.' Well, I had a key to the apartment and Miss Nette would always keep the refrigerator full of food she'd cooked for us. So we'd go home and we'd warm up something from Miss Nette, or if she was there, she would fix something for us, and we'd eat and sit around and play guitars."[52]

One time Benson drove up to Johnny Lee's grocery store and was shocked to see that Lightnin' "had a gun to a guy's head . . . and he had a Pearl beer in his other hand. And he walked over to my truck, still pointing the gun at the guy, handed me the beer through my truck window, and said, 'Hold this beer for me, baby, while I kill this motherfucka.' And I'm looking at the windshield at him, and he's arguing with the guy. 'Who told you to drink my liquor?' and the guy says, 'Lee,' a cousin of Lightnin's, who lived out in Sunnyside. 'Well, who told you to drink out of the bottle? Why couldn't you drink out of the cap? You're supposed to drink out of the cap so they can tell that you're not greedy. . . . You can't turn the bottle up.' See the guy had taken a drink from the bottle, and Lightnin' was going to kill him. Lee was so drunk; he was wallowing all over this hood of his car. He couldn't even stand up. And Lightnin' said, 'Who told you to drink out of the bottle?' And the guy said, 'My mama.' And Lightnin' said, 'You're right, because if you had said my mama, you'd be dead right now.' And Lightnin' started pistol whipping Lee and then he come back to me and said, 'C'mon, baby let's go.' And he got in his car and I followed him around to his apartment."[53]

Benson believed that Lightnin' wasn't "as hard as he put on to be. But Lightnin' would kill you. He was from that generation that would kill somebody, but when you did anger him, he was dangerous. But he was a very sweet man. He could be very tender."[54] Michael Point, a white hippie writer and blues fan, who sometimes served as Lightnin's driver in the 1970s, recalled that often times when he arrived early to pick up Lightnin' for a gig, "He'd be out on the porch with all these neighborhood kids around him, and he'd be playing a kids' concert for them, all cheerful and positive—Sesame Street versions of his songs. It's the last thing he'd want anyone to know."[55]

When Lightnin' was in the white world, he was often more withdrawn; he didn't say much, but he was nonetheless self-assured and confident in his own ability to do whatever he pleased on stage. On April 10, 1979, Lightnin' appeared in his fourth and final program at Carnegie Hall in a show called Blues 'n' Boogie that was organized by Christophe De Menil and her production company in New York. Anton J. Mikofsky, a blues fan and photographer, was hired to write the program notes and worked as a kind of consultant for De Menil. "She had a definite idea of who she wanted to book," Mikofsky says, "but was open to suggestions. Her vision was that the superstar would be Clifton Chenier, the great zydeco accordion player from Louisiana. He hadn't been in New York City since maybe the 1950s, when, I think, he played the Apollo, so this would be a comeback for him. And she arranged for Big Mama Thornton to be a special surprise guest with Clifton Chenier. And the second billing would either be John Lee Hooker or Lightnin' Hopkins. As it turned out, the way the program reads, John Lee Hooker is second billing, and Lightnin' Hopkins is third billing."[56]

Mikofsky had seen Lightnin' on different occasions over the previous four or five years, and had had a chance to speak to him backstage. At the Village Gate, Mikofsky remembered one night seeing John Belushi at Lightnin's show. "He was a big blues fan," Mikofsky said, "long before he did *The Blues Brothers*, and he would hang out backstage, and instead of being a journalist or worshipping fan, he would take over. He was like a take-charge kind of guy, an aggressive type, not in a bad way necessarily, but one time, as I remember it, he set himself up as a kind of doorman. He was going to screen whoever was going to get access to the dressing room; he was the real boss of the door. He would keep the riff-raff out of Lightnin's dressing room. Fortunately, I was already inside."[57]

Mikofsky found Lightnin' to be very friendly, "but at the same time, he had a certain reserve. He was very laconic. I used to wonder about the older black guys, if it was growing up in a segregated society, where you had to kow-tow a little bit. You didn't want to be another Emmett Till. But once you got to know these old black musicians, they warmed up a lot. Lightnin' definitely felt that way with real blues fans that were sincere, or other musicians. For example, there was a piano in a rehearsal room back stage. This is Carnegie, and he actually sat down and he started playing piano a little bit. He was a little more versatile than people think. . . . Lightnin' was definitely chatting with people . . . I didn't feel any animosity or resentment or anything, but I know that maybe at some point in the past in the South, they had to be cautious or careful of what they did or what they said. Or adopt a kind of glowering personality like Howlin' Wolf, who felt he had to be more aggressive."[58]

When Lightnin' got to New York City for the Carnegie Hall show with Benson and Wrecks Bell, whom he had asked to come along as his bass player, Mikofsky was sensitive to Lightnin's performance style and needs on stage and volunteered his services to find an appropriate drummer for the gig. "Lightnin' felt," Mikofsky says, "that he should be at least a trio, and drums would certainly round out his sound . . . and the best one that was available was Charles 'HoneyMan' Otis. He was, I think, from New Orleans, a very funky drummer. He had worked with a lot of various bands and black artists. So I fixed them up . . . and they got along famously. And they actually did very well together."[59]

On stage, Lightnin' was at ease. Bell had played bass with Lightnin' on numerous occasions, but hadn't really traveled much with him. "We brought him because Lightnin' basically liked him," Benson says. "But he had been in a fight, and his face was all bandaged up. And I think we had to lend him the money to get a tuxedo, but it all worked out in the end."[60]

During the show, Benson was backstage talking with John Lee Hooker. Hooker asked if Benson wouldn't mind letting Lightnin' know that he had a special request, and much to Hooker's amazement, Benson acted on it immediately. He crept out on the stage in the middle of the set and whispered in Lightnin's ear that Hooker wanted him to sing "Mr. Charlie." "John Lee stuttered," Benson says, "and that was one of his favorite songs [because it's about a boy who stutters and gets beyond it by singing]. So it seemed like the moment I said the words 'Mr. Charlie', Lightnin' hit the note and launched into the song."

For Christophe De Menil, Carnegie Hall was more than a concert; it was a social and media event. She planned a pre-party at Windows on the World on the 107th floor of the North Tower of the World Trade Center, and an after party at the restaurant One Fifth. "*Look* magazine," Benson says, "even made some arrangement to take Lightnin' on a carriage ride through Central Park and I had to go to do the sound check. Lightnin' didn't really like it. . . . He would have preferred to sit around the hotel and shoot the bull with Clifton and John Lee and the rest rather than being out on some publicity thing." The Carnegie Hall show was nearly sold out, though Mikofsky said it was never his impression that De Menil ever thought she was going to make money. Benson recalls, "All the New York press came out—it was a hell of an affair. Paul Simon was on the guest list. George Plimpton and Lee Radziwill were there. Lightnin' didn't much care for the party at Windows on the World, but he liked One Fifth. In the middle of that party, everybody got sort of schnockered and women started taking their clothes off on the dance floor, and Lightnin' was entranced. They were all getting naked and he was sitting back in a corner there."[61]

Lightnin's performance at Carnegie Hall was high profile, and on June 20, 1979, the mayor of Houston issued a proclamation to celebrate "Lightnin' Hopkins Day" as part of the Juneteenth Blues Festival, which included a parade down Dowling Street in the Third Ward that culminated with free concerts in Miller Outdoor Theater at Hermann Park. On August 3 and 4, Lightnin' was one of the headliners at ChicagoFest, and on October 10, he appeared at the Armadillo in Austin. Lightnin' was also invited back to New York to perform at the Lone Star Cafe by Christophe De Menil, who also provided Lightnin' with lodging at her residence at Sutton Place.

In 1980, Benson says he sensed that Lightnin' was having health problems, but he wasn't really sure. He had noticed how Lightnin' had trouble finding the right food to eat for years, but it didn't really click until later when he started having more serious symptoms. He didn't eat much and he was getting thinner. Eventually Benson realized that Lightnin's touring had declined not only because he didn't like traveling, but because it simply became too difficult physically. However, Lightnin' did not want to stop performing.

For Lightnin's sixty-eighth birthday, Benson says, Antoinette and Ron Wilson, who had accompanied him on his tour to Sweden and Germany, gave Lightnin' a 1980 Gibson Custom Les Paul Silverburst guitar. By then Lightnin' had established his guitar preferences and had become somewhat of a guitar collector. For years he played a small Harmony flat-top and a Gibson J-50 outfitted with a DeArmond soundhole pickup. But in the 1960s, he began using a Gibson J160E that he purchased at Ray Henning's Heart of Music store in Austin, though he also liked to perform with his red Guild Starfire and Fender Stratocaster and sometimes even used a wah-wah pedal.[62]

In June 1980, Lightnin' was invited again to be a headliner at the Juneteenth Blues Festival, which was an event that had honored him the previous year and whose director, Lanny Steele, Lightnin' liked a great deal. Onstage, no one knew exactly what to expect. Steve Ditzell, a guitarist for Koko Taylor's band, was sitting backstage when Lightnin' was about to go on. "I remember that day very well. I met him back stage and shook his hand. Well, he was getting ready to go do a gig, so [was] very reserved at that moment. He had a little 100-ml flask, one of the smaller ones, and he was working on that. He said, 'That's just enough,' and he was with his wife [Antoinette]. They were both real cordial. You know, musicians before they play, they tend to be kind of withdrawn, because you're psyching yourself; you're getting ready to do a show. That's the state of mind he was in."[63]

Muddy Waters had finished his set to loud applause, but this was Houston and the anticipation was building for Lightnin'. He wasn't going to be upstaged. He was the headliner. "It was great," Ditzell said. "He came out there and sat on one of those metal folding chairs. And he had a black Stratocaster and he had it turned up loud, and he just had a bass player and a drummer, and he sang into that mike, and when he wasn't singing into that mike, he rocked back on that chair, back on the last two legs; thought he was going to tip over backwards a couple of times. And he would hit these notes with that Stratocaster, just grin at the sky. . . . It was fantastic. There were maybe four thousand people there and they were all just crazy over Lightnin' Hopkins. . . . He was absolutely fuckin' great. In fact, I've told friends of mine thinking back over the years, when I've been asked what is the one performance that stands out over anybody, and it was Lightnin' Hopkins that day. He just tore that place up."[64]

Lightnin' then traveled to Montreal, where he was recorded live at the Rising Sun Celebrity Jazz Club on July 22, 1980, by Doudou Boicel, the Canadian impresario who had also recorded him at the same venue on June 23, 1977. Clifford Antone then invited Lightnin' to play at his club in Austin as part of a benefit for Clifton Chenier. While in Austin, Antone recalled,

Lightnin' liked to go fishing on Town Lake. "It was actually just an excuse to get out there and drink some beer," Antone said. "He played at my club three or four times."

Lightnin' returned to New York City to play at Tramps on August 8, and again from September 16 to 18, October 31, and November 1. Benson says that Tramps was owned by a Texan, who was able to pay well and take good care of him and Lightnin' while they were there. Robert Palmer in an article in the *New York Times* prior to the October 31 show at Tramps, however, recounted an interaction he observed between Lightnin' and an unnamed club owner, in which Lightnin' demanded payment before playing. "He was flashing a gleaming, gold-toothed smile," Palmer said, "and his powder blue suit was the brightest thing in the dingy nightclub basement, but his eyes were hidden behind dark sun glasses and it was impossible to read what was in them. He took a swallow of whisky, shook his head slowly from side to side, and looked up at the club owner, who was standing in the doorway of the dressing room. 'You've got one more show to do, Lightnin',"" he said. Mr. Hopkins tapped a bulge in his hip pocket significantly; it could have been a wallet or a flask, but on the other hand . . . 'If you want it now, Lightnin', that's no problem,' said the club owner. Mr. Hopkins smiled even more broadly. 'Yes,' he said, 'I want it now.' The club owner disappeared and Mr. Hopkins leaned back in his chair, emitting a short, dry laugh."[65]

Lightnin' made his last trip out of the country to appear at the fourth annual Festival de Blues en México on October 15, 16, and 18, 1980. He had never been to Mexico City and Antoinette traveled with him. Lightnin' was a headliner on a bill that included his old friend Willie Dixon, as well as Carey Bell, Eddie Clearwater, and Edwin Helfer. Jim O'Neal, who was then editor of *Living Blues* magazine, put the lineup together, and for Lightnin', he hired Aaron Burton on bass and Steve Cushing on drums, both of whom were from Chicago. Cushing says he didn't have much trouble following Lightnin', though Burton had a little more difficulty because Lightnin' changed his tempo unpredicatably. "When he came on stage, which was about the only time we saw him, he already had his guitar out of the case and he was carrying his guitar, it was a hollow body, by the neck, and he was wearing these beautiful cowboy boots and he had a bottle, I think it was Jack Daniels in the other hand. And he was with the most beautiful black woman [Antoinette] I had ever seen in my life. And she was over sixty years old. She was really statuesque. She made a real impression. I don't remember if she was light-skinned or dark, but I do remember she had silver highlights in her hair."[66]

As Lightnin' walked past Cushing and Burton, he said hi, but "that's basically all he said," Cushing recalls. "He never told us what to play or anything to do. He just expected that we'd be together enough to follow him. God, the guy had been playing for decades, so he'd probably been in every situation you could imagine. And the fact that we weren't lost was probably a relief to him. He wasn't hard to play behind. For a drummer, especially if you play a double shuffle, you're always on the beat. The people who have problems are the melody instruments because they have to be in a certain key at a certain time. So it was much harder for Aaron Burton on bass than it was for me. Well we were scrambling trying to keep up with him, but we did. I guess we were just sort of laughing between ourselves at how Lightnin' would jump. And when Lightnin' jumped time, actually, it didn't matter, I'd be right there with him."[67]

Lightnin's set didn't last very long. "I was really surprised," Cushing says, "because we played really long sets in Chicago, and I guess, this was as close to the big time as I ever got, but if he played half an hour, I think that would have been stretching it." The audience wanted to hear more music, and Lightnin's conversational approach didn't work very well because most of the people listening didn't speak English. This was especially true when Lightnin' did "Mr. Charlie," which was clearly one of his concert favorites, but he did finally realize that there was a language problem and just played the songs.[68]

In 1981, Lightnin' stayed mostly around Houston, playing on January 7 at the Rock House and later in the spring appearing at the Juneteenth Blues Festival on June 17. By then he was getting weaker. On July 1, he returned to the Rock House, where he was recorded for the last time, accompanied by Larry Martin on bass and Andy McCobb on drums. In his set, Lightnin' performed several of the songs that had become his standard fare, including "Trouble in Mind," "Mojo Hand," "Pa and Mama Hopkins," "Watch Yourself," and "Baby, Please Don't Go."[69] Within weeks, he was diagnosed with cancer of the esophagus and went into the hospital for surgery, forcing him to cancel a fourteen-day British and European tour. Benson says his recovery went smoothly and he slowly regained his strength. On November 8 and 9, his performances at Tramps were sold out. "They had to turn people back," Harold told a United Press International reporter.[70] But when he got back to Houston, his health declined rapidly.

On Wednesday, January 27, Lightnin' was admitted to St. Joseph's Hospital for further treatment. While he was in the hospital, Antoinette, Benson, Harold, and other family members and close friends visited him frequently. His daughter Anna Mae Box came often to Houston to spend time with Lightnin'.

Box had been estranged from Lightnin' for years. He had left her mother, Elamer Lacy, when she was only five years old. And even though Lightnin' probably knew she lived somewhere in East Texas, and she knew he was likely in Houston, they never made any effort to find each other until Box's eldest daughter, Bertha, heard that he was playing at the Jewish Community Center in Houston in 1973. "Bertha had a girlfriend who worked at the Jewish Community Center," Box said, "and this girl told my daughter that my daddy was going to play there. She didn't know that was Bertha's grandfather. She said, 'Lightnin's going to play at the Jewish Community Center Friday night.' And so Bertha told her, 'That's my grandfather. And I'm going to come over there to see him.' See I didn't know where he was or nothing. So Bertha went over there. And he called me that night. She gave him my telephone number, and he called me. Sure did."[71]

After that first conversation, Box called him often: "His voice was just . . . He had the most beautiful voice. And I just loved to hear him say hello." Lightnin' was delighted to see Box, and they visited each other fairly often. "Daddy would come up here, and I'd take him fishing. He liked to fish. And he'd be all dressed up, sitting in his chair with his leg crossed. And they would harass him and say, 'Lightnin', you know you didn't come to fish, not dressed up like that.' But he'd just sit there with that hook in the water.[72]

"You take a person that want to relax his mind and get things off his mind, well, maybe, say, worried about something that happened. Get him a little old tree, go to the tree and get him a hook and bait and go to fishin' he'll forget about that. . . .That's why the doctor tell lots of these old people it would be a lots of help to them to go to the creek and just fish. It don't matter if it's just a little minnow bitin'. You done forgot all about what's goin' on. I think the doctor is right there 'cause it gives you so much relax. You get on the creek fishin' you forget about what's worryin' you. Sometimes I get up there and get under a shade tree and kind of doze off. But I don't never sleep so sound that anything shake my post, you see I have it right there on my leg there."[73]

Sometimes Lightnin' would call Anna Mae in advance before driving up to Centerville. "He'd call me and tell me when he was coming," Box said, "and I'd always try to cook. He liked for me to cook him black-eyed peas. And I would cook them. Fry some pork chops. His companion [Antoinette] come down one weekend and spent the night with me. Her and Daddy."[74]

Bertha also saw Lightnin' in Houston almost daily. "She would go on her lunch hour over to Daddy's house. Daddy liked pinto beans and chicken and dumplings. And this lady friend of his [Antoinette] would always cook that kind of stuff for him. And my daughter would go over and eat dinner. She'd go over there to his apartment. He liked to play dominoes. He just liked to entertain his friends, just, you know, a bunch of them sitting around in the house, laughing and talking."[75]

Box had become part of Lightnin's inner circle, though she really didn't know Antoinette or Harold very well. Seeing Lightnin' in the hospital was painful. "He wasn't at hisself," Box said, "and so he just listened to his music. You cut it off, he would say something." Box believed that Lightnin' had a belief in God, because when she was with him in the hospital he "was so low. And I just believe that he—he just knew the Lord. He couldn't help but to know him because my grandmother taught all of that in her home."[76]

Lightnin's song "Death Bells," recorded for Gold Star as early as 1948, had a haunting tone, which Box believed expressed his deep-seated belief, but also his uncertainty.

> Sound like I can hear this morning
> Death bells ringing all in my ear (x2)
> Yes, I know that I'm gonna leave on a chariot
> Wonder what kind's gonna carry me from here

Box spent as much time as she could with Lightnin', but it was difficult because she had to commute from Crockett, and she had a daughter who was still in school. Antoinette kept vigil at the hospital, and was there with Benson on the day Lightnin' died, January 30, 1982. "When he got sick before he died,"

Benson says, "it was like a marble falling off a table; it was very sudden. He was always complaining about not being able to eat solid foods and wanting soups and those kinds of things. And then when we came back from Tramps, he started really getting weak, but he seemed like, I never did get to see him suffer as such. Then Miss Nette called me and said that he was in St. Joseph's hospital and that I should come down there quickly. And when I got to the hospital, Miss Nette was crying. So I went to his deathbed and Miss Nette, and my current wife, I had just met her before that, waited outside. And I went into the intensive care unit and they had him all hooked up to various breathing machines and apparatus, and Miss Nette would say, 'Lightnin' loved you; he loved you,' and he did, he genuinely did, I felt he genuinely loved me. We were like relatives, and I went into the hospital room, and his eyes were open, but he wasn't conscious seemingly, but it seemed as if he was trying to talk to me, and to express to me how much he had cared for me because we loved each other. That's why it was so important to me. It wasn't Lightnin' the musician, it was Lightnin' the man. And I stood there and I held his hand until the nurses asked me to leave and then I went back out and it wasn't any time before they pronounced him dead."[77] The cause of death was cancer of the esophagus.

Benson helped Antoinette make the necessary preparations for the wake and funeral, and Antoinette asked him to do the eulogy. Lighntin' had often called Benson a "pronouncer," meaning that he was good with words, especially as it related to introducing Hopkins on stage. "At one point," Benson says, Antoinette was "rather distraught about the whole thing, but she was very strong through most of the public part of it when other people were around."[78]

On Tuesday, February 3, a wake was scheduled at Johnson's Funeral Chapel at 2301 McGowen Street in the Third Ward. Throngs of people began showing up early in the afternoon, soon after Lightnin's eighteen-gauge steel casket was opened for viewing. Lightnin' was dressed in a brown pinstriped suit and was surrounded by three wreaths shaped like guitars. "Upwards of 1,000 mourners," Marty Racine reported in the *Houston Chronicle*, "paid their final respects." The tone was "quiet and low-keyed, as friends, fans, and family formed a line around the block waiting to file past the open casket."[79] An organ played quietly in the background, and the mourners expressed their condolences to Antoinette and members of Lightnin's family and closest friends. Rocky Hill, a local Houston

musician who had played with Lightnin' on different occasions, brought his guitar, pulled over a stool, and started playing "Amazing Grace" and, according
to Racine, "a standard blues on acoustic bottleneck guitar." Hill's performance
lasted about five minutes, and afterward he told a friend that it was the "hardest
gig I've ever done." Racine wrote, "The blues bothered some mourners. One
remarked, 'Nat King Cole sang the blues, too, but they didn't play the blues
at his funeral.'"[80] In fact, Benson said, Antoinette was annoyed, but she didn't
want to confront Hill. He was not asked to perform, and for family and friends,
Hill's "musical tribute" was inappropriate. Yet according to Bob Claypool of the
Houston Post, Antoinette had in fact "asked Rocky . . . to play some music" at
the wake, but after viewing the body, "Rocky said, 'I can't . . . I won't make it,'"
and stepped away. After a while, John Lomax Jr. said, "We're gonna mourn anyway, and it's better mourning with music than without it," and Hill picked up his
guitar and played "Amazing Grace," but didn't sing. He "just played—played it
slow and haunting, and yes, very, very *bluesy*, and anyone who heard had to be
touched. And when he finished, he walked out into the hallway and cried."[81]

"Miss Nette took affront," Benson said, "And she really asked me to ask
him to cease and desist and leave, because she thought that he was desecrating
the wake. But I didn't ask him to leave. I didn't confront him. We didn't want
a scene. But she was very distraught about it, and she thought it was very disre-
spectful. She didn't say anything either, because she's a very tactful woman."[82]

However, the presence of Hill, Billy Gibbons, and numerous other white
performers and fans at Lightnin's wake accentuated the cultural divide in which
he thrived and, to some extent, was able to bridge through his blues. As Harold
said in the *Houston Chronicle*, Lightnin' was essentially a private man: "He didn't
socialize in crowds, only performed in them."[83]

Lightnin's funeral was at 11:00 A.M. on the day after the wake at the Johnson
Funeral Home Chapel, located at 5730 Calhoun Road in Houston, with Reverend Johnny Kelly officiating. Lightnin's family and closest friends were there,
including Antoinette, David Benson, Dr. Harold, as well as his sister, Emma
Hopkins from Centerville; his daughter, Anna Mae Box from Crockett; and two
other children, whose mothers are unknown and who Lightnin' never talked
about in any interview or conversation: his daughter Celestine from Fort Worth,
and his son, Charles, who Benson said he learned about at the funeral, was

studying to become a minister in Houston.[84] For the funeral, Benson recalls, "I had Miss Nette's car, a Buick Riviera, and I did some running around for her. We all showed up at Miss Nette's house. We met and then we went to the funeral. I drove her car and she went in the car that the funeral home provided. And there were probably 100–150 people at the funeral, not nearly as many that had gone to the wake. It was sunny, as I remember, that day. We went to the cemetery. It was nice and bright. Albert Collins showed up. He came to the house, and we had a big dinner, fried chicken and all the fixins and everything after the funeral, and stayed over there with Miss Nette probably until late at night."[85]

Lightnin' was buried at Forest Park Cemetery. Some years later, a small plaque was placed as a memorial marker with the epitaph: "Here lies Lightnin' who stood famous and tall. He didn't hesitate to give his all." Presumably Antoinette wrote the epitaph, though Benson wasn't sure. "I've never gone back to the cemetery," Benson says, "I just can't."

Lightnin' declared in his will that he was "not now married, having been divorced from my former wife for over thirty years," a statement which was confusing especially since it didn't identify to which "wife" he was referring. Moreover, no divorce documents relating to any of Lightnin's "marriages" have ever been found. Lightnin' appointed Antoinette Charles as the independent executrix of the will, and bequeathed to his son, Charles Lewis Hopkins, his "Chevrolet Truck, and any of my clothes he desires and the sum of $100; to his daughter Celestine Hopkins, the sum of $2,000; to his daughter Anna Mae Box, the sum of $3,000" and "quarterly payments of $100 out of his royalty checks for as long as they are paid to his estate"; and to his "beloved friend and confidant," Antoinette Charles, the remainder of his property, "whether separate or community, and wherever situated, including the house at 4357 Knoxville in Houston, Texas and my savings and certificate of savings at South Main Bank and Houston United Bank, and my 1970 Cadillac."[86]

Lightnin's will is signed only with his initials, which seems unusual, if he were of "sound mind," considering that he was able to sign his full name on other documents in previous years. In addition, there are no other references to Lightnin' ever living at 4357 Knoxville in Houston. Anna Mae Box was shocked when she learned the details of the will. "He told me that I would be taken care of the rest of my life because I would draw royalties from his records, you know. He really thought that. You can just put too much confidence and faith in people. Don't always work out the way you want it to." Box felt that Antoinette had seized the moment and "taken control," getting Lightnin' to sign the will two days before he died. Box got a lawyer and contested the will but to no avail. The will was probated on March 16, 1983. "They bought my lawyer out," Box said in resignation, "I just prayed and I told the Lord, 'If it's for me to have anything, I'll get it. If not, I won't get it.' But I thank the Lord. You take crumbs from the table, and if you're right, it's going to work out for you." Years later, Box did admit that Antoinette was "a wonderful person. Anybody that take care of my daddy like she did, I love her. I do."[87]

While the circumstances surrounding Lightnin's death have left many questions unanswered, it is clear that Antoinette, over the thirty-five years of their affair, did help Lightnin' considerably, loving him, cooking for him, encouraging him to control his drinking, and providing a companionship that ultimately stabilized his life. Antoinette was his wife in every sense except legal. About Antoinette, Lightnin' once said, "If I had wings as an angel, I'd tell you where I'd fly. I'd fly to the heart of Antoinette and that's where I'd give up to die."[88]

Lightnin', Benson says, was more affectionate than he would ever admit. Benson saw Lightnin' and Antoinette hug and sometimes kiss each other in public. "They were close," Benson said, "and there was no stand-offishness about it. Now in that generation of black people, you don't see public kinds of things. But in terms of his warmth toward her, it was undeniable the love he had for her and she had for him." However, Antoinette also explained to Benson that Lightnin' had some bad relationships before they got together.

Ultimately, had Antoinette not worked with Harold, and to a lesser extent, Benson, to assist in managing his bookings and keeping track of his recording contracts, he would not have been able to keep up with the revenues associated with his music. By the 1960s some of his records, like those on Arhoolie and Prestige, were not only earning royalties from record sales, but he was beginning to realize income from his compositions via their publishers. However, after Lightnin's death the amount of his royalties increased exponentially. For example, between 1962 and 1982, Lightnin's Prestige albums earned approximately $8,410 in artist royalties and $1,580 in songwriter royalties after fees and expenses were recouped. But since 1983, Antoinette, as Lightnin's heir, has received (from Prestige and its subsequent owners Fantasy and the Concord Music Group) in excess of $47,000 in artist royalties and $245,000 in songwriter royalties from airplay and covers (most notably by Huey Lewis in 1994 and Van Morrison in 2003).[89] By comparison, Lightnin's artist royalties from Arhoolie sales, after fees and expenses were recouped, have been relatively low: about $3,900 between 1962 and 1982, and more than $42,000 from 1983 to the present. However, the songwriter royalties from Strachwitz's publishing company Tradition Music have been significantly less: about $2,100 during Lightnin's lifetime, and about $6,000 since his death. While these figures are illuminating, they provide a limited view of Lightnin's earning power. It's difficult to establish how much, if anything, Lightnin' was paid in royalties from his other contracts, especially since he usually sold his songs outright and wanted to be paid a flat fee of $100 per song. But this was not always the case. Prestige agreed to pay Lightnin' an advance of only $500 for each album with a 20-cents-per-LP royalty, and Arhoolie paid about the same.

Yet of all the white producers who recorded Lightnin', Benson said Lightnin' liked Chris Strachwitz the best. "He thought he was the most real, most genuine, and fair person. He thought that Chris genuinely had come through and tried to give what was due to the people who produced the music. He thought Chris was not up to no good, and that he had always proven out what he said. He didn't have too much respect for anybody else in that business, but he never said anything about Chris."[90]

For Strachwitz, his working relationship with Lightnin' was an outgrowth of his personal response to the music. In a condolence letter to Antoinette, sent four days after Lightnin' died, Strachwitz wrote: "Meeting him first in 1959 was really a pilgrimage on my part to visit the man I admired most in my life. His voice and music had haunted me since I first heard him sing on his records over the radio in Los Angeles. I think I bought every 78 that came out by him and when I had a chance to go to Houston in 1959 I went. . . . Once I heard Sam playing in the beer joints making up these songs about anything that happened that day and about the folks right there in front of him I just couldn't believe my ears! I had never heard anything quite like it in my life and have never heard anyone since then who could do this with the intensity Lightning put into his singing. That's what started me thinking about wanting to make records."[91]

Over the years Strachwitz had a satisfying relationship with Lightnin', even though he not only paid relatively small advances, but his recordings were never big sellers. Strachwitz said, "I liked being with Lightnin', and I feel we were able to connect in a very personal way. From the first time I met him, I had a sense that he was impressed or moved by the fact that I was simply a fan of his music and was so enthusiastic about him that I came all the way from California just to meet him, because all the other white guys that came his way were simply there to record him. And this held true through our years of knowing each other and carried into my interest in recording him and trying to get him booked in California. It wasn't just a business thing. We'd hang out with each other. I'd drive to Los Angeles to pick him up after he finished at the Ash Grove, and took him to Berkeley, where he stayed often, first in my apartment, and then at my house, sometimes with Antoinette. I spent a lot of time with him. I took him fishing; we went to Golden Gate Racetrack to watch them ponies run. I'd make him eggs for breakfast. He liked my down-home cooking. In the early days in the 1960s, I was totally devoted to Lightnin' and the other musicians (such as Mance Lipscomb and Fred McDowell) that I brought out here.

"One time I was driving Lightnin' to play at the Little Theatre in Carmel, California and I stopped at my mother's house. She actually cooked a chicken for us—although she was not known to cook much at all! My sister Frances—who was working in Germany when I went with Lightnin' with the AFBF in '64—remembered meeting us back stage in Frankfurt and when I introduced her to Lightnin'—he at once told her how our mother cooked a chicken for us when he played in Carmel!

"But by the 1970s, I didn't see Lightnin' as often. He became so busy and played extended gigs at bigger venues, like the Fillmore. And by then, he had recorded tons of stuff. The last time I saw him was in San Francisco a year before he died. He played so good—that electric box sounded like those sides he did for Herald—some of my favorites."[92]

Strachwitz felt that Antoinette had essentially saved Lightnin's life, and in his condolence letter to her, he wrote: "I . . . want to let you know how he admired and loved you. . . . He would always tell me how you got him off the wine and really saved him—I am sure Sam would have left us much earlier if you had not been with him over the years—but you had a strong influence on him in many ways."[93]

In assessing Lightnin's legacy, it is difficult to come to a definitive conclusion. John Corry, writing in the *New York Times* in 1980, wrote that "Sam 'Lightnin' Hopkins . . . may just possibly be the single greatest influence upon rock guitarists," though this was clearly an overstatement.[94] It's not to say that he didn't have an impact upon many blues and blues/folk/rock musicians. Stevie Ray Vaughan, Jimmie Vaughan, Anson Funderburgh, and Billy Gibbons, among other white blues rockers, as well as singer/songwriters Townes Van Zandt, Steve Earle, John David Bartlett, and Bernie Pearl, have certainly acknowledged his influence, as did his cousin Albert Collins, Juke Boy Bonner, Johnny Copeland, Joe Hughes, Texas Johnny Brown, and Freddie King.

Moreover, Lightnin' influenced blues players in not only Southern states, such as Texas, Louisiana, and Mississippi, but in other regions of the country and abroad. In Baton Rouge, for example, Lightnin' Slim (a.k.a. Otis Hicks) even appeared to have taken his nickname from Hopkins. Lightnin' was an effective songwriter, who had a fairly simple guitar style that could be readily grasped and imitated by beginning blues guitarists.[95]

"A lot of times you have people," Benson remarked, "especially white musicians, who have used Lightnin' as a way to push their own career. Everybody can go back and say Lightnin' influenced them, and say 'I played with Lightnin' Hopkins,' but Lightnin' was the kind of guy who let anybody come up on the stage, not that they could stay now, because if they couldn't play, or they pissed him off, he'd chase them off the stage as quick as he would let them on. So anybody could come to any show, and say, 'Lightnin', can I play with you tonight?' And he'd say, 'C'mon, get on up there.' So when people come back and say, 'I played with Lightnin' Hopkins,' they weren't necessarily the people who were steady. For example, Rusty [Hill], a red-headed guy, was a bass player Lightnin' preferred cause Rusty had a family. He would drive his own car to wherever Lightnin' went, and Lightnin' liked Rusty. So he would always get me to go find Rusty to play. Tommy Shannon, who played with Stevie Ray, was another one he liked. He played with Lightnin' all the time. So he would tell me to find Tommy to play bass. Lightnin' thought of Stevie [Ray Vaughan] the way he thought of all these other guys. And he knew Jimmie [Vaughan] before he knew

Stevie because we played at the Texas Chitlin' Cook-off at Manor Downs in Austin with the Thunderbirds. They were all just young. Lightnin' didn't care too much for young guys, period. He thought they were pretty much full of shit like he had been at that age. And then, by them being young white guys, he didn't really trust them as such. He thought they were good bands, but they were white kids mimicking something. It was rarefied. It was imitation."[96]

Lightnin' understood his importance as a bluesman, though he was sometimes prone to gross exaggeration. During the shooting of *The Blues According to Lightnin' Hopkins*, he stated that not only had he "learned B. B. King the notes that he make. He learned them off Po' Lightnin'," but that "the last of the blues is left here and the ones that's trying to do it right now they . . . after Po' Lightnin' Hopkins."[97] A decade later, Lightnin' reiterated this point in an interview in the *New York Times* and maintained that "the last of the blues is almost gone . . . and the ones who doin' it now got to either get a record or sit 'round me and learn my songs, 'cause that all they can go by."[98]

Throughout his career, Lightnin' mythologized himself, especially when he began to have a white audience, in part because he wanted to impress his listeners with the vast scope of his experience, but also due to the fact that certain myths were nurtured and fueled by collectors and the media. The perpetuation of misinformation as it relates to Lightnin's life underscores the complexities and difficulties in separating the myth from the man. On one hand, Lightnin' wanted to please those around him, whether his family, girlfriends, wives, friends, or record producers or blues fans, but at the root, he was a survivor. If survival meant leaving town, violating a contract, or not showing up for a gig, he did what he needed to do. "He didn't really care," Harold recalled. "He'd always say, 'Let him sue me, Doc.'"[99]

He often referred to himself as "Po' Lightnin'" in his songs to elicit sympathy as he carried on in a talking blues about anything that came into his mind. But he wasn't just speaking for himself. He was every man who had suffered and struggled and fought to make a living and to find some joy in the midst of the hardships of daily life. The songs he wrote gave voice to the swirling emotions of the world around him, the fears, anxieties, and aspirations of his generation of American Americans. He soaked up what was around him, whether it was what people said or what he heard, and he put it all into his blues. The lyrics spoke with a raw honesty and a bitter irony about the foibles of everyday life, but imbedded in the words there was at times a humor and genuine compassion for what he knew his listeners might be faced with and going through.

Lightnin's music accentuated the social injustices and intense emotions that informed the civil rights era, although Lightnin' himself was not known to participate in rallies or marches. Few of his songs were topical in nature, although "Slavery" and "Tim Moore's Farm" were protest songs, and he did sing about World War II, the Korean War, and the Vietnam War. Principally, Lightnin' voiced the yearnings and adversities of African Americans who moved away from the sharecropper farms and boll weevil–ravaged cotton fields of East and Central Texas to Houston's Third Ward. But by the late 1960s, when his audience had become predominantly white, it was difficult for him to gauge what his white listeners were feeling. They didn't whoop and holler and call out to him in the way people in a juke joint in the Third Ward might have done. White listeners may have misunderstood some of the metaphors and subtlety in his songs, and perhaps missed the innuendos and humor, though they were nevertheless captivated by his on-stage presence—his spiffy suits, polished shoes, gold-capped teeth, and Ray-Ban sunglasses.

When asked why he wore sunglasses all the time, he simply said, "I'm a hidin' man. I been hidin' all my life." He sometimes said he wore sunglasses because of a "lazy eye," but he told others that bright lights bothered him. However, he knew that sunglasses made him cool; other musicians tried to copy his style, but he had essentially defined the look. "They taken my habit to try to take my stuff," Lightnin' maintained, "and ain't but one thing they can do and that is wear shades. Because they can't do what I do. They tries . . . all these cats here be hip by Lightnin' Hopkins."[100]

When Hopkins would say, "Lightnin' change when Lightnin' change," he was not only telling his sidemen they needed to be ready, he was expressing exactly who he was. In performance, he had a general sense of where he wanted to go, but didn't know exactly how he was going to get there until he started into a song. At its best, his blues were a seamless dialogue between words and guitar, a largely improvised conversation not only between him and his instrument, but also between him and those who were listening. It's difficult to tell which lyrics are his, and which are from other sources, but in performance it didn't seem to matter.

Lightnin' did not want to be told what to do; he spoke his mind through his music. Lightnin' worked when and where he wanted to, and as he gained a white audience, the interest in his music among younger African Americans declined. Nevertheless, his concerts at college campuses were attended widely and introduced young audiences to down-home blues, which evoked a sense of the place that African Americans carried with them as they migrated away from country to the city, looking for new opportunities and a better way of life. As Chris Strachwitz has pointed out, even though Lightnin' spent most of his adult life in Houston, he remained "a real country man."

Sam Charters described Lightnin' as "the last singer in the grand style. He sang with sweep and imagination, using his voice to reach out and touch some-one who listened to him."[101] For filmmaker Les Blank, Lightnin' was "clown and oracle, wit and scoundrel. Like Shakespeare, he had an understanding of all people and all their feelings. Whether he was singing other people's songs, or as it more often happened, making a song up as he played, Lightnin' Hopkins was a man of all colors and classes, and of all times. He was an eloquent spokesman for the human soul which dwells in us all."[102]

While it is tempting to romanticize Lightnin' as a bluesman, one must not lose sight of the extent to which he was plagued by his own personal problems. He drank too much and was ostensibly an alcoholic, who in "Watch Yourself" sang: "I got to get drunk every day to please my mind." But according to Carroll Peery and others, he was never a sloppy drunk. "He didn't lose control of himself when he was drinking," Peery said, "because he didn't drink that heavily at any one time. But he drank pretty constantly. When I first met him he was drinking gin and then when we got a little bit of money, he switched to more expen-sive types of alcohol. He always drank whiskey [Canadian Club], but he started drinking it more consistently after he became more secure economically."[103]

As much as Lightnin's creativity may have declined in his later years when he was paid more for playing less and often repeating himself, or re-recording old songs, he was nonetheless a professional who was at any moment capable of a great performance that could surprise and wow even the most jaded. Lightnin', like his contemporaries Muddy Waters and John Lee Hooker, was an entertainer with an uncanny sense of drama. His movements on stage were measured; he knew he was a "star" for the people who bought the tickets and packed the clubs and festivals where he was often a headliner, and he played what they wanted to hear. Even when he was sloppy, or maybe had too much to drink, he was still worth seeing, especially if one had never seen him before. Everyone who came into contact with Lightnin' Hopkins remembered him. His presence was indelible and imbued those around him with a mix of emotions, from admiration to disdain. While he was generally respected for his blues, his personality was often inscrutable.

Through his songs, he led young and old alike into his past, but could push them back in an instant with a terse phrase or a swipe of his hand. In performance, the audience hung on to every word, from the moment he stepped onto the stage and tipped his hat to the instant when he picked up a guitar and began to play. And when he reared back and muttered a few words, or pulled out a flask of whiskey to take a long sip, no one was impatient. During his last years just about everyone who came to see him knew his songs, but they also knew what they were about to hear would take shape as it was performed. He rarely sang a song the same way twice, and the structure of his songs was often sprawling and rough. If the lyrics were ragged and the metaphors skewed, it rarely mattered; for his devotees, his blues were pure, and he was an oracle.

In the end, regardless of the myths, and the inevitable mix of fact and fiction, Lightnin' was happy that his music had reached such a wide audience. "I don't think in his younger days," Benson said, "he even imagined that there would be so many young people, so many white people, who would have such a genuine appreciation of his sound. He thought it was naive, but it was genuine. By the end of his life, his music had become sonorous, more than it was an exemplification of a particular social context. It became almost nostalgic, even as it related to the suffering. He knew that the people who bought his records and came to hear him play genuinely cared. They loved it, but it was artificial to the extent that it had been disconnected and removed from the reality that had generated it."

When asked once about what made him different than anyone else, Lightnin' replied, "A bluesman is just different from any other man that walks this earth. The blues is something that is hard to get acquainted with. Just like death. The blues dwell with you everyday and everywhere."[104]

Discography

Andrew Brown and Alan Balfour

The first attempt at compiling a Lightnin' Hopkins discography was made by the pioneering blues researcher Anthony Rotante in 1955 for *Discophile* magazine in England. Lightnin's style of blues must have seemed archaic enough at the time for Rotante to feel safe in referring to the subject of his piece in the past tense, unaware that a folk-blues renaissance was just a few years away. After a brief period of inactivity, Lightnin' began recording in earnest again, and (in Colin Escott's memorable phrase) "the world would never again want for a Lightnin' Hopkins record." By the time of his final studio recording in 1974, he had long since become established as one of the most recorded blues singers of the postwar era.

At the start of Lightnin's career in 1946, recording sessions in the music industry usually followed a predictable pattern: musicians (often members of the musician's union) would gather in a studio with a contracted artist and producer, and would, over the course of three hours or so, record two to eight masters. The musicians would get paid union fees for their work. If their contract called for it, the artist would repeat this scenario two or three times a year. Re-creating such sessions for a discography decades later can be challenging, but there was usually a logic that can be reconstructed without too much effort—particularly if session sheets and union files exist that can help identify dates, locations, and personnels.

None of this applies to Lightnin' Hopkins, who ignored exclusive contracts, did not join the musician's union until the latter stage of his career, and would record as many songs per session as he could get paid for. Session sheets and company files no longer exist for the majority of his recording sessions—and probably, in many cases, never existed in the first place. The chaotic and confusing nature of his discography is testament to the idiosyncratic nature of both Lightnin' and the small, independent producers who recorded him.

How do you bring order out of chaos? We have taken a fresh approach that considers the nature of Lightnin's recordings above the strict rules of discography, rules that sometimes don't even apply to his sessions (and introduce confusion of their own). It is thus divided into two main parts: the years when Lightnin' was a singles artist (1946–1954), and the period in which he was primarily an album artist (1959–1974). Within that scope, we have endeavored to make it as accurate and accessible as possible.

Our methodology is as follows:

Session dates. All sessions have been listed chronologically in the order in which they were recorded. Educated guesses and estimates are required for nearly everything Lightnin' recorded before 1959, and quite a few dates in the 1960s are speculative as well. We have broken down the sessions to a suggested chronology, but it should be emphasized that the 1946 to 1954 period is *only* suggested. Some singles sessions in which we have listed two songs to have been recorded may have been longer, etc. More difficult questions about longer sessions (such as those for the Sittin' In With and Herald labels) are addressed within the discography.

Location. We have tried to establish the city and studio in which Lightnin' made each of his recordings. It's well documented that the majority of them were recorded in Houston at Gold Star or ACA Studios. In other cases, we only know the city.

Personnel. Precisely who plays on Lightnin's recordings was largely pinned down by researchers in the 1960s. Some unknown musicians remain, however, and are unlikely to be identified at this point. We have corrected and updated the known personnel of earlier discographies as much as recent (and recently discovered) research allows. To cite one example: for the past forty years it has been written that Frankie Lee Sims plays slide guitar on Lightnin's 1949 "Jail House Blues," but we now know from the unpublished research of Laurence Schilthuis that the instrument heard on this session is a steel guitar, played by Harding "Hop" Wilson.

For the album era, each session has been considered individually in relation to the album. Where an album was recorded over different sessions, and featured different personnel, we have either listed the collective personnel, or, when it made more sense, specified which song a particular musician was playing on.

Instrumentation. Long-held misconceptions in popular writing about when Lightnin' started playing electric guitar have, we feel, made it necessary to establish whether he was playing acoustic or electric guitar on his sessions. Most of his early sessions feature Lightnin' playing a hollowbody electric guitar. After he became established as a folk-blues artist in 1959, he would often record with an acoustic guitar, or (especially live) an acoustic guitar outfitted with an electric pickup. In some cases, the aural differences between acoustic guitar sessions and acoustic-electric ones are not noticeable enough to make a definitive judgment.

Song Order. The exact song order for most sessions is not known. Therefore, we have arranged sessions to reflect the chronology of songs as they were issued, rather than by master numbers (which serve no purpose in this context). For singles, this means clusters of two songs per side of a 78 rpm or 45 rpm record. In the case of albums, the song order reflects the sequencing of side one and side two of the original albums. Titles in italics represent songs originally unissued from the particular session.

Song Titles. A great deal of what Lightnin' recorded was later reissued with altered song titles—by accident or design. (To give only one example, generations have been listening to a song titled "I Can't Stay Here in Your Town," unaware that they are actually hearing the original "Rocky Mountain Blues.") Other songs were mistitled upon release. A complete list of such titles supercedes the purpose of this discography; we have only noted when his singles were reissued with altered titles during his early (1946–1954) singles period.

Releases. Only original issues (or reissues from the same era, in the case of the earliest singles) are listed. We have not tried to address the hundreds of configurations in which these songs have been reissued (and often retitled) since their initial release. Rereleases of the same single have been divided by a slash. Single 45 rpm releases pulled from albums are divided from their LP release number by a semi-colon and a "(45)" prefix.

Album Sessions. Beginning with his Folkways album in 1959, most of Lightnin's sessions were specifically recorded as albums, or with an album concept in mind. Our discography reflects this change by listing album titles above the session, arranged with the earliest session date for that album (if there were more than one). While this method doesn't eliminate all possible confusion, we feel it makes the most sense in organizing and assimilating this material. Albums that feature sessions that were recorded more than one year apart have been further subdivided by session date. For Various Artists LPs, only Lightnin's songs have been listed.

Mono/Stereo. All of Lightnin's records prior to the early 1960s were released in monaural. Some of his 1960s albums were available in mono and stereo; these usually have been reissued on compact disc with only the stereo versions. A minority were only available in stereo. As a side point, a large number of Lightnin's early recordings were reissued after 1959 with added reverb to disguise their age. The listener should be aware that many reissues in the compact disc era are still using these inferior, altered sources rather than the original masters or singles.

Release Dates (Albums). Lightnin's singles were usually released a short time after they were recorded. Albums, on the other hand, were often released months, years, and decades after they were recorded. With this in mind, we have tried to establish release dates for all of Lightnin's original albums. In a few cases, this creates a conflict with the chronology by session dates (*The Rooster Crowed in England* LP is listed before the Folkways album; the latter was released first, but the *Rooster* LP features two songs recorded in 1954), but overall we feel this is the least confusing method of listing these sessions. Estimated release dates on LPs have been based on advertisements and reviews found in *Billboard*, *Sing Out!*, *Blues Unlimited*, *Blues and Rhythm*, *Jazz Journal*, *Cashbox*, *The American Folk Music Occasional*, *Mother*, *Juke Blues*, and *Soul Bag*.

Lightnin's work as a session musician for other artists (Thunder Smith, L. C. Williams, J. D. Edwards, et al.) has not been included.

In compiling this discography, we have been indebted to all those who came before us: Anthony Rotante, Chris Strachwitz, Mack McCormick, John Holt, Mike Leadbitter, Neil Slaven, Simon Napier, Frank Scott, Chris Smith, and Les Fancourt. For this revision we have been assisted, directly or indirectly, by Dave Sax, Chris Strachwitz, Mack McCormick, Paul Drummond, Mary Katherine Aldin, Richard Flohil, Chris Smith, Don Logan, Stefan Wirz, Bill Bellmont, Ed Pearl, Bernie Pearl, Roger Armstrong, and Alan Govenar. The Huey Meaux Papers at the Center For American History (University of Texas) contain relevant paperwork from the Gold Star era that was crucial in establishing the early chronology. The unpublished research of Laurence Schilthuis, who interviewed both Hopkins and Hop Wilson in 1974, was also helpful. We have also relied upon the following books:

Fancourt, Les and Bob McGrath. *The Blues Discography, 1943–1970*. West Vancouver, Canada: Eyeball Productions, 2006.

Holt, John. *Lightnin' Hopkins*. London: Texas Blues Society, 1965.

Leadbitter, Mike and Neil Slaven. *Blues Records 1943–1966*. New York: Oak Publications, 1968.

Ruppli, Michel. *The Aladdin/Imperial Labels: A Discography*. Westport, Connecticut: Greenwood Press, 1991.

Smith, Chris. *That's the Stuff: The Recordings of Brownie McGhee, Sonny Terry, Stick McGhee, and J.C. Burris*. Shetland, Scotland: The Housay Press, 1999.

Whitburn, Joel. *Billboard Top R&B Singles, 1942–1999*. Menomonee Falls, Wisconsin: Record Research, Inc., 2000.

November 9, 1946. Radio Recorders Studio, 7000 Santa Monica Blvd., Hollywood, CA.
Producer: Eddie Mesner

Sam "Lightnin'" Hopkins, vocal/acoustic guitar with Wilson "Thunder" Smith, piano; unknown drums.

"Katie Mae Blues"	Aladdin 167
"That Mean Old Twister"	Aladdin 167
"Rocky Mountain Blues"	Aladdin 168
"I Feel So Bad"	Aladdin 168
"I Feel So Bad" (alternate take)	*Score LP 4022*

Note: This was a split session with "Thunder" Smith.

c. May 1947. Quinn Recording Company, 3104 Telephone Rd., Houston, TX.
Producer: Bill Quinn

Vocal/electric guitar with Joel Hopkins, acoustic rhythm guitar.

"Short Haired Woman"	Gold Star 3131/Modern 20-529
"Big Mama Jump"	Gold Star 3131/Modern 20-529
"Short Haired Woman" (alternate take)	*Dart LP 8000*

Note: While some Gold Star sessions may have consisted of four songs or more, sonic differences suggest that usually only two songs were released from a particular session at a time. Unissued titles were later sold to Modern, Dart, and Arhoolie (see below).

c. June 1947. Quinn Recording Company, 3104 Telephone Rd., Houston, TX.
Producer: Bill Quinn

Vocal/electric guitar.

"Shining Moon"	Gold Star 613/Modern 20-543
"Ida May"	Gold Star 613/Modern 20-543

c. July 1947. Quinn Recording Company, 3104 Telephone Rd., Houston, TX.
Producer: Bill Quinn

Vocal/electric guitar.

"Mercy"	Gold Star 616/Modern 20-552
"What Can It Be"	Gold Star 616/Modern 20-552

August 15, 1947. Probably Radio Recorders Studio, 7000 Santa Monica Blvd., Hollywood, CA.
Producer: Eddie Mesner

Vocal/electric guitar with Wilson "Thunder" Smith, piano; unknown drums.

"Short Haired Woman"	Aladdin 3005
"Big Mama Jump"	Aladdin 3005
"Fast Mail Rambler"	Aladdin 204
"Thinkin' and Worryin'"	Aladdin 204
"Down Now Baby"	Aladdin 209
"Play With Your Poodle"	Aladdin 209

c. October 1947. Quinn Recording Company, 3104 Telephone Rd., Houston, TX.
Producer: Bill Quinn

Vocal/electric guitar.

"Lonesome Home"	Gold Star 624/Modern 20-568
"Appetite Blues"	Gold Star 624/Modern 20-568

c. November 1947. Houston, TX.

Vocal/electric guitar.

"Picture on the Wall"	Aladdin 3015
"Woman, Woman"	Aladdin 3028
"You're Not Going to Worry My Life Anymore"	Aladdin 3117
"Can't Get That Woman Off My Mind"	*Imperial LP 94000*

c. February 25, 1948. Commercial Recording Studio, 1120 Chenevert, Houston, TX.

Vocal/electric guitar.

"Sugar Mama"	Aladdin 3015
"Nightmare Blues"	Aladdin 3028
"Daddy Will Be Home One Day"	Aladdin 3117
"Lightnin's Boogie"	Score 4002
"Whiskey Head Woman"	Score 4002
"Morning Blues"	Aladdin 3035
"Have to Let You Go"	Aladdin 3035
"Baby Child"	Aladdin 3052
"Changing Weather Blues"	Aladdin 3052
"Shotgun Blues"	Aladdin 3063
"Rollin' Blues"	Aladdin 3063
"Moonrise Blues"	Aladdin 3077
"Honey Honey Blues"	Aladdin 3077
"Abilene"	Aladdin 3096
"Miss Me Blues"	Aladdin 3096
"My California"	Aladdin 3262
"So Long"	Aladdin 3262
"Mistreater Blues"	RPM 388
"I Just Don't Care"	*Score LP 4022*
"See See Rider"	*Imperial LP 9180*

"Baby You're Not Going to Make a Fool Out of Me"	*Imperial LP 9186*
"Come Back Baby"	*Imperial LP 9186*
"Someday Baby"	*Imperial LP 9211*
"Tell It Like It Is"	*Imperial LP 9211*
"Miss Loretta"	*Imperial LP 9211*
"Howling Wolf Blues"	*Imperial LP 94000*

Note: The February 1948 Aladdin sessions probably occurred over several days; only one exact date (February 25) is documented. "Mistreater Blues," recorded during these sessions, ended up with Bill Quinn and was among the masters he sold to Modern/RPM Records in 1951.

Most LP/CD reissues of the above titles have added reverb not present on the original records.

c. March 1948. Quinn Recording Company, 3104 Telephone Rd., Houston, TX.
Producer: Bill Quinn

Vocal/acoustic guitar.

"Walking Blues"	Gold Star 634/Modern 20-594
"Lightning Blues"	Gold Star 634/Modern 20-594

c. August 1948. Quinn Recording Company, 3104 Telephone Rd., Houston, TX.
Producer: Bill Quinn

Vocal/electric guitar.

"No Mail Blues"	Gold Star 637/Modern 20-621
"Ain't It a Shame"	Gold Star 637/Modern 20-621

c. September 1948. Quinn Recording Company, 3104 Telephone Rd., Houston, TX.
Producer: Bill Quinn

Vocal/electric guitar.

"Tim Moore's Farm"	Gold Star 640/Modern 20-673
"You Don't Know"	Gold Star 640/Modern 20-673

c. September 1948. Quinn Recording Company, 3104 Telephone Rd., Houston, TX.
Producer: Bill Quinn

Vocal/electric guitar.

"Treat Me Kind"	Gold Star 641
"Somebody Got to Go"	Gold Star 641

c. November 1948. Quinn Recording Company, 3104 Telephone Rd., Houston, TX.
Producer: Bill Quinn

Vocal/electric guitar.

"Baby Please Don't Go"	Gold Star 646
"Death Bells"	Gold Star 646

c. February 1949. Quinn Recording Company, 3104 Telephone Rd., Houston, TX.
Producer: Bill Quinn

Vocal/electric guitar.

"Mad with You"	Gold Star 652
"Airplane Blues"	Gold Star 652

c. March 1949. Quinn Recording Company, 3104 Telephone Rd., Houston, TX.
Producer: Bill Quinn

Vocal/electric guitar with unknown saxophone, piano, bass.

"Unsuccessful Blues"	Gold Star 656/Lightning 104/Dart 123
"Rollin' Woman Blues"	Gold Star 656

Note: Lightning 104 dates from 1955. The Dart release is a 1960 reissue of Lightning 104.

c. July 1949. Quinn Recording Company, 3104 Telephone Rd., Houston, TX.
Producer: Bill Quinn

Vocal/electric guitar with Harding "Hop" Wilson, steel guitar.

"Jail House Blues"	Gold Star 662/Sittin' In With 644
"T" Model blues"	Gold Star 662/Sittin' In With 644
"Traveler's Blues"	*Dart LP 8000*

c. October 1949. Quinn Recording Company, 3104 Telephone Rd., Houston, TX.
Producer: Bill Quinn

Vocal/electric guitar with L. C. Williams, tap dancing*.

"Lightning Boogie"*	Gold Star 664/Harlem 2324
"Unkind Blues"	Gold Star 664

Note: "Lightning Boogie" retitled "Mad Man's Boogie" on Harlem 2324.

c. October 1949. Quinn Recording Company, 3104 Telephone Rd., Houston, TX.
Producer: Bill Quinn

Vocal/electric guitar

"Fast Life Woman"	Gold Star 665/Harlem 2331
"European Blues"	Gold Star 665

Note: "Fast Life Woman" retitled "Fast Life" on Harlem 2331.

Late 1949. Quinn Recording Company, 3104 Telephone Rd., Houston, TX.
Producer: Bill Quinn

Vocal/electric guitar/electric organ*.

"Automobile"	Gold Star 666/Jax 318
"Zolo Go"*	Gold Star 666/Jax 318
"Organ Boogie"*	Arhoolie LP 2007
"Automobile Blues"*	Arhoolie LP 2010

Note: "Zolo Go" retitled "Organ Blues" on Jax 318. Both issues omit the spoken introduction, which has been restored on the Arhoolie reissues. "Automobile" retitled "Automobile Blues" on Jax 318.

Early 1950. Quinn Recording Company, 3104 Telephone Rd., Houston, TX.
Producer: Bill Quinn

Vocal/electric guitar.

"Old Woman Blues"	Gold Star 669/Harlem 2336
"Untrue Blues"	Gold Star 669/Harlem 2336/ Lightning 104/Dart 123

Note: "Old Woman Blues" retitled "Good Old Woman" on Harlem 2336. "Untrue Blues" retitled "Untrue" on Harlem 2336 and mistitled "Grievance Blues" on Lightning 104 and Dart 123. Lightning 104 dates from 1955. The Dart release is a 1960 reissue of Lightning 104.

Early 1950. Quinn Recording Company, 3104 Telephone Rd., Houston, TX.
Producer: Bill Quinn

Vocal/electric guitar.

"Henny Penny Blues"	Gold Star 671
"Jazz Blues"	Gold Star 671

1950. Quinn Recording Company, 3104 Telephone Rd., Houston, TX. Producer: Bill Quinn

Vocal/electric guitar.

"Jackstropper Blues"	Gold Star 673/Harlem 2331
"Grievance Blues"	Gold Star 673/Harlem 2324

Note: "Jackstropper Blues" retitled "The Jackstropper" on Harlem 2331. "Grievance Blues" retitled "Nobody Cares For Me" on Harlem 2324.

1947–1951. Quinn Recording Company, 3104 Telephone Rd., Houston, TX. Producer: Bill Quinn

Vocal/electric guitar

From previous Gold Star sessions and/or unissued Gold Star sessions.

"Goodbye Blues (Somebody's Got to Go)"	Arhoolie LP 2007
"Glory Be Blues (Blue bird Blues)"	Arhoolie LP 2007
"Seems Funny Baby"	Arhoolie LP 2007
"Cooling Board (Thunder and Lightnin' Blues)"	Arhoolie LP 2007
"Going Home Blues"	Arhoolie LP 2007
"All I Got is Gone"	Arhoolie LP 2010
"Grosebeck Blues" (take 2)	Arhoolie LP 2010
"Grosebeck Blues" (take 3)	Arhoolie LP 2010
"Grosebeck Blues (Penitentiary Blues)" (take 4)	Dart LP 8000
"Racetrack Blues"	Dart LP 8000

1947–1951. Quinn Recording Company, 3104 Telephone Rd., Houston, TX. Producer: Bill Quinn

Vocal/electric guitar/piano.

From previous Gold Star sessions and/or unissued Gold Star sessions.

"Beggin' You to Stay"	RPM 337
"Bad Luck and Trouble"	RPM 337
"Bad Luck and Trouble" (incomplete take)	P-Vine (Japan) CD 3056
"Jake Head Boogie"	RPM 346
"Lonesome Dog Blues"	RPM 346
"Jake Head Boogie" (alternate take)	P-Vine (Japan) CD 3056
"Lonesome Dog Blues" (alternate take)	P-Vine (Japan) CD 3056
"Don't Keep My Baby Long"	RPM 351
"Last Affair"	RPM 351

"Don't Keep My Baby Long" (unedited take)	*P-Vine (Japan) CD 3056*
"Last Affair" (incomplete take)	*P-Vine (Japan) CD 3056*
"Needed Time" (*sic* – Needy Time)	RPM 359
"One Kind Favor"	RPM 359
"Needed Time" (alternate take)	*Kent LP 9008*
"Another Fool in Town"	RPM 378
"Candy Kitchen"	RPM 378
"Candy Kitchen" (overdubbed guitar)	*P-Vine (Japan) CD 3056*
"Black Cat"	RPM 388
"Santa Fe"	RPM 398
"Some Day Baby"	RPM 398
"Drifting Blues"	*P-Vine (Japan) CD 3056*
"Ticket Agent"	*Kent LP 9008*
"Ticket Agent" (alternate take)	*P-Vine (Japan) CD 3056*
"House Upon the Hill"	*Kent LP 9008*
"Tell Me (Pretty Mama)"	*Crown LP 5224*
"Give Me Back That Wig"	*Crown LP 5224*
"Give Me Back That Wig" (alternate take)	*P-Vine (Japan) CD 3056*
"Everyday I Have the Blues" (incomplete take)	*Ace(UK) CD 697*
"Everyday I Have the Blues"	*Kent LP 9008*
"War News Blues"	*Kent LP 9008*

Note: Billboard *announced in September 1951 that Bill Quinn had shut down Gold Star Records and sold thirty-two masters of Hopkins and Lil' Son Jackson to Modern Records. These titles were presumably recorded over the course of Hopkins's tenure with Gold Star Records, with perhaps the majority of them dating from 1949–50. There are twenty titles by Hopkins (not including alternate or incomplete takes), plus one ("Mistreater Blues") from the February 1948 Aladdin sessions that was acquired by Quinn and issued on the flipside of RPM 388.*

Reverb was added to most titles; the P-Vine reissue (which compiles all of the RPM/Modern Hopkins masters) restores them to their original state.

c.1950. Houston, TX.

Vocal/electric guitar.

"Black Cat Bone"	*Specialty LP 2149*
"Disagreeable"	*Specialty (UK) LP 5013*
"Dark and Cloudy"	*Specialty LP 2149*
"Sold Out to the Devil"	*unissued*
"Ain't No Monkey Man"	*unissued*
"Racetrack Blues"	*unissued*

Note: *This session was unissued at the time it was recorded, only appearing on albums in the early 1970s. Roger Armstrong (Ace Records, UK) has documented three additional masters from this session that have never been released. The titles listed are provisional.*

Early 1951. New York, NY.
Producer: Bob Shad

Vocal/electric guitar; unknown bass.

"Gotta Move"	Sittin' In With 599
"Prayin' Ground Blues"	Sittin' In With 599
"Long Way From Texas"	Sittin' In With 611
"Tell Me Boogie"	Sittin' In With 611
"Mad As I Can Be" (alternate take of "Tell Me Boogie")	Mainstream (UK) CD 901
"Give Me Central 209"	Sittin' In With 621
"New York Boogie"	Sittin' In With 621
"Coffee Blues"	Sittin' In With 635/Jax 635
"New Short Haired Woman"	Sittin' In With 635/Jax 635

Note: Most LP/CD reissues of the Sittin' In With recordings, including those below, feature added reverb that does not appear on the original records.

1951. Houston, TX.
Producer: Bob Shad

Vocal/electric guitar; Donald Cooks, bass; L. C. Williams, tap dancing*.

"You Caused My Heart to Weep"	Sittin' In With 642/Jax 642
"Tap Dance Boogie"*	Sittin' In With 642/Jax 642
"Dirty House Blues"	Sittin' In With 647
"Bald Headed Woman"	Sittin' In With 647
"New Worried Life Blues"	Sittin' In With 649/Jax 649
"One Kind of Favor" (*sic* – One Kind Favor)	Sittin' In With 649/Jax 649
"Papa Bones Boogie"*	Sittin' In With 652
"Everything Happens to Me"	Sittin' In With 652
"Freight Train Blues"	Sittin' In With 658
"Broken Hearted Blues"	Sittin' In With 658
"I Wonder (Why)"	Sittin' In With 660/Jax 660
"I've Been a Bad Man"	Sittin' In With 660/Jax 315/Jax 660
"No Good Woman"	Jax 315
"(Lightnin's) Gone Again"	Sittin' In With 661/Jax 661
"Down to the River"	Sittin' In With 661/Jax 661
"Contrary Mary"	Jax 321/Harlem 2321
"I'm Begging You"	Jax 321/Harlem 2321
"You Do Too"	Mercury 8252
"Everybody's Down on Me"	Mercury 8252

"Worried Blues"	Time LP 1385
"Don't Think I'm Crazy"	Time LP 70004
"Broken Hearted Blues"	Mainstream (UK) CD 905
"Why Did You Get Mad at Me"	Mainstream (UK) CD 905
"What Kind of Heart Have You"	Mainstream (UK) CD 905
"What Must I Do"	unissued
"Walked to the River"	unissued

Note: The above sessions were probably recorded on different occasions over the course of 1951 (and possibly 1952) by Shad. "I've Been a Bad Man" retitled "Mad Blues" on Jax 660. "Contrary Mary" retitled "Crazy Mary" on Harlem 2321. "Broken Hearted Blues" on Mainstream CD 905 is a completely different song than the "Broken Hearted Blues" issued as Sittin' In With 658. Mercury 8252 credited to "Lightening" (sic) Hopkins."

Summer 1951. Probably ACA Recording Studio, 5520–22 Washington Ave., Houston, TX. Producer: Bob Shad

Vocal/acoustic guitar with Donald Cooks, bass.

"Sad News from Korea"	Mercury 8274
"Let Me Fly Your Kite"	Mercury 8274
"Gone with the Wind"	Mercury 8293
"She's Almost Dead"	Mercury 8293
"Ain't It a Shame"	Mercury 70081
"Crazy 'Bout My Baby"	Mercury 70081
"My Mama Told Me"	Mercury 70191
"What's the Matter Now"	Mercury 70191

Note: These singles were credited to "Lightening Hopkins."

July 29, 1953. Probably ACA Recording Studio, 5520-22 Washington Ave., Houston, TX. Producer: Bob Shad

Vocal/electric guitar with Donald Cooks, bass; Connie Kroll, drums. Overdubbed crying*.

"Merry Christmas"	Decca 48306
"Happy New Year"	Decca 48306
"Highway Blues"	Decca 48312
"Cemetery Blues"*	Decca 48312
"I'm Wild About You Baby"	Decca 48321
"Bad Things on my Mind"	Decca 48321
"The War is Over"	Decca 28841
"Policy Game"	Decca 28841

Note: All Decca pressings are credited to "Lightening Hopkins." Most reissues of "Cemetery Blues" use the original master, without the overdubbed "crying" as originally issued.

Original issues are on black Decca labels. "Merry Christmas" b/w "Happy New Year" was reissued in the early 1960s with the multi-colored Decca label.

c. November 1953. Probably ACA Sound and Film Studio, 5520-22 Washington Ave., Houston, TX. Producer: H. M. Crowe

Vocal/electric guitar.

"Late in the Evening"	TNT 8002
"Lightnin' Jump"	TNT 8002
"Leavin' Blues"	TNT 8003; 8010
"Moanin' Blues"	TNT 8003; 8010

Note: TNT 8010 is a c.1956 reissue of TNT 8003, credited to "Lightin' Hopkins."

c. April 1954. ACA Sound and Film Studio, 5520-22 Washington Ave., Houston, TX.

Vocal/electric guitar with Donald Cooks, bass; Ben Turner, drums; Ruth Ames, vocal*.

"Don't Think 'Cause You're Pretty"	Herald 425, 504, LP 1012
"Lightnin's Boogie"	Herald 425, 504, LP 1012
"Life I Used to Live"	Herald 428, 547, LP 1012
"Lightnin's Special"	Herald 428, 547, LP 1012
"Sick Feeling Blues"	Herald 436, 542, LP 1012
"Moving On Out Boogie"	Herald 436, 542
"Early Mornin' Boogie"	Herald 443, 531
"Nothin' but the Blues"	Herald 443
"They Wonder Who I Am"	Herald 449
"Evil Hearted Woman"	Herald 449, LP 1012
"My Baby's Gone"	Herald 456, LP 1012
"Don't Need No Job"	Herald 456
"Blues for My Cookie"	Herald 465
"Had a Gal Called Sal"	Herald 465
"Lonesome in Your Home"	Herald 471, LP 1012
"Hopkins' Sky Hop"	Herald 471
"Grandma's Boogie"	Herald 476, 531
"I Love You Baby"	Herald 476

"That's Alright Baby"*	Herald 483
"Finally Met My Baby"*	Herald 483
"Shine on Moon"	Herald 490
"Sittin' Down Thinkin'"	Herald 490, LP 1012
"Remember Me"	Herald 497
"Please Don't Go Baby"	Herald 497
"Bad Boogie"	Ace 516/Herald 520, LP 1012/Parade 8020
"Wonder What is Wrong with Me"	Ace 516/Herald 520
"Walkin' the Streets"	Chart 636/Parade 8020
"Mussy Haired Woman"	Chart 636
"Walkin' and Drinkin'"*	unissued
"God Made Man"*	unissued

Notes: These sessions probably occurred over several days in or around April 1954. Reverb was added to all songs except "Walkin' the Streets" and "Mussy Haired Woman."

Herald 483 credited to "Lightnin' Hopkins with his Protégé Ruth (Blues) Ames."

Ten songs from these sessions were retitled and reissued by Herald in the late 1950s. These are detailed below.

"Don't Think 'Cause You're Pretty" was edited and retitled "Blues Is a Mighty Bad Feelin'" on Herald 504.
"Lightnin's Boogie" retitled "Boogie Woogie Dance" on Herald 504.
"Life I Used to Live" retitled "Gonna Change My Ways" on Herald 547.
"Lightnin's Special" retitled "Flash Lightnin'" on Herald 547.
"Sick Feeling Blues" retitled "I'm Achin'" on Herald 542.
"Moving On Out Boogie" retitled "Let's Move" on Herald 542.
"Early Mornin' Boogie" retitled "Hear Me Talkin'" on Herald 531.
"Grandma's Boogie" retitled "Lightnin's Stomp" on Herald 531.
"Bad Boogie" (Ace 516) retitled "My Little Kewpie Doll" on Herald 520 and Herald LP 1012.
"Wonder What is Wrong with Me" (Ace 516) was edited and retitled "Lightnin' Don't Feel Well" on Herald 520.

Two songs from these sessions were also retitled and reissued on Parade in the late 1950s / early 1960s: "Bad Boogie" retitled "Work with Me and I'll Work with You" on Parade 8020, and "Walkin' the Streets" retitled "Street Walking Woman" on Parade 8020.

Herald LP 1012 (Lightnin' and the Blues), which technically may not qualify as a reissue, was released in 1960.

The Rooster Crowed in England

1954. ACA Sound and Film Studio, 5520-22 Washington Ave., Houston, TX.

Vocal/piano.

"Met the Blues on the Corner"	77(UK) LP 12/1
"Goin' to Galveston"	77(UK) LP 12/1

February 26, 1959; May 12, 1959; July 13, 1959; July 16, 1959; July 20, 1959. Houston, TX.
Producer: Mack McCormick

Vocal/acoustic guitar.

"Hello, England!"	77(UK) LP 12/1
"Beggin' Up & Down the Streets"	77(UK) LP 12/1
"When the Saints Go Marching In"	77(UK) LP 12/1
"Hard Headed Children"	77(UK) LP 12/1
"Dig Me in the Morning"	77(UK) LP 12/1
"Have You Ever Seen a One-Eyed Woman Cry?"	77(UK) LP 12/1
"Black Snake"	77(UK) LP 12/1
"How Many Days Must I Wait"	77(UK) LP 12/1
"If You Ever Been Mistreated"	77(UK) LP 12/1
"Back to Arkansas"	77(UK) LP 12/1
"Children's Boogie"	77(UK) LP 12/1
"Blues for Queen Elizabeth"	77(UK) LP 12/1

The Rooster Crowed in England was released (in the United Kingdom only) in early 1960. It was issued with a two-page insert by Mack McCormick.

Note: "Met the Blues on the Corner" and "Goin' to Galveston" are sourced from an ACA acetate acquired by Mack McCormick.

Lightnin' Hopkins

January 16, 1959. 2803 Hadley Street (Hopkins's apartment), Houston, TX.
Producer: Sam Charters

Vocal/acoustic guitar.

"Penitentiary Blues"	Folkways LP 3822
"Bad Luck and Trouble"	Folkways LP 3822
"Come, Go Home with Me"	Folkways LP 3822
"Trouble Stay 'Way From My Door"	Folkways LP 3822
"See That My Grave Is Kept Clean"	Folkways LP 3822
"Goin' Back to Florida"	Folkways LP 3822
"Reminiscences of Blind Lemon" (speech)	Folkways LP 3822
"Fan It"	Folkways LP 3822
"Tell Me, Baby"	Folkways LP 3822
"She's Mine"	Folkways LP 3822
"One Kind Favor"	*RBF LP LP 202*

(incomplete alternate take of "See That My Grave Is Kept Clean")

Lightnin' Hopkins was released in 1959. It was issued with a four-page insert by Sam Charters.

Country Blues

February 16 and 26, 1959. Houston, TX.
Producer: Mack McCormick

Vocal/acoustic guitar. Luke "Long Gone" Miles, vocal assistance*.

"Long Time"	Tradition LP "1035
"Rainy Day Blues"	Tradition LP 1035
"Baby!"*	Tradition LP 1035
"Long Gone Like a Turkey Thru the Corn (Long John)" [sic]	Tradition LP 1035
"Prison Blues Come Down on Me"*	Tradition LP 1035
"Backwater Blues (That Mean Old Twister)"	Tradition LP 1035
"Gonna Pull a Party"	Tradition LP 1035
"Bluebird, Bluebird"	Tradition LP 1035
"See See Rider"	Tradition LP 1035
"Worrying My Mind"	Tradition LP 1035
"Till the Gin Gets Here"	Tradition LP 1035
"Bunion Stew"	Tradition LP 1035
"You Got to Work to Get Your Pay"	Tradition LP 1035
"Go Down Old Hannah"	Tradition LP 1035
"Hear My Black Dog Bark"	Tradition LP 1035

Country Blues was released in early 1960.

Autobiography in Blues

February 16 and 26, 1959. Houston, TX.
Producer: Mack McCormick

Vocal/acoustic guitar.

"In the Evening, the Sun is Going Down"	Tradition LP 1040
"Trouble in Mind"	Tradition LP 1040
"Mama and Papa Hopkins"	Tradition LP 1040
"The Foot Race Is On"	Tradition LP 1040
"That Gambling Life"	Tradition LP 1040
"When the Saints Go Marching In"	Tradition LP 1040
"Get Off My Toe"	Tradition LP 1040
"75 Highway"	Tradition LP 1040
"Bottle Up and Go"	Tradition LP 1040
"Short Haired Woman"	Tradition LP 1040
"So Long Baby"	Tradition LP 1040
"Santa Fe Blues"	Tradition LP 1040

Autobiography in Blues was released in early 1960.

Various Artists — A Treasury of Field Recordings, Volume I

July 13, 1959. Houston, TX.
Producer: Mack McCormick

Vocal/acoustic guitar.

"Corinne, Corinna"   77(UK) LP 12/2/Candid LP 8026

A *Treasury of Field Recordings, Volume One* was released in the United Kingdom in 1960. It was reissued in slightly altered form in the United States on Candid Records in 1962. The 77 release was issued with a sixty-page booklet of notes by Mack McCormick; the Candid LP reprints the notes (in edited form) within a gatefold cover.

Note: This various artists LP includes the Dudley Alexander Washboard Band, Ed Badeaux, George Coleman (Bongo Joe), John Lomax, Jr., Joel Hopkins, and others.

Various Artists — The Unexpurgated Folk Songs of Mcn

July 16, 1959. Houston, TX.
Producer: Mack McCormick

Vocal/acoustic guitar.

"The Dirty Dozens"   (no label) LP 1/Raglan LP 51

The Unexpurgated Folk Songs of Men was released in December 1963. It was reissued on Raglan in 1964. Both were issued with a sixteen-page insert by Mack McCormick. Contrary to rumors, there was no Arhoolie reissue in the 1970s.

Note: This various artists LP includes John Lomax, Jr., Ed Badeaux, Mance Lipscomb, and Buster Pickens (all uncredited).

Various Artists — A Treasury of Field Recordings, Volume 2

July 16, 1959; January 25, 1960. Houston, TX.
Producer: Mack McCormick

Vocal/acoustic guitar/piano*; Melvin "Jack" Jackson, speech/piano*.

"Tom Moore's Farm"   77 (UK) LP 12/3
"The Slop"*   77 (UK) LP 12/3

A *Treasury of Field Recordings, Volume Two* was released (in the United Kingdom only) in 1960. It was issued with a sixty-page booklet of notes by Mack McCormick.

Note: This various artists LP includes John Lomax, Jr., Gozy Kilpatrick, George Coleman (Bongo Joe), and Mance Lipscomb (credited as "Anonymous").

Various Artists—Blues from East Texas

November 19, 1959. Houston, TX.
Producer: Mack McCormick

Vocal/acoustic guitar; acoustic bottleneck guitar*; Mack McCormick speech on **.

"Long Way from Texas"	Heritage(UK) LP 1001
"Whiskey, Whiskey"*	Heritage(UK) LP 1001
"Getting Out of the Bushes Tap Dance"	Heritage(UK) LP 1001
"Suicide Blues"	Heritage(UK) LP 1001
"Look Out Settegast, Here Me and My Partner Come"**	Heritage(UK) LP 1001

Blues From East Texas was released (in the United Kingdom only) in early 1960.

Note: Blues From East Texas was a split LP with Joel Hopkins on one side and Lightnin' on the other. It was limited to an edition of ninety-nine copies.

Unissued songs from Mack McCormick sessions, 1959–60

Vocal/acoustic guitar. Luke "Long Gone" Miles, vocal*.

"Blues Jumped the Rabbit"	*unissued*
"Blues Come Late in the Evening"	*unissued*
"Red River Valley"	*unissued*
"Ella Speed"	*unissued*
"Motherless Child"	*unissued*
"Jack o'Diamonds"	*unissued*
"Make Me Some Changes Soon"	*unissued*
"Farmer's Wife Come Creeping in Her Sleep"	*unissued*
"No Hair at All"	*unissued*
"Sad Hours of Night"	*unissued*
"Boogie Improvisation"	*unissued*
"Oh My Baby Take Me Back (Candy Man)"	*unissued*
"Minnie Lee"	*unissued*
"Mister Charlie Your Rolling Mill is Burning Down"	*unissued*
"Natural Blues"	*unissued*
"Houston Boogie"	*unissued*
"When Mother's Dead and Gone"	*unissued*
*"Black and Evil"**	*unissued*
*"Walkin' with Frankie"**	*unissued*

Various Artists—Down South Summit Meetin'

July 6 or 7, 1960. World Pacific Studios, Los Angeles, CA.
Producer: Ed Michel

Lead vocal*/backing vocal/acoustic guitar, with (collectively) Sonny Terry (a.k.a. Sanders Terrell), vocal/ harmonica; Walter "Brownie" McGhee, vocal/guitar; Big Joe Williams, vocal/guitar; Jimmy Bond, bass.

"First Meeting"	World Pacific LP 1296
"How Long Has It Been Since You Been Home"*	World Pacific LP 1296
"Ain't Nothing Like Whiskey"	World Pacific LP 1296
"Penitentiary Blues"	World Pacific LP 1296
"If You Steal My Chickens, You Can't Make 'em Lay"	World Pacific LP 1296
"Wimmen From Coast to Coast"	World Pacific LP 1296
"New Car Blues"	Society (UK) LP 1015
"You Gonna Need Somebody to Go Your Bond"	Society (UK) LP 1020
"I've Been 'Buked"	Society (UK) LP 1020
"Chain Gang Blues"	Verve-Folkways LP 3011
"Razor Sharp Blues"	Verve-Folkways LP 3011
"Four Friends Blues"	unissued
"Friends and Pals"	unissued
"Blues From the Bottom"	unissued

Down South Summit Meetin' was released in September 1960.

Note: The songs from this session have been reissued in countless forms and configurations, often with altered titles, since 1960. There has never been an issue of the complete World Pacific session.

Though purporting to be a live recording at the Ash Grove Club in Los Angeles, Ash Grove owner Ed Pearl, who was present at this session, has confirmed that the songs for this album (and subsequent issues of material recorded at this session) were recorded entirely at World Pacific Studios, and overdubbed with applause to make them sound live.

Various Artists—Blues Hoot

July 6 or 7, 1960; August 1961. Live at the Ash Grove Club / World Pacific Studios, Los Angeles, CA.
Producer: Ed Michel

Lead vocal/solo acoustic guitar*, with Sonny Terry, vocal/harmonica; Walter "Brownie" McGhee, vocal/ guitar; Big Joe Williams, vocal/guitar; Jimmy Bond, bass.

"Introduction to Big Car Blues"*	Davon LP 2015
"Big Car Blues"*	Davon LP 2015
"Coffee House Blues"*	Davon LP 2015
"Stool Pigeon Blues"*	Davon LP 2015

"Ball of Twine"*	Davon LP 2015
"Three Aces on the Bottom of the Deal"	Davon LP 2015
"Right on that Shore"	Davon LP 2015

Blues Hoot was released in 1961.

Note: This various artists LP is related to the Down South Summit Meetin' *LP above. The Hopkins solo set was recorded live at the Ash Grove Club; this set is mixed with the World Pacific studio session (see above) and a solo session by Brownie McGhee and Sonny Terry, not included here.*

The actual date of Lightnin's solo set is in dispute. It has long been written that it occurred on July 6, 1960, but the DCC Compact Classics reissue of Blues Hoot *states, "Recorded in August 1961 and released as Davon 2015 in 1961." Ash Grove owner Ed Pearl supports the 1961 date.*

Various Artists—Conversation with the Blues

August 12, 1960. Houston, TX.
Producer: Paul Oliver.

Speech.

"Ain't No Easy Thing"	Decca (UK) LP 4664

Conversation with the Blues was released (in the United Kingdom only) in 1965.

Note: This various artists LP includes Mance Lipscomb, Buster Pickens, John Lee Hooker, Robert Lockwood, Sunnyland Slim, Otis Spann, J. B. Lenoir, and others.

c. October 1960. Houston, TX.

Vocal/guitar with Luke "Long Gone" Miles, vocal/harmonica; L. C. Williams, vocal/drums

"When Mother's Dead and Gone"	*unissued*

Pete Seeger—Sing Out with Pete!
October 14, 1960. Live at Carnegie Hall, New York, NY.

Vocal/acoustic guitar with Pete Seeger, vocal/banjo; Joan Baez, vocal; Bill McAdoo, vocal/probably acoustic guitar; possibly Elizabeth Knight, vocal.

"Oh Mary, Don't You Weep"	Folkways LP 2455

Sing Out With Pete! was released in 1961.

Note: The People's Song Library collection in the Walter P. Reuther Library of Labor and Urban Affairs at Wayne State University in Detroit, Michigan, holds a program of this concert. Curator William Lefevre reports that "the program lists Elizabeth Knight. However, a hand-written note in the records lists the performers and the times they were to perform versus the actual times they performed. Elizabeth Knight is not listed on that note, but Joan Baez is listed as having performed twice."

Last Night Blues / Got to Move Your Baby

October 26, 1960. Van Gelder Studio, Englewood Cliffs, NJ.
Producer: Kenneth Goldstein

Vocal/acoustic guitar with Sonny Terry, vocal*/harmonica; possibly J. C. Burris, harmonica**; Leonard Gaskin, bass; Belton Evans, drums.

"Rocky Mountain Blues"*	Bluesville LP 1029
"Got to Move Your Baby"**	Bluesville LP 1029; (45) 813
"So Sorry to Leave You"	Bluesville LP 1029; (45) 813
"Take a Trip with Me"**	Bluesville LP 1029
"Last Night Blues"**	Bluesville LP 1029; (45) 821
"Lightnin's Stroke"**	Bluesville LP 1029
"Hard to Love a Woman"	Bluesville LP 1029; (45) 817
"Conversation Blues"*	Bluesville LP 1029

Last Night Blues was released in 1961. It was reissued under the new title *Got to Move Your Baby* c.1964.

Note: According to Chris Smith (in his book That's the Stuff: The Recordings of Brownie McGhee, Sonny Terry, Stick McGhee, and J. C. Burris)*, J. C. Burris—although uncredited on the album sleeve—is the possible harmonica player on the four songs noted above. This is based on Burris's claim to Gérard Herzhaft that he played on some titles at the session and Smith's aural assessment. To compound the confusion, Smith notes that "Hopkins addresses the harp player as 'J.C.' on 'Rocky Mountain Blues' and 'Hard to Love a Woman', but aurally it's Terry on those titles."*

Lightnin'—The Blues of Lightnin' Hopkins

November 9, 1960. Van Gelder Studio, Englewood Cliffs, NJ.
Producer: Kenneth Goldstein

Vocal/acoustic guitar with Leonard Gaskin, bass; Belton Evans, drums.

"Automobile Blues"	Bluesville LP 1019
"You Better Watch Yourself"	Bluesville LP 1019
"Thinkin' About an Old Friend"	Bluesville LP 1019
"The Walkin' Blues"	Bluesville LP 1019; (45) 821
"Back to New Orleans"	Bluesville LP 1019; (45) 817
"Katie Mae"	Bluesville LP 1019; (45) 825
"Down There Baby"	Bluesville LP 1019
"Mean Old Frisco"	Bluesville LP 1019
"Shinin' Moon"	Bluesville LP 1019
"Come Back Baby"	Bluesville LP 1019

Lightnin'—The Blues of Lightnin' Hopkins was released in 1961. It was reissued c.1964.

Mojo Hand

November 1960. New York, NY.
Producer: Bobby Robinson

Vocal/acoustic guitar/piano*; Delmar Donnell, drums; unknown bass; unknown female vocal**.

"Mojo Hand"	Fire LP 104; (45) 1034
"Glory Be"	Fire LP 104; (45) 1034
"Have You Ever Loved a Woman"*	Fire LP 104; (45) Sphere Sound 701
"Santa Claus"	Fire LP 104
"Black Mare (Trot)"	Fire LP 104
"Coffee for Mama"	Fire LP 104
"Awful Dream"	Fire LP 104
"Sometimes She Will"	Fire LP 104
"Shine on Moon"	Fire LP 104
"How Long Has the Train Been Gone"	(45) Sphere Sound 701
"Bring Me My Shotgun"	*Krazy Kat (UK) LP 7410*
"Just Picking"	*Krazy Kat (UK) LP 7410*
"Last Night"	*Krazy Kat (UK) LP 7410*
"Shake That Thing"	*Krazy Kat (UK) LP 7410*
"Walk a Long Time"	*Krazy Kat (UK) LP 7410*
*"I'm Leaving with You Now"***	*Krazy Kat (UK) LP 7410*
"Houston Bound"	*Relic CD 7058*
"Baby I Don't Care"	*Relic CD 7058*
"Twixt and Between"	*unissued*

Mojo Hand was released in 1962.

Lightnin' in New York

November 15, 1960. Nola Penthouse Studio, New York, NY.
Producer: Nat Hentoff

Vocal/acoustic guitar/piano*.

"Mister Charlie Pt. 1"	Candid LP 8010; (45) 603
"Mister Charlie Pt. 2"	Candid LP 8010; (45) 603
"I Have Had My Fun, If I Don't Get Well No More"	Candid LP 8010
"Mighty Crazy"	Candid LP 8010
"Wonder Why"	Candid LP 8010
"The Trouble Blues"	Candid LP 8010
"Your Own Fault Baby to Treat Me the Way You Do"*	Candid LP 8010
"Lightnin's Piano Boogie"*	Candid LP 8010

"Take It Easy"*	Candid LP 8010
"Black Cat"	Candid LP 8019
"Rainy Highway"	*Mosaic LP 139*
"When My First Wife Quit Me"	*Mosaic LP 139*
"Walk On"	*Mosaic LP 139*
"Lightnin's Guitar Boogie"	*Mosaic LP 139*
*"Come Go Home With Me"**	*Mosaic LP 139*

Lightnin' in New York was released in 1961.

The Mosaic reissue contains the complete Candid session, including five unissued titles, and was released as a limited-edition box set with Otis Spann's complete Candid sessions.

Walking this Road by Myself

July 7, 1961; February 17, 1962; February 20, 1962. ACA Recording Studio, 3619 Fannin St., Houston, TX.
Producer: Mack McCormick

Vocal/acoustic guitar with (collectively) Edwin "Buster" Pickens, piano; Billy Bizor, harmonica; Donald Cooks, bass; Joe "Spider" Kilpatrick, drums.

"Black Gal"	Bluesville LP 1057
"Baby Don't You Tear My Clothes"	Bluesville LP 1057
"Good Morning Little Schoolgirl"	Bluesville LP 1057
"Coffee Blues"	Bluesville LP 1057
"How Many More Years I Got to Let You Dog Me Around"	Bluesville LP 1057
"Black Cadillac"	Bluesville LP 1057
"Walkin' This Road by Myself"	Bluesville LP 1057
"The Devil Jumped the Black Man"	Bluesville LP 1057
"Worried Life Blues"	Bluesville LP 1057
"Happy Blues for John Glenn" (Pts. 1 & 2 on 45)	Bluesville LP 1057; (45) 820

Walking This Road By Myself was released in 1962.

Blues in My Bottle

July 26, 1961. ACA Recording Studio, 3619 Fannin St., Houston, TX.
Producers: Mack McCormick and Kenneth Goldstein

Vocal/acoustic guitar.

"Buddy Brown's Blues"	Bluesville LP 1045
"Wine Spodee-O-Dee"	Bluesville LP 1045

"Sail On, Little Girl, Sail On"	Bluesville LP 1045; (45) 814
"Death Bells"	Bluesville LP 1045; (45) 814
"DC-7"	Bluesville LP 1045
"Going to Dallas to See My Pony Run"	Bluesville LP 1045
"Jailhouse Blues"	Bluesville LP 1045
"Blues in My Bottle"	Bluesville LP 1045
"Beans, Beans, Beans"	Bluesville LP 1045
"Catfish Blues"	Bluesville LP 1045
"My Grandpa Is Old Too"	Bluesville LP 1045

Blues in My Bottle was released c.1961.

August 16, 1961. ACA Recording Studio, 3619 Fannin St., Houston, TX.

Vocal/electric guitar with Elmore Nixon, piano; Robert Ingram, drums; unknown bass.

"Got Me a Louisiana Woman"	Ivory 91272; Vee-Jay LP 1044
"War Is Starting Again"	Ivory 91272; Vee-Jay LP 1044
"The World's in a Tangle (War Is Starting Again)"	*Magnum CD (UK) 093*
"Good as Old Time Religion"	*Magnum CD (UK) 093*

Note: "The World's in a Tangle" (a retitling of "War Is Starting Again") on Magnum CD 093 contains an extra verse, and does not fade out, as the Ivory single does.

Lightning Strikes

Probably 1961. Probably Gold Star Studio, 5628 Brock St., Houston, TX.

Vocal/acoustic guitar; separate session* (with electric guitar) with Elmore Nixon, piano; Robert Ingram, drums; unknown bass.

"Got Me a Louisiana Woman"*	Vee-Jay LP 1044; (45) Ivory 91272
"Want to Come Home"	Vee-Jay LP 1044; (45) Dart 152
"Please Don't Quit Me"	Vee-Jay LP 1044
"Devil Is Watching You"	Vee-Jay LP 1044
"Rolling and Rolling"	Vee-Jay LP 1044
"War Is Starting Again"*	Vee-Jay LP 1044; (45) Ivory 91272
"Walkin' Round in Circles"	Vee-Jay LP 1044
"Mary Lou"	Vee-Jay LP 1044; (45) Dart 152
"Heavy Snow"	Vee-Jay LP 1044
"Coon Is Hard to Catch"	Vee-Jay LP 1044

Lightning Strikes was released in 1962.

Note: Lightning Strikes *was probably produced by H. W. "Pappy" Daily and/or Bill Quinn and Lola Cullum. Only the Dart single was initially issued (in 1961); Vee-Jay Records subsequently purchased the master tapes and released the entire session on this album, with the addition of the Ivory single, which was also released prior to the LP (see above).*

Reverb was added to all songs on the Vee-Jay LP.

Lightnin' Sam Hopkins

November 26, 1961; December 2, 1961; January 23, 1962. Berkeley, CA., and ACA Recording Studio, 3619 Fannin St., Houston, TX.
Producers: Chris Strachwitz and Mack McCormick (uncredited)

Vocal/electric guitar/piano with Gino Landry, bass; Victor Leonard, drums; Joe "Spider" Kilpatrick, drums*.

"Meet You at the Chicken Shack"*	Arhoolie LP 1011
"Once Was a Gambler"	Arhoolie LP 1011; (45) Joliet 205
"Speedin' Boogie"	Arhoolie LP 1011
"Ice Storm Blues"*	Arhoolie LP 1011
"California Showers"	Arhoolie LP 1011
"Burnin' in L.A."	Arhoolie LP 1011
"Do the Boogie"	Arhoolie LP 1011
"Bald Headed Woman"	Arhoolie LP 1011
"Goin' Out"	Arhoolie LP 1011

Lightnin' Sam Hopkins was released in November 1962.

Note: A listing of unissued songs from the Berkeley sessions for this LP is not available. Joliet 205 retitled "Once a Gambler."

Lightning Hopkins—Side One with His Brothers Joel and John Henry/ Side Two with Barbara Dane

November 26, 1961. Berkeley, CA.
Producer: Chris Strachwitz.

Vocal/organ with Barbara Dane, vocal

"Jesus, Won't You Come by Here"	Arhoolie LP 1022

February 16, 1964. Waxahachie, TX.
Producer: Chris Strachwitz

Vocal/acoustic guitar with John Henry Hopkins, vocal/acoustic guitar/solo vocal*; Joel Hopkins, vocal/ acoustic guitar/solo vocal**.

"Hot Blooded Woman Blues"	Arhoolie LP 1022
"See About My Brother John Henry"	Arhoolie LP 1022
"Black Hannah"	Arhoolie LP 1022
"I Walked from Dallas"**	Arhoolie LP 1022
*"Tell Me, Tell Me"**	*Arhoolie CD 340*
"Little Girl"	*Arhoolie CD 340*
"I Got a Brother Up in Waxahachie"	*Arhoolie CD 340*
"Come Down to My House"	*Arhoolie CD 340*
"Grosebeck Blues"	*Arhoolie CD 340*
"The Dice Game" (speech)	*Arhoolie CD 340*
"I Want to Go Fishing"	*Arhoolie CD 340*
*"Doin' Little Heifer"**	*Arhoolie CD 340*
"Hey Baby Hey"	*Arhoolie CD 340*
*"Saddle Up My Gray Mare"**	*Arhoolie CD 340*
*"Little Letter"**	*unissued*
"Mary"	*unissued*
*"Hey Mr. Buzzard"***	*unissued*
"Mama, Don't Treat Your Daughter Mean"	*unissued*
"Good Times Here, Better Down the Road"	*unissued*

June 18, 1964. Live at the Cabale Club, Berkeley, CA.
Producer: Chris Strachwitz

Vocal/acoustic guitar with Barbara Dane, vocal/acoustic guitar.

"Sometimes (I Believe) She Loves Me"	Arhoolie LP 1022
"You Got Another Man"	Arhoolie LP 1022
"I'm Going Back, Baby (Back Behind the Sun)"	Arhoolie LP 1022
"Mother Earth"	Arhoolie LP 1022
"Baby, Shake That Thing"	*Arhoolie CD 451*
"It's a Lonesome Old Town"	*Arhoolie CD 451*
"Don't Push Me ('Til You Find Out What I Want)"	*Arhoolie CD 451*
"Let Me be Your Rag Doll"	*Arhoolie CD 451*
"Mama Told Papa"	*Arhoolie CD 451*

March 17, 1965. Houston, TX.
Producer: Chris Strachwitz

Vocal/acoustic guitar with Joel Hopkins, acoustic guitar.

"Going Back to Baden-Baden"   Arhoolie LP 1022

Lightning Hopkins—With His Brothers Joel and John Henry/With Barbara Dane was released in 1966.

Po' Lightnin'

November 26, 1961. Berkeley, CA.
Producer: Chris Strachwitz

Vocal/organ*/piano**.

"My Baby's Gone"*   Arhoolie LP 1087
"Candy Kitchen"**   Arhoolie LP 1087

May 20, 1969. Berkeley, CA.
Producer: Chris Strachwitz

Vocal/electric guitar with Francis Clay, drums. Add Jeff Carp, harmonica; Johnny "Big Moose" Walker, piano; Paul Asbell, guitar; Chester "Gino" Skaggs, bass on *.

"Mojo Hand"   Arhoolie LP 1087
"Rock Me Baby"*   Arhoolie LP 1087
"Hello Central"   Arhoolie LP 1087
"Ain't It Crazy"   Arhoolie LP 1087
"My Starter Won't Start This Morning"   Arhoolie LP 1087
"One Kind Favor I Ask of You"   Arhoolie LP 1087
"Little Girl"   Arhoolie LP 1087
"Baby Please Don't Go"   Arhoolie LP 1087

"My Baby's Gone"   *Arhoolie CD 390*
"Come on Baby"   *Arhoolie CD 390*

Po' Lightnin' was released in 1983.

Note: The 1969 portion of this LP had been previously released on the Lightnin'! *LP on Poppy (see below).*

Various Artists—Texas Blues, Volume 2

November 26, 1961. Berkeley, CA.
Producer: Chris Strachwitz

Vocal/electric guitar with Geno Landry, bass; Victor Leonard, drums.

"Hurricanes Carla and Esther"	Arhoolie LP 1017
"I'm Feeling Bad"	Arhoolie LP 1017

Texas Blues Volume 2 was released in 1968.

Note: This various artists LP includes Mance Lipscomb, Mercy Dee, Billy Bizor, Alex Moore, Smokey Hogg, and others.

Various Artists—Blues and Trouble Vol. 2

November 26, 1961. Berkeley, CA.
Producer: Chris Strachwitz

Vocal/electric guitar.

"Wine Drinkin' Woman"	Arhoolie LP 1012

Blues and Trouble Vol. 2 was released in 1963.

Note: This various artists LP includes Lil' Son Jackson, Mercy Dee, Robert Shaw, and others.

December 2, 1961. Berkeley, CA.
Producer: Chris Strachwitz

Vocal/acoustic guitar.

"Hello (Austria)"	*Document (Austria) LP 577*

Note: This was a private acetate made for a fan in Austria, not intended for public release.

Smokes Like Lightnin'

January 1962; February 17, 1962; February 20, 1962. ACA Recording Studio, 3619 Fannin, Houston, TX.
Producer: Mack McCormick

Vocal/electric guitar with (collectively) Edwin "Buster" Pickens, piano; Donald Cooks, bass; Joe "Spider" Kilpatrick, drums

"T Model Blues"	Bluesville LP 1070
"You Cook All Right"	Bluesville LP 1070
"Jackstropper Blues"	Bluesville LP 1070
"Never Miss Your Water"	Bluesville LP 1070
"Let's Do the Susie Q"	Bluesville LP 1070
"Smokes Like Lightning"	Bluesville LP 1070
"My Black Name"	Bluesville LP 1070
"Ida Mae"	Bluesville LP 1070
"Prison Farm Blues"	Bluesville LP 1070

Smokes Like Lightnin' was released in 1963.

Various Artists—Bad Luck 'n' Trouble

**January 23, 1962. ACA Recording Studio, 3619 Fannin St., Houston, TX.
Producer: Mack McCormick.**

Vocal/piano with Joe "Spider" Kilpatrick, drums.

"Candy Wagon"	Arhoolie LP 1018

Bad Luck 'n' Trouble was released in 1965.

Note: This various artists LP includes Clifton Chenier, Bukka White, Mercy Dee, K. C. Douglas, and others.

Lightnin' and Co.

**February 17, 1962; February 20, 1962. ACA Recording Studio, 3619 Fannin St., Houston, TX.
Producer: Mack McCormick**

Vocal/electric guitar with (collectively) Billy Bizor, vocal/harmonica*; Edwin "Buster" Pickens, piano; Donald Cooks, bass; Joe "Spider" Kilpatrick, drums.

"My Baby Don't Stand No Cheating"	Bluesville LP 1061; (45) 825
"You Is One Black Rat"	Bluesville LP 1061
"The Fox Chase"*	Bluesville LP 1061
"Mojo Hand"	Bluesville LP 1061
"Mama Blues"*	Bluesville LP 1061
"Sinner's Prayer"	Bluesville LP 1061; (45) 822
"Angel Child"	Bluesville LP 1061; (45) 822
"I Got a Leak in This Old Building"	Bluesville LP 1061
"Pneumonia Blues"	Bluesville LP 1061
"Have You Ever Been Mistreated"	Bluesville LP 1061

Lightnin' and Co. was released c.1962.

Hootin' the Blues

May 17, 1962. Live at the Second Fret, Philadelphia, PA.

Vocal/acoustic-electric guitar.

"Blues Is a Feeling"	Prestige Folklore LP 14021
"Me and Ray Charles"	Prestige Folklore LP 14021
"In the Evening"	Prestige Folklore LP 14021
"Ain't It Crazy"	Prestige Folklore LP 14021
"Last Night I Lost the Best Friend I Ever Had"	Prestige Folklore LP 14021
"Everything"	Prestige Folklore LP 14021
"I Work Down on the Chain Gang"	Prestige Folklore LP 14021
"Meet Me in the Bottom"	Prestige Folklore LP 14021

Hootin' the Blues was released in January 1964.

Goin' Away

June 4, 1963. Gold Star Studio, 5628 Brock St., Houston, TX. Overdub session: June 21, 1963. Van Gelder Studio, Englewood Cliffs, NJ.

Vocal/acoustic guitar with (overdubbed) Leonard Gaskin, bass; Herbie Lovelle, drums.

"Business You're Doin'"	Bluesville LP 1073; (45) 823
"Wake Up Old Lady"	Bluesville LP 1073; (45) 823
"Goin' Away"	Bluesville LP 1073; (45) 824
"You Better Stop Here"	Bluesville LP 1073; (45) 824
"Stranger Blues"	Bluesville LP 1073
"Don't Embarrass Me, Baby"	Bluesville LP 1073
"Little Sister's Boogie"	Bluesville LP 1073
"I'm Wit' It"	Bluesville LP 1073

Goin' Away was released in 1963.

Various Artists—Look, It's Us!

c.1963. Gold Star Studio, 5628 Brock St., Houston, TX.

Vocal/acoustic guitar.

"Trouble in Mind"	Jester LP

Look, It's Us! was released c.1963.

Note: This various artists LP (a promotional album for the Jester Club in Houston) includes Guy Clark, Scott and Vivian Holtzman, Frank Davis, and Kay (K.T.) Oslin.

Live at Swarthmore College

April 6, 1964. Live at Swarthmore College, Philadelphia, PA.

Vocal/acoustic-electric guitar.

"Baby Please Don't Go"	Prestige CD 7-4406
"My Black Cadillac"	Prestige CD 7-4406
"It's Crazy"	Prestige CD 7-4406
"Mojo Hand"	Prestige CD 7-4406
"My Babe"	Prestige CD 7-4406
"Short Haired Woman"	Prestige CD 7-4406
"Mean Old Frisco"	Prestige CD 7-4406
"Trouble in Mind"	Prestige CD 7-4406
"The Twister"	Prestige CD 7-4406
"Green Onions"	Prestige CD 7-4406
"Sun Goin' Down"	Prestige CD 7-4406
"Come Go Home with Me"	Prestige CD 7-4406
"I'm a Stranger"	Prestige CD 7-4406

Live at Swarthmore College was released in 1992.

Down Home Blues

May 4, 1964. Gold Star Studio, 5628 Brock St., Houston, TX. Overdub session: Date unknown, Van Gelder Studio, Englewood Cliffs, NJ.

Vocal/electric guitar/electric bottleneck guitar* with (overdubbed) Leonard Gaskin, bass; Herbie Lovelle, drums.

"Let's Go Sit on the Lawn"	Bluesville LP 1086; (45) 326
"I Woke Up This Morning"*	Bluesville LP 1086
"I Got Tired"	Bluesville LP 1086
"I Like to Boogie"	Bluesville LP 1086; (45) 326
"I Asked the Bossman"	Bluesville LP 1086
"I'm Taking the Devil of a Chance"	Bluesville LP 1086
"Just a Wristwatch on My Arm"	Bluesville LP 1086
"I Was Standing on 75 Highway"	Bluesville LP 1086
"Get It Straight"	Bluesville LP 1086

Down Home Blues was released in 1964.

Soul Blues

May 4 and 5, 1964. Gold Star Studio, 5628 Brock St., Houston, TX. Overdub session: Date unknown, Van Gelder Studio, Englewood Cliffs, NJ.

Vocal/acoustic-electric guitar with (overdubbed) Leonard Gaskin, bass; Herbie Lovelle, drums.

"The Howling Wolf"	Prestige LP 7377
"Darling Do You Remember Me"	Prestige LP 7377
"I'm a Crawling Blacksnake"	Prestige LP 7377
"I'm Gonna Build Me a Heaven of My Own (Pts. 1 & 2)"	Prestige LP 7377; (45) 405
"My Babe"	Prestige LP 7377
"Too Many Drivers"	Prestige LP 7377
"Rocky Mountain Blues"	Prestige LP 7377
"I Mean Goodbye"	Prestige LP 7377
"Black Ghost Blues"	Prestige LP 7377
"Lonesome Graveyard"	Prestige LP 7377

Soul Blues was released in 1966.

The American Folk Blues Festival 1962–1966

September 28, 1964. Live at the American Folk Blues Festival, (possibly) Hamburg, Germany. Producer: Horst Lippmann

Vocal/acoustic-electric guitar with Willie Dixon, bass; Clifton James, drums.

"Mojo Hand"	Hip-O Select CD 1003

The American Folk Blues Festival 1962–1966 was released in 2003.

Note: This various artists CD includes performances by Howlin' Wolf, Muddy Waters, Sonny Boy Williamson, Lonnie Johnson, Memphis Slim, and others.

Various Artists—American Folk Blues Festival—1964

October 9, 1964. Live at the American Folk Blues Festival, Musikhalle, Hamburg, Germany. Producer: Horst Lippmann

Vocal/acoustic-electric guitar.

"Ain't It a Pity"	Fontana (Germany) LP 885.411
"Baby Please Don't Go"	Fontana (Germany) LP 885.411

The American Folk Blues Festival—1964 was released (in Germany only) in 1964.

Note: This various artists LP includes performances by Sonny Boy Williamson, Sunnyland Slim, Howlin' Wolf, Sleepy John Estes, and others.

My Life in the Blues

December 2, 1964. Live, unknown location. New York, NY.
Producer: Sam Charters

Vocal/acoustic-electric guitar.

"I Don't Want to do Nothing with You"	Prestige LP 7370
"You Is One Black Rat"	Prestige LP 7370
"Just Boogyin'"	Prestige LP 7370
"Take Me Back"	Prestige LP 7370
"I Was Down on Dowling Street"	Prestige LP 7370

Speech.

"I Growed Up with the Blues"	Prestige LP 7370
"My Family"	Prestige LP 7370
"I Learn About the Blues"	Prestige LP 7370
"I First Come to Houston"	Prestige LP 7370
"I Meet Texas Alexander"	Prestige LP 7370
"There Were Hard Times"	Prestige LP 7370
"I Make My First Record and Get My Name"	Prestige LP 7370
"My Thoughts on the Blues"	Prestige LP 7370

My Life in the Blues (a double LP) was released July 1965.

Live at the Bird Lounge

1964. Live at the Bird Lounge, 2305 S. Shepherd, Houston, TX.

Vocal/acoustic-electric guitar, "Curly Lee" (Billy Bizor), vocal/harmonica*.

"I Heard My Children Crying"	Guest Star LP 1459
"Leave Jike Mary Alone"	Guest Star LP 1459
"You Treat Po' Lightning Wrong"	Guest Star LP 1459
"I'm Gonna Meet My Babe Somewhere"	Guest Star LP 1459
"There's Good Rockin' Tonight"	Guest Star LP 1459
"Don't Treat That Man 'Way You Treat Me"	Guest Star LP 1459
*"Little Rose"**	*Collectables LP/CD 5206*
"With You on My Mind"	*Collectables LP/CD 5206*
"Sam Talking to the Group"	*Collectables LP/CD 5206*
"Sam and Curley Talking"	*Collectables LP/CD 5206*
*"Possum Hunt"**	*Collectables LP/CD 5206*
"Sam Talking and Strumming"	*Collectables LP/CD 5206*

"Love Me or Leave Me"   *Collectables LP/CD 5206*
"Load the Train"*   *Koch CD 9850*
"Baby Don't Tear My Clothes"   *Koch CD 9850*

Live at the Bird Lounge was released c.1964.

The King of the Blues

c.December 1964. Houston, TX.
Producer: Aubrey Mayhew

Vocal/electric guitar.

"This Time We're Gonna Try"   Pickwick LP 3013
"Christmastime Is Coming"   Pickwick LP 3013
"Come on Baby, Let's Work Awhile"   Pickwick LP 3013
"The Jet"   Pickwick LP 3013
"I Don't Need You Woman"   Pickwick LP 3013
"I Wish I Was a Baby"   Pickwick LP 3013
"The Crazy Song"   Pickwick LP 3013
"Lightnin's Love"   Pickwick LP 3013
"Take It If You Want It"   Pickwick LP 3013
"How Have You Been?"   Pickwick LP 3013

Probably from this session:
"From Man to Man"   *Collectables LP/CD 5203*
"Little Boy Blue"   *Collectables LP/CD 5203*
"That Man from New York City"   *Collectables LP/CD 5203*
"I Got a Letter"   *Collectables LP/CD 5204*
"Gonna Move Off This Street"   *Collectables LP/CD 5204*
"How Can You Love Me and Another Man, Too"   *Collectables LP/CD 5204*
"Chicken Minnie"   *Collectables LP/CD 5205*

The King of the Blues was released in August 1965.

Various Artists—Ball and Chain

March 18, 1965. Houston, TX.
Producer: Chris Strachwitz

Vocal/guitar with Harold "Frenchie" Joseph, drums.

"Gabriel"	Arhoolie LP 1039
"Money Taker"	Arhoolie LP 1039; (45) 513
"Come on Baby"	Arhoolie LP 1039; (45) 513
"Prison Blues"	Arhoolie LP 1039
"Mama's Fight"	Arhoolie LP 1039; (45) 508
"My Woman"	Arhoolie LP 1039; (45) 508

Ball and Chain was released in 1969.

Note: This various artists LP also includes Big Mama Thornton and Larry Williams.
    "Prison Blues" only appears on later pressings of this LP; it is excluded from first pressings.

Various Artists—Great Bluesmen/Newport

July 24, 1965. Live at the Newport Folk Festival, Newport, RI.

Vocal/electric guitar with Sam Lay, drums.

"Cotton Field Blues"	Vanguard LP 77/78
"Shake That Thing"	Vanguard LP 77/78

Great Bluesmen/Newport was released in 1976.

Note: This various artists double LP includes Son House, Skip James, John Lee Hooker, Mississippi John Hurt, and others.

Various Artists—Blues with a Feeling

July 24, 1965. Live at the Newport Folk Festival, Newport, RI.

Vocal/electric guitar.

"The Woman I'm Loving, She's Taken My Appetite"	Vanguard CD 2-77005
"Come On, Baby"	Vanguard CD 2-77005
"Baby Please Don't Go"	Vanguard CD 2-77005

Note: This various artists CD includes Son House, Bukka White, Skip James, Muddy Waters, Mississippi John Hurt, and others.

Blues With a Feeling was released in 1993.

Live at Newport

July 24, 1965. Live at the Newport Folk Festival, Newport, RI.

Vocal/electric guitar with Sam Lay, drums*.

"Where Can I Find My Baby?"	Vanguard CD 79715
"Baby Please Don't Go"	Vanguard CD 79715
"Mojo Hand"	Vanguard CD 79715
"Trouble in Mind"	Vanguard CD 79715
"The Woman I'm Loving, She's Taken My Appetite"	Vanguard CD 79715
"Come on Baby"	Vanguard CD 79715
"Cotton Patch Blues"	Vanguard CD 79715
"Instrumental"*	Vanguard CD 79715
"Jealous of My Wife"*	Vanguard CD 79715
"Every Day About This Time"*	Vanguard CD 79715
"Shake That Thing"*	Vanguard CD 79715

Note: Vanguard CD 79715 purports to reissue the complete Newport performance. However, "Cotton Patch Blues," while the same song as "Cotton Field Blues" on the Great Bluesmen/Newport LP, is a completely different performance, with no drummer present.

Live at Newport was released in 2002.

Lightnin' Srikes

October 4 and 5, 1965. Los Angeles, CA.

Vocal/electric guitar with Don Crawford, harmonica (overdubbed)*; Jimmy Bond, bass; Earl Palmer, drums.

"Mojo Hand"*	Verve-Folkways LP 9022
"Little Wail"*	Verve-Folkways LP 9022
"Cotton"	Verve-Folkways LP 9022
"Take Me Back (Baby)"	Verve-Folkways LP 9022
"(Really) Nothin' But the Blues"	Verve-Folkways LP 9022
"Hurricane Betsy"*	Verve-Folkways LP 9022
"Guitar Lightnin'"	Verve-Folkways LP 9022
"Woke Up This Morning"	Verve-Folkways LP 9022
"Shake Yourself"*	Verve-Folkways LP 9022
"Down Home Blues"	*Saga(UK) LP 8001*
"Lightnin's Blues"	*Saga(UK) LP 8001*
"Goin' to Louisiana" (alternate take of "Mojo Hand")	*Saga(UK) LP 8001*

Lightnin' Strikes was released in 1966.

Note: First pressings of this LP were released with a photo of Reverend Gary Davis on the cover.

Lightnin' Hopkins

October 4 and 5, 1965. Los Angeles, CA.

Vocal/electric guitar with Don Crawford, harmonica (overdubbed)*; Jimmy Bond, bass; Earl Palmer, drums; John "Streamline" Ewing, trombone **.

"Shaggy Dad" [sic "Shaggy Dog"]	Verve-Folkways LP 3013
"I'll Be Gone"**	Verve-Folkways LP 3013
"Shining Moon"	Verve-Folkways LP 3013
"Shake It Baby"	Verve-Folkways LP 3013
"Goin' Back Home"	Verve-Folkways LP 3013
"Good Times"	Verve-Folkways LP 3013
"What'd I Say"*	Verve-Folkways LP 3013
"Don't Wake Me"	Verve-Folkways LP 3013
"Talk of the Town"	Verve-Folkways LP 3013

Lightnin' Hopkins was released in 1967.

That's My Story: The Blues of Lightnin' Hopkins, Vol. I

October 4 and 5, 1965. Los Angeles, CA.

Vocal/electric guitar with Don Crawford, harmonica (overdubbed)*; Jimmy Bond, bass; Earl Palmer, drums; John "Streamline" Ewing, trombone**.

"Last Night"	Polydor(UK) LP 545019
"Rain"**	Polydor(UK) LP 545019
"Fugitive Blues"	Polydor(UK) LP 545019
"G String Blues"	Polydor(UK) LP 545019
"Grandma Told Grandpa"	Polydor(UK) LP 545019
"Goin' to Dallas"	Polydor(UK) LP 545019
"Keep Movin' On"	Polydor(UK) LP 545019
"That's My Story"	Polydor(UK) LP 545019
"Dillon's Store"**	Polydor(UK) LP 545019

That's My Story was released (in the United Kingdom only) in 1970.

Blue Lightnin'

c.1965. Probably Robin Hood Brian Studio, Tyler, TX. Producer: Stan Lewis

Vocal/acoustic-electric guitar with Elmore Nixon, piano; unknown bass and drums.

"Found My Baby Crying"	Jewel LP 5000; (45) 825
"Move On Out, Pt. 1"	Jewel LP 5000

"Back Door Friend"	Jewel LP 5000; (45) 788
"Fishing Clothes"	Jewel LP 5000; (45) 788
"Morning Blues" [a.k.a. "Moaning Blues"]	Jewel LP 5000
"Gambler's Blues"	Jewel LP 5000
"Wig Wearing Woman"	Jewel LP 5000; (45) 796
"Move On Out, Pt. 2"	Jewel LP 5000; (45) 796

Blue Lightnin' was released in 1967.

Note: The Blue Lightnin' *LP contains two tracks from Modern—"Lonesome Dog Blues" and "Last Affair."*

Various Artists—The Second Annual Berkeley Blues Festival, Concert and Dance

April 15, 1966. Live at the Berkeley Blues Festival, Berkeley, CA. Producer: Chris Strachwitz

Vocal/guitar with Francis Clay, drums.

"Last Night"	Arhoolie LP 1030
"Going to Louisiana (Mojo Hand)"	Arhoolie LP 1030
"Black Cadillac"	Arhoolie LP 1030
"Short Haired Woman"	Arhoolie LP 1030
"Lightnin's Boogie"	Arhoolie LP 1030
"If You Don't Want Me"	*Arhoolie CD 484*
"I Feel So Good"	*Arhoolie CD 484*

The Second Annual Berkeley Blues Festival, Concert and Dance was released in 1967.

Note: This various artists LP includes performances by Mance Lipscomb and Clifton Chenier.

Texas Blues Man

December 18, 1967. 3124 Gray, Apt. 14 (Hopkins's apartment), Houston, TX. Producer: Chris Strachwitz.

Vocal/electric guitar; electric bottleneck guitar*.

"Tom Moore Blues"	Arhoolie LP 1034
"Watch My Fingers"	Arhoolie LP 1034
"Little Antoinette"	Arhoolie LP 1034
"Love Is Like a Hydrant"	Arhoolie LP 1034
"Cut Me Out Baby"	Arhoolie LP 1034
"Take a Walk"	Arhoolie LP 1034
"Slavery"	Arhoolie LP 1034

"I Would If I Could"*	Arhoolie LP 1034
"Bud Russell Blues"	Arhoolie LP 1034
"At Home Blues"	Arhoolie LP 1034
"Gin Bottle Blues"	*Arhoolie CD 403*
"I'm Leaving You Now"	*Arhoolie CD 403*

Texas Blues Man was released in 1968.

Free Form Patterns

January 3 and 4, 1968. International Artists Studios, 5628 Brock St., Houston, TX.
Producer: Lelan Rogers

Vocal/electric guitar with Elmore Nixon, piano*; Billy Bizor, harmonica/vocal**; Earl "Duke" Davis, bass; Danny Thomas, drums.

"Mr. Charlie Pt. 1"	International Artists LP 6
"Mr. Charlie Pt. 2"	International Artists LP 6; (45) 127
"Give Me Time to Think"	International Artists LP 6
"Mr. Dittas' Grocery Store"	International Artists LP 6
"Open Up Your Door"*	International Artists LP 6
"Cooking's Done"	International Artists LP 6
"Got Her Letter This Morning"	International Artists LP 6
"Rain Falling"	International Artists LP 6
"Mini Skirt"*	International Artists LP 6
"Fox Chase"**	International Artists (45) 127
"Black Ghost"	*International Artists LP 13*
"Interview"	*International Artists LP 13*

Free Form Patterns was released in 1968.

Note: First pressings of Free Form Patterns *have a lettered cover with liner notes by Lelan Rogers; Lightnin's name is misspelled "Lightin'" throughout. The rarer second pressings have a painted portrait cover, unattributed liner notes, and corrected spellings.*

The flipside of International Artists (45) 127 is credited to Billy Bizor.

Talkin' Some Sense

January 17, 1968. ACA Recording Studio, 1017 Westheimer, Houston, TX.
Producer: Don Logan

Vocal/electric guitar with George "Wild Child" Butler, harmonica; Elmore Nixon, piano; Lawrence Evans, bass; unknown drums.

"Uncle Stan, the Hip Hit Record Man"	Jewel LP 5001, (45) 825
"Long Way from Home"	Jewel LP 5001
"I'm Tired of Trouble"	Jewel LP 5001
"Vietnam War Pts. 1 & 2"	Jewel LP 5001
"Lightnin' Strikes One More Time"	Jewel LP 5001
"Walkin' Blues"	Jewel LP 5001
"Talkin' Some Sense"	Jewel LP 5001
"Lonesome Lightnin'"	Jewel LP 5001
"My Suggestion"	Jewel LP 5001
"You're Gonna Miss Me"	Jewel LP 5001
"The Purple Puppy"	Jewel LP 5001
"Racetrack"	*Westside (UK) CD 228*
"My Money Is What You Want"	*Westside (UK) CD 228*

Talkin' Some Sense was released in 1968.

Lightnin' Hopkins Strikes Again!

**April 11 and 12, 1968. ACA Recording Studio, 1017 Westheimer, Houston, TX.
Producer: Roy Ames**

Vocal/electric guitar with Cedric Haywood, piano; Lawrence Evans, bass; Ben Turner, drums.

"Born in the Bottom"	Home Cooking LP 102
"Mojo Hand"	Home Cooking LP 102
"Feel Like Balling the Jack"	Home Cooking LP 102
"A Man Like Me Is Hard to Find"	Home Cooking LP 102
"Go Ahead"	Home Cooking LP 102
"I Wonder Where She Can Be Tonight?"	Home Cooking LP 102
"Old Man"	Home Cooking LP 102
"Crying for Bread"	Home Cooking LP 102
"Rainy Day in Houston"	*Rattlesnake(Germany) LP 55001*
"Stinking Foot"	*Rattlesnake(Germany) LP 55001*
"I Got a Letter This Morning"	*Collectables CD 5262*
"How Does It"	*Collectables CD 5262*
"Lonesome Life"	*Collectables CD 5262*
"Pine Gum Boogie"	*Collectables CD 5262*
"Wake Up the Dead"	*Collectables CD 5262*
"Walking and Walking"	*Collectables CD 5262*
"Shake That Thing"	*Amhearst CD 662033*

Lightnin' Hopkins Strikes Again! was released in 1975.

Various Artists—Soul . . . In the Beginning

April 11 and 12, 1968. ACA Recording Studio, 1017 Westheimer, Houston, TX.
Producer: Roy Ames

Vocal/electric guitar with Cedric Haywood, piano; Lawrence Evans, bass; Ben Turner, drums.

"December 7, 1941"	Avco Embassy LP 33006
"Mojo Hand"	Avco Embassy LP 33006

Soul . . . In The Beginning was released in 1970.

Note: *This various artists LP includes Clifton Chenier, T-Bone Walker, Billy Bizor, Calvin Johnson, and Johnny Winter.*

Billy Bizor—Blowing My Blues Away

April 15, 1968. ACA Recording Studio, 1017 Westheimer, Houston, TX.
Producer: Roy Ames

Vocal/electric guitar with Billy Bizor, harmonica; Elmore Nixon, piano; "Duck" Davis, guitar; Harold Chevalier, bass; Ben Turner, drums.

"Vietnam War"	Home Cooking LP 111
"You Just Got to Miss Me"	Home Cooking LP 111

Blowing My Blues Away was released in 1988.

The Great Electric Show and Dance

1969. ACA Recording Studio, 1017 Westheimer, Houston, TX.
Producer: Don Logan

Vocal/electric and acoustic guitar, with unknown fuzz guitar (probably overdubbed), harmonica, piano, bass and drums.

"You're Too Fast"	Jewel LP 5002; (45) 809
"Love Me This Morning"	Jewel LP 5002; (45) 819
"I'm Comin' Home"	Jewel LP 5002; (45) 809
"Ride in Your New Automobile"	Jewel LP 5002; (45) 803
"Breakfast Time"	Jewel LP 5002; (45) 807
"Lovin' Arms"	Jewel LP 5002; (45) 803
"Rock Me Mama"	Jewel LP 5002; (45) 819
"Mr. Charlie Pt. 1"	Jewel LP 5002; (45) 816

"Mr. Charlie Pt. 2"	Jewel LP 5002; (45) 816
"Play with Your Poodle"	Jewel LP 5002; (45) 807
"Little School Girl"	*Capricorn CD 42014*
"My Daddy Was a Preacher"	*Capricorn CD 42014*
"A Death in the Family"	*Capricorn CD 42014*
"I Hate I Got Married"	*Westside(UK) CD 228*
"Jail House Blues"	*Westside(UK) CD 228*
"Katie Mae"	*Westside(UK) CD 228*
"Sail on Little Girl"	*Westside(UK) CD 228*
"West Texas Blues"	*Westside(UK) CD 228*
"Walk Me"	*Westside(UK) CD 228*
"Little Boy Blue"	*Westside(UK) CD 228*
"Pneumonia Blues"	*Westside(UK) CD 228*
"Huntin' in the Morning"	*Westside(UK) CD 228*
"Letter to My Back Door Friend"	*Westside(UK) CD 228*
"Bass Player's Go Go"	*unissued*

The Great Electric Show and Dance was released in 1970.

Note: Don Logan has confirmed that this album was recorded at ACA in Houston, not Muscle Shoals Sound Studio in Muscle Shoals, Alabama, as has long been written. The Westside CD reissue further confirms this location since ACA engineer Bill Holford can be heard announcing most takes.

A fourth album for Jewel is alleged to have been recorded; no information is available.

California Mudslide (and Earthquake)

May 1969. Los Angeles, CA.
Producer: Bruce Bromberg

Vocal/electric guitar/piano*/organ** with John Howard, bass+; Bill Brown, drums+.

"California Mudslide"	Vault LP 129
"Rosie Mae"	Vault LP 129
"Los Angeles Blues"*	Vault LP 129
"Easy on Your Heels"+	Vault LP 129; (45) 965
"New Santa Fe"	Vault LP 129
"Jesus, Would You Come by Here"**	Vault LP 129
"No Education"	Vault LP 129; (45) 965
"Antoinette's Blues"*	Vault LP 129
"Change My Way of Livin'"	Vault LP 129
"Los Angeles Boogie"**	Vault LP 129
"Call on My Baby"	Vault LP 129

California Mudslide (And Earthquake) was released c.1969.

Lightnin'!

May 20, 1969. Berkeley, CA.
Producer: Chris Strachwitz

Vocal/guitar with Francis Clay, drums. Add Jeff Carp, harmonica; Johnny "Big Moose" Walker, piano; Paul Asbell, guitar; Chester "Gino" Skaggs, bass on *.

"Hold Up Your Hand"	Poppy LP 60002
"My Starter Won't Start This Morning"	Poppy LP 60002
"What'd I Say"	Poppy LP 60002
"One Kind Favor"	Poppy LP 60002
"Baby Please Don't Go"	Poppy LP 60002
"Trouble in Mind"	Poppy LP 60002
"Annie's Blues"	Poppy LP 60002
"Baby"	Poppy LP 60002
"Little and Low"	Poppy LP 60002
"I Hear You Callin'"	Poppy LP 60002
"Mojo Hand Pt. 1"	Poppy LP 60002
"Mojo Hand Pt. 2"	Poppy LP 60002
"Have You Ever Had a Woman"	Poppy LP 60002
"Ain't It Crazy"	Poppy LP 60002
"Black and Evil"	Poppy LP 60002
"Rock Me Baby"*	Poppy LP 60002
"Hello Central"	Poppy LP 60002
"Back Door Friend"*	Poppy LP 60002
"Little Girl, Little Girl"	Poppy LP 60002
"It's Better Down the Road"	Poppy LP 60002

From above session:

"Lightnin' Declares"	Tomato CD 2098
"Last Night I Lost the Best Friend I Ever Had"	Tomato CD 2098
"Baby, Please Lend Me Your Love"	Tomato CD 2098
"Short Haired Woman (speech)"	Tomato CD 2098
"Short Haired Woman"	Tomato CD 2098
"Cigar (speech)"	Tomato CD 2098
"Pneumonia Blues"	Tomato CD 2098
"What'd I Say"*	Tomato CD 2098
"Katie Mae"*	Tomato CD 2098
"Black Cadillac"	Tomato CD 2098
"One for the Gamblin'"	Tomato CD 2098
"I Gave Up Card Playin' (speech)"	Tomato CD 2098
"I Once Was a Gambler"	Tomato CD 2098
"Where Did You Stay Last Night?"	Tomato CD 2098
"Careless Love"	Tomato CD 2098
"Black Lightnin' (speech)"	Tomato CD 2098
"Lightnin' Slow Blues"	Tomato CD 2098

Lightnin'! (a double LP) was released in 1970.

Lightning Hopkins in Berkeley

May 20, 1969, and December 8, 1969. Berkeley, CA.
Producer: Chris Strachwitz

Vocal/electric guitar with Francis Clay, drums.

"Send My Child Home to Me"	Arhoolie LP 1063
"Wipe Your Feet on the Floor"	Arhoolie LP 1063
"Sellin' Wine in Arizona"	Arhoolie LP 1063
"Please Settle in Viet Nam"	Arhoolie LP 1063; (45) Joliet 205
"Up on Telegraph Avenue"	Arhoolie LP 1063
"Brand New Lock"	Arhoolie LP 1063
"Little and Low Blues"	Arhoolie LP 1063

Lightning Hopkins in Berkeley was released in 1973.

Note: Several songs on this album had been previously released on the Lightnin'! *LP on Poppy; only those unique to this LP have been listed.*

Blues Is My Business—Live 1971, Previously Unreleased, Vol. I

1971. Live, unknown location.

Vocal/guitar with unknown bass and drums.

"I Got a Feeling"	Edsel (UK) CD 353
"Walking All Night Long"	Edsel (UK) CD 353
"I Crawled By Your Window"	Edsel (UK) CD 353
"Take Me Back"	Edsel (UK) CD 353
"Blues Is My Business"	Edsel (UK) CD 353
"Mojo Hand"	Edsel (UK) CD 353
"Pinetop's Boogie"	Edsel (UK) CD 353
"Throw This Old Dog a Bone"	Edsel (UK) CD 353
"Cook My Breakfast"	Edsel (UK) CD 353
"You Can Look at Me"	Edsel (UK) CD 353

Blues is My Business—Live 1971, Previously Unreleased, Vol. 1 was released in 1993.

You're Gonna Miss Me—Live 1971, Previously Unreleased, Vol. 2

1971. Live, unknown location.

Vocal/guitar with unknown bass and drums.

"Rock Me Baby"	Edsel (UK) CD 357
"Put Your Red Dress On"	Edsel (UK) CD 357
"Lightnin' (He) Can Do It"	Edsel (UK) CD 357
"Lightnin' Boogie"	Edsel (UK) CD 357
"Mr. Charlie"	Edsel (UK) CD 357
"Baby Please Don't Go"	Edsel (UK) CD 357
"Lightnin's Gone Again"	Edsel (UK) CD 357
"One-Eyed Woman"	Edsel (UK) CD 357
"Hardly Trying"	Edsel (UK) CD 357
"You're Gonna Miss Me When I'm Gone"	Edsel (UK) CD 357

You're Gonna Miss Me—Live 1971, Previously Unreleased, Vol. 2 was released in 1993.

Note: Edsel CD 353 & CD 357 reissued as one CD on Edsel CD 8011.

It's a Sin to Be Rich

May 16 and 17, 1972. Village Recorder Studio, Los Angeles, CA.

Vocal/electric guitar/piano* with John Lee Hooker, guitar**/speech+; Jesse Edwin Davis, guitar; Luther Tucker, guitar; Mel Brown, guitar/piano/organ; Charlie Grimes, guitar; David Cohen, guitar; Clifford Coulter, piano/melodica***/bass; Michael White, violin; Joe Frank Corola, bass; Lonnie Castile, drums.

"Roberta"	Verve CD 517 514
"Katie Mae" + ***	Verve CD 517 514
"Howlin' Wolf" [spoken]	Verve CD 517 514
"The Rehearsal"**	Verve CD 517 514
"It's a Sin to be Rich, It's a Low-Down Shame to be Poor"	Verve CD 517 514
"Y'all Escuse Me" [sic]	Verve CD 517 514
"Just Out of Louisiana"	Verve CD 517 514
"Get Out Your Pencil" [spoken]	Verve CD 517 514
"I Forgot to Pull My Shoes Off"	Verve CD 517 514
"Turn Me On"*	Verve CD 517 514
"Candy Kitchen"**+	Verve CD 517 514

It's a Sin to be Rich was released in 1993.

The Legacy of the Blues Vol. 12

1974. Houston, TX.
Producer: Sam Charters

Vocal/electric guitar/electric bottleneck guitar* with Ira James, harmonica; Carl "Rusty" Myers or Ozell Roberts, bass/guitar; Larry "Bones" McCall, drums.

"Please Help Poor Me"*	Sonet (Sweden/UK) LP 672
"Way Out in Abilene"	Sonet (Sweden/UK) LP 672
"Don't You Call That Boogie"	Sonet (Sweden/UK) LP 672
"Swing in the Backyard"	Sonet (Sweden/UK) LP 672
"The Hearse Is Backed Up to the Door"*	Sonet (Sweden/UK) LP 672
"That Meat's a Little Too High"	Sonet (Sweden/UK) LP 672
"Let Them Little Things be True"	Sonet (Sweden/UK) LP 672
"I Been Burning Bad Gasoline"	Sonet (Sweden/UK) LP 672
"Don't You Mess with My Woman"	Sonet (Sweden/UK) LP 672
"Water Fallin' Boogie"	Sonet (Sweden/UK) LP 672

The Legacy of the Blues Vol. 12 was released (initially in Sweden and the United Kingdom only) in 1975.

Various Artists—New Orleans Jazz and Heritage Festival 1976

April 11, 1976. Live at the New Orleans Jazz and Heritage Festival, New Orleans Fairgrounds, New Orleans, LA.

Vocal/guitar with Big Will Harvey, bass; unknown, drums.

"Mojo Hand"	Island (UK) LP 9424
"Baby Please Don't Go"	Island (UK) LP 9424
"All Night Long"	Island (UK) LP 9424

New Orleans Jazz and Heritage Festival 1976 was released in 1977.

Note: This various artists LP features Lee Dorsey, Ernie K-Doe, Professor Longhair, Irma Thomas, and others.

The Rising Sun Collection, Vol. 9

June 23, 1977. Live at the Rising Sun Celebrity Jazz Club, Montreal, Canada.

Vocal/electric guitar with Phillip Bowler, bass; Walter Perkins, drums.

"Trouble in Mind"	Just a Memory (Canada) CD 009-2
"Have Mercy"	Just a Memory (Canada) CD 009-2
"Cook My Breakfast"	Just a Memory (Canada) CD 009-2
"It's Hard to Love a Woman"	Just a Memory (Canada) CD 009-2

"Get Up/Katie Mae"	Just a Memory (Canada) CD 009-2
"Goin' to Louisiana"	Just a Memory (Canada) CD 009-2
"Forgot What to Say"	Just a Memory (Canada) CD 009-2
"Lightnin's Boogie"	Just a Memory (Canada) CD 009-2
"Coming Back Home"	Just a Memory (Canada) CD 009-2
"Early in the Morning Blues"	Just a Memory (Canada) CD 009-2
"My Babe Don't Stand No Cheatin'"	Just a Memory (Canada) CD 009-2
"Rock Me Baby"	Just a Memory (Canada) CD 009-2

The Rising Sun Collection Vol. 9 was released in 1996.

Various Artists—Mighty Crazy

Probably June 19, 1978. "The Juneteenth Blues Spectacular," Miller Outdoor Theater, Houston, TX. Producer: Tom Usselmann

Vocal/electric guitar with unknown bass, drums.

"I Love My Biscuits"	Catfish (UK) CD 225
"Key to the Highway"	Catfish (UK) CD 225
"Come In"	Catfish (UK) CD 225
"Messin' Around"	Catfish (UK) CD 225
"Mighty Crazy"	Catfish (UK) CD 225
"Lightnin' Does It"	Catfish (UK) CD 225
"Lawd Have Mercy"	Catfish (UK) CD 225
"Catfish Blues"	Catfish (UK) CD 225

Mighty Crazy was released in 2002.

Note: This is a split CD between Hopkins and Big Mama Thornton. Although there is no date or location listed, a former Catfish Records producer recalled that it had been recorded for one of the annual Juneteenth Blues Spectaculars in Houston by Tom Usselmann, owner of the Lunar #2 label. The most probable year in which it was recorded is 1978, as it was the only time Lightnin' appeared with Big Mama Thornton and Juke Boy Bonner at the festival. Usselmann released a posthumous LP of Bonner recorded at that year's festival.

Various Artists—The Rising Sun Collection

July 22, 1980. Live at the Rising Sun Celebrity Jazz Fest, Salle Wilfrid-Pelletier, Place des Arts, Montreal, Canada.

Vocal/electric guitar with Louisiana Red, guitar; Johnny "Big Moose" Walker, piano; unknown, bass; Styve Homnick, drums.

"Lightnin's Blues"	Just a Memory (Canada) CD 0011
"Blues Ain't Nothin' But a Feelin'"	Just a Memory (Canada) CD 0011

"Trouble in Mind"   Just a Memory (Canada) CD 0011

The Rising Sun Collection was released in 1996.

Note: This various artists CD also includes Louisiana Red, Brownie McGhee, and Sonny Terry.

Forever—Last Recordings

July 1, 1981. Live at the Rock House, Houston, TX.

Vocal/electric guitar with Larry Martin, bass/guitar; Andy McCobb, drums.

"Intro"   Paris (French) LP 3368
"Watch Yourself" (1st version)   Paris (French) LP 3368
"Houston Rock"   Paris (French) LP 3368
"Baby Please Don't Go"   Paris (French) LP 3368
"Pa and Ma Hopkins"   Paris (French) LP 3368
"Mojo Hand"   Paris (French) LP 3368
"Don't Let That Bad Sun Shine Down on Me"   Paris (French) LP 3368
"Watch Yourself" (2nd version)   Paris (French) LP 3368
"Rock Me Baby"   Paris (French) LP 3368
"My Babe"   Paris (French) LP 3368
"Trouble in Mind"   Paris (French) LP 3368

Forever—Last Recordings was released in 1983.

Significant Early Reissues

Lightnin' Hopkins Strums the Blues (Score) 1958
The first Hopkins album, this collects together some of the Aladdin material, with reverb added to the masters.

Last of the Great Blues Singers (Time) 1960
The first reissue of the Bob Shad/Sittin' In With material, with reverb added to the masters.

Lightnin' and the Blues (Herald 1012) 1960
Twelve of the Herald singles.

Lightning Hopkins Sings the Blues (Crown) c.1960
RPM/Modern singles.

Lightning Strikes Again (Dart 8000) 1961
The first reissue of the Gold Star material.

Early Recordings Vol. 1 (Arhoolie 2007) 1965
Early Recordings Vol. 2 (Arhoolie 2010) 1971
The first comprehensive reissues of the Gold Star material.

Endnotes

Introduction

1. Interview by Les Blank, Skip Gerson, John Lomax Jr., Audio outtakes from *The Blues According to Lightnin' Hopkins,* Flower Films, 1969.
2. Interview outtakes from *The Blues According to Lightnin' Hopkins,* 1969.
3. David Evans, *The NPR Curious Listener's Guide to Blues* (Perigree/Penguin, 2005), pp. 124–125. For more information, see David Evans, "Musical Innovation in the Blues of Blind Lemon Jefferson," *Black Music Research Journal,* Vol. 20, No. 1 (Spring 2000), pp. 83–116.
4. Jas Obrecht, ed., *The Postwar Blues Guitarists: Rollin' & Tumblin',* (San Francisco: Miller Freeman Books, 2000), p. 74.
5. www.hawkeyeherman.com/pdf/Lightnin-Hopkins-BluesLife.pdf.
6. Sam Swank, interview by Alan Govenar, September 30, 2008.
7. Cecil Harold, M.D., F.A.C.S. letter to Alan Govenar, February 16, 2008.
8. Bryan Wooley, "Birthing the Blues: East Texas provided plenty of material for Clyde Langford and others who sang of love, sex, drinking, prison, poverty and death," *Dallas Morning News,* November 12, 2000.

I. Early Years

1. Ray Dawkins interview by Alan Govenar, March 14, 2008.
2. "Going Home Blues (Going Back and Talk to Mama)," an unissued Gold Star recording released on *The Gold Star Sessions, Vol. 1,* Arhoolie LP 2007 and Arhoolie CD 330.
3. Frances Jane Leathers, *Through the Years: A Historical Sketch of Leon County and the Town of Oakwood,* Privately printed, 1946.

4. W. D. Wood, *A Partial Roster of the Officers and Men Raised in Leon County, Texas*, Privately printed, 1899.

5. J. Y. Gates and H. B. Fox, *A History of Leon County* (Centerville: Leon County News, 1936).

6. "Texas Mob Lynches Slayer," *New York Times*, April 6, 1910.

7. *Handbook of Texas Online*. www.tsha.utexas.edu/hanbook/online.

8. Gates and Fox.

9. Sam Hopkins, interview by Sam Charters, "My Family," track from *My Life in the Blues*, Prestige LP 7370.

10. Ibid.

11. For more information on Abe Hopkins and the Hopkins family, see www.rootsweb.ancestry. com/–txhousto/biographies/hopkins_Lightnin.htm; Timothy J. O'Brien, "Sam Hopkins: Houston Bluesman, 1912–1960," M.A. Thesis, University of Houston, 2006. O'Brien writes that Sam's mother's maiden name was Frances Washington. Ray Dawkins says her maiden name was Davis. However, the Leon County Web site about Lightnin', the one that presents solid census research on Abe, says her maiden name was Frances Washington, but she is also listed as Frances Sims pre-1903, and speculates that she may have been married before Abe.

12. Thirteenth Census of the United States. Population Series: T635: 1828, p. 24.

13. Sam Hopkins interview by Sam Charters, "My Family," track from *My Life in the Blues*, Prestige LP 7370.

14. Clyde Langford, interview by Alan Govenar, March 21, 2008.

15. Ibid., February 7, 2008.

16. Ibid., February 6, 2008. For more information on the practice through which African Americans were sentenced to forced labor, see Douglas A. Blackmon, *Slavery By Another Name: The Re-Enslavement of Black People in America from the Civil to World War II* (New York: Doubleday, 2008).

17. Sam Hopkins interview by Sam Charters, "My Family," track from *My Life in the Blues*, Prestige LP 7370.

18. Ibid.

19. Lee Gabriel, April 1, 2000.

20. Ibid.

21. Ibid.

22. Ibid.

23. Ibid.

24. Lorine Washington interview by Alan Govenar, March 14, 2008.

25. Interview outtakes from *The Blues According to Lightnin' Hopkins*, 1969.

26. Paul Oliver, *Conversation with the Blues* (Cambridge: Cambridge University Press, 1997), p. 44.

27. Paul Oliver, *Vocal Traditions on Race Records* (Cambridge: Cambridge University Press, 1984), pp. 25–26.

28. Henry Thomas (*Ragtime Texas*), Vocalion 1230, Chicago, June 13, 1928. Reissued on Mack McCormick, "Henry Thomas," album notes and transcriptions, Herwin 209.

29. Clyde Langford interview by Alan Govenar, February 7, 2008.

30. Interview outtakes from *The Blues According to Lightnin' Hopkins*, 1969.

31. Sam Hopkins interview by Sam Charters, "My Family," track from *My Life in the Blues*, Prestige LP 7370.

32. Sam Hopkins, interview by Sam Charters, "I Learn About the Blues," track from *My Life in the Blues*, Prestige LP 7370.

33. Interview outtakes from *The Blues According to Lightnin' Hopkins*, 1969.

34. Mack McCormick, "A Conversation with Lightnin' Hopkins, Part 1," *Jazz Journal* 13, no. 11 (November 1960), pp. 22–24.

35. Over the years, Mary Allen College expanded its curriculum, but the school ultimately ceased operation in the late 1970s.

36. Blind Lemon Jefferson's two religious songs were "I Want to Be Like Jesus in My Heart" and "All I Want is That Pure Religion," Paramount 12386.

37. Laura Lippman, "Blind Lemon sang the Blues: Wortham man recalls his memories of musician," *Waco Tribune-Herald*, June 2, June 2, 1982, 11A.

38. Sam Hopkins, interview by Sam Charters, "I Growed Up with the Blues," track from *My Life in the Blues*, Prestige LP 7370.

39. For more information on Blind Lemon Jefferson, see Alan B. Govenar and Jay F. Brakefield, *Deep Ellum and Central Track: Where the Black and White Worlds Converged* (Denton: University of North Texas Press, 1998), pp. 61–85, and *Black Music Research Journal*, Vol. 20, No. 1, Spring 2000.

40. Interview outtakes from *The Blues According to Lightnin' Hopkins*, 1969.

41. Ibid.

42. Ibid.

43. Mack McCormick, "A Conversation with Lightnin' Hopkins, Part 2," *Jazz Journal* 14, no. 1 (January 1961), p. 18.

44. Lightnin' Hopkins, "Needed Time, RPM 359.

45. Lightnin' Hopkins, "When the Saints Go Marching In," Tradition LP 1040/77 "Jesus Won't You Come by Here," with Barbara Dane, Arhoolie LP 1022, "Jesus Won't You Come by Here," Vault LP 129, "I've Been 'Buked (and Scorned)" AoF LP 241 (Davon LP 2015), "Prayin' Ground Blues," Sittin' In With 599, "Devil is Watching You," Vee-Jay LP 1044, "Sinner's Prayer," Bluesville LP 1061; (45) 822, "I'm Gonna Build Me a Heaven of My Own," Prestige LP 7377. Lightnin' also sang one verse of "Oh Mary, Don't You Weep," a song that was no doubt suggested by Pete Seeger on Folkways LP 2455.

46. Interview outtakes from *The Blues According to Lightnin' Hopkins*, 1969.

47. Ibid.

48. Ray Dawkins, interview by Alan Govenar, March 14, 2008.

49. The Leon County Historical Book Survey Committee, *History of Leon County, Texas* (Dallas, Texas: Curtis Media Corporation, 1986).

50. Mabel Milton, interview by Alan Govenar, March 14, 2008.

51. Interview outtakes from *The Blues According to Lightnin' Hopkins*, 1969.

52. Paul Oliver, *Conversation with the Blues* (Cambridge: Cambridge University Press, 1997), p. 57.

53. Mack McCormick, *Jazz Journal* 13, no.11 (November 1960), p. 23.

54. Sam Hopkins, interview by Sam Charters, "They was Hard Times," track from *My Life in the Blues*, Prestige LP 7370.

55. John Jackson and John Dee Holeman, interview by Alan Govenar, 1992 and Ed Pearl, interview by Alan Govenar, July 17, 2008.

56. Mack McCormick liner notes to the LP *Country Blues*, Tradition LP 1035.

57. For more information on the Leadbelly release legend, see Charles Wolfe and Kip Lornell, *The Life and Legend of Leadbelly* (New York: HarperCollins, 1992), pp. 85–87.

58. According to Anna Mae Box, Sam and Lightnin' had a second child who was stillborn.

59. Anna Mae Box, interview by Alan Govenar, January 29, 2002. Census records spell Elamer as Almer but this is incorrect, as evidenced by the marriage license in the possession of Anna Mae Box. The census also recorded another child, Maxine, born to Sam Hopkins and Diamond Lacy on June 5, 1934. Some researchers have mistakenly maintained that Almer (sic) and Diamond Lacy were the same person, when in fact they were not. There was a Sam Hopkins listed in the Houston city directory from 1943 onward. However, this Sam Hopkins was living with Diaman (sic) and working as a "helper Mosher Steel Co—r. 1308 Bailey [4th Ward]," By 1949, Sam and Diamond had apparently separated as only Sam Hopkins "(no wife) driver Universal Term Warehouse—r. 3417 Live Oak [3rd Ward]" appears in the city directory. In 1951 this Sam Hopkins had the same listing and there was a separate one for "Hopkins, Mrs. Diamond—waiter Simon Ice House—r. 1308 Bailey." In 1953, there were listings for Sam Hopkins (no wife), "Mrs. Diamond Hopkins—Paramount Laundry & Dry Cleaners—r. 1506 Victor," and "Saml Hopkins (Gloria) musician—r. 2703 Gray Ave. [3rd Ward]." So, in what appears to be a bizarre coincidence, a black man named Sam Hopkins in Houston County (next to Leon County) married a woman named Diamond Lacy, had a child named Maxine in 1934, and moved to Houston's Fourth Ward by 1943. By 1949, they were separated and this Sam Hopkins was living in the Third Ward, a couple of miles from the other Sam Hopkins. He had a steady job with the Universal Term Warehouse throughout the 1950s.

60. Sam Hopkins, interview by Sam Charters, "They was Hard Times," track from *My Life in the Blues*, Prestige LP 7370, 1965.

61. Interview outtakes from *The Blues According to Sam Hopkins*, 1969.

62. Anna Mae Box, interview by Alan Govenar, January 29, 2002.

63. Ray Dawkins, interview by Alan Govenar, March 14, 2008 and July 17, 2008.

64. Ibid.

65. "Ida Mae," Gold Star 613, recorded at Quinn Studio, Houston, 1947

66. Interview outtakes from *The Blues According to Lightnin' Hopkins*, 1969.

67. Mack McCormick liner notes to the LP *Smokes Like Lightning*, Bluesville LP 1070.

68. Mack McCormick liner notes to the LP *Country Blues*, Tradition LP 1035.

2. Travels with Texas Alexander

1. For more information, see http://blog.negroleaguebaseball.com/negro_league_blog/2006/08/negro_league_or.html#more.

2. For more information, see Alan B. Govenar and Jay F. Brakefield, *Deep Ellum and Central Track: Where the Black and White Worlds of Dallas Converged* (Denton: University of North Texas Press, 1998).

3. Paul Oliver, liner notes to "Texas Alexander, 11 August 1927 to 15 November 1928," Document MBCD-2001.

4. Oliver, Document MBCD-2001.

5. For more information, see Paul Oliver, *Blues Off the Record* (Kent, England: Baton Press, 1984); Texas Alexander, "Complete Recorded Works in Chronological Order," Volumes 1, 2, and 3, Document MDCD-2001, MDCD-2002, and MDCD-2003.

6. Sam Hopkins, interview by Sam Charters, "I Meet Texas Alexander," track from *My Life in the Blues*, Prestige LP 7370.

7. Sam Hopkins, interview by Sam Charters, *My Life in the Blues*, Prestige LP 7370.

8. Hopkins, *My Life in the Blues*, Prestige LP 7370.

9. Hopkins, Prestige LP 7370.

10. Paul Oliver, liner notes to "Texas Alexander, 9 June 1930 to 1950," Document MBCD-2003.

11. Mack McCormick, "A Conversation with Lightnin' Hopkins," *Jazz Journal* 13, no. 11 (November 1960), p. 23.

12. Hopkins, Prestige LP 7370.

13. Ibid.

14. Ibid.

15. Frank Robinson, interview by Alan Govenar, January 29, 2002.

16. Helen Oakley Dance, *Stormy Monday: The T-Bone Walker Story* (New York: Da Capo, 1987), p. 96.

17. Alan Govenar, *Texas Blues: The Rise of a Contemporary Sound* (College Station: Texas A&M University Press, 2008), p. 416.

18. Mack McCormick, "A Conversation with Lightnin' Hopkins," *Jazz Journal* (January 1961), pp. 16–19.

3. The Move to Houston

1. www.tshaonline.org/handbook/online/articles/HH/jch4.html.

2. Beginning in 1893 the *Texas Freeman* was published by Charles N. Love, with the help of his wife Lilla, in issues of four pages, later expanded to ten or twelve. Love advocated the annulment of the Jim Crow laws, equal pay for black teachers, the hiring of black postal workers, and the Carnegie Library for Negroes in Houston, completed in 1912. A weekly paper known as the *Houston Informer* was published by C. F. Richardson, Sr., from 1919 until January 3, 1931, when the paper was acquired by attorney Carter W. Wesley and two business partners and merged with the *Texas Freeman* to form the *Houston Informer and Texas Freeman*. Wesley expanded the paper into a chain of *Informer* newspapers in Galveston, Beaumont, Dallas, and Austin, Texas, and New Orleans and Shreveport, Louisiana, and Mobile, Alabama, and circulated a statewide edition in small Texas towns, including Groesbeck and Crockett. The *Informer* acquired a printing company, employed fifteen hundred people at its peak, and is credited with starting many black writers in their careers. The paper was subsequently published as a weekly and semiweekly that changed its name alternately to the *Informer* and *Informer and Texas Freeman*. In the 1990s the paper was known as the *Informer*, was published and edited by George McElroy. For more information, see www.tshaonline.org/handbook/online/articles/HH/eeh11.html.

3. Alan Govenar, *Texas Blues: The Rise of a Contemporary Sound* (College Station: Texas A &M University Press, 2008), p. 245.

4. "El Dorado" is spelled as two words in the text instead of the more common "Eldorado" because it was always spelled as two words in the *Informer* during the early years of its existence.

5. www.artshound.com/venue/detail/58 and http://projectrowhouses.org/El Dorado-ballroom.

6. Lightnin' Hopkins, *Walkin' This Road By Myself*, Bluesville 1057.

7. Ted Williams, "Serenading the News," *Houston Informer*, October 10, 1942.

8. Sam Hopkins, interview by Sam Charters, *My Life in the Blues*, Prestige LP 7370.

9. Interview outtakes from *The Blues According to Lightnin' Hopkins*, 1969.

10. Clyde Langford, interview by Alan Govenar, September 30, 2008.

11. Mack McCormick, "A Conversation with Lightnin' Hopkins, Part 3," *Jazz Journal* 15, no. 2 (February 1961), p. 19.

12. "European Blues," Gold Star 665-B.

13. Samuel Charters, *Walking a Blues Road: A Blues Reader 1956–2004* (New York: Marion Boyars, 2004), p. 221.

14. Interview outtakes from *The Blues According to Lightnin' Hopkins*, 1969.

15. Anna Mae Box, interview by Alan Govenar, January 29, 2002.

16. Interview outtakes from *The Blues According to Lightnin' Hopkins*, 1969.

17. Ibid.

18. "Mrs. Lola Ann Cullum's 'Radio Aggregation' Entertains at Glendale," *Houston Informer*, September 14, 1940.

19. Mike Leadbitter, "Mrs. Cullen Rediscovered," *Blues Unlimited* 46 (September 1967), pp. 7–8.

20. Johnny Brown, interview by Alan Govenar, July 22, 2008.

21. Ibid.

22. Ibid.

23. Sid Thompson, "Yer Nite Lifer," *Houston Informer*, September 12, 1946.

24. Ibid., October 5, 1946.

25. Mike Leadbitter, "Mrs. Cullen Rediscovered," *Blues Unlimited* 46 (September 1967), pp. 7–8.

26. Clyde Langford, interview by Alan Govenar, February 7, 2008.

27. Leadbitter, pp. 7–8. There was a comedy team named "Thunder and Lightnin'" (not Smith and Hopkins) that had worked as an opening act for Milton Larkin and his Harlem Swing-Apators performing at the "Big All-Colored Midnite Show" at the Majestic Theatre in Houston in September 1939. Nothing is known about this comedy team and whether or not the naming of Smith and Hopkins had anything to do with them. However, a black convict named "Lightnin'" at Darrington State Farm in Sandy Point, Texas, was recorded by the Lomaxes in 1933 and 1934. It was not Sam Hopkins; but it makes one wonder how common a nickname this was.

28. Frank X. Tolbert, "In Remembrance of Texas Bluesmen," *Dallas Morning News*, March 1, 1982.

29. Doyle Bramhall, interview by Alan Govenar, December 4, 2008.

30. Ray Dawkins, interview by Alan Govenar, March 14, 2008.

31. Brown, July 22, 2008.

32. Ibid.

33. Peppermint Harris to Hank Davis, liner notes to "I Got Loaded," Route 66 KIX 23.

34. Mack McCormick, quoted in Andrew Brown's liner notes to "Harry Choates, Devil in the Bayou," Bear Family BCD 16355 BH, 2002.

35. Advertisement for the "New Gulf Records," *Billboard*, September 8, 1945.

36. E-mail correspondence from Andrew Brown, June 3, 2009.

37. Mack McCormick, liner notes to *Lightnin' Hopkins: Autobiography in Blues*, Tradition LP 1040.

38. The exact chronology of Lightnin's releases in 1947 cannot be definitively established; this section relies on a probable chronology established by researcher Andrew Brown. It has long been assumed that Hopkins recorded "Short Haired Woman" for Aladdin first, then rerecorded it for Gold Star. (Strachwitz, liner notes to *Lightnin' Hopkins, The Gold Star Sessions, Vol. 1* [CD 330], 1990). But surviving paperwork from Bill Quinn's files (Meaux Papers, Center for American History, UT-Austin) supports the claim for Gold Star as the original label. No paperwork relating directly to Hopkins' sessions exists; however, a Quinn Recording Company contract for his cohort L. C. Williams does survive, upon which Quinn handwrote "Session 6/19/47." This almost certainly dates Williams's debut on the label, "Trying, Trying" b/w "You Never Miss the Water" (Gold Star 614) to a session on June 19, 1947. Lightnin' plays piano and guitar on this single, which, if recorded on June 19, puts him in Quinn's studio almost two months before the August 15, 1947 Aladdin session. Lightnin's single "Shining Moon" (Gold Star 613) would then logically predate the Williams single, and "Short Haired Woman" (which prefigured the start of the 600 series) would predate both of them. Lightnin's May 7, 1948, "Option on Contract" with Quinn, referencing an earlier (now lost) contract set to expire on May 21, provides further evidence of a probable May 1947 session date for his first session for Gold Star. (Fellow blues artists Andy Thomas and Luther Stoneham signed contracts with Quinn dated June 19, 1947, and Curtis Amy's contract is dated July 18, 1947. None of this paperwork was available to earlier researchers, hence the long-standing confusion over the dating of Gold Star's blues series.) Internal evidence on the flipside, "Big Mama Jump," also supports the chronology. During the song Lightnin' yells out, "Are you listenin', Mr. Crowe?" a reference to Houston record distributor H. M. Crowe (who was involved with Lightnin's career as late as the Herald sessions). In an interview years later with Chris Strachwitz, Lightnin' reminisced, "Now, he [Crowe] was sittin' there [in the studio]. He wanted me to do that. [Crowe] was the man runnin' with Quinn . . . Quinn's partner. He was a good fella." ("Mr. Crow [sic] and Mr. Quinn," on *The Best of Lightnin' Hopkins* [Arhoolie CD 499], 2001.) Lightnin' repeats the aside to Crowe on the Aladdin session, almost certainly in an effort to mimic his Gold Star version word for word rather than a personal acknowledgement of Crowe sitting in a Los Angeles recording studio. Finally, Quinn would have had no discernible reason to release a record that would have been readily available locally on the Aladdin label, yet Aladdin would have every reason to rerecord a breaking hit that a contracted artist of theirs had recorded, without their knowledge, for another label.

39. By 1950, after the recording ban was history, the local union's rules had relaxed to the point that country musicians who couldn't read music were now admitted. Houston's African Americans would charter their own, segregated local of the AFM. The small labels continued on as before, however, with the tacit understanding between them, the AFM locals, and the union musicians that records made cheaply, and against union rules, were preferable to no records made at all.

40. Gold Star 646.

41. Brown, July 22, 2008.

42. Chris Strachwitz, interview by Alan Govenar, May 20, 2009.

43. SugarHill studios now occupies the Quinn's old residence and the second Gold Star building, not the one on Telephone Road where Lightnin' did most of his recording.

44. Andy Bradley, interview by Alan Govenar, August 11, 2008.

45. Ibid.

46. Strachwitz, May 20, 2009. Strachwitz also recalled that Quinn told him that he had difficulty finding out how records were pressed. He tried to contact the pressing plants of several major labels, but they refused to help him. He checked encyclopedias, but didn't find much information and apparently learned the process on his own.

47. In 1948, Eddie Henry, who owned record shops on Dowling Street in the Third Ward and on Lyons Avenue in the Fifth Ward and was, according to the *Informer*, one of the larger record distributors in the Southwest, started his own label. He put out releases by such local musicians as Conrad Johnson, Little Willie Littlefield, and Clarence Green, but never had any hits and shut down his label a year later. Sol Kahal, a doughnut shop operator and musician from Vermont, moved to Houston in 1948 and started the Freedom label, first acquiring some of Eddie's masters, and then producing a blues, country, and gospel series, which lasted until late 1951 or early 1952. Goree Carter, Sammy Harris, L. C. Williams, Lonnie Lyons, Big Joe Turner, and even Texas Alexander recorded for Freedom. Around 1947, Macy Lela Henry and her husband, Charlie, got their start as record distributors, but then started the Macy's label in 1949, probably the first to be run by a woman in the South. Over the next two years, Macy's had about sixty country releases, and twenty blues, but with two significant regional hits, Lester Williams's "Wintertime Blues" and Clarence Garlow's "Bon Ton Roulet."

48. For more information see Alan Govenar, *The Early Years of Rhythm and Blues* (Atglen, Pennsylvania: Schiffer Publishing, 2004) and Galen Gart and Roy C. Ames, *Duke/Peacock Records: An Illustrated History and Discography* (Milford, New Hampshire: Nickel Publications, 1990).

49. Bill Minutaglio, "Saying Goodbye," *Houston Chronicle*, February 2, 1982.

50. E-mail correspondence from Bill "Rascal" McCaskill, September 1, 2008.

51. Johnny Brown, July 22, 2008.

52. The "Race Records" chart was introduced by *Billboard* in 1945 as a catchall for all African American recordings to replace the chart called "Harlem Hit Parade," which had been in use since 1942. In 1949 the "Race Records" chart was renamed "Rhythm and Blues."

53. *Billboard*, February 25, 1949.

54. Mack McCormick, liner notes to *A Treasury of Field Recordings*, Vol. 2, pp. 37. For more information see Bruce Jackson, *Wake Up Dead Man: Afro-American Worksongs from Texas Prisons* (Cambridge: Harvard University Press, 1972). Also, Joseph "Chinaman" Johnson's recording of "Three Moore Brothers" appears on Bruce Jackson's 1966 LP "Negro Folklore from Texas State Prisons," Elektra EKL-296.

55. *Billboard*, August 13, 1949.

56. Huey P. Meaux Papers, 1940–1994, Center for American History, University of Texas at Austin, box 96-384/23.

57. For more information see Alan B. Govenar and Jay F. Brakefield, *Deep Ellum and Central Track: Where the Black and White Worlds Converged* (Denton: University of North Texas Press, 1998), p. 26.

58. "The government excise tax on discs calls for a 10 percent fee at the first level of sale." *Billboard*, February 7, 1948, p. 19. Also, "House Comm. Exempts Penny Machines From Excise Tax; See Other Levies Remaining," *Billboard*, May 6, 1950, p. 107. E-mail correspondence from Andrew Brown, June 6, 2009.

59. "When the US Government slapped a $26,000 fine and penalty on Gold Star Records, Bill (Quinn) quit record production and went back to operating a custom studio . . ." (Chris Strachwitz, liner notes to *Texas Blues: Bill Quinn's Gold Star Recordings* [Arhoolie CD 352], 1992.) In this account Strachwitz explains that Quinn "was under the impression that the pressing plants were paying this tax but apparently not so." Since Quinn was pressing his own records, this doesn't make sense; it is far more likely that the twenty-six-thousand-dollar penalty was based upon the cumulative total sale and distribution of Gold Star records since the label's formation in 1946, and Quinn had simply never paid the tax. According to Strachwitz, the fine was eventually settled at a mere $250. E-mail correspondence from Andrew Brown, June 6, 2009.

60. *Billboard*, September 22, 1951.

61. Quinn never gave a reason why he discontinued the 600 blues series long before he discontinued the Gold Star label itself. Frustrations with Lightnin' and Lil' Son Jackson may have contributed to its demise. Other Houston labels like Freedom, Peacock, and Macy's were now recording black music in earnest and driving musicians away from Quinn. Perhaps more importantly, his talent scout for blues artists, distributor and record store owner Eddie Henry, moved away from Houston in or around 1950. E-mail correspondence from Andrew Brown, June 6, 2009.

62. Bob Shad, liner notes to *Lightning Hopkins Dirty Blues*, Mainstream MRL 326.

63. Johnny Brown in Roger Wood, *Down in Houston: Bayou City Blues* (Austin: University of Texas Press, 2003) p. 18.

64. Arnold Shaw, *Honkers and Shouters* (New York: Collier Books 1986) p. 142–143.

65. Bob Shad, liner notes to *Lightning Hopkins Dirty Blues*, Mainstream MRL 326.

66. Hal Webman, "Rhythm and Blues Notes," *Billboard*, February 9, 1952.

67. Mack McCormick, liner notes to *A Treasury of Field Recordings*, Vol. 2, p. 51.

68. Johnny Brown, July 22, 2008.

69. Policy originated, according to blues historian Paul Oliver, among racketeers in Chicago around 1885 and was especially popular among poor African Americans because of the possibility of a large return for a small stake. Over time, policy became a traditional subject in blues, and songs about the game were recorded by musicians as diverse as Papa Charlie Jackson, Yodeling Kid Brown, Kokomo Arnold, Tommy Griffin, and Cripple Clarence Lofton.

70. *Billboard*, January 16, 1954.

71. *Billboard*, February 4, 1956.

72. Herald 520.

73. The headquarters for the Royal Amalgamated Association of Chitterling Eaters of America, Incorporated for the Preservation of Good Country Blues was in Town Creek, Alabama, where the Grand National Convention was each August.

74. *Tri-State Defender*, August 21, 1954, p. 15.

75. Louis Cantor, *Wheelin' on Beale* (Pharos Books, New York, 1992), pp. 121–123.

76. Cantor, p. 123, 154–168.

77. Hunter Hancock, "Huntin' With Hunter: The Story of the West Coast R&B Disc Jockey," *Blues & Rhythm*, No. 166, February 2002, pp. 12–14.

78. Charles Shaar Murray, *Boogie Man: The Adventures of John Lee Hooker in the American Twentieth Century*, (New York: St. Martin's Griffin, 2002).

79. Wood, p. 16.

80. Mack McCormick, "A Conversation with Lightnin' Hopkins, Part 3" *Jazz Journal* 14, no. 2 (February 1961), pp. 18–19.

4. Rediscovery

1. Allan Turner, "History as Close as a Turntable," *Houston Chronicle*, Section 7, November 16, 1986.

2. John A. Lomax Jr., "The Life and Times of John Lomax, Jr.," *Houston Folklore Bulletin*, 5:5, John Avery Lomax Family Powers, 1842, 1853–1986, Center for American History, University of Texas at Austin, Box 3D 218. Others involved in founding the Houston Folklore Group include Ed Badeaux, Chester Bower, and Harold Belikoff. "Hootenanny at the Alley, July 20, 1959" program. Lomax Family Papers Box 3D 215.

3. Richard Carlin, *Worlds of Sound: The Story of Smithsonian Folkways* (New York: HarperCollins, 2008), pp. 28–31.

4. Samuel Barclay Charters IV, *Jazz: New Orleans 1885–1957*, Jazz Monographs No. 2, February 1958 (Bellville, NJ: Walter C. Allen). This monograph is not a book per se. It was privately published and was an index to "the Negro musicians of New Orleans."

5. Sam Charters, interview by Alan Govenar, March 13, 2008.

6. Samuel B. Charters, liner notes to *Lightnin' Hopkins*, Folkways LP 3822.

7. Chris Strachwitz, interview by Alan Govenar, July 12, 2009.

8. Ibid.

9. Charters, Folkways LP 3822.

10. Samuel B. Charters, *The Country Blues* (New York: Da Capo, 1975), pp. 254–261.

11. Carlin, pp. 111–133.

12. Sam Charters, March 13, 2008.

13. Ibid.

14. Ibid.

15. Ibid.

16. Ibid.

17. Undated correspondence from Sam Charters to Moses Asch. Moses and Frances Asch Collection, Smithsonian Center for Folklife and Cultural Heritage, Lightning Hopkins file.

18. Sam Charters, interview by Alan Govenar, March 13, 2008.

19. Strachwitz, July 12, 2009.

20. Mack McCormick, in Chris Strachwitz's, "Lightnin' Hopkins Discography, Pt. 2," *Jazz Monthly*, no.10 (December 1959), p. 14.

21. Strachwitz, July 12, 2009.

22. Ibid.

23. In the early twentieth century, *hootenanny* referred to things whose names were forgotten or unknown and was synonymous with *thingamajig* or *whatchamacallit*. It was also an old-country word for *party*. In various interviews, Seeger said that he first heard the word *hootenanny* in the late 1930s in Seattle, Washington, where Hugh DeLacy's New Deal political club used it as a name for their monthly music fundraisers. In New York City, Seeger and the Almanac Singers (1940–41) adopted the word *hootenanny* to describe their folk music events, as did other groups focused on traditional music, including People's Songs (1946–1949), People's Artists (1949–1956), and *Sing Out!* magazine (1957).

24. Kyla Bynum, interview by Alan Govenar, August 30, 2008.

25. Ibid.

26. Mack McCormick, Liner notes to *The Rooster Crowed in England*, 77 (UK) LP 12/1.

27. Ibid.

28. Timothy O'Brien, MA thesis, p. 64.

29. This show was in the original Alley Theatre location that only held about two hundred people, not the existing Alley Theatre, built in 1968, which seats eight hundred.

30. Interview with McCormick, Timothy O'Brien, MA thesis, p. 65.

31. "Hootenanny Scores Hit," *Houston Post*. Arhoolie Records clipping file.

32. Bill Byers, "'Hootenanny' Singers Win Applause at Alley Program," *Houston Chronicle*, July 21, 1959.

33. Mack McCormick, undated letter to John Lomax Jr. papers. Op cited. Box 3D folder 318.

34. John S. Wilson, "Lightnin' Hopkins Rediscovered," *New York Times*, August 23, 1959.

35. Kyla Bynum, interview by Alan Govenar August 30, 2008.

36. Charlotte Phelan, "Song Maker," *Houston Post*, August 23, 1959.

37. Mack McCormick, liner notes to *Lightnin' Hopkins, Country Blues*, Tradition LP 1035. What McCormick apparently didn't understand at the time was that a good portion of Lightnin's repertoire was probably gleaned from phonograph records.

38. Mack McCormick, liner notes to *Lightnin' Hopkins, Country Blues*, Tradition LP 1035.

39. Patrick B. Mullen, *The Man Who Adores the Negro: Race and American Folklore* (Champaign, IL: University of Illinois Press, 2008), p. 122.

40. Benjamin Filene, p. 116.

41. Sam Charters, *The Country Blues*, New York: Da Capo Press, 1975, p. 266.

42. Mack McCormick, "Lightnin' Hopkins: Blues," *The Jazz Review*, Vol. 3, no. 1 (January, 1960). Reprinted in *Jazz Panorama: From the Pages of Jazz Review*, edited by Martin Williams, New York: Crowell-Collier Press, 1962, p. 313.

43. Isabelle Ganz, interview by Alan Govenar, August 28, 2008.

44. Kyla Bynum, interview by Alan Govenar, August 30, 2008.

45. For more information on *Sweatt v. Painter*, see Robert D. Bullard, *Invisible Houston: The Black Experience in Boom and Bust* (College Station, TX: Texas A&M University Press, 1986), pp. 126–129.

46. Benny Joseph, interview by Alan Govenar, 16, 1989. For more information, see *Houston Post*, March 9, 1960, Section 1, p. 1, *Houston Post*, March 17, 1960, and *Houston Informer*, March 19, 1960.

47. Jim Mousner, "Houston Negroes: Despite Problems Their Life is Sunnier," *Houston Post*, April 24, 1960.

48. For more information, see Alwyn Barr, *Black Texans: A History of Negroes in Texas, 1528–1971* (Austin: Jenkins, 1973). Howard Beeth and Cary D. Wintz, eds., *Black Dixie: Afro-Texan History and Culture in Houston* (College Station, TX: Texas A&M University Press, 1992).

49. *The Rooster Crowed in England*, 77 (UK) LP 12/1.

50. Mack McCormick, liner notes to *The Rooster Crowed in England*, 77 (UK) LP 12/1.

51. Ibid.

52. Phelan, August 23, 1959.

53. *Country Blues*, Tradition LP 1035 and *Autobiography in Blues*, Tradition LP 1040. Diane Guggenheim (a.k.a. Diane Hamilton) founded (and funded) the Tradition label, after signing the Clancy Brothers, the company began to earn profits. When the Clancy Brothers were signed by Columbia in 1961, the label ceased to be viable, and the catalogue was sold, possibly to Translantic, and then to Everest Records in the 1980s.

54. Robert Shelton, "An Earthy Shirt-Sleeve Type of Folk Art," *New York Times*, January 30, 1960.

55. Mack McCormick, in Chris Strachwitz, "Lightnin' Hopkins Discography, Pt. 2," *Jazz Monthly*, no. 10 (December 1959), p. 14.

56. *The Unexpurgated Folk Songs of Men*, USFOM, a label created by McCormick and Strachwitz and released in December 1963, and later reissued by them on Raglan LP 51.

57. Mack McCormick, liner notes to *The Unexpurgated Folk Songs of Men*, Raglan LP 51.

58. "The Dirty Dozens," from *The Unexpurgated Folk Songs of Men*, Raglan LP 51.

59. *A Treasury of Field Recordings Vols. 1 and 2*, 77 LA-12-3; Dobell's Jazz Record Shop, 77 Charing Cross Road, London; and D.K. Wilgus, "Record Reviews," *Journal of American Folklore*, Vol. 79, No. 314 (October–December, 1966), 632–633.

60. Lightning Hopkins, letter to Ed and Folkways Records, November 26, 1959, Moses and Frances Asch Collection, Smithsonian Center for Folklife and Cultural Heritage, Lightning Hopkins file.

61. Memo, February 10, 1960, Ibid.

62. Moses Asch, letter to Ed and Folkways Records, November 26, 1959, Ibid.

63. Lightning Hopkins, letter to Moses Asch, December 12, 1959, Ibid.

64. In an interview with Timothy O'Brien, McCormick claimed that he had in fact written to Folkways to produce a record with Hopkins, and the Sam Charters "showed up." O'Brien, p. 70.

65. *John A. Lomax, Jr. Sings American Folk Songs*, Folkways LP 3508, 1956; Mack McCormick, letter to Ed Badeaux, Moses and Frances Asch Collection, Smithsonian Center for Folklife and Cultural Heritage, Lightning Hopkins file.

66. Sam Charters letter to Moses Asch, January 13, 1960, Ibid.

67. Ibid.

68. It was reissued in 1967 under the new title *The Roots of Lightnin' Hopkins* and is still available as a CD today.

5. The Blues Revival Heats Up

1. Anthony Rotante, "Sam 'Lightnin' Hopkins: A Discography," Discophile (UK) #45, December 1955.

2. Chris Strachwitz, "Lightnin Hopkins Discography—Pt. 1," *Jazz Journal* 5, no. 9 (November 1959), pp. 25–26, and Chris Strachwitz, "Lightnin Hopkins Discography—Pt. 2," *Jazz Journal* 5, no. 10 (December 1959), pp. 13–14.

3. Jeff Todd Titon, "Reconstructing the Blues: Reflections on the 1960s Blues Revival," in *Transforming Tradition: Folk Music Revivals Examined* edited by Neil V. Rosenberg Champaign, IL: University of Illinois Press, 1993, p. 225.

4. Mack McCormick, interview by Andrew Brown, January 23, 2006.

5. Ibid.

6. Interview outtakes from *The Blues According to Lightnin' Hopkins*, 1969.

7. John Lomax Jr., letter to B. J. Connors, June 3, 1960. Lomax papers, Center for American History, University of Texas at Austin. Box 3D 318.

8. Mack McCormick, interview by Andrew Brown, January 23, 2006.

9. Chris Strachwitz, interview by Alan Govenar, May 20, 2009.

10. Alfred Frankenstein, "UC Folk Festival is Skillfully Shaped," *San Francisco Chronicle*, July 4, 1960.

11. Lightnin' Hopkins, interview by Barbara Dane on KPFK-FM, Los Angeles, CA, July 8, 1960.

12. Barbara Dane, interview by Alan Govenar, March 27, 2008.

13. Ibid.

14. *Billboard*, Vol. 79, No. 16, February 29, 1964, p. 7.

15. Ed Pearl, interview by Alan Govenar, July 17, 2008.

16. For more information, see Charles Wolfe and Kip Lornell, *The Life and Legend of Leadbelly*. New York: HarperCollins, 1992, p. 2.

17. John Lomax Jr., interview by Barbara Dane, July 8, 2008.

18. Pearl, July 17, 2008.

19. For more information, see Chris Smith, *That's the Stuff: The Recordings of Brownie McGhee, Sonny Terry, Stick McGhee and J. C. Burris* (Shetland: The Housay Press, 1999).

20. Ed Pearl, interview by Andrew Brown, e-mail correspondence, June 9, 2009.

21. Hopkins and McGhee were already quite familiar with each other; they had both recorded for Bobby Shad, and McGhee had actually recorded a song "Letter to Lightnin' Hopkins" in 1952, in which he referenced Hopkins' "Hello Central," and how he was going to Houston to see Lightnin's women.

22. Dane, March 27, 2008.

23. "Down South Summit Meetin'," *Billboard*, October 24, 1960.

24. Chris Strachwitz, interview by Alan Govenar, July 18, 2008.

25. Paul Oliver, interview by Alan Govenar, September 5, 2008.

26. Ibid.

27. Ibid., June 3, 2009.

28. Ibid., September 5, 2008.

29. Ibid.

30. Ibid.

31. Pete Seeger, interview by Alan Govenar, August 29, 2008.

32. Ibid.

33. Letter from John A. Lomax, Jr. to Irwin Silber, August 1, 1960. Courtesy Center for American History, University of Texas at Austin.

34. Institute of Jazz Studies, Rutgers University, Newark, New Jersey, Lightnin' Hopkins file.

35. Robert Shelton, "Lightning Strikes," *New York Times*, October 15, 1960.

36. Ibid.

37. Seeger, August 29, 2008.

38. Nat Hentoff, "A Long Way from Houston," *Reporter* December 8, 1960, pp. 63–64.

39. Ibid.

40. Pete Welding, "Jazz Notes: Lightnin' Hopkins," *Coda* 3, no. 10 (February 1961), pp. 28–29 and Pete Welding, "Lightnin'," *Down Beat* (July 20, 1961), pp. 18–19.

41. Welding, *Coda*, p. 29.

42. "Lightnin' Hopkins—A Description," *Jazz Journal*, October 1959, p.5.

43. Robert Shelton, "Lightning Hopkins at the Village Gate," *New York Times*, October 24, 1960.

44. The first Bluesville release was with Al Smith and was followed by Brownie McGhee and Sonny Terry, Willie Dixon, Lonnie Johnson, and Roosevelt Sykes, among others.

45. *Last Night Blues*, Bluesville LP 1029.

46. Mack McCormick, liner notes to *Last Night Blues*, Bluesville LP 1029.

47. Ibid.

48. Joe Goldberg, liner notes to *Lightnin': The Blues of Lightnin' Hopkins*, Bluesville LP 1019.

49. "Lightnin'," *Billboard*, Vol. 73, No. 16, April 24, 1961, p. 28.

50. CBS Television Network press release, November 4, 1960, Institute of Jazz Studies, Lightnin' Hopkins file.

51. John Sebastian's son, also named John Sebastian, was about sixteen years old at the time and sat behind the camera in the studio to watch this television production. Lightnin', he said, made a very strong impression upon him. The young Sebastian went on to establish himself as musician and songwriter, performing at Woodstock and with the Lovin' Spoonful. In time he became friends with Lightnin', inviting him stay in the apartment he shared with Nick Lore in New York City, carrying his guitar to gigs, and sometimes interceding on his behalf with club owners. For more information, see www.classicbands.com/JohnSebastianInterview.html.

52. The Candid recordings were out of print for about twenty-five years when Alan Bates acquired the masters and renamed his Black Lion Productions company Candid. Bates then worked to make the Candid titles available again on CD.

53. Nat Hentoff, liner notes to *Lightnin' in New York*, Candid LP 8010.

54. "Lightnin' in New York," *Billboard*, April 3, 1961.

55. Harold Leventhal letter to George Hoefer [*Down Beat* magazine], September 23, 1960. Institute of Jazz Studies, Lightnin' Hopkins file.

56. Mitch Greenhill, interview by Alan Govenar, October 10, 2008.

57. Ibid.

58. Ibid.

59. John Broven, "Bobby's Happy House of Hits: The Story of Bobby Robinson and His Famous Labels, Part 2," *Juke Blues* No. 16, (Summer 1989), p. 11.

60. For more information on Bobby Robinson, see John Eligon, "An Old Record Shop May Fall Victim to Harlem's Success," *New York Times*, August 21, 2007; and Timothy Williams, "In Harlem, 2 Record Stores Go the Way of the Vinyl," *New York Times*, January 21, 2008.

61. Broven, p. 11.

62. "Mojo Hand" charted in the first week: 49, second week: 37, third week: 27, fourth week: 26, fifth week: 36. For more information see George Albert, Frank Hoffman and Lee Ann Hoffman, *The Cashbox Black Contemporary Singles Charts, 1960–1984*, (Metuchen, Jersey: Scarecrow Press, 1986).

63. "Mojo Hand," *Billboard*, Vol. 73, No. 3, p. 40.

64. Chris Strachwitz, May 21, 2009.

65. Art D'Lugoff, interview by Alan Govenar, August 2008.

66. Nat Hentoff, liner notes to *Lightnin' in New York*, Candid LP 8010.

67. Benson, January 30, 2002.

68. *Billboard*, March 31, 1958.

69. *Lightnin' Hopkins Strums the Blues*, Score LP 4022.

70. *Lightnin' and The Blues*, Herald LP 1012.

71. Charles Edward Smith, "Lightnin' Strikes Thrice," *Saturday Review*, December 3, 1960, p. 60.

72. McCormick, Mack. "Lightnin' Hopkins: Blues." *Jazz Review* [USA] 3:1 (January 1960): 14–17. Reprinted in *Jazz Panorama*, edited by M. T. Williams, pp. 311–318. New York: Crowell-Collier, 1962.

73. Nat Hentoff, liner Notes to *Lightning Hopkins: The Last of the Great Blues Singers*, Time LP 70004.

74. Hentoff, Time LP 70004.

75. Agreement between Prestige Records, Inc. and Sam Lightning Hopkins, May 19, 1961. Courtesy Prestige Music Archives/Concord Music Group, Inc.

76. Joe Kessler, interview by Alan Govenar, September 3, 2009.

77. Carroll Peery, interview by Alan Govenar, May 22, 2009.

78. Ibid.

79. Ibid.

80. Ibid.

81. Lola Cullum's name is misspelled "Cullen" on the labels, undoubtedly the source for the confusion over her name that Mike Leadbitter reported on in *Blues Unlimited* magazine and his book *Nothing But the Blues*. See Leadbitter, *Nothing But the Blues*, (London: Hanover Books, 1971) p.170. Leadbitter also alleged that Lola Cullum had briefly been a talent scout for Quinn in Gold Star's heyday. Leadbitter, *Nothing But the Blues* (London: Hanover Books, 1971) p.172.

82. Quinn and Cullum didn't record enough songs for an album, so the *Lightnin' Strikes* LP had to be filled out with two songs from a completely different, electric session that Lightnin' had made for the local Ivory label.

83. Chris Strachwitz, interview by Alan Govenar, July 18, 2008.

84. Ibid.

85. Ibid.

86. Contract between Chris A. Strachwitz and L. Sam Hopkins, November 26, 1961.

87. Chris Strachwitz, interview by Alan Govenar, October 2, 2008. Strachwitz did not release any Lightnin' 45s until 1965, when he issued "Mama's Flight," backed by "My Woman" with drummer Harold "Frenchie" Joseph (Arhoolie 45-508) and "Come On Baby" and "Money Taker."

88. Chris Strachwitz, July 18, 2008.

89. "Meet You at the Chicken Shack" and "Ice Storm Blues" appeared on Arhoolie LP 1011, and "Candy Wagon," on Arhoolie 1018, but Lightnin's version of "Down Home Blues" was never released.

90. Sam Charters, "Po' Lightnin': Some Thoughts about Lightnin' Hopkins," booklet in *Lightnin' Hopkins: The Complete Prestige/Bluesville Recordings*, Fantasy, 1991, p. 25.

91. Ibid.

92. "Good Morning Little School Girl" had been a Don and Bob hit, but Lightnin' was no doubt more familiar with Sonny Boy Williamson's 1937 version.
93. Charters, p. 27.
94. Ibid.
95. Lorine Washington, interview by Alan Govenar, March 14, 2008.
96. Mabel Milton, interview by Alan Govenar, March 15, 2008.
97. Lightnin' Hopkins, interview by Barbara Dane on KPFK-FM, Los Angeles, CA, July 8, 1960.
98. McCormick, January 23, 2006.
99. Letter from Sam Charters to Mack McCormick, September 30, 1963; Letter from M. Richard Asher to Mack McCormick, October 16, 1963; Letter from M. Richard Asher to Mack McCormick, October 28, 1963; Letter from Mack McCormick to Mr. Asher, stamped Received November 1, 1963; Letter from Samuel Charters to Mack McCormick, November 7, 1963; Letter to from Sam Charters to Mack McCormick, November 12, 1963; Letter from Samuel Charters to Mack McCormick, November 18, 1963; Letter from Sam Charters to Mack McCormick, November 20, 1963.
100. Letter from Samuel B. Charters to John W. Moore, January 24, 1964. In Houston, Bill Holford's ACA studio merged with Gold Star for a brief period in 1965–66.
101. Bill Belmont, interview by Alan Govenar, May 21, 2009.
102. Undated letter form Mack McCormick to Sam Charters.
103. Letter from Samuel Charters to Mr. McCormick, February 27, 1964.
104. Undated letter from Mack McCormick to Sam Charters, stamped "Received March 16, 1964."
105. Charters, p. 27.

6. The Touring Intensifies

1. Robert Shelton, "Two Guitarists at Village Gate," *New York Times*, March 31, 1962.
2. Shelton, 1962.
3. Lawrence Cohn, Liner Notes to *Lightnin' Hopkins: Hootin' the Blues*, Prestige 7806.
4. Liner notes to *Lightnin' Hopkins, Mojo Hand*, Fire LP 104.
5. Ibid.
6. Chris Strachwitz, interview by Alan Govenar, May 20, 2009.
7. On *Lightnin' Hopkins, Rare Performances 1960–1979*, Vestapol DVD 13022, this footage is incorrectly dated 1960. The clip of Lightnin' Hopkins was excerpted from *On the Road Again: Down Home Blues, Jazz, Gospel and More*, produced and directed by Sherwin Dunner and Richard Nevins with footage shot by Dietrich Wawzyn.
8. Dan Morgenstern, interview by Alan Govenar, February 3, 2009.
9. Morgenstern, February 3, 2009.
10. Morgenstern, February 3, 2009.
11. Joe Nick Patoski, "Remembering Lightnin' Hopkins," *Texas Music*, Issue 24, Fall 2004. Patoski also recalled a performance by Lightnin' on an unspecified date at Jay's Lounge and Cockpit near Cankton, Louisiana, where "the loser of the cockfights staged around back wound up in the gumbo. Hopkins was opening for Clifton Chenier on a weeknight, playing in front of a packed house that remained orderly despite a throng gathered outside that was even larger than the one inside, packed onto the wooden dance floor. All it took was Hopkins hitting a few licks on his guitar, while the other players—mostly Chenier's Red Hot Louisiana Band—started to percolate

behind him. Before he could finish the first verse, a rock crashed through a window near the stage, followed by a mass of people pouring through the opening, oblivious to the broken shards of glass. Hopkins glanced over to the window, flashed a flicker of a smile, and kept on playing, never missing a beat. It's anything he hadn't seen before. He knew as well as anyone what his music could do."

12. Gordon Dougherty, "Lightnin' 1963 Flashbacks: A Folk Junkie's Out-Of-Place Encounter with a Blues Legend," *Austin American-Statesman*, August 22, 1996.

13. Ibid.

14. For more information, see *The American Folk Blues Festival, 1962–1966*, Vols. 1 and 2, Reelin' In The Years Productions, 2003.

15. Chris Strachwitz, interview by Alan Govenar, October 10, 2008.

16. Strachwitz, October 10, 2008.

17. Ibid., September 4, 2008.

18. George W. Lyons, "No Lyon," *Blues Unlimited* 123 (January/February 1977), p. 12.

19. Ibid.

20. Barbara Dane, interview by Alan Govenar, March 27, 2008.

21. Ibid.

22. Ibid.

23. Jesse Cahn, interview by Alan Govenar, May 30, 2008.

24. Ibid.

25. Ibid.

26. Dane, March 27, 2008.

27. Chris Strachwitz, interview by Alan Govenar, October 10, 2008.

28. Ibid.

29. Rob Bowman, liner notes to *The American Folk Blues Festival 1962–1966*, Reelin' In The Years Production, 2003.

30. *The Hopkins Brothers: Lightning, Joel and John Henry*, Arhoolie CD 340.

31. Strachwitz, October 10, 2008.

32. Francis Hofstein, interview by Alan Govenar, April 8, 2008.

33. Alan Balfour, "Death of a Legend," *New Musical Express [UK]*, February 6, 1982.

34. Derrick Stewart-Baxter, "Blues," *Jazz Journal*, December 1964, pp. 28–29.

35. Paul Oliver, "Festival Blues, The American Blues Festival, 1964," *Jazz Monthly*, Christmas 1964, pp. 4–6.

36. Val Wilmer, "Blues '64," *Jazz Beat* (November 1964), pp. 36–37.

37. Kay Pope, "The European Odyssey of Lightnin' Sam Hopkins," *Houston Chronicle Sunday Magazine*, November 22, 1964, p. 14.

38. "Down Home Blues," *Billboard*, Vol. 76, No. 40 (October 3, 1964), p. 24.

39. Dane, March 27, 2008.

40. Mitch Greenhill, interview by Alan Govenar, October 10, 2008.

41. Chris Strachwitz, September 4, 2008.

42. Ibid.

43. Ibid. October 10, 2008.

44. For a discography of blues singers who appeared at the Newport Folk Festival, see www.wirz.de/music/newpofrm.htm.

45. Strachwitz, October 10, 2008.

46. The *Live at Newport* recordings were released on Vanguard CD 79715 in 2002.

47. Vanguard CD 79715.

48. Strachwitz, October 10, 2008.

49. Lay, October 9, 2008.

50. Verve-Folkways LP 9022 was also issued as Verve LP 5014, Saga LP 8001, and Boulevard LP 4001.

51. Stan Lewis, interview by Alan Govenar, August 7, 2008.

52. Colin Escott, liner notes to Lightnin' Hopkins, *Fishing Clothes, The Jewel Recordings, 1965–69*, Demon Music Group, 2001.

53. Lewis, August 7, 2008.

54. Ibid.

55. "Wig Wearing Woman," Jewel 766 and Jewel LP 5000, reissued on Lightnin' Hopkins, *Fishing Clothes, The Jewel Recordings, 1965–69*, Demon Music Group, 2001.

56. Lightnin' recorded this song twice for Jewel; the first version is the one with acoustic-electric guitar that was released as a single, for which Robin Hood Brians was likely the engineer. The second version, which has a very electric guitar lead, was an unissued take from *The Great Electric Show and Dance* album. The voice heard at the beginning of this track is Bill Holford at ACA in Houston.

57. "(Letter to My) Back Door Friend," Jewel 788 and Jewel LP 5015, reissued on Lightnin' Hopkins, *Fishing Clothes, The Jewel Recordings, 1965–69*, Demon Music Group, 2001.

58. Lightnin' Hopkins, "I'm Going to Build Me a Heaven of My Own," on Lightnin' Hopkins, *Soul Blues*, Prestige LP 7377.

59. John Holt, letter to Folkways Records, June 6, 1965, Moses and Frances Asch Collection, Smithsonian Center for Folklife and Cultural Heritage, Lightning Hopkins file.

60. Paul Oliver, "The World of Lightnin' Hopkins," The Texas Blues Society, December 1965, pp. 7–9.

61. Rubenstein's M & I Department Store was located in the 2100 block of Dowling, and his third store was called Well Worth's in the 2700 block of Dowling. At the time, many of the stores on Dowling were Jewish owned and serviced the African American community, which Mansel pointed out by saying, "They had for decades. Blacks couldn't shop downtown, and the Jewish-owned businesses helped people out—the shoe stores, furniture stores, and even the Dowling Theatre." The loan offices and pawnshops functioned as banks for some blacks, who had great difficulty borrowing money.

62. Strachwitz, October 19, 2008.

7. Mojo Hand: An Orphic Tale

1. J. J. Phillips, e-mail correspondence, October 13, 2008.

2. Ibid., May 28, 2009.

3. Ibid., June 2, 2009.

4. Here, the events in Phillips's life are contrary to the immediate infatuation that the fictional Eunice experiences when she hears the recording by Blacksnake Brown.

5. Phillips, June 2, 2009.

6. Ibid. October 23, 2008.

7. Ibid., May 27, 2009.

8. Ibid., May 28, 2009.

9. J. J. Phillips, interview by Alan Govenar, October 14, 2008.

10. Ibid.

11. Ibid., October 13, 2008.

12. *Live at the Bird Lounge* Guest Star LP 1459. In December 1964, Lightnin' recorded another song, titled "Chicken Minnie," that was apparently about Phillips, though Phillips didn't hear it until 2009.

13. J. J. Phillips, interview by Alan Govenar, June 3, 2009.

14. Ibid.

15. Ibid., October 23, 2008.

16. Ibid. May 23, 2009.

17. Ibid., May 23, 2009.

18. Ibid., October 14, 2008. In *Mojo Hand*, this cafe became the basis for the Raleigh Palace Bar.

19. Ibid.

20. Ibid.

21. Ibid. In *Mojo Hand*, Phillips based the character of X. L. Millson on Billy Bizor.

22. Ibid.

23. J. J. Phillips, e-mail correspondence, May 27, 2009.

24. Ibid., May 23, 2009.

25. Ibid., October 13, 2008.

26. Ibid.

27. Ibid.

28. Mrs. Frook and Mrs. Johnson in *Mojo Hand* are based on two of the older women that Phillips met in Hattie's shop. Hattie's store became the artificial flower shop in the novel.

29. Phillips, May 20, 2009.

30. J. J. Phillips, letter to Albert Murray, 2002.

31. J. J. Phillips, interview by Alan Govenar, May 31, 2009.

32. Ibid., May 28, 2009.

33. Ibid., October 14, 2008.

34. Ibid

35. Ibid., October 23, 2008.

36. Ibid.

37. Ibid., June 3, 2009.

38. Ibid., October 14, 2008.

39. Ibid.

40. Ibid.

41. Ibid., October 23, 2008.

42. Ibid.

43. Ibid., May 28, 2009.

44. Harriet Doar, "Blue Notes and Voodoo," *Charlotte Observer*, November 6, 1966.

45. Jane Phillips, *Mojo Hand*, New York: Simon & Schuster Pocket Books, 1969.

46. Albert Murray, *The Omni-Americans*, New York: Outerbridge & Dienstfrey, 1970, 125–126.

47. Phillips, October 23, 2008.

8. An Expanding Audience

1. Ken Sharp, "Backstage Pass: It Don't Come Easy for Ringo Starr," *Goldmine*, May 22, 2008.
2. Les Blank, interview by Alan Govenar, May 30, 2008.
3. Les Blank, *Dizzy Gillespie*, Flower Films, 1965.
4. Les Blank, *God Respects Us When We Work, But Loves Us When We Dance*, Flower Films, 1968.
5. Les Blank, interview by Alan Govenar, May 30, 2008.
6. Ibid.
7. Ibid.
8. Ibid.
9. Ibid.
10. Ibid.
11. Ibid.
12. Ibid.
13. Ibid.
14. Mike Leadbitter, *Nothing But the Blues*, London: Hanover Books, 1971, p. 168.
15. Roger Greenspun, "The Screen: 2 Studies of Popular Music Groups Open," *New York Times*, December 21, 1970.
16. Mike Leadbitter, liner notes to *Lightnin' Hopkins: King of Dowling Street*, Liberty/UA Records [UK], LP 83254.
17. Chris Strachwitz, interview by Alan Govenar, May 20, 2009.
18. Harold V. Ratliff, "Texas System to Lose Stand By, Colorful, Towering Bud Russell, Prison Transfer Agent, Retires," *Dallas Morning News*, May 25, 1944.
19. Arhoolie LP 1034.
20. Carroll Peery, interview by Alan Govenar, May 22, 2009.
21. Bill Minutaglio, "Saying Goodbye," *Houston Chronicle*, February 2, 1982.
22. "Legendary Blues Artist Dies of Pneumonia at 60," *Houston Chronicle*, February 1, 1982.
23. Between 1965 and 1970, International Artists released twelve albums and thirty-nine singles and was primarily known for its roster of Texas psychedelic rock bands, including the 13th Floor Elevators, Red Crayola, and Bubble Puppy.
24. Mansel Rubinstein, interview by Alan Govenar, May 7, 2009.
25. John David Bartlett, interview by Alan Govenar, October 26, 2008.
26. Duke Davis, interview by Paul Drummond, e-mail, May 6, 2009. For more information, see Paul Drummond. *Eye Mind: The Saga of Roky Erickson and The 13th Floor Elevators*. Port Townsend, WA: Process, 2007.
27. Other Houston shows from this period (listed in the *Houston Post*'s "Nowsounds Calendar") are: January 26 and 27, 1968 at Love Street Light Circus, with the Starvation Army Band; and March 23 and 24, 1968 at Love Street Light Circus, with the Shaydes.
28. Danny Thomas, interview by Paul Drummond, e-mail, May 6, 2009.
29. Bartlett, October 26, 2008.
30. Don Logan, interview by Alan Govenar, August 7, 2008.
31. Ibid.
32. Ibid.

33. Ibid.

34. John Lomax, Jr. and Alan Lomax also appeared at the event ("A Tribute to the Lomax Family" was part of the program). Muddy Waters and Skip James were featured as well. For a full text of the program and a full listing of the roster of the 1968 Festival of American Folklife, see www. archive.org/stream/1968festivalofam00fest/1968festivalofam00fest_djvu.txt.

35. Ed Pearl, interview by Alan Govenar, July 16, 2008.

36. Bromberg, October 14, 2008.

37. Ibid.

38. Tony Joe White liner notes to *California Mudslide (and Earthquake)*, Vault LP 129.

39. Robert Earl Hardy, *A Deeper Blue: The Life and Music of Townes Van Zandt*, Denton, TX: University of North Texas Press, 2008, p. 62.

40. Adam Machado, liner notes to *Hear Me Howling*, Arhoolie CD 518 and Arhoolie CD 519.

41. Strachwitz, May 20, 2009.

42. Alan Govenar, *Texas Blues: The Rise of a Contemporary Sound*, College Station, TX: Texas A&M University Press, 2008.

43. Logan, August 7, 2008.

44. Ibid.

45. Ibid.

46. Dan Morgenstern, *Living with Jazz*, edited by Sheldon Meyer, New York: Pantheon Books, 2004, p. 511.

47. Dick Waterman, *Between Night and Day*, San Rafael, CA: Insight Editions, 2004.

48. Ibid.

49. David Benson, interview by Alan Govenar, November 14, 2008. See also, Sam Charters, "Po' Lightnin': Some Thoughts about Lightnin' Hopkins," booklet in *Lightnin' Hopkins: The Complete Prestige/Bluesville Recordings*, Fantasy, 1991, p. 29.

50. Ed Pearl, July 16, 2008.

51. Ibid.

52. Ibid.

53. Bernie Pearl, interview by Alan Govenar, July 17, 2008.

54. Ibid.

55. Ibid.

56. Ibid., July 16, 2008.

57. Ibid.

58. Ibid., July 17, 2008.

59. Ibid.

60. The other contenders were "Blues Piano Orgy" with Little Brother Montgomery, Roosevelt Sykes, and Sunnyland Slim; "Walking the Blues" by Otis Spann; and "Live at Soledad Prison" by John Lee Hooker, with whom Lightnin' recorded on May 16 and 17, 1972, for an album that was not released until 1993 on a CD called *It's a Sin to Be Rich* (Gitanes 517 514-2). The CD was a mishmash of recordings that included not only Lightnin' and John Lee Hooker, but Jesse Ed Davis on guitar; Luther Tucker, guitar; Mel Brown, guitar/piano/organ; Charlie Grimes, guitar; David Cohen, guitar; Clifford Coulter, piano/melodica; Michael White, violin; Joe Frank Corolla, bass; and Lonnie Castille, drums.

9. The Last Decade

1. Mack McCormick, liner notes to *Robert Shaw, Texas Barrelhouse Piano*, Almanac LP 10, 1966.
2. Leadbitter, liner notes to *Lightnin' Hopkins: King of Dowling Street*, Liberty/UA Records [UK] 83254.
3. David Benson, interview by Alan Govenar, November 7, 2008.
4. Ibid.
5. Ibid., January 30, 2002.
6. Joe Kessler, interview by Alan Govenar, September 3, 2009.
7. Benson, January 30, 2002.
8. Ibid.
9. Ibid., November 7, 2008.
10. Ibid., January 30, 2002.
11. Kessler, September 3, 2009.
12. Sam Charters, March 13, 2008.
13. "Lightnin' Hopkins," Vol. 12 of *Legacy of the Blues*, GNP Crescendo. 1992.
14. Benson, January 30, 2002.
15. Robert Palmer, "Jazz: Master," *New York Times*, May 15, 1977.
16. Over the years, Lanny Steele and his SumArts organization hosted hundreds of blues and jazz artists, from John Lee Hooker, Muddy Waters, Koko Taylor, Big Mama Thornton, and Albert King to Milt Larkin, Eddie "Cleanhead" Vinson, Alex Moore, Clarence "Gatemouth" Brown, Albert Collins, Johnny Copeland, and Texas Johnny Brown. For more information, see Jim Sherman, "Goodbye to Lanny Steele," *Houston Press*, November 3, 1994 and "Houston Celebrates Juneteenth with Parade of Black Progress," in *Chronicle-Telegram* [Elyria, OH], June 19, 1977, p. A-10.
17. Benson, January 30, 2002.
18. Ibid.
19. *The Rising Sun Collection, Vol. 9*, featuring Lightnin' Hopkins, vocal/electric guitar, Phillip Bowler, bass; and Walter Perkins, drums, Just a Memory CD 009-2, released in 1996.
20. Benson, November 7, 2008.
21. Ibid.
22. Ibid.
23. Ibid.
24. Ibid.
25. Ibid.
26. Norbert Hess, "Europe," *Living Blues* 36 (January/February 1978); and Norbert Hess, interview by Alan Govenar, May 14, 2009.
27. Benson, January 30, 2002 and November 7, 2008.
28. Ibid., November 7, 2008.
29. Ibid., January 30, 2002.
30. Ibid., November 7, 2008.
31. Timothy J. O'Brien. "Lightnin' Hopkins: Houston Bluesman, 1912–1960," MA thesis, University of Houston, 2006, p. 88.

32. Michael Hall, "Let There be Lightnin'," *Texas Monthly*, June 2007.

33. Benson, November 7, 2008.

34. Ibid., January 30, 2002.

35. Mark Pollock interview by Alan Govenar, October 14, 2008.

36. Anson Funderburgh interview by Alan Govenar, October 15, 2008.

37. Ibid.

38. Ibid.

39. Ibid.

40. Doyle Bramhall, interview by Alan Govenar, October 14, 2008.

41. Ibid.

42. Funderburgh, October 15, 2008.

43. Bramhall, October 14, 2008.

44. Funderburgh, October 15, 2008.

45. Bramhall, October 14, 2008.

46. Tim Schuller, "Lightnin' Hopkins at the Granada Theater, Dallas, Texas" *Living Blues* (November/ December 1977).

47. Tim Schuller, "Lightnin' Hopkins at the Granada Theater, Dallas, Texas" *Living Blues* (November/ December 1977).

48. Benson, November 7, 2008.

49. Ibid.

50. Ibid., January 30, 2002.

51. Ibid., November 7, 2008.

52. Ibid.

53. Ibid.

54. Ibid.

55. Michael Hall, "Let There Be Lightnin'," *Texas Monthly* (June 2007).

56. Anton J. Mikofsky, interview by Alan Govenar, August 28, 2008.

57. Mikofsky, August 28, 2008.

58. Ibid.

59. Ibid.

60. Benson, November 7, 2008.

61. Ibid.

62. Kessler, September 3, 2009. For more information, see *Lightnin' Hopkins: Rare Performances, 1969–1979*, Vestapol Videos 13022.

63. Steve Ditzell, interview by Alan Govenar, April 17, 2009.

64. Ibid.

65. Robert Palmer, "Lightnin' Hopkins at 68: Still Singing Those Blues," *New York Times*, October 31, 1980.

66. Steve Cushing, interview by Alan Govenar, December 14, 2008.

67. Ibid.

68. Ibid.

69. Lightnin's last recordings were not released until 1983 on *Forever—Last Recordings*, Paris (French) LP 3368.

70. "Legendary Blues Artist Dies of Pneumonia at 69," United Press International, *Houston Chronicle*, February 1, 1982.

71. Anna Mae Box, January 29, 2002.

72. Ibid.

73. Ibid.

74. Ibid.

75. Ibid.

76. Ibid.

77. Benson, November 7, 2008.

78. Ibid.

79. Marty Racine, "1,000 Mourners Pay Tribute to Musician Lightnin Hopkins," *Houston Chronicle*, February 4, 1982.

80. Ibid.

81. Bob Claypool, "Respects Offered at 'Last Call' for Hopkins," *Houston Post*, February 2, 1982.

82. Benson, November 7, 2008.

83. *Houston Chronicle*, February 1, 1982.

84. All efforts to find Lightnin's children Charles and Celestine have been unsuccessful.

85. Benson, November 7, 2008.

86. Sam L. Hopkins, Last Will and Testament, January 27, 1982, filed with the Harris County Clerk in Houston on February 19, 1982.

87. Box, January 29, 2002.

88. Interview outtakes to *The Blues According to Lightnin' Hopkins*, 1969.

89. Huey Lewis covered "Good Morning Little School" for his LP *Four Chords and Seven Years Ago*, released on November 1, 1994. He insisted that he was covering Lightnin's version of the song, even though Sonny Boy Williamson had recorded it first. Van Morrison covered Lightnin's "Better Watch Yourself" in his song "Stop Drinking," released on October 21, 2003.

90. Benson, November 7, 2008.

91. Letter from Chris Strachwitz to Antoinette Charles, February 3, 1982.

92. Chris Strachwitz, interview by Alan Govenar, May 22, 2009.

93. Letter from Chris Strachwitz to Antoinette Charles, February 3, 1982.

94. John Corry, "Sam Hopkins Returns," *New York Times*, September 16, 1980.

95. David Evans, e-mail correspondence, June 16, 2009.

96. Benson, November 7, 2008.

97. Interview outtakes from *The Blues According to Lightnin' Hopkins*, 1969.

98. Wolfgang Saxon, "Sam (Lightnin') Hopkins, 69, Blues Singer and Guitarist," *New York Times*, February 1, 1982.

99. Bill Minutaglio, "Saying Goodbye," *Houston Chronicle*, February 2, 1982.

100. Interview outtakes to *The Blues According to Lightnin' Hopkins*, 1969.

101. *Houston Chronicle*, February 1, 1982.

102. Les Blank, "Lightnin' Hopkins, 1912–1982," *Living Blues* 53 (Summer–Autumn 1982), p. 15.

103. Carroll Peery, interview by Alan Govenar, May 22, 2009.

104. Interview outtakes to *The Blues According to Lightnin' Hopkins*, 1969.

Selected Bibliography

Adins, Georges. "Souvenirs de Houston." *Rhythm & Blues Panorama* no. 32 (1964): 16–22.

———. "With Lightnin' in Oakland." *Blues Unlimited* no. 74 (July 1970): 16–17.

Albert, George and Frank Hoffman. *The Cash Box Black Contemporary Singles Charts, 1960–1984*. Metuchen, NJ: Scarecrow Press, 1986.

Albertson, Chris. *Lightnin' Hopkins: Down Home Blues*. USA: Prestige PR 1086, c.1964.

———. *Lightnin' Hopkins: Soul Blues*. USA: Prestige PR 7377, 1965; USA: Original Blues Classics OBCCD-540-2, 1991.

———. *Lightnin' Hopkins in New York*. USA: Barnaby Z 30247, 1970.

Atherton, Mike. *Lightnin' Hopkins: Remember Me: The Complete Herald Singles*. UK: Ember EMBCD 006, 2000.

Balfour, Alan. *Big Boy Crudup/Lightnin' Hopkins: Previously Unissued 1960–62 Recordings*. UK: Krazy Kat 7410, 1982.

———. *Lightnin' Hopkins: Blues is My Business*. UK: Edsel EDCD 353, 1992. Notes reprinted with *Lightnin' Hopkins Live 1971*. UK: Demon DIAB 8011, 1999.

———. "Lightning Hopkins: Blues Walkin' Like a Man." *Subway (Leading to and from the Underground)* no. 3 (6 November 1967): 5–6; no. 4 (13 November 1967): 5–6; no. 5 (20 November 1967): 5–6; no. 6 (27 November 1967): 5–6.

———. *Lightnin' Hopkins: Free Form Patterns*. UK: Charly CD 294, 1991.

———. *Lightnin' Hopkins: Lightnin' Strikes Back*. UK: Charly CRB 1031, 1981.

———. *Lightnin' Hopkins: Move on Out*. UK: Charly CRB 1147, 1986.

———. *Lightnin' Hopkins: You're Gonna Miss Me*. UK: Edsel EDCD357, 1992. Notes reprinted with *Lightnin' Hopkins Live 1971*. UK: Demon DIAB 8011, 1999.

————. *Sittin' in with Lightnin' Hopkins*. USA: Mainstream MDCD905, 1991; USA: Legacy/Mainstream JK53626, 1993.

Barr, Alwyn. *Black Texans: A History of African Americans in Texas 1528–1995*. Norman, OK: University of Oklahoma Press, 1996.

Bastin, Bruce. "Houston '65." *Blues Unlimited* no. 34 (July 1966): 4–5.

Batey, Rick. "Soul Food and Tasty Blues Bites: Lightnin' Hopkins." *The Guitar Magazine* 7, no. 4 (February 1997): 22.

Beeth, Howard and Cary D. Wintz. *Black Dixie: Afro-Texan History and Culture in Houston*. College Station, TX: Texas A&M University Press, 1992.

Bentley, Chris. "Lightnin' Hopkins: Last of the Great Blues Singers: 'A Folk Poet in the True Sense of the Word.'" *Juke Blues* no. 40 (1998): 36–40.

————. "Vanity Dresser Boogie." *Roll Street Journal* no. 24 (1989): 18–19.

Berg, Arne. *Rhythm & Blues Panorama Special: Lightnin' Hopkins*. Stockholm: Panorama, c.1964.

Blackmon, Douglas A. *Slavery By Another Name: The Re-Enslavement of Black People in America from the Civil to World War II*. New York: Doubleday, 2008.

Birkerts, Sven. "Lightnin' Hopkins: The Bluesman as (Comic) Antihero." *Oxford American* no. 50 (Summer 2005): 10–12.

Boicel, Rouè-Doudou. *Lightnin' Hopkins: The Rising Sun Collection*. Canada: Just a Memory RSCD 0009, 1995.

Bowden, Dan, ed. *Mel Bay Presents Lightnin' Hopkins: Blues Guitar Legend*. Pacific: Mel Bay, 1995.

Bromberg, Bruce. *Lightnin' Hopkins: Los Angeles Blues*. USA: Rhino RNLP 103, 1982.

Bruynoghe, Yannick. "Hopkins, Sam Lightning" in *Jazz Era: The Forties* edited by Stanley Dance. New York: Da Capo, 1961.

Broven, John. *Record Makers and Breakers*. Champaign, IL: University of Illinois Press, 2009.

Bullard, Robert D. *Invisible Houston: The Black Experience*. College Station, TX: Texas A&M University Press, 1987.

Byers, Bill. "'Hootenanny' Singers Win Applause at Alley Program," *Houston Chronicle*, July 21, 1959.

Cantor, Louis. *Wheelin' on Beale*. New York: Pharos Books, 1992.

Cantwell, Robert. *When We Were Good: The Folk Revival*. Cambridge, MA: Harvard University Press, 1996.

Carlin, Richard. *Worlds of Sound: The Story of Smithsonian Folkways*. New York: Smithsonian Books/HarperCollins, 2008.

Charters, Samuel B. *The Legacy of the Blues*. New York: Marion Boyars, 1975.————. *The Country Blues*. New York: Da Capo, 2003.

————. "Lightnin'." *Walking a Blues Road: A Blues Reader 1956–2004*, New York: Marion Boyars, 2004.

————. *The Legacy of the Blues. Vol. 12: Lightnin' Hopkins: Texas's Blues Legend Considers His World, His Life and Times*. UK: Sonet SNTF 672, 1974; USA: GNP Crescendo GNPS 100022, 1976.

————. *Lightnin' Hopkins*. USA: Folkways FS 3822, 1959, Smithsonian/Folkways SF 40019, 1990.

————. *Lightnin' Hopkins: The Complete Prestige/Bluesville Recordings*. Prestige 7PCD-4406-2, 1991.

————. *The Roots of 'Lightnin'' Hopkins*. Verve Folkways FVS 9000, 1965; Folkways FTS 31011, 1968.

————. *Lightnin' Hopkins: The Swarthmore Concert*. USA: Original Blues Classics OBCCD-563-2, 1993.

Cohen, Ronald D., ed. *Wasn't That a Time! Firsthand Accounts of the Folk Music Revival*. Metuchen, NJ: The Scarecrow Press, 1995.

Cohn, Lawrence. *Lightnin' Hopkins: Hootin' the Blues*. Prestige/Folklore 14021, 1964. Prestige PRT-7806, 1972.

Cortese, Bob. "A Telephone Interview with Lightnin' Hopkins." *Whiskey, Women and ...* no. 8 (March 1982): 18–20.

Cummings, Tony. "Lightnin' Hopkins: His British Releases." *Soul: The Magazine for the R&B Collector* no. 5 (1966).

Dahl, Bill. *Blues Kingpins: Lightnin' Hopkins*. Virgin 72435-82740- 2-8, 2003.

———. *Hello Central: The Best of Lightnin' Hopkins*. Columbia/Legacy CK 86988, 2004.

———. *Lightnin' Hopkins & the Blues Summit*. Fuel 2000 302 061 101-2, 2001.

———. *Lightnin' Hopkins: Freeform Patterns*. Fuel 2000 302 061 315-2, 2003.

Dance, Helen Oakley. *Stormy Monday: The T-Bone Walker Story*. New York: Da Capo, 1987.

Dane, Barbara. *Barbara Dane and Lightning Hopkins: Sometimes I Believe She Loves Me*. Arhoolie CD 451, 1996.

Darwen, Norman and Tamara Shad. "Bobby Shad: The Record Man, The Sittin' In With Story," *Blues & Rhythm* no. 100 (June/July 1995), 16–30.

Davis, John T. *Austin City Limits: 25 Years of American Music*. New York: Billboard Books, 2000.

Demêtre, Jacques. *Lightnin' Hopkins: Blues in My Bottle*. France. Vogue/Prestige BL.12504, 1972.

DeVinck, Richard, ed. *Lightnin' Hopkins: Vital Blues Guitar: Authentic Tablature Transcriptions Off the Original Recordings*. Ojai, CA: Creative Concepts, 1992.

Drummond, Paul. *Eye Mind: The Saga of Roky Erickson and The 13th Floor Elevators, The Pioneers of Psychadelic Sound*. Port Townsend, WA: Process, 2007.

Drust, Greg. *Mojo Hand: The Lightnin' Hopkins Anthology*. USA: Rhino R2-71226, 1993.

Edwards. David Honeyboy. *The World Don't Owe Me Nothin'*. Chicago: Chicago Review Press, 1997.

Escott, Colin and Tony Rounce. *Lightnin' Hopkins: Fishing Clothes: The Jewel Recordings, 1965–1969*. UK: Westside WESD228, 2001.

Evans, David. "Lightnin' Hopkins." *The NPR Curious Listener's Guide to Blues*. New York: Perigee, 2005.

Filene, Benjamin. *Romancing the Folk: Public Memory and American Roots Music*. Chapel Hill, NC: University of North Carolina Press, 2000.

Ford, Robert. *A Blues Bibliography*. Florence, KY: Routledge, 2007.

Gates, J. Y. and H. B. Fox. *A History of Leon County*. Centerville: Leon County News, 1936.

Goldberg, Joe. *Lightning: The Blues of Lightnin' Hopkins*. Bluesville BV-1019, 1960.

Goldsmith, Peter J. *Making People's Music: Moe Asch and Folkways Records*. Washington: Smithsonian Press, 1998.

Govenar, Alan. *Meeting the Blues: The Rise of the Texas Sound*. New York: Da Capo, 1995.

———. *Living Texas Blues*. Dallas: Dallas Museum of Art, 1985.

———. *Texas Blues: The Rise of a Contemporary Sound*. College Station, TX: Texas A&M University Press, 2008.

———. *The Early Years of Rhythm and Blues: The Photography of Benny Joseph*. Atglen, PA: Schiffer Publishing, 2004.

Govenar, Alan B. and Jay F. Brakefield. *Deep Ellum and Central Track: Where the Black and White Worlds of Dallas Converged*. Denton, TX: University of North Texas Press, 1998.

Hall, Michael. "Mack McCormick Still Has the Blues," *Texas Monthly* (April 2002).

———. "Let There be Lightnin'," *Texas Monthly* (June 2007).

Hancock, Hunter. "Huntin' With Hunter: The Story of the West Coast R&B Disc Jockey," *Blues & Rhythm*, no. 166 (February 2002): 12–14.

Hentoff, Nat. *Lightnin' Hopkins: Blues Train.* Mainstream MDCD 901, 1991.

———. *Lightnin' Hopkins: Lightnin' in New York.* USA: Candid 8010, 1960.

———. *Lightnin' Hopkins: The Blues.* USA: Mainstream MRL 311, 1973.

———. "A Long Way from Houston." *Reporter* (December 8, 1960): 63–64, 66.

Hobus, André. "Lightnin' Hopkins." *Jazz, Blues & Co* no. 28/29 (1979): 12–13.

Holt, John, Paul Oliver, and Frank Scott. *Lightnin' Hopkins.* Texas Blues Society (December 1965).

Holt, John. "Lightnin' Hopkins Discography." Pts. 1–6. *Blues World* no. 12 (January 1967): 24– 26; 13 (March 1967): 6–9; 14 (May 1967): 11–14; 15 (July 1967): 18–21; 16 (September 1967): 4–7; 18 (January 1968): 27–-29.

———. "Nothin' But the Blues." *Blues World* no. 3 (June 1965): 2–4.

Leadbitter, Mike. *Lightnin' Hopkins: King of Dowling Street.* UK: Liberty LBL 83254, 1969.

———. *Lightnin' Hopkins: Lonesome Lightnin'.* UK: Polydor 2941 005, 1973. Entry in Robert Ford, *A Blues Bibliography.* Florence, KY: Routledge, 2007.

———. "Mike's Blues: Hopkinstipation." *Blues Unlimited* no. 69 (Jan 1970): 21.

———. *Nothing But the Blues.* London: Hanover Books, 1971.

Leon County Historical Book Survey Committee, ed. *History of Leon County, Texas.* Dallas: Curtis Media Coporation, 1986.

Lewis, Grover. "Lookin' for Lightnin': A Blues Odyssey." *Village Voice* (c.1969). Reprinted in *Blues World* no. 24 (July 1969): 2–9. Reprinted again in eds. J. Reid and W. K Stratton's *Splendor in the Short Grass: The Grover Lewis Reader.* Austin: University of Texas Press, 2005.

Lewis, Paul. "Blues on the Silver Screen: Two Films About Lightnin' Hopkins." *Blueprint* no. 68 (November 1994): 19.

Lewis, Stan and Richard DeVinck. *Lightnin' Hopkins: The Ultimate Texas Bluesman.* Ventura, CA: Bluetab Entertainment, 1995.

Lomax, John A. "Lightning Hopkins." *Space City News* 1, no. 2 (June 19, 1969): 17–18.

Louis, Big Joe. *Sam "Lightnin'" Hopkins: Jake Head Boogie.* UK: Ace CDCHD 697, 1999.

McCormick, Mack. "A Conversation with Lightnin' Hopkins. Pt 1." *Jazz Journal* 13, no. 11 (November 1960): 22–24

———. "A Conversation with Lightnin' Hopkins. Pt 2." *Jazz Journal* 14, no. 1 (January 1961): 16–19.

———. "A Conversation with Lightnin' Hopkins. Pt 3." *Jazz Journal* 14, no. 2 (February 1961): 18–19.

———. "Lightnin' Hopkins." *Jazz: Metodická Publikace Urcená Clenum Jazzové Sekce* no. 23 (1978): 44–45.

———. *Lightnin' Hopkins: Autobiography in Blues.* Tradition LP 1040, 1960; Tradition TCD-1002, 1996.

———. "Lightnin' Hopkins: Blues." *Jazz Review [USA]* 3, no. 1 (January 1960): 14–17. Reprinted in *Jazz Panorama*, edited by M. T. Williams, New York: Crowell-Collier, 1962.

———. *Lightnin' Hopkins: Blues in My Bottle.* Bluesville BV-1045, c.1961; Original Blues Classics OBC-506, 1984; UK: Ace CH 290, 1984.

———. *Lightnin' Hopkins: Country Blues.* Tradition LP 1035, 1959; USA: Tradition TCD 1003, 1996.

———. *Lightnin' Hopkins: Got to Move Your Baby.* Prestige PRT 7831, 1972.

———. *Lightnin' Hopkins: How Many More Years I Got.* Fantasy FCD-24725-2, 1981.

———. *Lightnin' Hopkins: Last Night Blues*. Bluesville BV-1029, 1961; UK: Fontana 688 301, 1962; USA: Bluesville BV-SP 101; USA: Original Blues Classics OBCCD-548-2, 1992.

———. *Lightnin' Hopkins: Lightnin' and Co*. Bluesville BV-1061, 1962.

———. *Lightnin' Hopkins: Smokes Like Lightning*. Bluesville BV-1070, 1975; Original Blues Classics OBCCD-551-2, 1992.

———. *Lightnin' Hopkins: Walkin' This Road by Myself*. Bluesville BV-1057, 1962; UK: Ace CH 256.

———. "Sam 'Lightnin'' Hopkins: A Description." *Jazz Monthly* 5, no. 8 (October 1959): 4–6. Reprinted in *Sing Out!* 10, no. 3 (October/November 1960): 4–8.

———. *Sam "Lightnin'" Hopkins: The Rooster Crowed in England*. UK: 77 Records LA 12-1, 1960.

MacLeod, Doug. "Doug's Back Porch: Two Statues Named Sam." *Blues Revue* no. 93 (April/May 2005): 35–36.

Michel, Ed. *Down South Summit Meetin'*. World-Pacific WP-1296, 1960; Liberty/World Pacific 1817, 1970.

Milward, John. *Lightnin Hopkins: Live at Newport*. Vanguard VCD 79715, 2002.

Morgenstern, Dan. *Lightnin' Hopkins: Goin' Away*. USA: Bluesville BV-1073, 1963.

Mullen, Patrick B. "The Prism of Race: Two Texas Performers." *Southern Folklore Quarterly* 54, no. 1 (1997): 13–25.

———. *The Man Who Adores the Negro: Race and American Folklore*. Champaign, IL: University of Illinois Press, 2008.

Murray, Charles Shaar. *Boogie Man: The Adventures of John Lee Hooker in the American Twentieth Century*. New York: St. Martin's Griffin, 2002.

Obrecht, Jas. "Lightnin' Hopkins." *Guitar Player* 31, no. 10 (October 1997): 60–61, 63, 65–66, 68, 70. Reprinted in *Rollin' and Tumblin'*, edited by J. Obrecht. San Francisco: Miller Freeman Books, 2000.

O'Brien, Timothy J., "Lightnin' Hopkins: Houston Bluesman, 1912–1960," MA thesis, University of Houston, 2006.

Oliver, Paul. "Lightnin Hopkins."*Conversation with the Blues*. Cambridge: Cambridge University Press, 1965: 43–44, 55–56, 74–75, 183.

———. "Hopkins, Lightnin'" in *The New Grove Dictionary of Music and Musicians*. Vol. 8, edited by S. Sadie, p. 690. London: Macmillan, 1980. Reprinted in *The New Grove Dictionary of Music and Musicians*. Vol. 11. 2nd ed., edited by S. Sadie, p. 700. New York: Grove, 2001.

———. *Lightnin' Hopkins/John Lee Hooker: Live Recordings from Bird Lounge, Houston Texas*. Denmark: Storyville SLP 174, 1965.

———. *Songsters and Saints: Vocal Traditions on Race Records*.Cambridge, MA: Cambridge University Press, 1984.

———. Liner notes to Texas Alexander, "Complete Recorded Works in Chronological Order," Volumes 1, 2, and 3, Document MDCD-2001, MDCD-2002, and MDCD-2003.

Palmer, Robert. "Lightnin' Hopkins at 68: Still Singing Those Blues." *New York Times* (October 31, 1980): 14.

Phelan, Charlotte. "Song Maker." *Houston Post* (August 23, 1959).

Phillips, J. J. *Mojo Hand*. New York: Trident, 1966. Reprint, New York, Pocket, 1969. Restored edition: *Mojo Hand: An Orphic Tale*. Berkeley, CA: City Miner, 1985. London: Serpent's Tail, 1987. *La Tour d'Aigues: Éditions de l'aube*, 1991.

Ritz, David. *Blues Masters: The Very Best of Lightnin' Hopkins*. Rhino R2 79860, 2000.

Rogers, Lelan. *Lightnin' Hopkins: Freeform Patterns*. International Artist IA-LP-6, 1968.

Rotante, Anthony. "Sam 'Lightnin'' Hopkins Discography." *Discophile* no. 45 (December 1955): 3–7; *Discophile* no. 46 (April 1956): 11; *Discophile* no. 47 (April 1956): 3-7; *Discophile* no. 56 (October 1957): 18; *Discophile* no. 59 (April 1958): 8–9.

Russell, Tony, ed. "Lightnin' Hopkins." *The Blues Collection* no. 31 (1992).

Rye, Howard and Alan Balfour. "Lightnin' Hopkins: The Aladdin Recordings." *Collectors Items* no. 30 (June 1985): 12–13.

Sharp, Ken. "Backstage Pass: It Don't Come Easy for Ringo Starr," *Goldmine* (May 22, 2008.)

Shaw, Arnold. *Honkers and Shouters: The Golden Years of Rhythm and Blues*. New York: Collier Books, 1978.

Slaven, Neil. *Lightnin' Hopkins: All the Classics, 1946–1951*. UK: JSP SPCD 7705, 2003.

Smith, Charles Edward. "Lightnin' Strikes Thrice." *Saturday Review* 43 (December 3, 1960): 60.

Sokolow, Fred. "Lightning Strikes." *Acoustic Guitar* no. 26 (September/October 1994): 84, 90–91.

Spanckeren, Kathryn van. "Folk Poetry through Film: Film-Maker Les Blank and Bluesmen Lightnin' Hopkins and Mance Lipscomb." *Tampa Review* 1 (1988): 65–67.

Stewart-Baxter, Derrick. "Blues in the Country." *Jazz Journal* 12, no. 4 (April 1959): 3–4.

Strachwitz, Chris. *The Hopkins Brothers: Sam, Joel and John Henry*. Arhoolie D-340, 1991.

———. *Lightning Hopkins*. Blues Classics BC-30, 1984.

———. "Lightnin' Hopkins Discography." *Jazz Monthly* 5, no. 9 (November 1959): 25–26; no. 10 (December 1959): 13–14.

———. *Lightnin' Hopkins: Early Recordings. Vol. 1*. USA: Arhoolie R-2007, 1975. *Vol. 2*. Arhoolie R-2010, 1971.

———. *Lightnin' Hopkins: Po' Lightnin'*. Arhoolie 1087, 1983; Arhoolie CD 403, 1995.

———. *Lightnin' Hopkins: The Gold Star Sessions. Vol. 1*. Arhoolie CD-330, 1990. *Vol. 2*. Arhoolie CD-337, 1990.

———. *Lightnin' Sam Hopkins*. USA: Arhoolie F 1011, 1962.

———. *Lightning Hopkins with His Brothers Joel and John Henry*. Arhoolie F 1022, 1966. Templeton, Ray. "Lightnin Hopkins: A Short Introduction." *Blues & Rhythm* no. 24 (November 1986): 14–15.

———. "Lightnin' in Bluesville." *Blues & Rhythm* no. 67 (February 1992): 8–9.

Titon, Jeff Todd. *Early Downhome Blues: A Musical and Cultural Analysis* Champaign, IL: University of Illinois Press, 1979.

———. "Reconstructing the Blues: Reflections on the 1960s Blues Revival," in *Transforming Tradition: Folk Music Revivals Examined*, edited by Neil V. Rosenberg, p. 225. Champaign, IL: University of Illinois Press, 1993.

Tonneau, Serge. "Discography." *Rhythm & Blues Panorama* no. 32 (December 1964).

Waterman, Dick. "Lightning Hopkins" in *Between Midnight and Day*, New York: Thunder Mouth, 2003.

Welding, Pete. "Jazznotes: Lightnin' Hopkins." *Coda* 3, no. 10 (February 1961): 26–28.

———. "Lightnin'." *Down Beat* 28, no. 15 (July 20, 1961): 15, 64.

———. *Lightnin' Hopkins: The Complete Aladdin Recordings*. Aladdin/EMI CDP-7-96843-2, 1991.

West, Sarah Ann. *Deep Down Hard Blues: A Tribute to Lightnin' Hopkins*. Lawrenceville, GA: Brunswick, 1995.

Wheat, John. "Lightnin' Hopkins: Blues Bard of the Third Ward" in *Juneteenth Texas: Essays in African American Folklore*, edited by Frances E. Abernethy, Patrick B. Mullen, and Alan B. Govenar. Denton, TX: University of North Texas Press, 1996.

White, Tony Joe. *Lightnin' Hopkins: California Mudslide (And Earthquake)*. Vault LP SLP-129, 1969; UK: Ace CDCHM 546, 1994.

Wilds, Mary. "Sam 'Lightnin" Hopkins" in *Raggin' the Blues*. Greensboro, NC: Avisson, 2001.

Wolfe, Charles and Kip Lornell. *The Life and Legend of Leadbelly*. New York: HarperCollins, 1992.

Wilson, John S. "Lightnin' Hopkins Rediscovered." *New York Times* (August 23, 1959): B8.

Wood, Roger and James Fraher. "Learning About Lightnin': The Soil Beneath My Feet" in *Down in Houston*. Austin: University of Texas Press, 2003.

Obituaries

Billboard 94 (February 13, 1982): 72.

Black Perspective in Music 10, no. 2 (Fall 1982): 228.

Coda no. 183 (April 1982): 37.

Creem 13 (May 1982): 14.

Down Beat 49, no. 5 (May 1982): 11.

Goldmine no. 71 (April 1982).

Guitar Player 16, no. 4 (April 1982): 10.

International Musician 80 (May 1982): 11.

Jazz Magazine [France] no. 306 (April 1982): 28.

JazzTimes (April 1982): 8.

Living Blues no. 52 (Spring 1982): 57.

Neue Zeitschrift für Musik no. 3 (March 1982): 69.

Newsweek 99 (February 15, 1982): 92.

Pickin' the Blues no. 2 (February 1982): 4.

Rolling Stone no. 385/386 (December 23, 1982–January 6, 1983): 90.

Time [USA] 119 (February 15, 1982): 65.

Times [UK] (February 3, 1982): 10.

Variety 306 (February 3, 1982): 133.

Alvarez, Rafael. "Lightnin' Will Strike the Blues No More." *The Sun [Baltimore]* (February 2, 1982).

Applebone, Peter. "Another Man Done Gone." *Texas Monthly* 10, no. 3 (March 1982): 98, 100, 102, 104.

Balalas, Alain. "Lightnin' Hopkins (1912–1982)." *Bulletin du Hot Club de France* no. 298 (June 1982): 22–23.

Balfour, Alan. "Death of a Legend." *New Musical Express* (February 6, 1982): 8.

Blank, Les. "Lightnin' Hopkins, 1912–1982." *Living Blues* no. 53 (Summer/Autumn 1982): 15.

Brasso, Paul and Jørgen Bennetzen. "Nekrolog: Bed for Lightning." MM: *Tidskrift för Rytmisk Musik* 15, no. 3 (April 1982): 18.

Charters, Samuel. "Lightnin' Hopkins: Vielleicht der Kreativste Blues—Sanger aller Zeiten." *Blues Forum* no. 6 (2nd Quarter 1982): 4–8.

Claypool, Bob. "Sam 'Lightnin'" Hopkins (1912–1982)." *Second Line* 34 (Spring 1982): 10–11.

Dauer, Alfons M. "Lightnin' Hopkins: Der Chantefable-Blues." *Blues Forum* no. 5 (lst Quarter 1982): 18–23.

———. "Mister Charlie: A Type of Chantefable—Blues in Commemoration of Samuel 'Lightnin'" Hopkins (1912–1982)." *Jazzforschung/Jazz Research* 15 (1983): 115–145.

Demêtre, Jacques. "L'Heritage de Lightnin' Hopkins." *Jazz Hot* no. 393 (March 1982): 24–25.

Federighi, Luciano. "Blues for Lightnin' Hopkins." *Musica Jazz* 38, no. 3 (March 1982): 9.

Herzhaft, Gérard. "Good Bye Sam." *Soul Bag* no. 88 (April/May 1982): 39.

Hess, Norbert. "Lightnin' Hopkins." *Jazz Podium* 31, no. 3 (March 1982): 4–5.

Loder, Kurt. "Lightnin' Hopkins, 1912–1982: A Classic Blues Life." *Rolling Stone* (March 18, 1982): 17–18.

Minutaglio, Bill. "Saying Goodbye," *Houston Chronicle*, February 2, 1982.

Obrecht, Jas, Billy Gibbons, B. B. King, and Johnny Winter. "Requiem for a Bluesman: Lightnin' Hopkins: Remembrances by B .B. King, Johnny Winter and Billy Gibbons." *Guitar Player* 16, no. 6 (June 1982): 48, 50, 52, 54, 56.

Ola, Akinshiju. "Hopkins: His Music Lives." *Guardian [UK]* 34, no. 20 (February, 17 1982): 55.

Palmer, Robert. "A Requiem for Hopkins: True Poet of the Blues." *New York Times* (February 17, 1982): C17.

Saxon, Wolfgang. "Sam (Lightnin') Hopkins, 69; Blues Singer and Guitarist." *New York Times* (February 1, 1982): B4.

Solding, Staffan. "Lightnin' Hopkins, 1912–1982." *Jefferson* no. 55 (Spring 1982): 44–45.

Stenbeck, Lennart. "Sam 'Lightnin'" Hopkins." *Orkester Journalen* 50, no. 3 (March 1982): 5.

———. "Lightnin' Hopkins: Bluesman och Ordkonstnär." *Orkester Journalen* 50, no. 10 (October 1982): 17–18.

Turner, Bez. "Lightnin' Hopkins." *Blues Unlimited* no. 142 (Summer 1982): 23.

Vacher, Peter. "Lightnin' Hopkins." *Jazz Journal* 36, no. 3 (March 1983): 14.

Wisse, Rien. "Lightnin' Hopkins Overleden." *Block* no. 42 (April/May/June 1982): 11–12.

Index

About the Author

Alan Govenar is a writer, a photographer, a filmmaker, and the president of Documentary Arts, a nonprofit organization he founded in 1985 to present new perspectives on historical issues and diverse cultures. Govenar is a Guggenheim Fellow, has directed more than two dozen films, and is the author of thirty books, including *The Blues Come to Texas: Paul Oliver and Mack McCormick's Unfinished Book*; *Everyday Music*; *Untold Glory: African Americans in Pursuit of Freedom, Opportunity and Achievement*; *Stompin' at the Savoy: The Story of Norma Miller*; and *Texas Blues: The Rise of a Contemporary Sound*. His off-Broadway musicals *Texas in Paris* and *Lonesome Blues* are represented by Columbia Artists for national touring. He lives in Dallas, Texas, and New York City.